BEYOND BLURRED LINES

BEYOND BLURRED LINES

Rape Culture in Popular Media

Nickie D. Phillips

ROWMAN & LITTLEFIELD
Lanham • Boulder • New York • London

cart. Cherry had to run beside it on every trip, and soon he was panting with his tongue hanging out.

" Don't be silly, Cherry," Daisy told him. " You don't have to go every time! "

But Cherry raced off without listening.

" Did you know he was a trick dog? " Ernest asked Shusai. " Here, Cherry," he called. " See no evil, hear no evil, speak no evil." At the words, the little dog shut his eyes, put his nose down and put one paw over an ear. But only for a minute. Then he opened his eyes and looked so mischievous that they all laughed and laughed. " It's really your trick," Ernest explained. " It's like the monkeys you gave us."

" Here, Cherry," said Daisy. " Shake hands." And Cherry put up his paw. " He's the smartest dog in Morioka, and I guess in the whole world," she said.

After breakfast, the ricksha men appeared at the door. Nishima-san clapped his hands and beckoned, and one of them came forward with a big package.

" Poate-san," said Nishima-san, " be pleased to accept this insignificant present for yourself and your honorable wife."

When the wrappings were taken off there was an antique bronze *hibachi,* or firebox, beautifully etched and

Published by Rowman & Littlefield
A wholly owned subsidiary of The Rowman & Littlefield Publishing Group,
Inc.
4501 Forbes Boulevard, Suite 200, Lanham, Maryland 20706
www.rowman.com

Unit A, Whitacre Mews, 26-34 Stannary Street, London SE11 4AB

British Library Cataloguing in Publication Information Available

Library of Congress Cataloging-in-Publication Data Available

ISBN 978-1-4422-4627-0 (cloth : alkaline paper)

♾ ™ The paper used in this publication meets the minimum requirements of
American National Standard for Information Sciences Permanence of Paper
for Printed Library Materials, ANSI/NISO Z39.48-1992.

Printed in the United States of America

CONTENTS

ACKNOWLEDGMENTS

This book may bear my name, but many others helped me along the path to bringing it to fruition. They certainly deserve credit and praise here. I'd like to give special thanks to Jeffrey Cohen, Gennifer Furst, Tammy Garland, Kishonna Gray, Emily Horowitz, Chris Krebs, Alyce McGovern, and Staci Strobl for offering support, comments, and constructive criticism on various drafts. Thanks to Andrea Auther, Wendy Galgan, and Esther Klein for listening to my rambling thoughts and offering encouragement along the way.

Thanks to Provost Timothy Houlihan and Rich Relkin at St. Francis College for your support and to the college for the generous funding for student assistants whose help was invaluable at the outset of this project, including Trang Cao, Rosa Casiano, Ellie Marcus, and Eva Nieves.

I'd like to thank Kathryn Knigge and Melissa McNitt at Rowman & Littlefield for their support and assistance ushering the book through production.

Thanks to everyone, including Michelle, Maria, Lamar, Ashley, and others, at Root Hill Cafe for the best iced mocha lattes in Brooklyn.

Most importantly, special thanks to my family and to KT for endless hours of listening and for lending editing skills to the book; you continue to amaze. And finally, I'd like to dedicate the book to Patrick Tucker for being a brave soul and to Bernice Tucker for being a lovely soul.

I

RAPE CULTURE

The Evolution of a Concept

In the spring of 2014, Elliot Rodger, a twenty-two-year-old in Isla Vista, California, embarked on a stabbing and shooting spree, killing six, wounding thirteen, and ultimately killing himself. Later, it was found that Rodger had left a manifesto, "My Twisted World," in which he expressed misogynist, racist, and violent rhetoric directed at women and others that he believed had thwarted his attempts to become sexually active. He had also posted a video on YouTube entitled "Retribution" that contained similar comments. In it, Rodger's sense of entitlement is palpable as he describes that he *deserves* a girlfriend and that he was rabidly jealous of other couples. Beyond the obvious alarming nature of Rodger's words, the strangest aspect of the video is his unsettling delivery and maniacal laughter. The *Daily Mail* tabloid newspaper described Rodger in the video as behaving as if he were "delivering a movie."[1]

In response to the events, film critic Ann Hornaday of the *Washington Post* indicted the entertainment industry, specifically Hollywood movies, for perpetuating a culture of entitled womanizers. She wrote, "If our cinematic grammar is one of violence, sexual conquest and macho swagger . . . no one should be surprised when those impulses take luridly literal form in the culture at large."[2] She was immediately met with scorn. Hornaday specifically called out director Judd Apatow's movies and mentioned *Neighbors* (a comedy starring Seth Rogen). Both Apatow and Rogen quickly took to Twitter to lambaste her for her "idiotic thoughts."[3]

Many readers, including *New York Times* op-ed columnist Frank Bruni, condemned Hornaday for "a question too far," for suggesting that Hollywood had influence on Rodger's behavior.[4] In fact, she received so much criticism from her column that she posted a video response on the *Washington Post* website reiterating how Rodger's comments, coupled with the production values of his YouTube video clip, seemed to embody so much of the entertainment culture he had been exposed to growing up.

Much of the criticism against Hornaday was in direct response to the idea that Hollywood fare directly *causes* violence, yet Hornaday's point was more nuanced. She critiqued the entertainment business as overwhelmingly run by men, and as having a culture that objectifies women and portrays any scenario in which the "shlubby arrested [male] adolescent" does not get the girl as grossly unfair. Hornaday also homed in on a point perhaps more significant than whether popular culture directly causes violence: she suggested that the prevalent portrayals "drastically limit our collective imagination."[5]

While many were quick to criticize Hornaday, others echoed her comments. Using the hashtag #YesAllWomen, many Twitter users reacted to the Rodger incident by emphasizing that his misogynist statements about women were not necessarily "shocking" but, rather, indicative of the attitudes and statements by men that many women face daily. The hashtag, a response to the antifeminist #NotAllMen that was spawned to point out that "not all men" are responsible for violence against women, began trending after the incident.[6] The BBC noted that the #YesAllWomen hashtag was used by more than 250,000 people in less than twenty-four hours after the incident. Within just three days, it had been tweeted 1.2 million times and had made 1.2 billion impressions.[7] Feminist writer Jessica Valenti wrote of the incident and the subsequent outpouring of commentary on social media, "I want to believe that a misogynist shooting people dead in the street will matter to people for more than the length of the news cycle."[8]

While the Rodger case faded from the news cycle, the debates spurred by his crimes are part of a broader public dialogue around the concept of "rape culture." While the term has been used among feminist scholars for decades to describe the cultural normalization of sexual violence, it has only recently, primarily since 2013, been a significant part of the *popular discourse*, or "collective imagination" to quote Hornaday. Using a cultural criminological framework, this book aims to show how the concept of rape culture has entered into our collective imagination, effectively providing a cultural space for the notion that violence against women is often ignored, implicitly condoned, or explicitly encouraged in the United States. Drawing on news articles, websites, blogs, and other social media, the book contends that the current intensified discourse about rape culture has created a media-cultural environment that ultimately impacts politics and policy making.

This chapter explores the contested meanings of the term and the subsequent backlash against its usage. As a means of providing a backdrop to the larger discussion about public discourse around the topic, the chapter shows how the term's rise in popularity does not necessarily correspond to increases in actual rates of violence against women in the United States—at least according to official statistics. Although the use of the term skyrocketed in 2013, conservative pundits and others quickly leveled a backlash against its use. Many were critical of the term for forging a perceived link between "microaggressions"—the constant exposure to misogyny, harassment, objectification, and nonphysical aggression experienced by women on a daily basis—and sexual violence.

RAPE CULTURE AND FEMINIST FURY

When she was crowned Miss USA in June 2014, Nia Sanchez from Nevada was asked about the problem of sexual assaults on campuses and why colleges have swept so many allegations "under the rug." Sanchez, a fourth-degree black belt in Tae Kwon Do replied,

> I believe that some colleges may potentially be afraid of having a bad reputation . . . but I think more awareness is very important so women can learn how to protect themselves. Myself, as a 4th degree black belt, I have learned from a young age that you need to be confident and be able to defend yourself and I think that is something that we should start to really implement for a lot of women. [9]

Sanchez's remarks sparked a wave of controversy on the Internet and social media, with some critics suggesting that she was promoting "rape culture," a term introduced by feminist scholars in the 1970s to highlight the cultural normalization of sexual violence against women. [10] Sanchez's statements prompted a barrage of tweets about sexual assault on campus, victim blaming, and the perils of placing responsibility for rape on women themselves to learn self-defense to the exclusion of men's responsibility. [11]

Conservative websites soon joined the fray, contending that feminists were apoplectic about her comments. The *Independent Journal Review* claimed the controversy had sparked "feminist fury." The publication questioned why feminists would be in an "uproar" over "mak[ing] sure women are empowered to defend themselves." [12]

Journalist Katie Pavlich, writing for *Townhall*, suggested that women were "freaking out" in response to what appeared to be commonsense advice. She objected to the notion that the primary focus on preventing rape should be to teach men not to rape. Instead, Pavlich advocated for both self-defense and education and suggested that "leftist feminists" who minimize the value of women learning self-defense are promoting victimhood. She wrote,

> Modern feminism can't survive without victims so naturally, preventing victimhood through self-defense is unacceptable. Telling women they don't need self-defense to prevent rape is exactly what moves "rape-culture" forward. [13]

But were these conservative pundits wagging the dog? Just how much feminist fury was actually directed toward Ms. Sanchez's comments? Writing for *Thoughts on Liberty*, a website devoted to "women libertarian voices," Rachel Burger pointed out that there was no feminist fury—at least not from prominent feminist bloggers who write for sites such as *Feministing*, *Bitch Media*, *Media Girl*, *Finally Feminism 101*, and *Feministe*. She wrote,

> I want to point out that no major individual or group is seriously accusing Ms. Sanchez of perpetuating rape culture. *It was not an issue until conservative media made it out to be.* (emphasis added) [14]

The controversy over Sanchez's remarks revealed a number of issues central to understanding how we discuss sexual violence in contemporary society. First, popular culture, however seemingly trivial, can deeply influence our ideas about sexual violence. In this case, a relatively innocuous comment made in a beauty pageant ignited a larger discussion about rape and rape prevention. Second, the concept of rape culture itself, once referenced primarily in academic settings, is now an explicit part of the dialogue surrounding sexual violence. Related, while discourse involving sexual violence and prevention strategies is not new, the Internet and social media have created opportunities for more voices to enter the debate. [15] Academia, teach-ins, and mainstream news media, though influential, do not dictate the terms of popular discussion. Instead, there is an array of feminist-focused blogs and websites that bring attention to sexual violence. The conversations reverberate from social media to mainstream media, creating a feedback loop. [16] This is not to say that the discussion is somehow centralized; it is not. In fact, the discourse is fragmented and originates from a variety of voices, making it difficult to pinpoint any clear, single feminist perspective or, conversely, any singular organized backlash.

Culture critic Alyssa Rosenberg characterized the issues involving sexual violence in media and popular culture as part of a new culture war, with "flash points" similar to the "same issues of identity politics that roiled universities in earlier decades." She wrote that unlike the earlier culture war that focused on issues of decency and morality, this culture war "is being waged over whether or not culture is political, and if so, what its politics ought to be and how they might be expressed." She described this new culture war as being waged in battlefields that are "low culture and the combatants are consumers, mass media critics and creators."[17]

Understanding this new reality requires us to examine how "low culture"—forms of popular culture often met with disdain—is a vital space for negotiating meanings of sexual violence. In the case of Sanchez, the pageant provoked responses that were fragmented and arose from different voices and perspectives demonstrating that best practices in sexual violence prevention remain very much in dispute. Yet some commentators blamed the "feminist agenda" for claiming that self-defense is an inadequate rape prevention strategy. In fact, feminists have long been instrumental in advocating self-defense as a useful rape prevention strategy.[18] This book focuses on how meanings of sexual violence are contested in "low culture," showing that ideas about sexual violence and its prevention are influenced by an array of experiences and social practices, including personal experience, shifting legal norms and criminal justice procedures, research, entertainment media, and news media representations, and how over the past few years, rape culture has emerged as a common conceptual tool for popular understandings of women's experiences of sexual violence.

THE ORIGINS OF RAPE CULTURE

It is unclear who first coined the term "rape culture," and there is some ambiguity to its definition. Generally, feminist scholars have used the term to describe how violence against women has been normalized in our society through a process of linking sexuality to violent aggression. The concept emerged from radical feminists during the 1970s, when our understandings of sexual violence and treatment of victims within the criminal justice system dramatically evolved. During this time, second-wave feminists began to focus attention on violence against women, drawing attention to behaviors that had historically been neglected, including domestic violence and marital rape.

Those involved in the anti-rape movement fiercely advocated for cultural awareness and legal reform around sexual assault, including amending laws historically rooted in property rights wherein women were treated as men's property. Law reform in the late 1970s and 1980s ushered in major changes in how rape cases were handled in the criminal justice system. Rape shield laws, for example, were enacted to prohibit evidence regarding the victim's past sexual history. Such evidence had been inappropriately used to determine whether the victim consented to the encounter. It was also used as a means of judging the victim's credibility. Other reforms included redefining rape to include a continuum of sexual assault with a range of penalties. It broadened the category of victim to include males, eliminated the corroboration requirement (which was justified based on the assumption "that women lie"), as well as the requirement of evidence of physically resisting the assault. However, despite these changes, legal reform alone was not enough to ensure that victims continue to be treated with respect and that justice is served.[19]

It was also during this time that our popular understandings of rape radically evolved. Although feminists had addressed issues of sexual violence, most give credit to Susan Brownmiller for bringing the topic to the masses in authoring the groundbreaking *Against Our Will*. The book provided a historical account of rape that reframed the crime from one of insatiable sexual lust to that of men maintaining power and control over women through sexual violence. From the problematic origins of rape laws that treated women as property rather than victims, to the use of rape as a tactic of war, to the difficulties of collecting accurate statistics on victims, to the debunking of rape myths, Brownmiller's book was extraordinarily influential and reached mainstream audiences. In 1975, she was named one of *Time* magazine's twelve Women of the Year.[20] Her work brought to the public consciousness the notion that through the potential for sexual violence, "*all men* keep *all women* in a state of fear."[21]

Some have argued that Brownmiller's work did suggest an essentialist, biological component of rape. Even if so, her work expanded our understanding of rape from that of an offender's individual psychopathology to a historical and cultural phenomenon rooted in patriarchy. Scholar Maria Bevacqua pointed out that while Brownmiller was not the first to suggest that rape be considered a crime motivated by domination and power rather than by "sex" (this she credited to Ruth Herschberger's work in 1948), she was the first to bring the idea to a wide audience.[22] Bevacqua explained that such a perspective provided cultural space for shattering rape myths and reducing victim blaming. Other feminists, too, had begun to view heterosexual sex and rape as functioning on a continuum in which coercion operated in more subtle ways than just via physical force. Scholar Nicola Gavey wrote that even among feminists, the debate "over whether rape is about sex or whether it is about violence and power" continues.[23] Nonetheless, Brownmiller's comprehensive take on rape prompted a shift from thinking of the crime as an individual, aberrant act to understanding the historical and cultural context in which rape occurs. This lens contributed to an understanding of how sexual aggression and violence against women is implicitly condoned, if not explicitly encouraged, in contemporary society.

Brownmiller, and other radical feminists that organized in the 1960s and 1970s, considered sexual violence among their major concerns.[24] It was during these early decades of the feminist movement that rape crisis hotlines and centers for victims were developed and anti-rape campaigns, including "Take Back the Night" marches, were organized. It was radical feminist scholars who gave insight into the fact that incidences of violence against women are related to patriarchy and broader cultural attitudes permissive of misogyny. From this perspective, understanding the concept of rape culture requires a consideration of the fact that violence and aggression, and those who commit such acts, are products of the culture from which they emerge. Or, as cultural criminologist Mike Presdee noted, "crime and violence erupt out of social processes and come from *within social life*, not from outside of it."[25] The idea is that those who rape are not alien evil monsters that invade our idyllic landscape. Rather, they are products of the culture from which they emerge—a culture that in many ways condones aggression against women.

The feminist perspective of viewing violence against women as "a fundamental component of the social control of women" provided the theoretical framework that propelled social action around the issue, ultimately leading to massive changes in how victims were viewed and treated.[26] The feminist movement was instrumental in providing victims services, and the impetus for change was rooted in increasing cultural awareness. In her study of the anti-rape movement of the 1970s and 1980s, scholar Nancy Matthews wrote that the "overarching project of this movement was changing consciousness about rape."[27] Bevacqua documented the history of the feminist anti-rape movement and noted its success on a number of levels, including at the policy level and in terms of cultural attitudes. By the end of the 1990s, women were much more likely to have their complaints of sexual violence taken seriously by both the public and by authorities than in the 1960s and 1970s, and they were more likely to be treated compassionately. Bevacqua emphasized that the movement was pivotal to increasing cultural awareness. She wrote, "The importance of this outcome cannot be overstated: the way we, as a culture, understand rape today marks a radical break from the public consciousness of the late 1960s."[28]

The victims' rights movement converged with a number of unusual allies, including members of the tough-on-crime law enforcement community and the women's movement to provide more resources for victims and ushered in legal reform. Yet despite these concerted efforts, many scholars have documented that the reforms were minimal in terms of "concrete improvements in the actual outcome of rape cases."[29] In other words, legal reform was necessary but not sufficient for ameliorating the problem of sexual violence. As law scholar Stephen Schulhofer noted, "criminal law never functions independently of the culture in which it is set."[30]

As advocates attempted to make inroads in how rape was prosecuted, feminist scholars continued to explore the cultural climate that facilitated the crime. In her article "Deconstructive Strategies and the Movement against Sexual Violence," scholar Renee Heberle isolated what she believed to be the inception of the term "rape culture." She credited author Susan Griffin, who used it in a 1977 book chapter, "Rape: The All-American Crime," as "describ[ing] the general environment created by the threat and the experience of sexual violence whose terms women must internalize in order to live safely in the world."[31]

The term does not appear in Griffin's 1971 *Ramparts* article of the same title. However, in that piece, she explicitly argued that a culture that privileges patriarchal sex roles and oppressive attitudes toward women plays a dominant role in encouraging rape and stigmatizing victims. The solution, for Griffin, was to eliminate patriarchy.[32] She argued that sexuality and violence are intertwined in ways that promote false beliefs about rape—including that women desire to be raped. Griffin blamed the criminal justice system, which is primarily operated by white men, as further victimizing women by blaming them for their plight. Perhaps most important, Griffin set the stage for a broad, longstanding cultural critique in emphasizing that "the fact that rape is against the law should not be considered proof that rape is not in fact encouraged as part of our culture."[33]

Other scholars found different origins for the rape culture concept. Joetta Carr traced it to *Rape: The First Sourcebook for Women* published in 1974.[34] The book, edited by Noreen Connell and Cassandra Wilson and written by New York Radical Feminists, is largely culled from materials presented at the Speak Out on Rape and the New York Radical Feminist Rape Conference held in 1971. The book provided tips for the anti-rape movement, including best ways to organize and guidelines for consciousness raising that best lead to social action. What we think of today as "rape culture" was articulated in the text through women's experiences of victimization. Consciousness raising was essential at the time because experiences of rape were frequently unspoken. When women brought them to light, they were frequently blamed for their own victimization. Though many women had experiences to share, they had yet to connect their personal circumstances to broader social patterns of patriarchy, social institutions, and the legal reality that served to silence and marginalize women.

The consciousness-raising sessions that were popular in the 1970s were vital to empowerment. In those women-only circles, the personal became political. That is, women began to define their own experiences instead of relying on the dominant male perspective to understand themselves. This process encompassed taking a step back to survey the entire landscape to recognize how popular culture operates to reinforce the status quo.

A year after the publication of *Rape: The First Sourcebook for Women*, Cambridge Documentary Films released a film, *Rape Culture*. Co-producer Margaret Lazarus has said that as she recalls, the term evolved out of long discussions she and others had about what they sought to convey in the documentary. To her recollection, the film marked the first time the term was used.[35] The documentary included commentary from a collaboration between rape crisis workers and prisoners determined to combat rape. Influenced by radical feminism, the film suggested that the system of patriarchy serves to oppress women, and, as a result, all women are at risk for sexual violence. Feminist scholar and theologian Mary Daly, who was interviewed in the film, echoed that assessment. She suggested another term to describe the phenomenon, "rapism," a

> stronger and more accurate word to describe the disease of a phallo-centric society than sexism, because it really does get to the very act itself of penetration and violation and rapism of course, it's primary significance is the physical act itself which puts all of us into what you would call a state of siege, all women.[36]

The film did not shirk from interviewing offenders about their take on the pervasiveness of rape and how it is explicitly linked to normative heterosexual behavior. One prisoner, Gary Aston, explained,

> I think that in fact all men do rape. For example, I've never been convicted of rape but I would venture to say that there have been

occasions when I have raped my wife, probably my girlfriends, and so
forth. We have to deal with the total . . . process of socialization and
how men view women, what their attitudes about women are.

The documentary was a forerunner in its use of cinema and advertising
to help viewers understand why rape is so pervasive. It featured clips
from movies such as *Last Tango in Paris* and *Gone with the Wind*,
along with commercials containing scenes of implicit sexual violence to
show how such imagery promotes rape culture. Whereas today's viewers may view such scenes as relatively tame, the documentary was revelatory for its time.

Janet O'Hare, a counselor with New York Women against Rape who
was interviewed in the film, sought to convey how popular-culture imagery impacts survivors:

> One of the things that we see a lot as counselors is that people who
> have recently been assaulted all of a sudden become really sensitive
> to all these kinds of things, all the rape imagery in movies and books
> leaps out at them and they really feel traumatized by it and really
> vulnerable to it and they realize it's not really their problem, that it's
> everywhere.[37]

Feminists increasingly pointed to the plethora of depictions of rape in
television, film, and books as symptomatic of rape culture. They contended that such representations too often objectify and oppress wom-
en, and ultimately shape and influence pro-rape attitudes and behaviors. Added to this is the potential for these popular images to retrau-
matize survivors of sexual assault who inevitably come across them.
These themes continue to resonate among contemporary feminist critiques of rape culture.

It was unsurprising for feminists to learn that victims of sexual assault often fail to regain their sense of safety in society. Indeed, they
argued that even women who haven't been raped are often kept on
edge in their daily lives. Dianne Herman offered insight into this in
"Rape Culture," published in 1979 in *Women: A Feminist Perspective.*
Drawing from Griffin's notion of rape as a kind of terrorism that keeps
women in fear, Herman described sexual violence as occurring on a
continuum, ranging from "mini-rapes" to violent sexual attacks. She
wrote,

> Every woman knows the fear of being alone at home late at night or
> the terror that strikes her when she receives an obscene phone call.
> She knows also of the "mini-rapes"—the pinch in the crowded bus,

the wolf whistle from a passing car, the stare of a man looking at her bust during a conversation.[38]

Behaviors on this continuum—ranging from street harassment to unwanted sexual contact to rape—are the result of underlying gender role assumptions about how men are expected to be sexually aggressive and women passive. Here, we can see rape as operating on a continuum of heterosex—as an extension of normative heterosexual behavior that is culturally conditioned as aggressive. The consequences are that myths of men's sexuality (e.g., as insatiable, uncontrollable) and women's status as objects, coupled with their (socially constrained) sexual agency, contribute to a persistent fear of sexual violence, which in turn operates as a means of social control. Sexism, then, becomes part of our larger understanding about how rape functions in society. That is, the perpetuation of sexism rests at one end of the continuum of sexual violence and provides social scripts for how laws are constructed and for how society reacts to victims of sexual violence. For example, rape myths that revictimize women by assuming they are "asking for it" or that they are "maliciously vindictive" and frequently falsely accuse innocent men of rape derive from sexist treatment of women—including economic sexual exploitation. From this perspective, until women achieve some semblance of equitable social power, they will continue to be victims of sexual violence.[39]

In her work, Herman found popular culture to be an important influence in our understanding of the relationships between men and women. She wrote,

> The imagery of sexual relations between males and females in books, songs, advertising and films is frequently that of a sado-masochistic relationship thinly veiled by a romantic facade. Thus it is very difficult in our society to differentiate rape from "normal" heterosexual relations. Indeed our culture can be characterized as a rape culture because the image of heterosexual intercourse is based on a rape model of sexuality.[40]

Such assessments, now widely acknowledged in feminist teachings, were pioneering at the time. Of their significance, scholar Nicola Gavey wrote, "In historical context, these kinds of radical feminist analyses of rape were a brave and revolutionary attack on the masculinist discourses of sex and rape that had worked so long to support rape," and central to this shift was how feminists, activists and scholars, began to privilege women's voices and their experiences.[41] These sentiments are echoed in perhaps one of the most widely cited contributions to our understanding of the concept, the book titled *Transforming a Rape*

Culture by Emilie Buchwald, Pamela Fletcher, and Martha Roth, first published in 1995 (with a later edition in 2005). The book's purpose was to change attitudes and values that are rooted in patriarchy, are oppressive toward women, and contribute to sexual violence. They wrote,

> We saw with increasing clarity the extent of the problem: On TV programs and ads, in newspapers, novels, poetry, songs, opera, rock, and rap, on every billboard, in every shop window, on every museum wall we found evidence of rape culture.[42]

A clarion call to end rape, the book opened with feminist Andrea Dworkin's powerful essay declaring that there is no freedom while living in a world in which rape exists. With a sense of urgency, Dworkin dares the reader—the men—to stop rape. For Dworkin, rape is a product of women's oppression under male supremacy, though it is not inevitable. She contended that real equality would remain elusive until rape is eradicated.

Dworkin's quest for equality has remained unrealized. Third-wave feminists increasingly highlighted the failures of the criminal justice system to adequately address sexual violence and contended that such failures were symptomatic of rape culture. In her entry in the *Encyclopedia of Rape* published in 2004, scholar Robin Field defined rape culture as "one in which rape and other sexual violence against women and children are both prevalent and considered the norm."[43] Field cited various ways in which sexual violence had effectively been normalized, including through low arrest and conviction rates, the excuses commonly offered that absolve perpetrators of responsibility, the persistence of victim blaming, and the continuing acceptance of rape myths.[44]

Empowering women to claim sex for their own—as opposed to merely something that happens to them—has been a key focus for latter-day feminists. The anthology *Yes Means Yes! Visions of Female Sexual Power and a World without Rape* (2008), edited by Jaclyn Friedman and Jessica Valenti, focused on female empowerment and sexual agency as one strategy to combat rape. In his chapter, Brad Perry described rape culture as domination over the sexual autonomy of another. He wrote,

> Domination over the sexual autonomy of others can almost become fetishized, and operates from a societal level (e.g., restrictions on reproductive freedoms, forced sterilization policies, inadequate laws against rape, etc.) down through the interpersonal (e.g., a greater concern for the number of bedpost notches than for the people involved in the experiences, or the experiences themselves).[45]

Similarly, Friedman and Valenti wrote that "suppressing female sexual agency is a key element of rape culture," but they do not go on to specifically define rape culture. Instead, the authors pointed out that "rape culture has directly affected our lives," with one writer pointing to an incident of sexual assault and the other referencing catcalls, gropings, and "being labeled a 'slut.'"[46] Echoing the work of earlier feminists, this approach presented sexual violence as a continuum on which rape occupies one extreme.

Overall, the term "rape culture" is now widely used and assumed to be self-explanatory. In the process, however, it has devolved into a blanket term, its use frequently imprecise or abstract. In her review of Buchwald et al.'s 1995 edition of *Transforming a Rape Culture*, criminologist Kathleen Daly pointed out how broad and encompassing the term can be. She wrote that the authors declared

> that a rape culture exists, but they do not reflect on what the term means. At times it refers literally to rape; then it expands to include a continuum of sexual violence, and finally it refers to domination and exploitation in a diffuse and metaphorical sense.[47]

Rape culture is now part of popular discourse and continues to be defined in ways that encompass a range of attitudes and behaviors toward sexual violence. In her book *Asking for It: The Alarming Rise of Rape Culture—and What We Can Do about It*, Kate Harding pointed to our society's contradictory attitudes regarding rape—that is, we condemn it while condoning the behavior of celebrity criminals who have been convicted of the offense, for example, Mike Tyson. Just as second-wave feminists such as Andrea Dworkin correlated the lack of women's liberation with sexual violence, rape culture today continues to be viewed within the larger context of men's continuing oppression of women. That oppression is still inextricably connected to the ways women experience, and respond to, sexual violence.

FROM ACADEMIA TO URBAN DICTIONARY

There is an abundance of literature on sexual violence—for example, the history of rape reform legislation, victimology studies, and rape prevention—that implicitly, or explicitly, addresses rape culture. Before the 1980s, there were few instances of the term "rape culture" in scholarly literature. A search of databases shows that scholars gradually increased their use of it in dissertations, journal articles, and books beginning in the mid-1990s (see table 1.1). Yet the most significant increase in the term arose in mainstream newspapers and magazines between 2010 and 2014 (see figure 1.1). It was during this time that rape culture emerged as part of the broader popular discourse involving issues of sexual violence. According to a database search of newspaper and magazine articles published between January 1989 and mid-April 2014, the term experienced a growth rate of 1,871 percent in just four years (2010–2014), compared to the prior five-year period.

My data collection on the use of the term was sparked by work on a project with my colleague, sociologist Emily Horowitz. Interested in exploring how frequently the concept of rape culture appeared, we conducted searches covering both academic and mainstream media.[48] Our search for the term in scholarly journals turned up 224 articles published between the 1980s and April 2014.[49] While a search of the words "rape" and "culture" would certainly produce hundreds, if not thousands, more results, we wanted to see whether the phrase "rape culture" was becoming more frequent in the literature. The articles that contained the phrase spanned various disciplines, including criminology, philosophy, and critical pedagogy. Until 1994, the search revealed only nineteen journal articles that contained the phrase. The next two decades produced over two hundred (see the appendix for more details on the search methodology).

Table 1.1. Frequency of "Rape Culture"

	Books	Dissertations and Theses	Scholarly Articles	Newspaper/Magazines
pre-1989	1	12	5	3
1990–1994	3	22	14	10
1995–1999	2	134	47	5
2000–2004	3	162	45	19
2005–2009	6	164	51	7
2010–2014	9	282	62	138
Total	24	776	224	182

Books: 1979–March 19, 2014; keyword "rape culture"
Dissertations: 1979–March 19, 2014; "rape culture" anywhere, dissertations and theses
Scholarly articles: 1983–April 1, 2014; full-text "rape culture"
Newspapers/magazines: 1989–April 2, 2014; top ten "rape culture" full-text; other "rape culture" in title
Source: ProQuest and WorldCat

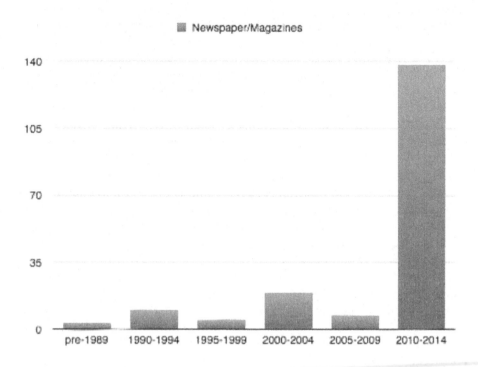

Figure I.I. Frequency of "Rape Culture" in Mainstream Sources. *Source: Pro-Quest.*

We coded each article according to its primary theme, with the acknowledgment that any given article might address several themes. For example, one article may focus on both victims as well as campus life. Overall, about 20 percent of the articles focused primarily on hookups, sports, fraternities, and campus or high school life. About 12 percent focused on rape culture in literature and mythology. About 10 percent discussed general awareness of violence against women and issues related to feminism, and about 8 percent centered on the topic of rape culture in popular culture. The remainder focused on issues such as theory and discourse around rape, global sexual politics, social science studies on behavior and attitudes around sex roles, and rape in prison. There has also been a notable increase since 1994 in the use of the term in dissertations, indicating solid academic acceptance of it.

In terms of books, WorldCat designated a total of twenty-four with the keyword "rape culture." Nine of the twenty-four were published in 2010–2014, and, notably, none of the books were written with the express purpose to question or critique the term. Rather, the term has clearly reached widespread usage in academic literature and is considered a valid concept, even if it is not always clearly defined. There is much more controversy surrounding the term in mainstream discourse.

We also found that there was a much sharper surge in use of the term in newspapers and magazines. According to our database search, there were 182 newspaper and magazine articles published between January 1989 and mid-April 2014 that contained the phrase "rape culture." Almost 88 percent of the articles originated in North America. Many used the term in the headline to point to rape culture as a problem, for example, "'Rape Culture' Puts Burden on Women, Experts Say," "Working to Eliminate a Rape Culture," and "The West Too Has a 'Rape Culture.'" Most commonly, rape culture was used to characterize the social environment on college campuses (38.5 percent) and in discussions of politics and popular culture (34 percent). The remaining articles addressed topics such as sports, military, global issues of violence against women, SlutWalk and other feminist activism, and general issues of concern to feminists.

Although many mainstream articles used quotation marks around the term, indicating that the concept itself was in question, of the total articles, only about 14 percent actually explicitly challenged it. Articles dealing with sexual assault on campuses were most likely to challenge the concept. For example, Heather MacDonald's 2008 article in the *Los Angeles Times* declared, "What campus rape crisis? Promiscuity and hype have created a phony epidemic at colleges" and, more than a decade earlier, Katie Roiphe's 1993 "Date Rape's Other Victim," which argued that the oft-cited statistical claim that one in four college women has been raped is an exaggeration. Most articles took the concept as a given and presented it as something to work toward eliminating.[50]

What is most remarkable about the mainstream news accounts is that sixteen months accounted for the publication of 64 percent of the total articles (117 of 182 appeared during 2013 and the first four months of 2014). Only 44 articles appeared before 2010, indicating how quickly the term diffused into mainstream conversation.

The increase in frequency of the term in mainstream news articles reflected the broader, general interest in the term, which exploded in 2013. To gauge the extent of the public interest in the term, I conducted a Google Trends search.[51] Google Trends is described as providing an "analysis of web searches 'from all Google domains to compute how many searches have been done for the terms you've entered, relative to the total number of searches done on Google over time.'"[52] The trend showed a massive spike in popularity beginning in January 2013 and extending beyond into 2016 (see figure 1.2). Although Google Trends does not calculate the absolute number of searches, it does indicate how popular the term is relative to other searches.

The massive interest in the term, relative to its virtual obscurity just a few years ago, reveals that an important cultural moment was occurring around "rape culture." Our focus on academic sources was initially useful for understanding how the concept is rooted in radical feminism. However, an exclusive focus on those sources would fail to convey the intensity with which the general public connects to the term—and the ways it is contested in society. Thus, the social meaning of rape culture is better understood by exploring how the term circulates among mainstream news sources, as well as how it is used in more ephemeral spaces such as blogs and social media. As of February 2016, there were several definitions of rape culture offered on *Urban Dictionary*. One simply stated,

> Rape Culture:
> Something that doesn't exist.
> *Rape culture is a completely made up concept.* (Posted May 16, 2014)

A second entry defined rape culture from a more feminist-oriented perspective:

> Rape Culture:
> Shaming victims of rape, making women feel bad for having consensual sex, making fun and trivializing rape and not embracing sex positivity so the unfortunate victims of rape who want to put their rapist behind bars will have fear that they will be blamed. (Posted July 3, 2011)

The "top definition" on *Urban Dictionary* is worth quoting in full as it encapsulates the contestation of the phrase,

Figure 1.2. Google Trends: Rape Culture. *Source: Google Trends. Accessed February 3, 2014, https://www.google.com/trends/explore#q=rape%20culture.*

Rape Culture:
The literal definition would posit a culture that advocates and nor-
malizes rape, which is blatantly not true of the Western world and
why people obviously deny it (because it doesn't exist).

Feminism's redefinition though . . . sigh . . . is a sub-ideology that
concerns the collective issues, cultural ingraining and disparagement
of rape. Basically a pseudo-theory that society has been groomed by
patriarchy to enable and excuse rape.

Despite numerous flaws and dogmatic principle, many feminists
and SJWs [social justice warriors][53] are pushing it as unequivocal
fact. Its flagship slogan is "Don't tell me what to wear, teach MEN
not to rape!"

Said slogan also defies reason.
A few tenets of this twaddle include:

- *dissent of rape culture is proof of rape culture*
- *questioning a rape accuser is victim blaming*
- *rape accusers never lie*
- *consent is black and white*
- *porn grooms men to rape*
- *trials that do not find a conviction are rape culture*
- *this urban dictionary definition is rape culture* (Posted August 26, 2014)[54]

It is here, in the low culture of a colloquial online resource, where we
see that "rape culture" is heavily contested in ways that reflect a spiral-
ing of the concept from its roots in radical feminism to a mockery of
feminism itself—perspectives that resonate throughout popular culture
in broader discussions of sexual violence.

SLUTWALK AND THE UNMOORING OF A CONCEPT

Academic interest in, and use of, the term "rape culture" has continued
to grow, but the concept did not reach the public consciousness until
the first decade of the twenty-first century. During this time, there
were several international and domestic events that were frequently
framed in the context of rape culture—in particular, by feminist-focused blogs and websites. In her article in the *Guardian*, journalist
Libby Brooks credited SlutWalk—a global movement featuring organized marches to end "rape culture"—for extricating the term from
academia into mainstream popular consciousness.[55]

SlutWalk was spawned in direct response to an event on a Canadian
college campus. During a safety forum at York University in 2011, po-

lice officer Michael Sanguinetti offered what he thought were sound words of advice to students on the prevention of sexual assault. According to *The Star*,

> "You know, I think we're beating around the bush here," the officer said . . . "I've been told I'm not supposed to say this, however, women should avoid dressing like sluts in order not to be victimized."[56]

Although only about ten people reportedly attended the safety forum, the words sparked a global movement and international conversation about victim blaming and rape myths.[57] The officer later apologized, but the underlying assumption inherent in his initial comment—that victims of sexual assault somehow initiate their own victimization—struck a nerve. In response, rallies known as "SlutWalks" were designed to bring attention to slut shaming (or "survivor shaming")[58] and to challenge rape myths. SlutWalks were organized in over two hundred communities in Canada, the United States, Europe, Mexico, Australia, South Africa, and Asia.[59]

SlutWalks were designed to be provocative; participants were often scantily clad, wrote on their bodies, and held signs that explicitly challenged the assumption that somehow a woman's attire initiates sexual assault. The *Huffington Post* described attendees at the 2011 Toronto SlutWalk:

> some wearing jeans and a T-shirt; others in outfits more appropriate for a Victoria's Secret fashion show: thigh-highs, lingerie, stilettos—and marched to police headquarters. Their goal: to shift the paradigm of mainstream rape culture, which they believe focuses on analyzing the behavior of the victim rather than that of the perpetrator.[60]

Taking a decidedly third-wave feminist sensibility, many participants embraced the term "slut" as a way of reappropriating the term and dressed accordingly—a sharp, in-your-face declaration that attire does not invite sexual assault and victim blaming must be challenged. Ray Filar, writing for the *Guardian* described how the feminism fueling SlutWalk was rooted in the Riot Grrrl movement. Filar wrote,

> it harks back to the dawn of the 1990s when musician Kathleen Hanna, unwilling figurehead for the riot grrrl movement and lead singer for Bikini Kill, went on stage with the word "slut" scrawled across her body. In doing this, she made a visceral, powerful statement about her sexuality. Her message was not "yes, I am a slut." It

was this: "by reclaiming the derogatory terms that you use to silence my sexual expression, I dilute your power."[61]

The third-wave feminist movement in the United States, a concept coined by writer Rebecca Walker in the aftermath of the 1991 Anita Hill sexual harassment case, embraced—and explicitly demanded—young women as essential participants in moving the feminist agenda forward.[62] Part of the third-wave movement encompassed that the "daughters" of the second-wavers recognize that their brand of feminism differed from that of their predecessors.[63] This new wave incorporated the second-wave credo of the personal as political. Yet the personal now encompassed the myriad ways that young women are feminists in an increasingly diverse, multicultural society.

While the first wave brought forth women's suffrage and the second wave carried the torch to raise awareness around legal and cultural issues vital to women's welfare and equality, by the dawn of the third wave, the term "feminist" had come to be disavowed by many; it was no longer perceived as necessary to self-identify as such. Rather, it was considered more important to live the values of a feminist—that is, to engage in activities that promote equality between the sexes—as opposed to explicitly self-describing as "feminist." In essence, terminology itself was viewed as less important than actions and behavior. In the increasingly postmodern and multicultural society, there was growing acceptance that feminism could be enacted in various ways that either challenged traditional notions of femininity and/or embraced them.

These ideas, however, have not always sat well with those vigilant regarding the dangers of "buying into" dominant patriarchal notions of sexuality. For some who align themselves with the second wave's philosophy, embracing conventional femininity can be tantamount to further perpetuating rape culture. In their book offering a framework for third-wave feminists to facilitate social change, Jennifer Baumgardner and Amy Richards addressed these and other concerns around the third-wave movement and warned that feminism may be in danger of irrelevance if it does not connect itself to a broader political agenda.[64]

Meanwhile, Baumgardner, and other scholars, have suggested that a fourth wave of feminism has arisen that is building a powerful movement that includes both virtual and material campaigns in the fight for gender equality.[65] This shift from traditional media to new media, including feminist-inspired websites, is where much of the rhetoric around rape culture flourishes.[66]

The dissonance between the second- and third-wave philosophies is evidenced by the response to such feminist actions as SlutWalk.[67] Although many have claimed it as an important, progressive movement, others have been more critical, particularly of its embrace of the term "slut" as political action.[68] Scholar Theresa O'Keefe wrote that Slut-Walks effectively depoliticize women's bodies. She writes,

> SlutWalk Toronto refused to adopt the label "feminist" and, as a consequence, there is no acknowledgement of patriarchy as a system of oppression, no mention of the exploitative nature of capitalism, and no reference to systemic racism, homophobia or heteronorma-tivity.[69]

Likewise, in her analysis of SlutWalk, scholar Kathy Miriam asks what it "means to trade on the very semantics of rape culture—male fantasy—to relay a message against rape?"[70] She wrote that the problem with SlutWalk is the focus on individualized empowerment—e.g., the "choice" to wear whatever one wants—over the focus on the collective and imperative to dismantle the structural obstacles that limit those very choices. She wrote, "The issue is not the absence or presence of agency, but the *power* to determine the 'rules' of the game."[71] For Miriam, SlutWalk is devoid of political significance and does not adequately challenge patriarchal capitalism, which severely limits the types of choices women, particularly women of color, may make in their so-called freedom to dress like a slut.[72]

Similarly, Tram Nguyen wrote that SlutWalk offers no actual challenge to the social structures that enable and promote sexual violence:

> These performances do little to disturb social understanding of a "slut"—instead, they reify and concretize the concept of "slut" as scantily clad, sexually immoral women. Moreover, these actions ultimately displace the somber and deadly issues of rape, domestic violence, sexual abuse, and street harassment.[73]

Perhaps most importantly, scholars have noted the resistance by women of color to the use of "slut" as emancipating.[74] Miriam points out that in response to SlutWalk, the Black Women's Blueprint website noted that the history of the sexualization of black women deprives them of the privilege of being able to march and "reclaim" *slut* as some sort of political action that will reduce sexual assault in their communities. Nguyen echoed this sentiment in commentary on the *Crunk Feminist Collective*, writing that the blog

> makes the important point that "white women and liberal feminist women of color who argue that 'slut' is a universal category of female experience, irrespective of race," effectively ignore the brutal history and realities with which many Black women live. . . . For Crunk

Feminists and other hip-hop feminists, the sexualization of Black women is deeply connected to the history of American slavery, and reclamation of the word "slut," "ho," or "bitch" does not serve the interest of emancipation and equality. [75]

Although the concept of rape culture was dislodged from its academic roots in global conversations about SlutWalk, it was not until a couple of years later that it more fully diffused into public conversations outside the context of activism. It was during 2013 that it began to be associated with various international and domestic high-profile events involving sexual violence. Much of the media coverage of it used those events as indicators that rape culture "exists" or "is real." On February 14, 2013, an article appearing in *The Nation* led with a photo from the SlutWalk protest in Berlin that included a sign reading "No Excuses for Rape & Violence." The article stated,

> But recent headline-grabbing instances of sexual assault, from Steubenville, Ohio, to Delhi, India, are prodding Americans to become self-aware about the role we play in propagating a culture that not only allows but justifies sexual violence against women. [76]

Similarly, Sarah Trotta, writing for *Everyday Feminism*, stated,

> We've been hearing a lot about rape culture these days. The brutal and lethal rape in India, the sheer malignance of the high school boys in Steubenville, the House of Representative's refusal to reauthorize the Violence Against Women Act. [77]

In her article, Trotta encouraged readers to acknowledge the more unobtrusive ways that rape culture is perpetuated, including via sexist advertising, sexist language, and body shaming, and to link those "small-scale infractions" to the more brutal and violent incidents of sexual violence that more frequently capture the media attention. In doing so, Trotta echoed the feminist contention that central to the understanding of the normalization of male aggression against women is the recognition that "everyday" sexual violence is pervasive in mass media. [78]

Feminist blogs, which have become central to the mainstream public's understanding of rape culture, frequently disseminate their message by citing explicit concrete examples of it in society. This is very much like how Friedman and Valenti's and Kate Harding's books explored the concept. [79] For example, *Shakesville*, a self-described progressive feminist blog, suggested that the following constitutes rape culture: unacceptable rates of sexual assault against both women and men, using rape as a tool of war, victim blaming, the use of rape jokes, the blurring of lines between persistence and coercion, the lack of education about rape, and the mistreatment of victims who report rapes. The site also called out popular entertainment for using gratuitous rape scenes and, conversely, for the tendency in popular culture to ignore rape completely so as to erase the reality of sexual assault faced by women.[80]

Other sites also offer everyday examples to show how women are devalued and sex is linked to violence. *Feministing* shared common examples from social media to illustrate that rape culture is not a myth, including citing tweets using the hashtag #HowToAskSomeoneOnADate:

> Well what works for me, is holding a really sharp knife next to their neck and begging them #HowToAskSomeoneOnADate
>
> Take a rag of chloroform and have her sniff it. Take her body then put it in the trunk #HowToAskSomeoneOnADate
>
> Roofies make it a lot easier #HowToAskSomeoneOnADate[81]

Similarly, the "Rape Culture" Pinterest page published by Sociological Images documented numerous examples of images that condone violence against women. This included a T-shirt with an image of "heart hands," followed by the caption "It's not rape; it's a snuggle with a struggle"; a drinking glass available on sale from Etsy with an inscription on the bottom reading "You've just been roofied"; and an image from Facebook of duct tape with a caption that reads, "Turning NO, NO, NO into MMM, MMM, MMM."[82]

MICROAGGRESSIONS AND "REAL TRAUMA"

The examples of rape culture mentioned above do not necessarily rise to the level of criminal behavior, but by highlighting them, a cultural casualness of misogyny is revealed. It is this everyday experience of misogyny and rape-permissive attitudes, comments, and behavior that may be considered "microaggressions," a term that, like rape culture, originated in academia and has over the past few years gained mainstream currency. Microaggressions, a concept that was introduced in the 1970s, originally referred to pro-racist behaviors described as "subtle, stunning, often automatic, and nonverbal exchanges which are 'put downs' of blacks."[83]

In their 1978 study of media portrayals of race, researchers Chester Pierce et al. argued that in mass media, blacks are frequently subject to microaggressions in ways that seem innocuous, but the "cumulative weight of their never-ending burden is the major ingredient in black-white interactions." For example, in television commercials, blacks are rarely presented as "exerting authority or displaying superior knowledge or dispensers of goods and favors." This in turn reflects that they have nothing of value to offer and that they are "dependent and subservient." The authors further found, in contrast, that whites were overwhelmingly used to represent ideal beauty standards. Here, the constant inundation of subtle racism results in all races accepting these representations as "unremarkable" and thereby complicit in the acceptance of skin color as an indicator of superiority and inferiority.[84] Similarly, critical race theorists define microaggressions as a "stunning small encounter with racism, usually unnoticed by members of the majority race."[85]

Microaggressions are best understood as arising in a culture in which blatant, explicit racism and sexism are generally frowned upon, but implicit and casual evidence of racism and sexism remains commonplace and condoned. In the context of race and the criminal justice system, criminologist Katheryn Russell-Brown distinguished between microaggressions as nonverbal exchanges that are "put-downs of Blacks" and macroaggressions, defined as "attacks, insults, or pejorative statements made against Blacks as a group" that may be nonverbal or directed toward a particular individual but "becomes a group offense once it is made public, repeated, and heard around the world."[86] History has shown that although explicit, structural mechanisms of discrimination may be dismantled and abolished, such as the slave codes, black codes, and Jim Crow statutes, these advancements do not mean that equality has been achieved and that discrimination has been eliminated. In fact, rather than ushering in a colorblind (and sexist-free) world, informal and subtle instances of racism and sexism continue to thrive.[87]

The Tumblr *Microaggressions: Power, Privilege, and Everyday Life* invites people to submit write-ups of their experiences with microaggressions. The entries are simple comments that when taken in isolation may seem somewhat innocuous, but when taken together reveal how commonly these put-downs occur. For example,

> Working in my first bar job, I overheard the bar owner telling my manager to keep me on glass collection because he "only wanted the hot chicks working the bar." He also scolded her for hiring me in the first place—Apparently she was only supposed to hire thin girls.

"Don't you think your reaction was offensive to others as well?"—
White teacher to a black student who was offended that another
student described a neighborhood as "ghetto."

"Is she yours?"—Strangers to me, a white woman with a black
daughter.[88]

It is easy to see how examples of microaggressions could be dismissed
as hypersensitivity, especially among those who do not consistently experience insulting or degrading verbal or nonverbal gestures directed
toward them. In fact, the *New York Times* pointed out that comments
on articles about microaggressions "have been a mix of empathetic and
critical."[89]

There has been a palpable backlash against the increasing attention
to perceived microaggressions. In his article for *New York Magazine*,
Jonathan Chait argued that complaining about them is but one of the
many examples illustrating how the past few years have ushered in a
renewed era of political correctness, reminiscent of that in the 1980s
and 1990s, that has perverted free speech.[90] In his article for *The Federalist*, Paul Rowan Brian ridiculed the concept of microaggressions by
suggesting that it goes too far, and its "growing popularity as a concept
is problematic." Brian's most significant complaint seems to be that the
concept has emerged from the "ever-leftwards-winding corridors of Academia" into mainstream usage and his fears that virtually any offensive
behavior might be deemed a microaggression. He stated,

> The problem with terms and concepts like microaggression is that
> they lend an academic, politically-correct air to the whole topic of
> prejudice and to the language around the resolution of prejudice.[91]

From this perspective, in addition to being committed unintentionally,
microaggressions are problematic in that they maintain focus on what
are perceived weaknesses instead of strengths, are too broad in scope,
and potentially create a "culture of victimhood."[92] Bringing microaggressions to public attention has at times inspired particularly harsh
responses. Former police officer and marine veteran Chris Hernandez
wrote that those who are concerned with microaggressions are "whin-
ing" and "pathologically stupid." The implication is that those who have
experienced "real" trauma, such as war or other violent conflict, should
not be fazed by these "fake" traumas.[93]

One of the key differences between critics and supporters of the
concept is that the critics view its usage as potentially undermining the
real struggle with civil rights. That is, that it serves to divert attention

away from important issues to insignificant ones. On the flipside, those who support the usage of the concept see microaggressions as *part of* their everyday struggles. These everyday interactions do not have to rise to the level of violent conflicts to be impactful—their power derives from their cumulative impact.[94]

This is therefore how what might be considered one of the most innocuous of behaviors, a comment uttered by a stranger—"Smile"— can also be one of the most irritating. Angela Della Porta, writing for the *Stop Street Harassment* blog put it this way: "Men of every age seem to be so bothered that I don't constantly look ecstatic."[95]

Hearing the phrase is so commonplace, and so unwanted, that Tatyana Fazlalizadeh created an art series around street harassment titled "Stop Telling Women to Smile." She pastes posters in public places featuring her portraits of women she interviewed about street harassment. The paintings are accompanied by phrases such as "Women Don't Owe You Your Time or Conversation," "Women Are Not Seeking Your Validation," "Critiques on My Body Are Not Welcome," and "Stop Telling Women to Smile."[96] Fazlalizadeh said of her project,

> I think when we talk about street harassment we're talking about a type of power and privilege that's being exerted over women in public spaces. And whenever we talk about any type of oppression or privilege, there's always the other types of oppression or privilege that come in to play. That includes race, sexuality, class, gender, etc. How do queer women experience street harassment, how do trans women experience it?[97]

In an effort to document street harassment, ad agency owner Rob Bliss placed a hidden camera in his backpack and walked in front of a woman, actor Shoshana Roberts, for ten hours on the streets of New York City. In October 2014, *Hollaback*, a website devoted to ending street harassment, released a condensed (about two-minute) video clip that documented over one hundred catcalls. As of February 2016, the video had amassed nearly forty-two million views on YouTube. Although the video prompted conversations about street harassment, it also resulted in unanticipated consequences. Within a day, Roberts received numerous online rape threats. Roberts told the *Guardian*, "I got people wanting to slit my throat."[98] One threat read,

> So we reached a state where it's already harassment if you wish a woman a nice day as a male. well played feminism . . . well played. this woman wears a skintight tanktop with leggings and probably a push-up bra. what did she expect? why is she even wearing make-up

if she doesn't want to draw attention on her? this slut can fuck herself.[99]

And another: "stupid fucking cunt i seriously hope you get rape [*sic*]."[100]

Roberts told CNN that the catcalling depicted in the video was
typical of her daily experiences, and in response to the rape threats, she
told *The Forward*, "Unfortunately I have sexual assault in my past, and
unfortunately, I relive it when all of this comes up. . . . Luckily I've built
up a much thicker skin, but I am very fearful."[101]

The video clip also received criticism for its racist implications—that
is, that in the edited version, almost all the harassers were black or
Latino. When interviewed by Metro.co.uk, the video editor defended
the editing decisions and stated,

> We got a fair amount of white guys, but for whatever reason, a lot of
> what they said was in passing, or off camera. So their scenes were a
> lot shorter, but the numbers themselves are relatively even.[102]

Hollaback responded to the criticism,

> "We regret the unintended racial bias in the editing of the video that
> overrepresents men of colour." That day of filming included a line of
> white businessmen, "who were like, and excuse my language: I'd fuck
> the shit out of you."[103]

Telling women to smile and other forms of street harassment are pervasive behaviors that impact women every day, even if they do not rise to
the level of criminal behavior. What the concept of microaggression
allows is recognition that these experiences reveal a pattern of how
groups, in this case, women, continue to be marginalized in subtle ways.
This is despite more formalized moves over the past decades to address
structural inequality (e.g., increasing gender equality, the passage of
laws preventing racial discrimination, laws allowing gay marriage, etc.).
In this context, microaggressions have become symptomatic of rape
culture itself. Though they reside on the low-level, noncriminal end of
the continuum of sexual violence, they are nevertheless viewed as oppressive.

THE END OF RAPE CULTURE?

By 2014, the mainstream media had widely acknowledged rape culture
as a problem in America and featured the subject in a variety of articles

and television news programs. In their year-end "Make It a Year of Solutions" feature, CNN cited it as one of 2014's greatest problems. Author and political commentator Sally Kohn, in recounting the top stories that had captivated the public's attention, included the University of Virginia (UVA) rape allegation scandal and the numerous sexual assault allegations against the once-beloved comedian Bill Cosby (nearly sixty women have come forward as of July 2016). Kohn called for increased education around issues of consent and rape prevention efforts.[104] Similarly, Ann Friedman, writing for NYMag.com, declared 2014 "The Year Everyone (Finally) Started Talking about Sexual Assault."[105] It was during this year that President Barack Obama's Task Force to Protect Students from Sexual Assault released their first report, "Not Alone," claiming that "One in five women is sexually assaulted in college" and offered recommendations to reduce the violence.[106]

By the end of the year, however, a backlash had begun to build against the concept of rape culture. It actually came under attack as quickly as it had burst onto the scene and into the public's consciousness a year earlier. The backlash can be traced, in part, to November 2014, when *Rolling Stone* magazine published their article, "A Rape on Campus: A Brutal Assault and Struggle for Justice at UVA." That piece erupted in a firestorm of controversy when the victim's account was challenged[107] and the article was retracted.[108] Writing for *A Voice for Men*, a website devoted to men's rights, Jim Byset stated, "For me, 2014 will be remembered as the year that we did serious damage to [the myth of] rape culture. . . . Put bluntly, people aren't going to swallow the bullshit anymore."[109]

Similarly, journalist Cathy Young declared 2014 "The Year the Crusade against Rape Culture Stumbled," *Powerline* declared rape culture "debunked," and in March, Caroline Kitchens declared rape culture as "hysteria."[110] The *National Review* asked, "Who *Really* Created the Rape Culture?" and blamed leftists for creating "a sexual free-for-all" on American campuses.[111] Jay Ambrose, writing for the *Columbus Dispatch*, described the concern around sexual assault on campus as "an epidemic of hyperbole," suggesting that it is the culture of female sexual empowerment that is criminogenic. He stated,

> Female students have, in fact, been subjected to something awful. It includes big-time boozing and starts with a society that has taught that free-wheeling, emotionally detached sex for the fun of it is jim-dandy as long as they keep it safe. What obviously can follow is young men taking eager advantage of the situation.[112]

The concept of rape culture was not only challenged, but worse, was deemed a "moral panic"—a term popularized by sociologist Stanley Cohen in the 1970s in his pioneering work on the ways deviance is amplified by the media. The concept is used to describe how certain groups, or "folk devils," are considered threats to the social order. Their threat is portrayed far out of proportion to their actual deviance or criminality. While Cohen used the term to describe the media and public reaction to British youth subcultures in the 1960s, it has since been used to describe societal overreaction to everything from the threat of poisonous Halloween candy, to the threat of juvenile "super-predators," to the epidemic of so-called crack babies, among other scares. [113]

In one of her American Enterprise Institute videos, Christina Hoff Sommers, author of *Who Stole Feminism? How Women Have Betrayed Women*, equated the embrace of rape culture to the satanic child abuse scares of the 1980s. [114] Sommers wrote of the perceived panic in *Time*:

> Today's college rape panic is an eerie recapitulation of the daycare abuse panic. Just as the mythical "50,000 abducted children" fueled paranoia about child safety in the 1980s, so today's hysteria is incited by the constantly repeated, equally fictitious "one-in-five women on campus is a victim of rape"—which even President Obama has embraced. [115]

Journalist Judith Levine echoed that sentiment in an article she wrote for the *Boston Review* in which she addressed the response to the discredited *Rolling Stone* article. Levine critiqued feminist Jessica Valenti for alleging that "1 in 5 girl children are sexually assaulted" and pointed out that believing victims "en masse" is problematic. Levine suggested that the belief in all claims of rape is similar to the unquestioning belief that many held regarding children's false testimonies against ritual sexual abuse during the 1980s. She wrote,

> Shouldn't Valenti know that "believe the children"—all the children, even those coached by adults to lie—was the motto of the panic over the spectral crimes of "satanic ritual abuse," whose monsters were innocent people, some of whom died behind bars for crimes that never happened? [116]

By this time, the discrediting of rape culture was in full gear, with many characterizing those that embraced the concept as irrational, blinded by ideology, or, at the very least, naive. Reactionary responses were prevalent, such as Matt Walsh's article in *The Blaze*, which declared that rape culture does not exist, that college campuses "encourage" false allegations, and that "rape hoaxers are as despicable as rapists," because false claims "have the potential to completely ruin a man." Similarly, Barbara Kay's article for the *National Post* declared that "moral panic is oxygen to the rape-culture movement, a movement that seeks to demonize all men and victimize all women."[117]

Arguments embracing the concept of rape culture, and those seeking to debunk it, have been made before in contemporary society. They echo the same concerns that arose, for example, when the concept of "date/acquaintance rape" entered the public lexicon over twenty years ago. At that time, the anti-rape movement was targeted and their efforts condemned for their "overly broad feminist redefinitions of rape."[118] Bevacqua noted that in the 1990s, "self-described feminists" such as Camille Paglia, Katie Roiphe, and Christina Hoff Sommers led the charge that feminists themselves were part of the problem, as they had overstated the prevalence of rape. Decades later, these same debates continue.[119]

THE NUMBERS

As the concept of "rape culture" began to be questioned in late 2014, detractors scrutinized its statistical prevalence. Rape culture was called out as a fiction, hyperbolic, and a moral panic. The argument was that if rates of rape are low, there is no rape culture. The assumption follows that feminists "need" high rates of rape to claim victimhood status and thus "prove" we live in a rape culture. Conversely, those opposed to the use of the concept must dismiss high rates of sexual violence as hype to "prove" that we do not live in a rape culture. Despite the continuing debates, particularly around rates of sexual assaults on college campuses, there is some consensus that, in general, violence against women is a serious problem on a global scale.

GLOBAL SEXUAL VIOLENCE

Over the past several decades, researchers have worked to develop and refine measures of sexual violence. By all serious accounts, violence against women is considered a major global problem.[120] Among many feminist scholars, violence against women is broadly understood as a consequence of gender inequalities and gender discrimination, resulting in a range of victimizations, including sexual harassment, reproductive injustices, sexual exploitation, sexual assault, and rape.[121] Human rights organizations have documented high rates of sexual violence in various regions of the world. They point out that women and children disproportionately suffer when sexual violence is used as a weapon of war in conflict-ridden regions, as well as when those in positions of state power commit it [122] The World Health Organization (WHO) described violence against women as "a global public health problem of epidemic proportions, requiring urgent action."[123] Its study on "Global and Regional Estimates of Violence against Women" found that

> more than one in three women (35.6%) globally report having experienced physical and/or sexual partner violence, or sexual violence by a non-partner, the evidence is incontrovertible.[124]

SEXUAL VIOLENCE IN THE UNITED STATES

While violence against women, including sexual violence, is generally acknowledged as a serious global problem, there is much debate in the United States over the rates of sexual violence. Skeptics have questioned the reporting of government data sources, as well as that of researchers, particularly with regard to rates of rape on college campuses.[125] The media echoed similar arguments over the validity of sexual violence statistics in the late 1980s when the concept of acquaintance (or "date") rape first entered public consciousness. This new understanding shattered the myth that strangers are most frequently the perpetrators of rape. The public learned that, in fact, victims of rape usually know their assailants, and they can even be victimized by the person they are dating. The attention to acquaintance rape resulted in massive backlash that included victim blaming, debates around issues of consent and false allegations, and increased skepticism around rape statistics.[126] Over the past few years, these debates have raged again, frequently framed in the context of rape culture and often discussed in the context of rates of sexual violence on campuses.

Measuring the rates of sexual violence has proven challenging, and as a result public discourse around the concept of rape culture frequently centers on the validity of the data.[127] Much of the confusion centers on the methodology of the studies themselves—that is, how rape is defined and measured. Since there is no single, consistent definition of sexual violence among researchers, critics tend to point to conflicting findings regarding the incidence and prevalence rates as evidence that the problem of sexual violence is vastly exaggerated.[128] The definition of rape, like all crimes, is socially constructed, and the stated purpose of any given survey—whether it is designed to determine crime rates or to assess the effects of victimization and address issues of public health—will influence the way that sexual violence is defined and measured. Despite these issues, there is a growing consensus regarding the ways to best measure sexual violence.[129]

According to the Department of Justice report "Female Victims of Sexual Violence, 1994–2010" published in 2013, the "estimated annual rate of female rape or sexual assault victimizations declined 58%" from 1995 to 2010. In 2010, the annual rate of female rape or sexual assault victimization was 2.1 per 1,000 (approximately 91% of all victimizations from 1995 to 2010 involved female victims). The report found that 78 percent of the sexual violence involved a family member, intimate partner, friend, or acquaintance. The report is based on findings from the National Crime Victimization Survey (NCVS), which measures both reported and unreported victimizations. The study found that although reporting reached a high of 56 percent in 2003, by 2010 only 35 percent of victims reported to police.[130] Some common reasons for not reporting included fear of reprisal, perceiving the incident as a personal matter, believing that the police would not be helpful, and reporting the incident to another (nonpolice) official.

It is widely believed that sexual violence is vastly underreported and that the NCVS does not provide a wholly accurate estimate of the victimizations. In fact, the discrepancies between the NCVS and other sources are so variable that the Bureau of Justice Statistics convened an expert panel to address the confusion around methodology and data collection and to recommend best practices moving forward. The panel was charged with addressing the difficulties of defining and measuring sexual violence, examining issues of underreporting, and improving ways that respondents may report anonymously. Overall, the report concluded that the NCVS underestimates rape and sexual assaults and stated that the survey is "not an adequate vehicle for the goal of accurate measurement." The panel recommended development of a new survey that is specific to rape and sexual assault.[131]

Another major official source of crime data in the United States, the Uniform Crime Report (UCR), published by the Federal Bureau of Investigation (FBI), also reported a substantial decline in rape from a rate of 37.1 per 100,000 inhabitants in 1995 to 26.4 in 2014 (legacy definition).[132] However, as with the NCVS, there are several limitations to the UCR that should be taken into account. First, since the data contain only information about crimes reported to law enforcement, it is widely acknowledged that the numbers present an undercount. For example, some studies find that as many as 65 to 80 percent of victims do not report incidents to law enforcement.[133] Additionally, until 2012 the UCR contained a strikingly limited definition of rape: "the carnal knowledge of a female forcibly and against her will," which defined carnal knowledge as "penetration (however slight) of a penis into a vagina." This legacy definition eliminated many types of behavior that most would consider rape, including penetration by other objects, and the definition omitted male victims. After much debate and "decades of lobbying," revisions were made in an attempt to address the inadequacies of the definition.[134] As of January 1, 2013, the expanded, revised definition reads, "Penetration, no matter how slight, of the vagina or anus with any body part or object, or oral penetration by a sex organ of another person, without the consent of the victim." It is too soon to measure long-term trends that include the revised, more inclusive definition.

In addition to the definitional problems with the UCR, evidence of crime rate suppression has been found among various police departments across the country.[135] Since the UCR only contains information submitted to law enforcement, if those agencies downgrade offenses, the undercounts will be reflected in the data. For example, the *Village Voice* reported that in 2010, the "downgrading of sexual assaults from felonies to misdemeanors has become a growing problem," and the New York Police Department (NYPD) apologized to a female victim for downgrading her report of felony sexual assault to a misdemeanor, presumably in an effort to suppress crime numbers.[136] The downgrading was recognized as part of a larger, more systemic problem with how the pressures from Compstat, a police management strategy focused on reducing crime numbers and holding supervisors accountable, led to patterns of downgrading offenses within the NYPD.[137] Crime number manipulation and downgrading of offenses have also been found in other cities that have implemented "Compstat-like performance management systems in such locations as Philadelphia, Atlanta, New Orleans, Broward County and elsewhere."[138]

Despite the downward trend as reported by official sources, research still indicates a notable number of women and men that experience sexual violence in their lifetimes. In her review of the literature on lifetime prevalence rates of rape, attorney Jody Raphael used a narrow definition of rape defined as "forcible penetration" (vaginal, anal, or oral penetration) and found that in five studies from 1992 to 2010, lifetime prevalence rates of forcible penetration of women ranged from 10.6 to 16.1 percent. From the same studies, she found that forcible penetration of women within the last twelve months ranged from .3 to .74 percent.[139]

The 2011 National Intimate Partner and Sexual Violence Survey published by the Centers for Disease Control and Prevention (CDC) found that "19.3% of women and 1.7% of men have been raped during their lifetime," and slightly under 2 percent of women were raped during the twelve months preceding the survey. The study also found that

> an estimated 43.9% of women and 23.4% of men experienced other forms of sexual violence during their lifetimes, including being made to penetrate, sexual coercion, unwanted sexual contact, and noncontact unwanted sexual experiences.[140]

The study found that for female rape victims, the vast majority of the perpetrators (99 percent) were male, with about 80 percent of the male rape victims having male perpetrators. Further, consistent with other studies, the majority of victims knew their perpetrator. For the female victims, 78.8 percent of the rapes occurred before twenty-five years of age.[141]

Despite these findings, these statistics do not sit well with critics who charge that the rates of sexual violence are inflated.[142] For example, journalist Cathy Young attacked the CDC's report, mainly taking issue with the way rape is defined—a common criticism lodged against early studies of acquaintance rape. That is, that the definition includes instances of "incapacitated rape" (e.g., incidents in which the respondent was "drunk, high, drugged, or passed out and unable to consent") that may fall outside the legal definition of rape. She wrote,

> The CDC study—the second in two years—seems to support a radical feminist narrative that has been gaining mainstream attention recently: that modern America is a "rape culture" saturated with misogynistic violence.[143]

While the framing of criticisms over rape statistics *in the context of rape culture* is relatively new in popular discourse, the debate over the numbers themselves is not new. In fact, *Ms.* magazine characterized the recent debate over the numbers as the "Second Wave of Backlash against Anti-Rape Activism" following the well-documented backlash against acquaintance rape statistics in the late 1980s and 1990s.[144] Arguments challenging the validity of rape statistics, including the oft-cited "1 in 5" findings (which will be discussed in chapter 6), the definition of date rape, the role of intoxication, and the prevalence rates on college campuses have raged for several decades.[145] However, before addressing how the concept of rape culture was initially validated by high-profile instances of sexual assault on campuses, and then later discredited by those same instances, let's go back to 2013, the year that "rape culture" exploded into the public imagination.

2

THE MAINSTREAMING OF RAPE CULTURE

It was not until 2013 that "rape culture" became a framework in popular discourse for understanding the attitudes and behaviors pertaining to sexual violence. Three unrelated, high-profile events, in particular, ignited public interest in it: the Steubenville, Ohio, rape case; the New Delhi, India, gang rape; and the success of Robin Thicke's pop song "Blurred Lines." These events are by no means inclusive of all relevant events, nor are they even the "most important" events related to sexual violence. However, they are symbolic of what feminist scholars have for years described as rape culture. Taken together, these events culminated in awareness of the concept on three levels: (1) domestically, with regard to teen behavior, sports entitlement, and social media; (2) internationally, with regard to violence against women; and (3) in popular culture, with regard to narratives and images of sexual violence.

As previously discussed, in 2013, Google Trends showed an increase in searches for "rape culture" relative to other searches. Although Google Trends does not give an indication of the context for which individuals searched for "rape culture," it is reasonable to posit that the increase in popularity of the term was likely related to stories that dominated news media during the time period. For example, Google Trends shows a spike on the search "rape culture" during March 17–23, 2013. This corresponds to the trial of two juvenile boys in Steubenville, Ohio, accused of rape and posting incriminating photos and comments on social media. The term "rape culture" also peaked in November 2013, corresponding to a scandal known as the "New Zealand Roast Busters," which was described as alleged incidents where teen boys would

target teenage girls, ply them with alcohol until they're often close to
unconsciousness, gang-rape them, and then upload the evidence to
social media sites in an attempt to shame their victims.[1]

According to news reports, some of the victims were underage, as
young as thirteen. In response to the incidents, thousands protested
against the lack of criminal justice response.[2] According to the *New
Zealand Herald,* part of the focus of the protests was to "bust rape
culture." As one rape prevention advocate argued,

> My issue is that you have these people calling for their heads and
> "they need to go to prison" and it's like, sweet, put them in prison . . .
> it doesn't solve the problem. . . . You look around at how much
> advertising objectifies women, the prevailing attitudes towards vic-
> tim blaming and you can start to see how attitudes like this [exist].[3]

The *Herald* later reported that seven teen female victims made formal
complaints, although twenty-five additional girls declined to make formal statements.[4] Ultimately, no charges were filed in the case due to
lack of evidence.[5]

Although the Roast Busters case did not attract much media attention in the United States, other international cases did receive widespread notice. From September 8 to 14, 2013, Google Trends showed a
spike on the search "gang rape" and "Delhi" and "Delhi gang rape."[6] In
media accounts of the New Delhi rape case, the concept of rape culture
was frequently used as a means of placing the case within the larger
context of how women are treated in a patriarchal society. Lauren
Wolfe, writing for CNN, framed the case as an example of the larger
problem of global violence against women, pointing out that protests in
India, Egypt, and Somalia indicated a growing consciousness around
sexual violence. She wrote,

> This groundswell—what [activist Eve] Ensler calls "a catalytic mo-
> ment"—is the perfect chance for us to consider how we think about
> subjugation, rape, and degradation of women globally.[7]

"RAPE CULTURE ISN'T JUST INDIA'S PROBLEM"

On December 16, 2012, after an evening at the movie theater, a young
woman, Jyoti Singh, and her male friend, Awindra Pandey, were attacked on a private bus in New Delhi. He was beaten and she was
brutally tortured and gang raped; both were left to die on the street.

Singh was hospitalized and transported to Singapore for treatment but later died from her injuries; Pandey survived. On December 28, before the identity of the victim was known, the *New York Times* reported on the severity of her injuries:

> The woman, whose intestines were removed because of injuries caused by a metal rod used during the rape, has not been identified. She was flown to Singapore on Wednesday night after undergoing three abdominal operations at a local hospital. She had also suffered a major brain injury, cardiac arrest and infections of the lungs and abdomen.[8]

In the BBC documentary *India's Daughter*, which covered the aftermath of the incident in India, Doctor Rashmi Ahuja, who was at the hospital, explained Singh's condition:

> She was bleeding very much from her vagina . . . she was slapped on her face, she was kicked on her abdomen and she had multiple injuries over her body, over her private parts. There were multiple bite marks over her face, over her lips, over her limbs.[9]

Although police arrested the suspects, the case prompted thousands to protest and demand harsher anti-rape legislation and legal reform. Five perpetrators and one juvenile were arrested (one adult committed suicide while incarcerated). The four adults were sentenced to death, and the juvenile was sentenced to a maximum of three years. In this case, we can see how the victim fit the model of what criminologist Nils Christie deemed the "ideal victim"—one who, in the public imagination, is weak, engaged in respectable activity, devoid of blame, and a stranger to the perpetrator(s).[10] The *Guardian* explained the characteristics of the case and why it captured the public's attention and sympathy:

> The attack was of almost unprecedented brutality, committed by complete strangers on a Sunday evening, on the streets of Delhi itself. J was out with a friend watching a film. She was not in a village, nor was she working in a nightclub. She was thus seen as representative in a way that other victims, rightly or wrongly, had never been. Very soon she had been dubbed "Delhi's daughter" in the media, and thus neatly slotted into one of the three legitimate categories allowed to women in India: mother, spouse or child.[11]

The New Delhi rape case, along with other cases of sexual violence in India, such as the gang rape of a photojournalist on assignment in

Mumbai in August 2013, resulted in global media coverage. In their study of the sex crimes reported in the Indian press three months following the New Delhi rape case, researchers Daniel Drache and Jennifer Velagic found that the coverage tended to focus primarily on the personal attributes of the victim, the public outcry about the case, issues of women's safety, and legislative and police handling of the case.[12] Notably, much of the global news coverage moved away from individualized explanations of rape (i.e., a focus on the personality or psychopathology of the perpetrators) and instead focused on sexual violence as a social problem, while implicating broader social issues such as patriarchy, misogyny, and economic conditions as contributing factors.[13]

India itself has been described as the "rape capital of the world," though that moniker has been heavily criticized.[14] The *Washington Post* dubbed New Delhi the "'rape capital' of India, with more than 560 cases of rape reported in the city, but violence against Indian women is widespread and has deep roots."[15]

Similarly, *Gulf News* reported that "incidents of rape and murder have become routine in India," pointing to the statistics derived from the annual National Crime Records Bureau, which found 24,923 rape cases in 2012.[16] The *New York Times* reported that rapes had "increased by 25 percent in the past six years." Further, many believe that rape in India is vastly underreported and often met with insensitivity by officials.[17] Jason Burke, writing for the *Guardian*, described sexual harassment in India as "endemic" and reported that rape is "systematically blamed on irresponsible women behaving in 'un-Indian' ways."[18]

In this context, "rape culture" ultimately became synonymous with "Indian culture" on the global stage. Professor Meenakshi Gigi Durham concluded that U.S. media coverage of the New Delhi incident neglected to mention other cases of sexual assault that occurred in other countries, for example, the Steubenville, Ohio, rape case. She said this in effect singled out India "as a crucible for sexual violence, exacerbating global hierarchical power structures."[19] Professor Durham pointed out that the news reports "repeatedly referred to India as a place of great sexual danger to women, demonizing Indian men as morally degenerate while positioning Third World women as oppressed and victimized."[20]

In response to this type of critique, some journalists did make the distinction in their stories that rape is obviously not inherent to India's culture, but rather, there has been increased awareness and public discussion of sexual violence that has created the perception of an India rape culture.[21] *Gulf News* said that the rates of reported rape in India were actually lower than those in Western Europe and Latin America. However, it is not clear whether this was due to the underreporting of rape in India.[22] In fact, according to the *International Business Times*, reports of rape increased the first two months of 2015 and were on track to double over the year. This indicates that it is possible that more women are coming forward who would have previously remained silent.[23]

News coverage in North America also highlighted a perceived marginalization of women in India. Some stories positioned the violence as being part of a larger patriarchal society that links rape to shame, and, as a result, prevented victims from speaking out. Such articles frequently pointed to high rates of sexual harassment and sexual violence, low prosecution rates, and the mistreatment of victims in India.[24]

One blog post written by John Xenakis for the conservative blog *Breitbart* blamed the caste system for how poor, disadvantaged victims in India are more likely to be neglected by the justice system. The post posited that the case "is only tangentially a story about rape" and that the real concern is the caste system in India.[25] While the claim that this story is only "tangentially" about rape seems dismissive, the article does acknowledge that treatment by the criminal justice system varies by caste position and that sexual violence against lower-caste women is likely to go unacknowledged.[26] A number of attacks in India, including a 2014 incident in which two teen girls were raped, murdered, and left hanging from a tree in the state of Uttar Pradesh, brought renewed attention toward how the lower caste are less valued and considered "fair game" as victims.[27] In their study of Indian news media, Drache and Velagic found that in coverage of sexual violence, discussions of caste were specific to Dalit victims—those at the bottom of the caste system.[28]

Some scholars pointed to the depiction of the men in India as problematic. Researcher Tara Atluri described the news coverage of the New Delhi case as paradoxical in that on the one hand, young men in India were portrayed in ways that pathologized them, while on the other, they were portrayed as leaders of the progressive protest movement against sexual assault.[29] In fact, one study conducted by sociologist Jesna Jayachandran, which investigated the largely male reader responses to rape coverage in the *Times of India* during 2013, found that they expressed a desire for justice and called for harsh punishment. The researchers noted, however, that comments expressing general outrage and anger against incompetent policing with regard to sexual violence "rest comfortably alongside sexist jokes, patriarchal views on gender norms, sexuality."[30]

Such misogynistic attitudes, as well as the social movement that arose in response to the New Delhi case, were illuminated in the BBC-produced documentary film *India's Daughter*. It had been slated to be shown in India on International Women's Day in March 2015 but was instead banned by the government.[31] The documentary depicted Jyoti Singh's victimization through interviews with her parents, one of the convicted offenders, defense attorneys, and others with knowledge about the case. Statements made by one of the convicted men, as well as by defense attorneys, revealed entrenched misogynist views. In his interview, rapist Mukesh Singh blamed Jyoti for her torture, rape, and murder. He stated,

> You can't clap with one hand—it takes two hands. . . . A decent girl won't roam around at nine o'clock at night. A girl is far more responsible for rape than a boy. . . . Boy and girl are not equal. . . . About 20% of girls are good.

He continued, "When being raped, she shouldn't fight back. She should just be silent and allow the rape. Then, they'd have dropped her off after 'doing her,' and only hit the boy."[32] In addition, one defense attorney, A. P. Singh, shared his views about proper behavior for women,

> If my daughter or sister engaged in pre-marital activities and disgraced herself and allowed herself to lose face and character by doing such things, I would most certainly take this sort of sister or daughter to my farmhouse, and in front of my entire family, I would put petrol on her and set her alight.[33]

These types of attitudes clash profoundly with the progressive views held by those seeking reform in India. In fact, the case was widely regarded as a watershed moment in terms of encouraging victims to speak out about their experiences by linking it to rape culture.[34] Journalist Nilanjana Roy told BBC News,

> "Rape culture" in India is fuelled by an acceptance of inequality and of embedded violence; it may be the first time in decades that we are exploring these fault lines—of caste, class and gender—in such a mainstream fashion. . . . The rapes might not stop; but this conversation isn't stopping either.[35]

Ruchira Gupta's CNN article titled "Victims Blamed in India's Rape Culture" detailed how the system fails victims of sexual assault. She drew attention to the National Crime Records Bureau's reporting of increased incidences of sexual assault and the correspondingly low conviction rate of offenders. She wrote,

> In the course of my work with Apne Aap Women Worldwide, I have
> seen the steady creeping of a rape culture into the fabric of India. . . .
> The biggest challenge we face is the attitude of politicians, senior
> police officials, heads of foundations and even policy makers who
> view rape as a normal part of society. Many have told me: "Men will
> be men."[36]

In the aftermath of the protests, authorities in India also made comments that reinforced the perception that entrenched patriarchy in the
country was depriving women of their human rights.[37] According to the
Sydney Morning Herald, in 2014, Babulal Gaur, a minister of the ruling
Bharatiya Janata Party in India, told reporters that rape "is a social
crime which depends on men and women. Sometimes it's right, sometimes it's wrong."[38] In an article discussing how the caste system contributes to rape-permissive attitudes, *USA Today* reported a comment
from Uttar Pradesh chief minister Mulayam Singh Yadav, stating,
"'Boys will be boys,' he said. 'Sometimes they make mistakes.'"[39] This
"cult of masculinity," as described by Gupta, enables victim blaming
and is linked to larger structural issues:

> rape has too often become the weapon of choice for frustrated young
> men who blame women, increasingly visible in the workplace, for
> their unemployment, and who hope to regain jobs by frightening
> women back home through sexual violence.[40]

According to scholar Tara Atluri, what the media coverage around the
case was missing was discussion on the increasing sexual violence within
the context of an unstable global economy and global austerity.[41] Atluri
wrote that Prime Minister Manmohan Singh described "footloose mi-
grants" as a potential "menace to society."[42] She suggested that rather
than understanding the case through the lens of "tradition vs. moder-
nity," neoliberalism itself should be considered to have "gendered consequences at the level of both violence and resistance."[43] Part of such a
discussion would certainly implicate the justice system in relation to its
abysmal treatment of lower-class victims.

The news coverage generally avoided simplistic, individualistic explanations of rape but did so in a way that some considered problematic. In an analysis of the first two weeks of U.S. media coverage of the
case, including articles appearing in the *Wall Street Journal*, *USA Today*, and CNN, Professor Durham argued that the media "reinscribed
social geographies of power in terms of sex and gender" and, as a result,
minimized sexual violence in the First World.[44] For Durham, framing
India as a failed democracy lacking gender equality is troublesome because it does not acknowledge the frequency of sexual violence in other

locales and virtually eliminates opportunities for "cross-national collaborations, solidarity, and collective action against the worldwide problem of sexual violence against women."[45] Durham wrote,

> Overall, the news coverage invoked archetypes of the Third World as a primitive and undisciplined place populated by savage males and subordinate women, a space in which women's mobility is constrained and where state authority is complicit in rendering women vulnerable to sexual assault due to its incompetence in governing a modern democracy.[46]

Given that media coverage of sexual assault in America has a history of focusing on the victim's behavior and/or individual pathology of the offender, the media's shift of focus toward broader social and economic factors that influence sexual violence in this case might have been a welcome one had it provided for moments of domestic introspection. However, what the coverage demonstrated was that the concept of rape culture is more likely to be widely accepted domestically when it is directed to an "other" culture. As Professor Helen Benedict pointed out in her post on *Women under Siege*, what is striking about the media coverage of cases of sexual violence in India and other non-Western countries is that it allows the possibility for us to consider cultural factors that we neglect when covering domestic rape cases. She wrote,

> The bottom line is this: Just about any discussion of women's rights is still seen in the mainstream press as radical, opinionated, and biased, not as legitimate news. . . . Perhaps, though, we can take the discussions of cultural misogyny that *are* allowed about the military and about India (or any other country that isn't *us*), and apply them to our own culture—to ourselves.[47]

There were, however, some exceptions.[48] For example, one Canadian newspaper headline read, "Rape Culture Isn't Just India's Problem."[49] In a *National Post* article, "How India's Rape Culture Came to Canada," Canadian-born Afsun Qureshi wrote from personal experience:

> I know that the attitudes that spawned India's recent gang-rape tragedy don't just flourish in South Asia. Sadly enough, there are common threads of cultural-based misogyny wherever the Indo-Pak, and now Afghani, communities settle.[50]

He alleged that, in insular patriarchal communities, there is a tendency to protect perpetrators, at the expense of victims who are too often reluctant to contact the police.[51]

Ultimately, the protests regarding the victimization of women in India prompted the convening of the Verma Committee, which released its report on January 23, 2013. The committee recommended changes to the law, including expanding the definition of rape and harsher punishments for offenders. The report acknowledged that legal changes alone are insufficient and that attitudes that perpetuate gender bias must be altered. In their concluding remarks, the report stated, "The nation has to account for the tears of millions of women and other marginalized sections of the society which has been ignored owing to institutional apathy."[52]

In March 2013, the Criminal Law (Amendment) Act of 2013 was passed, demonstrating that the calls for an end to sexual violence had resulted in reliance on the state.[53] Many find the legal reforms, which include an expansion of the definition of rape; the outlining of punishments for acid attacks, sexual harassment, voyeurism, and stalking; and harsher punishments, such as possible life imprisonment for gang rape, to be improvements necessary for justice.[54] It remains to be seen how the legislation will be implemented on the ground and how it will impact women's lives.

JUSTICE FOR JANE DOE

The media coverage of the New Delhi rape case revealed that when sexual violence occurs in an "other" culture, it may be understood as a cultural and structural problem that implicates patriarchy, class, and neoliberalism. Meanwhile, another high-profile case occurred in our own backyard, in Steubenville, Ohio, which focused our attention primarily on teen behavior, misogyny, social media use, and online vigilantism. The case, and subsequent discussions of it on social media, collectively contributed to our understanding of Steubenville as symbolic of rape culture in the United States.

On March 13, 2013, a juvenile trial of two high school football players began in Steubenville, Ohio. Trent Mays, seventeen years old, and Ma'lik Richmond, sixteen years old, were accused of raping an intoxicated, unconscious sixteen-year-old girl, known as Jane Doe, during a night of partying in August 2012. The sexual assault was reported on August 14, and by August 22, two arrests were made. By March of the following year, both juveniles were adjudicated guilty of rape, with Mays guilty of an additional charge of distributing a nude photo of a minor. The same day as the verdict, two teen girls posted threats directed toward Jane Doe on social media and were subsequently arrested. Their tweets included the following:

> I'll celebrate by beating the s*** out of Jane Doe.

> You ripped my family apart, you made my cousin cry, so when I see you bitch it's going to be a homicide.

> She's the town whore anyways. She hasn't stopped drinking yet. just pray, cause God's gonna get her worse than anyone can.

The two later pled guilty to the charge of telecommunications harassment.[55]

The case easily conformed to what criminologists would describe as newsworthy and quickly captured the public's attention.[56] It involved allegations of sexual assault, teen alcohol consumption, accusations against players on a beloved football team and of a cover-up, Internet vigilantism, and visual spectacle. The photos and screenshots served as evidence in trial, as well as in the court of public opinion.

Public discourse surrounding the case ranged from extensive victim blaming, including questioning whether a rape actually occurred, to assertions that the incident proved that rape culture exists. There was critique of the mainstream media for its perceived callous disregard for the victim in the coverage following the verdict, as well as indictment of the use of social media for online vigilantism. Here's how the case was initially described by *Democracy Now!* on January 7, 2013:

> Well, according to both the *New York Times* and Anonymous, what they're saying happened was that a 16-year-old girl, who was from a neighboring town in West Virginia, was taken to a series of parties celebrating the end of the summer and the beginning of the football season. She was intoxicated or possibly date-raped, and unconscious even at one point, being carried by football players from party to party and allegedly sexually assaulted and raped both at parties and in between. Anonymous is saying that the sexual assaults may even have happened at the homes of assistant coaches to the football team, as well as the prosecutor.[57]

Over the next few months until the trial, rumors circulated as to what had happened that night. While mainstream media coverage of the Steubenville case was extensive, social media served as the primary avenue for uncovering details. In her article for the *New Yorker* published in August 2013, Ariel Levy corrected much of the misinformation that had come to dominate the narrative. She wrote,

In versions of the story that spread online, the girl was lured to the party and then drugged. While she was delirious, she was transported in the trunk of a car, and then a gang of football players raped her over and over again and urinated on her body while her peers watched, transfixed. The town, desperate to protect its young princes, contrived to cover up the crime. If not for [blogger Alexandria] Goddard's intercession, the police would have happily let everyone go. None of that is true.[58]

The teens did attend a series of parties, Jane Doe was raped (though there was no evidence she was urinated on), and there were witnesses that evening. In their coverage of the trial, Fox8 detailed the crime,

> According to prosecutors, Richmond and Mays each penetrated the victim's vagina with their fingers, an act that constitutes rape under Ohio law. They are not accused of having intercourse with the girl, although prosecutor Marianne Hemmeter said in opening statements that one photograph appears to show semen on the girl's body and DNA analysis of semen on a blanket she was lying on was a match for Mays.[59]

The Steubenville case was unique in that many details about the crime came to light when the boys, their teammates, and their schoolmates shared the information on social media. The most incriminating activities were recorded, though some of the footage would later be deleted. At trial, one witness recounted his involvement in the incident:

> He went on to describe how he [the witness] filmed—and then deleted from his iPhone—footage of one of the accused, Trent Mays, digitally penetrating her in the back of a car, how Mays put his penis in the mouth of the teenage girl and how he [the witness] viewed the notorious picture of her being carried by her arms and legs as a "bad joke."[60]

Some of the boys used Facebook, Twitter, and Instagram to comment on the activities that occurred the night of the rape, including posting pictures of the girl. One Instagram photo became emblematic—the one showing Mays and Richmond holding the unconscious girl by her wrists and legs, her head dangling to the ground.[61] Comments made about Jane Doe were amplified on social media and revealed the continuing presence of rape myths and victim blaming. Some of the incendiary statements included, "Song of the night is definitely Rape Me by Nirvana," "Some people deserve to be peed on," "Never seen anything this sloppy lol," and "I have no sympathy for whores."[62] The victim was ridiculed, blamed for the incident, and was referred to as Steubenville's "train whore."[63]

The rampant misogyny permeating the case, which can be characterized more broadly as "slut shaming," makes it an easy fit for the ideological camp that believes "rape culture exists."[64] Steubenville also serves as a cautionary tale for a number of societal problems—some new and some long prevalent—including the careless teen use of social media, the lingering confusion around the definition of rape and consent, and the perils of online vigilantism.

The boys' social media posts were online for all to see. However, they had not been widely disseminated until former Steubenville resident and blogger Alexandria Goddard scoured social media accounts after the arrests and reposted screenshots of them. Goddard blogged about the incident out of concern that the crime might be minimized or ignored. She pointed out that the accused were Steubenville football players, and that football is highly revered in the town. She stated,

> I have been following the twitter accounts of many of the football players and students about the attack, and quite frankly am a bit shocked that some of them are supporting the boys. This was tweeted about the victim. "You supposevly [*sic*] get 'raped and tweet happy shit #idontgetit #dumbbitch."[65]

Goddard was outspoken in her condemnation of the boys' behavior. She maintained that exposing rape culture was central to her understanding of and involvement in the case. Ariel Levy of the *New Yorker* quoted Goddard: "I don't think I've really grasped how huge it is. Internationally, and opening that dialogue that we do have rape culture and violence against women."[66]

In what was considered the first national exposure, the *New York Times* reported on the case in their article "Rape Case Unfolds on Web and Splits City" on December 16, 2012, citing Goddard's involvement in the case. The article outlined how the local community responded in ways that both blamed the victim and called out the "hero-worshiping culture" of the football team that created an atmosphere of entitlement and immunity around the players. For example, one volunteer coach was quoted in the article:

> The rape was just an excuse, I think. . . . What else are you going to tell your parents when you come home drunk like that and after a night like that? . . . She had to make up something. Now people are trying to blow up our football program because of it.[67]

According to *20/20*, the coach in charge of disciplining the players, Reno Saccoccia, learned of the incident before the police and questioned the team members. In a police interview broadcast on the program, Saccoccia stated that he asked the boys, "And I said, did you rape her? They said no. I said, did you ____ her. They said no. That was the end of our . . . that was it."[68] In fact, at trial, texts revealed that Mays was confident the coach would help him. According to *Yahoo! News*, Mays texted the following about Coach Saccoccia:

> "But I feel he took care of it for us," Mays continued. "Like, he was joking about it, so I'm not worried." . . . "I got Reno. He took care of it and ain't [expletive] going to happen, even if they did take it to court."[69]

Much of the discussion around the case centered on how Steubenville's reverence for football enabled residents to excuse and justify the actions of the players. The *New York Times* outlined how culturally important the football games have become in a community that falls below the median national income and has experienced massive job losses over the past several decades. In January, CNN echoed the sentiment by stating that "controversy has shaken the city, with some residents accusing outsiders of trying to ruin the reputation of the town's high school football team, one of the few bright spots in the economically depressed community of 18,000," although deeper discussion of economic factors was, in general, relatively rare.[70]

The notion of entitlement and the permissive attitudes by authorities and other community members has been understood by sociologist Michael Kimmel as part of the cultural dynamics that justify the participation of and condoning of sexual violence. In his book, *Guyland*, Kimmel analyzed how young men negotiate their transition from adolescence to adulthood according to the "Guy Code"—that is a "collection of attitudes, values, and traits that together composes what it means to be a man."[71] Per that code, dominant notions of masculinity, such as toughness, being daring, aggressiveness, and the suppression of emotion, are part of what it means to be a man.

While Kimmel was explicit that not every guy adheres to the types of masculinity required of the Guy Code, he did suggest that there are three cultural dynamics that allow, and at times encourage, harmful behavior such as sexual assault. First is the culture of entitlement, where young males feel superior and entitled to power. Since men (and women) are not always powerful in all situations, they feel threatened when their status is challenged. Kimmel described this as arising from an overconformity "to the hyperbolic expressions of masculinity that still inform American culture."[72] Second is the culture of silence, which allows sexual harassment and violence to go unchecked because of either the fear of being ridiculed or the fear of retaliatory violence. The effect of this culture of silence, according to Kimmel, is that it "gives the perpetrators and the victims the idea that everyone supports the Guy Code." Third is the culture of protection, in which family, friends, and community members rally around boys and men, protecting them from having to take responsibility for their behavior.[73] In the Steubenville case, there indeed appeared to be Guy Code dynamics at work. Journalist Juliet Macur described it while reporting on the case: "Many of the adults I spoke to in Steubenville feigned ignorance about the rape, including the high school's principal and football coach, or blamed the victim for what happened."[74] Further, revelations of an earlier rape case allegedly committed by Steubenville sports team members also lent weight to the suggestion that school officials were less than forthcoming about the incidents. The "other" Steubenville case involved a fourteen-year-old girl who alleged she was raped in an incident that reportedly "took place at a team coach's house." However, no charges were filed against the alleged perpetrators in this case.[75]

While that earlier Steubenville case remained largely buried, social media's ongoing documentation of the Jane Doe case held the public transfixed. The case gained further nationwide traction when Knight-Sec, a subgroup of the hacktivist collective Anonymous, became involved. KnightSec had obtained and released a twelve-minute video clip recorded on the night of the event. It showed Steubenville graduate Michael Nodianis, and others off camera, laughing, discussing the rape, and describing the unconscious victim as "deader than Caylee Anthony . . . deader than JFK . . . deader than Trayvon Martin," "Her puss is about as dry as the sun right now," and "They raped her quicker than Mike Tyson raped that one girl."[76]

"RAPE HAS GONE VIRAL"

In this case—and in an increasing number of similar cases—social media became the primary forum where the perpetrators publicized their actions. It also served as a forum for victim blaming and support for the perpetrators, even if pro-victim sentiment ultimately became the dominant mainstream media narrative.

An exploratory examination of tweets (#Steubenville) between January 23 through March 9, 2013, the time frame leading up to the trial of the boys, revealed how social media was used as a forum for misogyny and victim blaming.[77] Several common themes emerged from the tweets, including placing the case in the larger context of sexual violence against women, entitlement in sports, and rape culture. Writing for *Salon*, Irin Carmon argued that more victims are willing to speak out on social media and that "in the crudest journalistic terms, rape is having a moment, from India to Ohio." She quoted feminist Jaclyn Friedman's take on how the Internet serves as both condemnation of and support for victims of sexual violence:

> "When you talk on the Internet about being a survivor of sexual violence, two things will invariably happen," [Friedman] said. "You will be surrounded by support and you will be called hateful names and hear abusive things."[78]

In the case of Jane Doe, Twitter was used in a variety of ways, including to circulate mainstream news articles, to pass on information about the case, and to call for direct action—that is, to ask users to post information regarding rallies or other local actions.[79] Some on Twitter said the case pointed to perceived deficiencies in the criminal justice system that have enabled rape culture to flourish.

> In the #ohio #USA HUNDREDS+ Rape Kits sit on shelves, while rapists are Free to rape & abuse women??? That explains #steubenville

> In wake of #Delhi & #Steubenville, @totn looks at why so many rape cases go unreported http://t.co/lX6kegXt

> Why has #Steubenville attracted so much attention? Because world identifies with case. It's not about Steubenville, it's about rape culture.

> My reportage from 2 Feb 13: Rally Decries "Rape Culture" in #Steubenville—WTRF 7 News http://t.co/N6fTWyhO[80]

Ultimately, rape culture became a prominent lens through which to view the case.[81] Linking the Steubenville case to similar cases involving sexual violence and social media, *Bustle* declared, "Rape has gone viral in our country."[82] Journalist Ann Friedman weighed in by describing how with the increasing use of social media and the resulting exploitation, threats, and victim blaming, we are all complicit:

> Now that cases regularly crop up in which photos and videos of sexual assaults are circulated on social media, it's becoming harder to

argue that rape is anything but a public scourge. We are all bystanders. We all bear witness. [83]

In their video promoting a rally held at the Steubenville courthouse
before the trial, Anonymous explicitly made the connection between
the Steubenville rape case and the global epidemic of sexual assault
against women. In their call to action, the narrator stated that the rally
had two goals, which included "an end to all bullying, assault, violence
and rape against all people" and to "show community pride for the great
city of Steubenville." The narrator stated,

> A global revolution is taking place before our very eyes. From the
> friendly street of Steubenville to the historic city of New Delhi, vic-
> tims of assault and rape are realizing they do not need to live with
> this fear and oppression any longer. [84]

In addition to linking the case to broader issues of sexual violence,
various tweets echoed confusion regarding the definition of rape and of
consent. Under Ohio law, the definition of rape includes "digital penetration"—the use of fingers—and both boys were convicted of rape.
Some members of the public were perplexed by the use of the term.
For example, these tweets reflected the confusion:

> #Steubenville Speaking honestly, I'm 30+ years old and did not know
> that digital penetration was considered rape in Ohio. #NowIdo
>
> #steubenville its pretty clear she was raped! Not just digitally either!
> The texts prove this!!
>
> FBI def of rape yes #Steubenville victim was raped. Please stop
> saying digital penetration w/out consent isn't rape! http://t.co/
> J0VsTDXipSa [85]

According to the victim's testimony at trial, she, too, was unaware of the
law. Connor Simpson reported on the trial for *The Wire* and stated that
the day after the incident,

> she [the victim] sent a text message to one of the defendants, appar-
> ently Mays, insisting that she didn't want to go to the cops: "We know
> you didn't rape me," it said. The girl went on to say that she had not
> been aware at the time that digital penetration was also considered
> rape. [86]

The perception that digital penetration is not "rape" is not surprising given that state statutes vary. Even though legal reforms instituting a more expansive definition of rape have been in place for years, our cultural understandings of it continue to evolve.[87] The local prosecutor Jane Hanlin, who ultimately recused herself from the case, also discussed the confusion around rape and the role of social media. In an interview, Hanlin stated,

> It may also have helped that the teens seemed largely unaware that they'd been involved in a crime. They don't think that what they've seen is a rape in the classic sense. And if you were to interview a thousand teen-agers before this case started and said, "Is it illegal to take a video of another teen-ager naked?," I would be astonished if you could find even one who said yes.[88]

Since social media was so instrumental in piecing together what happened that night—including for the victim herself—it is unsurprising that the incident was primarily characterized as a "social media problem" instead of a sexual violence problem. This framing of the incident was dominant in the 20/20 broadcast titled "Steubenville: After the Party's Over."[89] Although the episode featured an interview with Ma'lik Richmond, family members, and other attorneys involved in the case, the episode centered on the role of social media and featured the former editor-in-chief of Seventeen Ann Shoket as an expert on teen use of social media. The voice-over stated, "Many here are saying *the real question* is what's going on everywhere with kids and cellphones and sex" (emphasis added). Trent Mays himself, as well as the judge presiding at the trial, recast the case as a problem of "teen use of social media" rather than a problem of sexual violence. When Mays addressed the court upon being adjudicated delinquent, his apology concentrated on the damage done by social media. He apologized by stating,

> I'd like to apologize to the family. . . . No pictures should have been sent around, let alone even taken. That's all, sir, thank you.

As for the judge, he cautioned that one of the lessons learned is for people to be aware of "how you record things on social media that are so prevalent today."[90]

For the Steubenville case, social media became part of the landscape in which the reality of sexual violence merged with its representation.[91] The boys validated their "real life" experience by way of conversations and dissemination of images on social media. This was then used against them as their incriminating evidence was collected and preserved by those outside their circle of friends, including by law enforcement. Further, the victim became aware of and experienced her "real life" victimization that was, in many ways, inseparable from her "virtual" victimization. Concurrently, social media was used as a forum for expressing public sentiment about the case, whether as a means of victim blaming or to demonstrate an allegiance to Jane Doe. This phenomenon is best illustrated by Dan Wetzel's report for *Yahoo! News* where the victim's real-life experience merged with the revelations of her experience with social media,

> The girl . . . became aware of the alleged assault when she was sent a gruesome picture of her that was circulating.
>
> "If that is [semen] on you that is [expletive] crazy," a friend texted her.
>
> "I hate my life," the girl texted the friend at a different point. "I don't even know what the [expletive] happened to me."
>
> Later she texted a friend, "I swear to God I don't remember doing anything with them. I remember hearing Trent's voice telling me to do something, but I said no."[92]

As criminologist Anastasia Powell pointed out in an article published in *Theoretical Criminology*, social media has been mobilized in a number of ways to shape the narrative on events surrounding sexual violence. This can include, for example, offenders disseminating images of their own criminal behavior for use as evidence in criminal trials, as a means of slut shaming and victim blaming, and as a means of achieving informal justice either by the victims themselves or by allies. The desire to shape the narrative via social media is particularly common in situations where the criminal justice system is viewed as inadequate or has previously failed the victim.[93] As with Steubenville, there is often a reciprocal relationship between social media and mainstream media. Social media is initially the source for various details of the case. Then, mainstream media report on the significance of social media, and subsequently social media echoes the mainstream media coverage.[94]

In this context, both Goddard and Anonymous engaged in the case as a means of pushing law enforcement to investigate a potential cover-up. They hoped to seek informal justice through their dissemination of (sometimes inaccurate) information, and by calling out misogyny and other symptoms of rape culture. Here, social media was more than an adjunct to law enforcement but rather was used as an extralegal tool by the victim's allies. For example, KnightSec, the offshoot of Anonymous, was instrumental in organizing protests, including at least three local rallies in support of Jane Doe and other survivors of sexual violence.[95] Meanwhile, there was also a counter-rally held in defense of the accused boys and the community at large.

As scholar Michael Salter pointed out, there are some limitations to using social media as a means of counter-hegemonic discourse, and not all victims are interested in going public in this way. Salter found that the outcomes vary according to the social position of the victim and her access to networks, resources, and activism. Social media may be used successfully to challenge victim blaming and slut shaming, particularly if the victim is "middle-class, well-educated, and articulate" and as long as the victim "presents a consistent coherent account of her experiences."[96] Salter highlighted a 2012 case eerily similar to Steubenville in which the victim, Savannah Dietrich, went public by tweeting about the case in defiance of a judge's order, including naming the boys responsible and criticizing the juvenile justice process. *Newsweek* described the case:

> Her ordeal began when two 16 year-old boys stripped off her bra and underwear after she had passed out at a party. The boys took turns pushing their fingers into her vagina, documenting their actions with cellphone photos. When Dietrich pressed charges, the boys pleaded guilty in a deal offered by the prosecutor, but she faced a new and unexpected problem: the judge ordered her not to talk about what had happened to her—an apparent infringement of her right to free speech, according to legal experts and to Dietrich herself.[97]

The boys' defense attorneys filed a motion that she be held in contempt of court, although they later withdrew the motion after media attention.[98] Among public opinion, Dietrich was generally met with support.[99] As a result of Dietrich's actions, a bill was passed that would clarify allowing juvenile victims to speak after the conclusion of their case.[100]

Another case, in Houston, Texas, involved a sixteen-year-old girl who went to a house party and was allegedly drugged and raped. She only became aware of what happened after seeing photos of her unconscious and naked body posted on social media. In response, social media users began posting photos of themselves mockingly in a sprawled position similar to that in which she was photographed. This prompted the meme #JadaPose that trended on Twitter.[101] Despite the overwhelming misogyny on display, the *Houston Press* reported that the reaction to #JadaPose was mostly that of support for the victim.

Most of the tweets we found, though, tended to be speaking out against #jadapose, calling it "childish," "pathetic" and further proof of the necessity of the #YesAllWomen hashtag, which spoke out against misogyny and violence against women and went viral in May 2014 after the Isla Vista, California, shootings.[102]

In a display of how social media may be used as resistance, counter hashtags such as #StandWithJada, #JusticeForJada, and #IAmJada arose as a result of the mocking and derision directed toward Jada.[103] Meghan Daum, writing for the *Los Angeles Times*, noted, however,

But for all the Take Back the Night-style rallying, there's no taking back the fact that the initial trolling gathered considerable momentum before anyone questioned it. . . . There is no magic bullet, no one watershed event, that's going to change "rape culture" overnight.[104]

Many connected Jada's incident to the Steubenville case, pointing to a larger cultural problem of victim blaming, slut shaming, and the dehumanization and objectification of women—all of which are considered aspects of rape culture.[105] In response to Jada's experience, *For Harriet*, a blog devoted to dialogue about African ancestry and black womanhood, wrote about the intersection of rape culture and black women's experiences:

It is time we accept that we live in a rape culture. . . . Black Girls and Black Women have a history of being sexually brutalized in this country. We must remember the lies that have been told about our Black female bodies: they signal a sexuality that is both criminal and irresistible; and if we are raped or assaulted, it is our fault. We must remember that these lies are told to do one thing: make our bodies a commodity to be consumed, discarded, and ignored. We must remember that these lies help perpetuate a rape culture that denies us our right to be Black and Woman and human.[106]

According to *The Root*, Jada and her mother came forward to "counter rape culture in social media."[107] In an interview with KHOU News in Houston, Jada explained why she decided to speak publicly and why she refused to let the incident define her:

"There's no point in hiding," she said. "Everybody has already seen my face and my body, but that's not what I am and who I am."[108]

In the Steubenville case, it was Goddard and Anonymous who most ferociously employed the Internet to defend and support Jane Doe.

Though the police made arrests relatively quickly on the basis of their own investigations, many credited Goddard with bringing attention to the case. Others suggested Goddard was spreading misinformation; indeed, she would later be sued for defamation by one of the boys and his family, though the suit was eventually dismissed. Similarly, Deric Lostutter (@KYAnonymous) of KnightSec, who would later be raided by the FBI for hacking-related crimes, was deemed both a "hero" and a misguided vigilante. In an interview with the *Brooklyn Rail*, Lostutter said he became involved with the Steubenville case because he was concerned about victims who have been silenced and neglected by the system.[109]

In a clear effort to enact what criminologist Powell described as "informal justice," Lostutter launched #OpRollRedRoll and published a video threatening to dox (i.e., reveal personal information such as social security numbers, addresses, etc.) Steubenville football players if they did not come forward and apologize.[110] In their profile of Lostutter, *Mother Jones* reported what became a common refrain among Jane Doe supporters when Lostutter's alleged crimes were discussed in comparison to the rape itself (as of May 26, 2015, Lostutter has not been charged):

> If convicted of hacking-related crimes, Lostutter could face up to 10 years behind bars—*far more than the one- and two-year sentences doled out to the Steubenville rapists.* (emphasis added)[111]

While some viewed Lostutter's actions regarding Steubenville as bold and courageous (or more pejoratively, that he acted as a "white knight"), Anonymous in general was frequently called out for their irresponsible treatment of the case. The group had unintentionally leaked the name of the victim and also used the site LocalLeaks, which basically served as a hub for leaked information about the case.[112] Journalist Cathy Young wrote that LocalLeaks contained information and rumors that were "entirely unsupported, and sometimes directly rebutted, by evidence presented at the trial three months later" and called out Anonymous for alleging a conspiratorial cover-up.[113]

Other recent cases sharing similarities with Steubenville include one involving Rehtaeh Parsons, a fifteen-year-old in Canada. It also involved an allegation of sexual assault, teens consuming alcohol, and the dissemination of texts and a photo of the victim that circulated through social media. In Parsons's case, no charges were filed, and she tragically committed suicide. According to the *New York Times*, "Her parents blamed, in part, the decision not to prosecute for her suicide."[114] Similarly, fifteen-year-old Audrie Pott took her own life following an inci-

dent at a house party in which she was unconscious and sexually assaulted by three boys who later shared photos.[115] The Daisy Coleman
case (fourteen years old, Maryville, Missouri) similarly involved teens,
alcohol, allegations of sexual assault, and attempted suicide. The progressive website *Think Progress* described the case:

> The 14-year-old was raped by a high school football player and left
> semi-unconscious in her front yard in the middle of a January
> night—and despite the evidence surrounding the incident, including
> a cell phone video of the assault, the charges against the boy were
> dropped.[116]

Ultimately, Coleman told her own story in *xoJane*, including how she
was harassed online, called a "skank and a liar," and "encouraged to kill
herself," which she did twice attempt.[117] In both cases, offshoots of
Anonymous became involved and agitated law enforcement, either
through publicizing the cases, threatening to dox the alleged offenders,
or organizing protests. The structure of Anonymous is complicated and
the motivations of its members are varied, and the ethical and legal
issues surrounding this type of extra-legal justice, though well documented, continue to be debated.[118] Here, what is important is that in
the context of rape culture, these types of cases continue to be frequently referenced as examples of how the accounts of victims of sexual
violence are frequently disbelieved; how victims are shamed, harassed,
threatened, and neglected by the system; and, as a result, how such
cases necessitate the intervention of allies.

After the judge adjudicated Trent Mays and Ma'lik Richmond guilty
on March 17, 2013, the aftereffects of the case continued to reverberate
in discourse on rape culture, most notably around criticism of the media
coverage itself.[119] Reporting on the verdict was frequently criticized,
particularly for its emphasis on how the case outcome would impact the
lives of the boys. It often neglected to mention how the rape impacted
the victim. As sociologist Lisa Wade noted,

> CNN says the boys were "promising students"
> ABC News makes excuses for the rapists
> NBC News laments the boys' "promising football careers"
> USA Today stresses that the victim was drunk[120]

Media coverage of the verdict was described as "sympathetic" to the
offenders, with one source declaring that "media outlets became active
participants in furthering victim-blaming rape culture."[121] For example,
one report in San Francisco's *SFGate* compared Trent Mays to the

television character Eddie Haskell, popularized on the late 1950s sit-com *Leave It to Beaver*. The article stated,

> Making mischief, getting his friends in trouble, sucking up to their parents as if he were the nicest boy who ever lived. If the writers had cast Eddie as the bad guy in a crime show instead of a sitcom, he might have resembled Trent Mays. [122]

After commenters expressed outrage at the comparison between Mays's behavior and the high jinks of Eddie Haskell, the writer issued a disclaimer stating that people "misunderstood" the point of the piece. [123] Most notable, however, was CNN's coverage of the verdict. It was roundly criticized for being insensitive and promoting rape culture. [124] A change.org petition calling for CNN to apologize reportedly gained almost three hundred thousand signatures. In a breaking news segment covering the verdict, CNN's Candy Crowley stated to her colleague Poppy Harlow, who covered the event, "I cannot imagine . . . how emotional that must've been sitting in the courtroom."

> Poppy Harlow: "I've never experienced anything like it Candy. It was incredibly emotional, incredibly difficult even for an outsider like me to watch what was happening as these two young men who had such promising futures, star football players, very good students, literally watched as they believed their life fell apart. One of the young men, Ma'lik Richmond, when that sentence came down, he collapsed. He collapsed in the arms of his attorney Walter Madison. He said to him, 'My life is over. No one is going to want me now.' . . . But I want to let the viewers listen because for the first time in this entire trial we have now heard from the two young men. Trent Mays stood up apologizing to the victim's family in court. After him, Ma'lik Richmond. Listen . . . [125]

CNN then played the footage of Mays and Richmond in court offering their apologies. Harlow then discussed Richmond's background, explaining that his father spoke in court about his history of alcoholism and how he felt responsible for his son's actions. Going further, she stated that this was the first time that Richmond's father had said "I love you" to his son. Crowley transitioned into her next discussion by querying, "What's the lasting effect, though, on two young men being found guilty in juvenile court of rape, essentially?" The CNN legal contributor stated that we have witnessed a "courtroom drenched in tears and tragedy" and that Harlow's description "sums it all up." The remainder of the segment focused on the impact of sex offender registrations. [126]

The judge declared that both boys would be required to register as sex offenders—a policy that many have long argued imposes undue stigma and collateral punishment on offenders. However, news reports have indicated that the boys may petition to be removed pending their progress at rehabilitation.[127] In fact, by 2015, both boys had been released from juvenile detention. Richmond was released in January 2014, and by August of that year he was back on the Steubenville high school football team. Mays was released one year later.

In his announcement regarding the adults who were indicted in the Steubenville cases, Ohio attorney general Mike DeWine took the opportunity to emphasize that problems such as teen alcohol consumption, partying, bad decisions, and acts of violence are not exclusive to Steubenville; rather, they are nationwide problems.[128] For DeWine, the case represented "blurred, stretched and distorted boundaries of right and wrong" in an "anything goes" culture in which social media makes it more difficult to hold individuals accountable. Ultimately, DeWine argued that adults have responsibility to intervene and must be held accountable.[129] But in the public's imagination, the so-called distorted boundaries around teen behavior, sports and entitlement, consent, and victim blaming were often considered not just symptomatic of an "anything goes culture" but the epitome of a "rape culture."

"I KNOW YOU WANT IT"

In 2013, Google listed the Video Music Awards (VMAs) as one of three top trending events on Google during the year. Only the Boston Marathon bombing attack and the government shutdown trended higher. The most talked-about performance of the VMAs was Robin Thicke and Miley Cyrus's controversial performance of Robin Thicke's hit pop song "Blurred Lines" (ft. TI & Pharrell).

On March 20, 2013, Robin Thicke released the video of "Blurred Lines," a massive hit that *Billboard* declared the "Song of the Summer." It earned numerous nominations at the American Music Awards, the MTV VMAs, and the Grammy Awards and an award for *Billboard*'s 2014 Top R&B and Top 100 song.[130] The song reached notoriety for its catchy melody, cocksure delivery, and what many would characterize as misogyny. In fact, the song and accompanying video seem to embody all of the problematic popular-culture representations of women that feminist scholars have long railed against. Within seven days of the video's release, the popular-culture website *The Frisky* posted the following pithy description,

> Nevertheless, this video has it all: barenaked models dancing poorly, T.I. pulling a lady's hair, blatant references to the size of Robin Thicke's penis, and the line "you're a good girl, I know you want it," which isn't the slightest bit rape-y or anything. [131]

The release of the song and video, and the subsequent reactions, prompted renewed discussion about how women are presented in popular culture and how these images promote a rape culture. By April 2, 2013, feminist blogger "feministinLA" posted, "Has anyone heard Robin Thicke's new rape song?"; by June 17, the *Daily Beast* headline read, "'Blurred Lines,' Robin Thicke's Summer Anthem, Is Kind of Rapey"; the following day, UPI caught up with their headline, "Robin Thicke's 'Blurred Lines' Dubbed 'Rapey' by Critics"; and, on June 21, the *Independent* published "Robin Thicke's Number One Single 'Blurred Lines' Accused of Reinforcing Rape Myths."

Thicke had released two versions of the video, one of which was deemed not safe for work (NSFW). Parodies of it quickly followed, many of which criticized the video's objectification of women. The parodies themselves were also scrutinized for being racy, in some cases even more so than the original song. Most notably, Mod Carousel's gender-swap parody was given an 18+ restriction, while Thicke's original video remains unrestricted on YouTube. Another parody video made by New Zealand law students gained over four million hits but was briefly pulled from YouTube for being too inappropriate. [132]

The director of Thicke's "Blurred Lines" video, Diane Martel, contended in an interview with *Grantland* that the video's intention was meant to be subversive. She explained, "I wanted to deal with the misogynist, funny lyrics in a way where the girls were going to overpower the men." She added that the performances by the women are "very, very funny and subtly ridiculing" and that the video is "meta and playful." [133] But, as *Jezebel* and others pointed out, the songwriter himself seemed unaware of the subversive nature of the video, and at one point he described the purpose of the video to be "derogatory towards women." [134] When Martel was asked about Thicke's comments on the video, she responded, "That's crazy. Maybe he wasn't thinking when he said that." [135]

In an interview with *GQ* magazine, Thicke explained the motivation for the song:

> We tried to do everything that was taboo. Bestiality, drug injections, and everything that is completely derogatory towards women. Because all three of us are happily married with children, we were like, "We're the perfect guys to make fun of this. . . . so we just wanted to turn it over on its head and make people go, 'Women and their

bodies are beautiful. Men are always gonna want to follow them around.'"[136]

Jimmy Johnson, writing for *Truthout*, placed the song, and the public's reaction to it, in the broader context of rape culture. He pointed to inconsistencies in Thicke's explanation of the song compared to its lyrics and what is portrayed in the video. For example, the *Hollywood Reporter* quoted Thicke in a BBC Radio 1 interview claiming that the song is about the strength of women and about how men and women are really "the same" and the lines between a "good girl and a bad girl" are blurred.[137] Johnson found Thicke's explanation of the song so puzzling that he struggled to make sense of it:

> His hatred of the blurred lines means he greatly prefers clear gender lines and hates his wife's strength and smarts. Alternately, Thicke wrote lyrics meaning the opposite of his intent and doesn't know it. Alternately again, Thicke wrote lyrics that fairly represented his intent which he misrepresented to the BBC. One of these has to be true.[138]

On July 1, when VH1 announced that Thicke would participate in a Twitter chat (#AskThicke), the website *BuzzFeed* compiled the many queries that poured in, including "Why are you such a misogynist?" and "What does it feel like to be an icon for sexism, predatory behaviour and sexual assault?" Another simply commented, "This won't end well."[139] Later in the year, controversy swirled again when Thicke performed the song on August 25, 2013, at the MTV VMAs with a scantily clad Miley Cyrus who gyrated against Thicke throughout the performance, or as Daniel D'Addario described in his review for *Salon*, Cyrus "twerked wildly all over the body of Robin Thicke, stroking his crotch with a foam finger." Basically, D'Addario pointed out that the VMAs were actually much less "sex positive" than they intended to be. He wrote,

> "Blurred Lines," the song and video, has been read by some as an ode to coercive sex—not an opinion I had shared until watching Cyrus thrust herself all over a tight-suited Thicke.[140]

Further, he stated that despite efforts to be gay friendly, the VMAs ultimately privileged heterosexual performers, while silencing queer performers.[141] The negative reaction to the performance, however, was less directed toward Thicke and more frequently directed at Cyrus, revealing continuing gender double standards. *Celebuzz* called the performance "awkwardly inappropriate," and Mika Brzezinski, a morning talk show host on MSNBC, stated that Cyrus was "obviously deeply troubled, deeply disturbed, clearly has confidence issues, and probably an eating disorder," and "someone needs to take care of her." Cohost Joe Scarborough concurred that Cyrus was "messed up."[142] Scarborough suggested that Cyrus's behavior during the performance was indicative of behaviors of other teen girls that, in effect, sets bad examples for young boys.[143]

Perhaps one of the more provocative responses was penned by Richard Cohen of the *Washington Post*. He called Cyrus a "cheap act" and "tasteless twit." But then he went further, suggesting that Cyrus perpetuates rape culture. He blamed her performance for contributing to a "teen culture" of "sexual exploitation"—the very things he saw in the Steubenville case. Cohen euphemistically described it as a case of "sexual mistreatment" in which "there weren't many young men involved— just two."[144] Others suggested that the VMA performance itself was likely intended as a subversive take on female objectification, albeit in ways that appropriated black culture. It was described by one critic as "coded racial condescension."[145] Nolan Feeney, writing for *The Atlantic*, suggested that Cyrus's embrace of her own sexuality, by "ramping it up" and "throwing it back" in Thicke's face and lap, might actually have been intended as a critique of "Blurred Lines'" female objectification. If so, Feeney acknowledged that the attempted critique was a failure, but further noted that Cyrus had taken the heat, and slut shaming, for the performance. Similarly, Soraya Chemaly, writing for *Alternet*, noted that Cyrus was only performing as men do regularly—using women as props and sexual objects. Chemaly wrote,

> Cyrus was cocky, she strutted around, she danced (really awkwardly), was brash and confident and made lewd gestures and creative use of her tongue. In addition, she, like her male peers, sexually and racially objectified other women who were onstage with her, almost all of whom were black—and she has come in for deserved criticism for this. . . . She acted like a man, objectified herself and other women, and appropriated several racial cultural signifiers when she did.[146]

Culture critic Alyssa Rosenberg placed the performance in the context of other young, white female pop performers who appropriate black culture and flirt with bisexuality as a means of appearing edgy and rebellious without having to deal with the day-to-day realities of marginalization.[147] The gamble Cyrus took with such a performance is that it was less frequently read as transgressive and liberating, and more commonly as desperate and crazy.

Given that pop music has long been criticized for its portrayal of women and, at times, rape-positive lyrics (e.g., Rick Ross's

"U.O.N.E.O."), it is telling that this particular song, "Blurred Lines," became so symbolic of the problematic depictions. The song's lyrics, at times explicit and violent, certainly were legitimate fodder for criticism. For example, "I know you want it. . . . I'll give you something big enough to tear your ass in two."

There is also a scene in the song's video in which a literal "stop sign" rested on the ass of one of the naked models. Added to this was the perception that the VMA performance provided yet another example of slut shaming and condemnation of women who are sexually aggressive in ways that only men are culturally permitted to be. But it wasn't simply the discourse about the song that made it culturally significant. It was that the public began to see the song as emblematic of everyday realities around sexual harassment and sexual violence. The collective experience of "Blurred Lines" (i.e., the song, video, performance, as well as reaction) struck a nerve with many survivors of sexual assault. In an effort to point out the ways in which the song actually contributed to the normalization of violence against women, the academic website *The Society Pages* juxtaposed the song lyrics with *Project Unbreakable* testimonials—a website that features photographs of women holding signs containing the written words spoken by their abusers. In these powerful images, we see how the words of the rapists eerily echo the song's lyrics. Among the many examples, one woman holds a sign reading, "I know you want it"; another holds a sign reading, "We both know you don't really mean it when you say no"; and another holds a sign reading, "Good girl."[148] In another effort to use the song to raise awareness, the *Mirror* reported that Robin Thicke's song influenced the anti-rape campaign #NoBlurredLines that was launched during "Freshers Week," with the aim of "changing attitudes to a 'no rape' culture."[149]

BEYOND BLURRED LINES

The gang rape case in India, the Steubenville case, and Thicke's "Blurred Lines" were not the only events of significance that propelled the concept of rape culture into public conversation during 2013. They did, however, converge to illustrate the ways that rape culture became an anchor for understanding sexual violence in various contexts. In 2013, the *Washington Examiner* ran this headline, "Time to End the Rape Culture," in reference to lyrics from award-winning hip-hop recording artist Rick Ross's song "U.O.N.E.O." that brags about drugging a woman and raping her unconscious body:

Put Molly all in her champagne, she ain't even know it
I took her home and I enjoyed that, she ain't even know it. [150]

That song's controversy was linked to the Steubenville rape case by journalist Gregory Kane, who suggested that the sense of entitlement to women's bodies is prevalent among "male rappers and athletes," where "rape—date, forcible and statutory—isn't seen as an aberration, but an obligation."[151]

Like Thicke and Ross, various celebrities and personalities have been called out over the past few years for normalizing and condoning sexual violence. This includes renowned evolutionary biologist and best-selling author Richard Dawkins, who was criticized for "embracing" rape culture after a series of tweets dismissive of rape victims.[152] In response to the tweets, the *New Statesman* ran an anonymous first-person account of rape, querying Dawkins directly with the headline: "I was raped when I was drunk. I was 14. Do you believe me, Richard Dawkins?" detailing the physical and psychological toll of rape trauma. Dawkins responded that he believed her account because she demonstrated "clear and convincing memories."[153] Similarly, Grammy-winning singer and self-described "Lady Killer" CeeLo Green was called out for a string of offensive tweets about rape.[154]

AMERICA'S DAD

At this point, rape culture had moved from an isolated, academic term embraced by radical feminists to the mainstream public, where it had begun to provide a framework for understanding a range of behaviors, from slut shaming to street harassment to online victim blaming to rape. It was in this context that one of the most explosive celebrity rape accusations in the past several decades captured the public's attention. In November 2014, during a stand-up show in Philadelphia, comedian Hannibal Buress made a remark about the perceived smugness of legendary comic Bill Cosby:

> Yeah, but you rape women, Bill Cosby, so turn the crazy down a couple notches. . . . I've done this bit on stage and people think I'm making it up . . . when you leave here, Google "Bill Cosby rape." That sh°° has more results than "Hannibal Buress."[155]

Those comments sparked a reemergence of interest in Cosby's past, including a lawsuit that Cosby settled in 2006 for an undisclosed amount. The case centered around an incident in which Cosby was accused of drugging and sexually assaulting a woman.[156] The earlier lawsuit was covered in the media, but it wasn't until Buress's comments set off a firestorm of controversy that a number of women came forward, alleging that they, too, were victimized by Cosby. As of July 2016, nearly sixty have said they were victimized by Cosby in a similar fashion.[157] Adding to the controversy was Cosby's own rape joke from a 1969 album (*It's True! It's True!*) in which he riffed on taking a trip to Spain to score some Spanish fly, a substance believed to be an aphrodisiac.[158]

The allegations against Cosby easily fit into the framework of rape culture. This was noted in a CNN article: "While I cannot definitively say that Cosby is guilty of the crimes of which he is accused, the conversation about him epitomizes some of the most pernicious aspects of rape culture," including victim-blaming and "shielding men from accountability."[159]

When women came forward to recount their experiences with Cosby, reactions to their stories sadly reinforced the myth that rape can be prevented if the victim simply acted differently. When one of Cosby's accusers, Joan Tarshis, told CNN host Don Lemon that Cosby forced her to give oral sex, Lemon instructed her, "You know, there are ways not to perform oral sex if you didn't want to do it."[160] Further, the Cosby allegations highlighted ways that women's voices are often silenced in regard to allegations of sexual violence. One of the women, aspiring actress Barbara Bowman, who did not testify in the civil suit against Cosby but who went public with her story a decade ago, pointed out in the *Washington Post* how disappointed she was that her story was validated only when a male comedian gave the narrative credence. She wrote, "Only after a man, Hannibal Buress, called Bill Cosby a rapist in a comedy act last month did the public outcry begin in earnest."[161]

In fact, it was not until Cosby's formerly sealed deposition was publicly released, wherein he admitted to obtaining "Quaaludes with the intent of giving them to young women he wanted to have sex with," that a criminal investigation into one of the cases was reopened. Cosby continues to maintain his innocence.[162] For some, Cosby's status made it difficult to reconcile his public persona with the allegations that he was a dangerous serial predator. Writer Britney Cooper explained this dilemma for those who have viewed Cosby as a cultural icon and found inspiration in not only his fictional television character Cliff Huxtable, but also his personal philanthropic work.[163] She wrote,

> Middle-class black folks love the Cosbys for the same reason that working-class black folks love Tyler Perry's Madea stories. In them, we feel seen and heard—recognized. But if that recognition comes

through the creative vision of men who really don't value women, do those representations not deserve our deepest skepticism? . . . His own crimes demonstrate in black-and-white the diseased, misogynistic, violent thinking at the heart of patriarchy. And as much as I might love "The Cosby Show," we should perhaps consider it "fruit of the poisonous tree."[164]

Compared to media reports of the civil lawsuit in 2006, public reaction against Cosby this time was intense. Part of the venom directed toward Cosby was due to his reputation for delivering moral lectures that demand young black men take responsibility for their actions—sentiments that were popular among many conservatives. Such narratives, however, struck many as wildly hypocritical. Cosby's "Pound Cake Speech" delivered in 2004 at the NAACP Awards is among his most well known. Jenée Desmond-Harris described the speech as including

a litany of things that poor black people were doing wrong: bad names, bad words, bad clothing, bad priorities, and bad parenting—basically all of the ways that younger black people, in his view, had failed the civil rights generation that came before them.[165]

In 2008, Ta-Nehisi Coates explained the appeal of Cosby's moralizing and revealed his own unease with parts of it by stating, "I'd take my son to see Bill Cosby, to hear his message, to revel in its promise and optimism. But afterward, he and I would have a very long talk." Notably, Coates took Cosby to task for his ahistorical approach to social problems among blacks in America, particularly those that involve the criminal justice system.[166]

The civil lawsuit was public knowledge, yet the allegations never really caught the public's attention. Race was cited as an explanation for the previous lack of public outcry. The *New Republic* declared, "No One Wanted to Talk about Bill Cosby's Alleged Crimes Because He Made White America Feel Good about Race."[167] In her interview with *Vanity Fair*, model and actress Beverly Johnson recounted her experience with Bill Cosby in which she alleged that he drugged her. She detailed her concerns about going public, specifically how she feared that doing so might impact the plight of black men in America. She wrote,

Still I struggled with how to reveal my big secret, and more importantly, what would people think when and if I did? Would they dismiss me as an angry black woman intent on ruining the image of one of the most revered men in the African American community over the last 40 years? Or would they see my open and honest account of being betrayed by one of the country's most powerful, influential, and beloved entertainers? As I wrestled with the idea of telling my story of the day Bill Cosby drugged me with the intention of doing God knows what, the faces of Trayvon Martin, Michael Brown, Eric Garner, and countless other brown and black men took residence in my mind. [168]

The specter of "black-man-as-rapist" has a long history. [169] From using false allegations of rape to justify the lynching of innocent black men to the continuing invisibility of black female victims in the press, the lingering history of prejudices within the criminal justice system continues to influence the reporting and response of sexual violence today. In fact, in her study of media accounts of rape, Professor Helen Benedict found that "the press has tended to cover the rape of white women by blacks more than any other type of sex crime." [170] Benedict also showed that media coverage frequently pitted white women against black men in ways that were counterproductive to both the plight of black men who have suffered a history of false accusations as well as anti-rape feminists. [171]

Although Johnson specifically mentioned young black men killed by law enforcement officers (as well as, in the case of Trayvon Martin, a citizen-vigilante who was later acquitted), it was Coates who later linked Cosby's situation directly to Black Lives Matter, the movement challenging unlawful police use of force and other injustices. He discussed how visible brutality can go unchecked in systems bolstered by fictive narratives that delegitimize victims. He stated,

> Much like it is impossible to understand the killing of Tamir Rice as murder without some study of racism, it is impossible to imagine Bill Cosby as a rapist without understanding the larger framework. (For instance, it took until 1993 for all 50 states to criminalize marital rape.) Rape is systemic. And like all systems of brutality it does not exist merely at the pleasure of its most direct actors. It depends on a healthy host-body of people willing to look away. [172]

Ultimately, the coverage of the allegations against Cosby may have resulted in a positive impact in terms of women coming forward to tell their stories. Rape, Abuse, and Incest National Network's (RAINN) vice president of communications, Katherine Hull Fliflet, claimed that the coverage "has already led to a significant increase in the number of survivors reaching out for help through the National Sexual Assault Hotline." [173] Additionally, when Jackie Fuchs, formerly known as Jackie Fox, of the all-female legendary rock band The Runaways, decided to go public with her allegation of being raped by music producer, and later band manager, Kim Fowley in 1975 after being given several Quaaludes, she specifically credited the women who came forward on the Cosby case as inspiration to tell her story.[174]

Fuchs alleged that the rape took place at a party where there were several bystanders, some of whom she described as "snickering," none of whom intervened. One witness stated, "It was really weird. Everybody was sitting in there alone with themselves. It felt like everyone was detached or trying to pretend like nothing was going on."[175] Fuchs's allegation prompted a barrage of commentary, particularly with regard to bystanders who remained silent.[176]

Although the reaction to Fuchs's revelation could be read as indicative of how our perceptions of rape have shifted over time—from that of an "inconvenience" that women are expected to endure, to the increasing willingness to consider acquaintance rape as "real rape"—there is still a palpable undercurrent of persistent rape myths.[177] Both the Cosby case and the Fuchs case demonstrate that there is still much reluctance to believe women who come forward with their accounts. Fuchs said that though she received much support, she was "shocked by some of the vitriol; more so by the fact that nearly all of it came from other women."[178]

As the Cosby case illustrated, even a pattern of accusations (at least fifty similar accounts) can amount to insufficient evidence of wrongdoing in the court of public opinion.[179] Actor and talk show host Whoopi Goldberg initially defended Cosby by stating, "The '80s, they weren't fun for everybody, clearly."[180] Similarly, one of Cosby's staunchest supporters, R&B singer Jill Scott, demanded "proof" of the allegations. She tweeted, "u know Bill Cosby? I do child and this is insane. Proof. Period."[181] After the deposition was released, *Gawker* reported, "Scott reversed course Monday, saying what she needed to believe Cosby might be guilty was for Cosby to literally admit to it."[182]

At the most basic level, the Cosby case demonstrates, in part, the power of (racial) representation in popular culture to shape our collective understanding of sexual violence. It uncovered our continuing discomfort of grappling with rape and race rooted in American history, revealed the persistence of rape myths, and brought to light our stubborn reluctance to come to terms with an overwhelming litany of personal testimonies.

It is ironic that it was a rape joke itself that (re-)ignited interest in the Cosby case—especially considering that a few years prior, humor referencing sexual violence was the focus of numerous heated debates on the ethics of joke telling.[183] In fact, 2012 had been declared by the *Daily Beast* as the "year of the rape joke."[184] However, a few years later, the ethical debate over rape jokes had largely subsided, most notably reframed by Jerry Seinfeld as overbearing political correctness, largely sustained by what he called ignorant college students who lack an understanding of racism and sexism.[185] Of course, comedians continued to tell rape jokes in a variety of contexts, but it was Amy Schumer (*Inside Amy Schumer*) who most notably shattered the rape joke taboo and delivered a series of rape culture jokes so searing that she was deemed a feminist icon.[186] One of Schumer's skits put Bill Cosby on trial in the "Court of Public Opinion" and played on the tension of trying to reconcile Cosby as an inspiring cultural icon and father figure with the overwhelmingly troublesome public accusations. In the skit, Schumer plays a lawyer "defending" Cosby in the courtroom by playing clips from the *Cosby Show* and distributing pudding pops. After playing a clip, she quips,

> Did anyone feel raped by that? . . . What about drugged? . . . I felt comforted by a familiar father figure . . .
>
> This is a court of public opinion. If convicted, the next time you put on a rerun of the Cosby Show you may wince a little, might feel a little pang. None of us deserve to feel that pang. We deserve to dance like no one's watching, and watch like no one's raping.[187]

By the beginning of 2014, the term "rape culture" reached such popularity that *BuzzFeed* devoted a column titled "What Is Rape Culture?" to addressing, among other issues, slut shaming, street harassment, rape jokes, and pick-up artists.[188] Musicians, entertainers, and public intellectuals became ensnared in debates around issues of consent, victim blaming, and rape myths. During the time period under study in which the concept emerged as a popular framework for understanding sexual violence (roughly late 2012–2015), popular culture itself became one of the primary sites through which rape culture was understood, negotiated, and contested.

3

"HEY TV, STOP RAPING WOMEN"

Game of Thrones remains HBO's most popular series ever—and among its most brutal. To give a sense of how disturbing viewers found it, *Salon* reported that "sexual violence is so pervasive on the show that nearly every woman on the show has been raped or threatened with rape."[1] So when controversy ensued over the rape scene in the season 4 episode "Breaker of Chains" (aired April 20, 2014), outsiders who weren't avidly watching the show were surprised. What made this rape different? Why the uproar over this particular episode? *Jezebel* writer Madeleine Davies attempted to explain why so many viewers found this particular incident shocking:

> As we unfortunately know all too well from real-life examples, being charming or admired and being a rapist are not mutually exclusive. And if anything, our trust in Jaime only made the horror, pain and hurt of what he did to Cersei (someone who trusts him more than anyone else) all the more relatable.[2]

Davies, like other television watchers, viewed that particular scene in the show as too close for comfort—as disturbingly relatable. Rather than perceiving popular culture as a distinct entity separate and apart from real life, this chapter considers the ways that our lived experiences reflect and influence it. Here, popular culture is viewed as part of our social fabric, as a cluster of images and representations that shape and influence our understandings of sexual violence. Moving away from a "media effects" type of analysis that would suggest there is a causal relationship between media violence and behavior, this chapter explores the social meanings of sexual violence. From this perspective, popular culture neither exerts an all-powerful force on its audience nor is it entirely insignificant. This chapter shows that in some ways, popular culture continues to be understood by some as a primary site for reproducing rape myths, objectifying women, celebrating male aggression, and conflating sexuality and violence. However, it also demonstrates that there is no monolithic understanding around the social meaning of sexual violence. Both our intellectual and affective engagement with popular culture inform our understanding and construction of "rape culture."

In early 2014, *Entertainment Weekly* issued an exasperated plea: "Hey TV: Stop Raping Women," suggesting that lazy writers were overusing rape as a plot line. Rather than develop complex characters that are nuanced, with various shades of being flawed, scriptwriters were accused of injecting "sexual horror" to liven up the plot.[3] *Salon* similarly declared that "starting around the turn of the decade [2010], rape on television morphed from a delicate topic to practically *de rigueur*." The *Los Angeles Times* declared simply that there was a "rape glut" on television.[4]

Over the past few years, sexual violence in television and film has generated a barrage of commentary. While this attention to violence against women in entertainment media is not particularly new, these more recent reactions have been particularly passionate. Media scholar Henry Jenkins wrote that increasingly media "are more focused on social exchanges and personal interactions in which the creation of the texts is secondary to the cementing of social bonds."[5] This analysis acknowledges the increasing tendency to move beyond various interpretations of the text itself (i.e., the television show, film, etc.) toward the exchange of ideas and how those exchanges contribute to our collective understandings of sexual violence. There is no single reading or interpretation of any given text. There is, however, generally a preferred reading, and at some point there is usually some general consensus around "what just happened." The focus of the remainder of this chapter is to explore responses to sexual violence in popular culture and offer an analysis of our construction, negotiation of, and collective understanding around "what just happened."

The debate surrounding violence in entertainment media is a longstanding one, with practically every generation decrying the nature and frequency of violence in popular culture. Historically, the debates have centered on whether violent content impacts behavior and/or attitudes and, consequently, on the limits of free speech and censorship.[6] While studies are mixed, it is reasonable to conclude that media do not directly "cause violence"—although it does impact attitudes and perceptions about violence, crime, and justice. In fact, we tend to look back on the biggest efforts to crack down on violence and sexual content in entertainment, including instituting industry moral guidelines like the Motion Picture Production Code, the Comics Code Authority, and the Parents Music Resource Center, as moments of paternalistic overreach.[7]

Author Harold Schechter forcefully argued that our attraction to violence in popular culture is not a new phenomenon and that we have long been fascinated with aggression and cruelty. Counter to what many believe, Schechter found that popular culture in the new millennium is actually *less brutal* than ever.[8] There are still those who argue that we are exposed to too much violence, particularly sexual violence. In her article titled "Maxing Out on Murder: Good Luck Finding a Decent TV Drama without Rape or Killing," writer Margaret Lyons reported just how pervasive violence is in primetime and found that of the 125 scripted dramas airing in 2013, 109 included "in detail a rape or murder."[9] By April 2014, cultural critic Alyssa Rosenberg declared, "Almost every buzzworthy drama now on television features a female main character who has been raped."[10] Tiffany Jenkins, writing for the *Independent* asked, "Is there too much rape on stage and TV?" She answered in the affirmative, arguing that our disproportionate focus on sexual violence is presented under the guise of "awareness raising" that too often devalues victims and presents men as a continuous threat toward women. The problem for Jenkins is that such portrayals give the impression that "we live in a culture of misogyny, that abuse is endemic and that all relationships are toxic. But it's not, it isn't and they aren't."[11]

The depiction of sexual violence in entertainment is a catch-22. If it is minimized or ignored, the public complains that the plot does not reflect the reality of our lives. Invariably, when it is incorporated into the story line, people complain that the depictions themselves are problematic or too frequent. Inherent in these reactions is the idea that popular culture is consequential. For criminologists, there is no question of whether popular culture matters in our collective understandings of crime and justice—it does. However, how and to what extent it matters is unsettled. It is therefore important to explore how popular culture serves as a resource for working through our collective moral anxieties about sexual violence at both an intellectual and affective level.

As *Washington Post* music critic Chris Richards stated, the larger popular-culture landscape has become central to our conversations about sexual violence. He wrote,

> In the social-media age, pop culture has become a safe place to talk about the most difficult subjects. We might flinch at reading about rape on our college campuses or in our military, but we're eager to

talk about it through the lens of *Game of Thrones* or a Lady Gaga video.[12]

Popular culture is so fully embedded in our contemporary daily existence that it is difficult to collectively process issues of sexual violence without influencing or reflecting on its messaging.

While we do hear the common refrain that there is too much rape on television, it is rare to hear that sexual violence should *never* be portrayed. There is a sense that such portrayals are necessary because they reveal a larger truth about the human condition. Journalist Michael Deacon, writing for the *Telegraph*, argued that because sexual violence against women is a reality, television shows must reflect that reality even if they are "intensely stressful" to watch. He wrote, "And if it's graphically disturbing—well, so it should be. There's no way to make palatable the truth about what men do to women."[13] Or, as this *Telegraph* headline stated, "If rape scenes on stage and screen aren't horrific then they aren't doing their job."[14]

The discourse dedicated to whether scenes of sexual violence are necessary encompasses several common themes. They include the questions of whether such depictions are merely prurient, whether they serve artistic purposes, and whether they hold educational value for teaching viewers about the realities of sexual violence. Conversations about portrayals of sexual violence rarely remain solely within the purview of popular culture. Instead, they tend to reverberate and clash against survivors' recollections of their own real-life experiences. They also tap into our emotional and affective responses to crime and justice, and they may even reinforce and/or contradict academic research. Ultimately, our conversations about popular culture are never fully removed from our lived experiences. In fact, after *Entertainment Weekly* published the aforementioned "Hey TV: Stop Raping Women" piece, which called for more nuanced portrayals of sexual violence, reader comments quickly turned to the validity of rape statistics, the difficulties of defining rape, and disagreements about how consent should be legally defined.[15]

Critics of portrayals of sexual violence often contend that these depictions just do not "get it right." Popular-culture portrayals of rape, much like its renderings of other crimes, do not necessarily reflect what we know empirically about sexual violence. All too often, they reinforce rape myths and perpetuate victim blaming.[16] As a result, there is much discussion about what makes for a "good" rape scene. For example, Rape, Abuse and Incest National Network (RAINN) advised that shows should maintain a focus on the aftereffects of rape as a means of showing audiences what happens "in real life."[17] The online news site *Huff-*

ington Post presented the following recipe for a good, responsible rape scene: the victim should be the focal point, rape as character development should be avoided, and victim blaming should be avoided.[18] Similarly, following the portrayal of rape in the Netflix show *Orange Is the New Black* that was perceived as particularly sensitive in its depiction of the aftermath of rape, writer Jada Yuan proposed a "Pennsatucky test" (modeled after the Bechdel test). Yuan said a good rape scene would answer the following:

> Is the victim's point-of-view shown? Does the scene have a purpose for existing for character, rather than plot, advancement? Is the emotional aftermath explored?[19]

Journalist Natasha Vargas-Cooper tapped into one of the most important aspects of our engagement with scenes of sexual violence—that of our affective response. For Vargas-Cooper, the scene, "should feel ugly and leave us cringing, disgusted, perhaps even a little violated ourselves for having witnessed such a thing."[20]

Here, the concern is not so much with rape as representation, but rather with our encounter with the images. In the following sections, I will show how our engagement is varied and complex, involving our intellectual understandings of rape, as well as recognizing the intensity with which we connect to the images. Taken together, these elements inform our collective understandings of sexual violence.

POWERING THROUGH TRAUMA

Over the years, pop-cultural portrayals of sexual violence have reflected our changing awareness of rape, rape myths, and legal reform. Scholar Lisa Cuklanz noted that rape portrayals on prime-time television during the late 1970s to mid-1980s predominantly consisted of the victim being assaulted by a stranger. This imagery adhered to the mythological concept of "real rape" (i.e., rape committed by a stranger, involving extreme violence, physical injury, and use of weapon).[21] It was not until the mid-1980s through the 1990s that portrayals generally shifted to include acquaintance and date rapes. This coincided with research that consistently showed that rape is more likely to be committed by someone known to the victim. Cuklanz found that over time, rape portrayals transitioned toward more sophisticated and complicated depictions. However, overall, they continued to reinforce "hegemonic masculinity," or the social hierarchy in which we privilege certain ways of "doing gender" over others. Doing gender encompasses the notion of gender not as a biological trait, but rather as an accomplishment—the product of daily social practices and behaviors that codify and manifest femininity or masculinity.[22] From this perspective, viewers are concerned less about the frequency of the violence and more about the way in which the violence is depicted. This is particularly true when the portrayals reinforce privileged forms of masculinities that intersect with race and class.

In her study of rape in prime-time television, Cuklanz found the portrayals problematic in that they virtually neglected the plight of the (almost always female) victim, preferring instead to focus on the heroic, male protagonist who seeks justice for the crime.[23] Cuklanz wrote, "The primary function of rape on prime-time episodic television, from 1976 through 1990, was to provide material for the demonstration of ideal masculinity in terms that worked to contain feminist arguments."[24] In other words, the focus was primarily on men who rescued women rather than an exploration of the women's experiences or any discussion of the causes of rape beyond extreme individual pathology. Cuklanz wrote, "Masculinity emerges as the solution to, rather than the cause of, the victimization of women through rape."[25]

Cultural critics have more recently echoed Cuklanz's findings. This includes television critic Sonia Saraiya's observation that over the past few years, plots have continued to reproduce hegemonic masculinity by "focus[ing] on the feelings of the men in the story, at the expense of the victims'."[26] Moreover, Cuklanz noted that there were some glaring omissions in the treatment of rape in prime time during the years under study, including the neglect of "gang rape, marital rape, adjudication of consent, and the underlying causes of rape," as well as the abysmal treatment of issues of race and rape.[27]

Currently, what remains missing from popular discourse is a robust discussion of the intersection of race, class, and rape, as well as an exploration of the ways that hegemonic masculinities serve to marginalize male victims of sexual violence.[28] One example of a male victim can be found in Amazon's *Transparent*, the first online show to win the Golden Globe Best Series Award for its sensitive portrayal of gender transition. Despite the show's pioneering nature, there was no significant public discussion of the portrayal of statutory rape involving Josh, one of the main characters in the show. As one recap/review in the *New York Observer* pointed out, there is no language for us to speak about Josh's experience.[29] Carrie Nelson, writing for the *Observer*, said,

> Was Josh sexually abused? Undeniably, yes. He was a minor having sex with an adult; even if he verbally agreed to every sexual act, minors can't consent, so we're talking about statutory rape at the

absolute minimum. And yet, the way Josh touched Rita during their
love scene in the pilot was filled with raw desire. Today, they are
both adults, capable of making their own choices, and Josh chooses
Rita.[30]

In her book *Watching Rape*, Sarah Projansky examined post-1980s rape
narratives in television and film and found that they were influenced by
a postfeminist discourse that has shifted the cultural consciousness
around rape. She suggested that although feminist activism had, among
other achievements, raised awareness and ushered in rape reform that
broadened the ways that rape is portrayed in popular culture (e.g., the
portrayal of acquaintance rape, increased attention to the traumatic
effects of rape, critique of the male gaze, and critique of the treatment
of victims by the criminal justice system), postfeminist portrayals were
quite limiting. She explained,

> postfeminism's version of feminism assumes that antirape activism is
> no longer necessary, ultimately holds women responsible for re-
> sponding to rape, often recenters white men in the name of feminist
> antirape activism, and perpetuates a long-standing tradition of ex-
> cluding women of color, particularly black women, from rape scenar-
> ios in ways that negate rape's complexity and frequency in their
> lives.[31]

The interplay between postfeminist discourse and rape narratives has
resulted in portrayals that are more complex, but that can also be more
confusing. For example, the shift from stranger rapes to acquaintance/
date rapes may be more in line with statistical findings, but the portrayals themselves may be more confusing in terms of our cultural understandings of consent. In other words, rape narratives may present some
feminist sensibilities and still be problematic for some viewers. Ultimately, according to Projansky, even rape narratives that are produced
from a feminist perspective and are designed to challenge rape myths
may also simultaneously serve to contribute to the "hatred for and violence against women."[32]

Critic Emily Nussbaum touched on this phenomenon when she
wrote about the rape of Charlotte (played by KaDee Strickland), the
tough, "self-reliant, sharp-tongued Southerner" on *Private Practice*
(2007–2013). The show was a spin-off of writer Shonda Rhimes's first
major breakthrough hit, *Grey's Anatomy*. Charlotte was considered
among Rhimes's most intriguing, powerful, and independent characters. She was raped by a mentally ill patient at her office, was taken to
the hospital, and stoically refused to report the crime to the police.

In her review of the episode, Nussbaum pointed out that the assault echoed other contemporary shows' portrayals of rape and the emerging "tough woman" trope,

> but it's peculiar that each shares with *Private Practice* this motif of a tough woman who tries to power through her trauma, a notion by now as fetishized as any notion of fragility. It's a plot twist with a prismatic ambiguity: You can view it as realistic (because it's true that few women report their rapes), as perversely affirming (there's a Wild West stoicism to these women, like cowboys who shrug off a beating), or as troubling—however great these series are, there's something punitive about seeing a succession of strong women who are ravaged and then go silent.[33]

The "tough woman" construct has been deconstructed before, particularly in discussions that highlight how strong female characters are often broken down by threats of rape or other sexual violence, either as shock value or to advance the plot of the men. Such scenes could be read as either distressing or empowering, or both. These dynamics were put in stark relief by writer Leigh Alexander in her article about gaming, gender, and heroes. She stated, "It seems that when you want to make a woman into a hero, you hurt her first. When you want to make a man into a hero, you hurt . . . also a woman first."[34]

Television critic Mary McNamara also alluded to the tough woman trope in entertainment, pointing out that the strong women characters who are broken down often survive to emerge stronger.[35] Writer and cultural critic Chauncey DeVega made a similar point in his article criticizing the portrayal of the African-American character Michonne in the television show *The Walking Dead*. DeVega skewered the show for its underdeveloped treatment of African-American characters, particularly in comparison to the comic books on which the show is based. DeVega was particularly incensed when the rape of Michonne as depicted in the comic book did not appear in the television show. DeVega wrote,

> Michonne, who was brutally raped by The Governor in *The Walking Dead* comic book series, has to suffer in order to have her revenge and triumph over him. *Michonne is made by pain; it tempers and refines her* like an alloy or fine blade of steel.
>
> If you remove her personal challenges, tragedies, and triumphs, you remove Michonne's power in *The Walking Dead*. This is disrespectful to the character. Considering that Michonne is one of the most compelling characters in any recent comic book, and who also

happens to be a person of color (a group marginalized in graphic novels), the insult is very much magnified. . . .

Michonne has to suffer at the hands of The Governor so that she can evolve and grow into an even more essential character who is (at least) as important and capable a leader as Rick. (emphasis added)[36]

By *not* subjecting Michonne to sexual violence in the television series, and instead choosing to threaten a fellow white female character with rape, DeVega suggested that the writers were perhaps fearful of the inevitable controversy that would likely arise. That is, by not depicting the rape, there was no opportunity to confront the historical treatment of black women at the hands of white men. As a result, the white, masculine postapocalyptic landscape remained uninterrogated.

Culture critic Eliana Dockterman noted that rape portrayals on television are increasingly more likely to be revealed as a character's back-story as opposed to a real-time occurrence. For Dockterman, the increased attention toward rape culture itself has prompted the plot device of revealing a character's secret past as a path for healing the victim. Or, alternatively, as video game show host Jace Hall more bluntly remarked, female characters "absolutely must have endured some kind of sexual trauma to become the badass she is now."[37]

In the second season of Netflix's *House of Cards*, Claire Underwood (played by Robin Wright) revealed she was raped by a boyfriend in college. Her assailant later became a high-ranking military general who was awarded medals by her husband, the president of the United States. The show is about power and corruption in Washington, D.C., and Claire is a manipulative liar, bordering on psychopathy, who, in partnership with her husband, will go to any lengths to gain and maintain power. Claire was in the uncomfortable position of publicly discussing her three abortions (two of which she described as "reckless" behavior as a teenager, and one as a decision made in concert with her husband so as not to interfere with their campaigning). Rather than reveal the truth, in a televised interview she falsely attributed the latter pregnancy to the rape by her former boyfriend. Another victim subsequently came forward and revealed that she, too, had been raped by the same man, bolstering Claire's credibility. Claire used her leverage to push for legislation to impose civilian oversight on cases of rape in the military. The bill is similar to New York senator Kirsten Gillibrand's real-life attempts to remove the decision to prosecute serious crimes in the military from the chain of command and implement independent prosecutors.[38]

The *Daily Beast* reported that Robin Wright's own activism in the fight against sexual violence in conflict zones was instrumental in bringing the plot to *House of Cards*.[39] However, reactions to the story line were mixed.[40] Some viewers were uncomfortable with the rape because they found it unnecessary for Claire's cruelty to be forged from sexual violence. *Entertainment Weekly* wrote,

> It's not that women like Claire don't get raped. Or that stories of abuse and survival and the cost of resilience aren't important ones. But on the flip side, can't we enjoy standing aghast in the face of Claire's ruthlessness without saddling her with such an excruciating foundation?[41]

As an example of how Claire fits the mold of the "tough woman" trope, *Bustle* praised her for powering through the incident and refusing to buckle to victimhood.

> She doesn't crumble at the sight of the man who temporarily stole her power—though she does quiver. She hasn't forgotten what happened to her or blocked it from her mind, but she also hasn't taken her attacker down. Instead, her revenge is that she's built a life of power and influence—however ruthless that life may be—and she's unwilling to let this man keep her from realizing her goals. Her silence isn't weakness, it's strength.[42]

Ultimately, the show prompted a "rape culture critical analysis" by the Colorado Coalition against Sexual Assault. The organization concluded that while the show should be praised for "accurately reflect[ing] the lifelong healing process and re-emergence of triggers that many sexual trauma survivors experience," it also conflated dishonesty (not about the rape, but about the abortion) in a way that likely contributes to questions of credibility around rape survivors.[43]

"WELL, IT BECOMES CONSENSUAL BY THE END"

Gross cruelty and indifference to human life are among the hallmarks of HBO's *Game of Thrones* as various characters battle for power and control. The tone of the series is set in the first episode, which includes gruesome deaths and rape. On a show known for its willingness to shock viewers by brutally killing main characters, as well as its overuse of "sexposition"—"the art of outlining all that tedious plot against a background of no-holds-barred sex"—it is the sexual violence that fuels most of the controversy around the show, particularly as it intersects with portrayals of powerful women.[44]

The show premiered in 2011, and by 2012, author Laurie Penny wrote that *"Game of Thrones* is racist rape-culture Disneyland with Dragons."* Two years later, the *New York Times* dedicated front-page coverage to the show's depictions of rape, with an article declaring that "the series's sexual violence has spilled into the mainstream and grown vehement," with sexual violence practically having evolved into "background noise."[45] Throughout its run, other headlines echoed similar sentiments:

> *Jezebel*: "Game of Thrones, Sex and HBO: Where Did TV's Sexual Pioneer Go Wrong?"

> *Salon*: *"Game of Thrones* glamorizes rape: That was not consent, and rape is not a narrative device"

> *Guardian*: *"Game of Thrones*: too much racism and sexism—so I stopped watching"

> *Forbes*: "Does Game of Thrones Have a Misogyny Problem?"[46]

Here is how *Bitch* magazine described how women were treated on the show in season 3:

> women used as numerous pawns in the titular game, treated like chattel, commanded to show men their "cunts," threatened with rape at nearly every turn, stabbed viciously in the uterus, and, in one case, crucified by crossbow.[47]

The constant threat, and realization, of sexual violence on the show fit easily into the larger discourse around rape culture, as evidenced by these tweets:

> #RapeCultureIsWhen a director films a rape scene and doesn't think they filmed a rape scene. #GameofThrones

> #YesAllWomen because rape on TV and in movies shouldn't be a "matter of perspective" or "only for shock value." #GameOfThrones #rapeculture

> Can't wait to wake up to 40 Jesebel [*sic*], AV Club, Kotaku, and BadAssDigest articles about "rape culture" #GameOfThrones[48]

Although the show had long included scenes of sexposition and sexual violence, it was the episode titled "Breaker of Chains" in the show's fourth season that unleashed a flurry of criticism surrounding the ethics and responsibility of portraying rape. In "Breaker of Chains," Cersei and her brother/lover Jaime meet at the sept where their dead son's body was on display. Here's how the *Hollywood Reporter* described the scene:

> As Cersei (Lena Headey) is mourning her son, Jaime (Nikolaj Coster-Waldau) comes in to comfort her and pay his respects. Things get hot and heavy between the siblings/lovers, but when Cersei attempts to put a stop to it, Jaime rapes her. To add another layer to the already disturbing scene, their son's dead body is just inches away.[49]

In the same article, the director Alex Graves described the scene as "rape" and "forced sex."[50] However, in another interview, Graves revealed that the scene was designed to be much more ambiguous. He stated, "Well, it becomes consensual by the end, because anything for them ultimately results in a turn-on, especially a power struggle."[51] *Hitfix*'s description of the scene also alluded to some of that ambiguity:

> It's an intense scene, and beautifully shot (just look at the glow surrounding Cersei after she's left alone in the sept with Jaime), and rekindles the sick, complex relationship between these two—an unholy union in the holiest of places.[52]

The revelation that the director perceived the scene as both "rape" and as "becoming consensual" contributed to the controversy and ultimately revealed larger confusion among the public about the issue of consent. Further, the actors involved in the scene, Lena Headey (Cersei) and Nikolaj Coster-Waldau (Jaime), both told *Entertainment Weekly* that the scene was "not rape" and "was never intended to be."[53] In an interview with the *Daily Beast*, Coster-Waldau provided more context:

> It took me awhile to wrap my head around it, because I think that, *for some people, it's just going to look like rape.* The intention is that it's not just that; it's about two people who've had this connection for so many years, and much of it is physical, and much of it has had to be kept secret, and this is almost the last thing left now. (emphasis added)[54]

The problem was that so many viewers disagreed—and perceived it as rape. A sample of headlines included,

> *Wired*: That Game of Thrones Scene Wasn't a 'Turn-On,' It Was Rape

Vulture: Yes, Of Course That Was Rape on Last Night's Game of Thrones

Salon: *Game of Thrones* glamorizes rape: That was not consent, and rape is not a narrative device

New Republic: Yes, That Scene in 'Game of Thrones' Was Rape. No, the Show Isn't Ruined.

AV Club: Rape of Thrones

Daily Beast: Why We Should Pretend the 'Game of Thrones' Rape Scene Never Happened

Jezebel: The Game of Thrones Rape Scene Was Unnecessary and Despicable[55]

Many viewed the rape as problematic because it was considered by some as "out of character" for Jaime, reasoning that although he might have acted malevolently in the past, he was no rapist, and this incident was perceived as having irrevocably changed his character arc in an irredeemable way. Others felt that, as with many rape portrayals on TV, the rape was simply unnecessary and failed to offer insight into the aftereffects and trauma that would continue to impact Cersei throughout her life.[56]

Notably, one of the main problems—for those who had read the books by George R. R. Martin—was that the scene in the book was overwhelmingly interpreted as consensual sex, while the scene on the show was overwhelmingly interpreted as rape.[57] This intertextual shift provoked discussions about whether the show was simply sensationalizing and exploiting sexual violence for shock value. The scene in the book has Cersei initially protest, but eventually she states,

> "Hurry . . . quickly, quickly, now, do it now, do me now. Jaime Jaime Jaime." Her hands helped guide him. "Yes," Cersei said as he thrust.[58]

In contrast, here's how feminist writer Roxane Gay described the scene from the show:

> There was no ambiguity to the scene. Cersei repeatedly said no. She said, "Stop." She said, "Not here." She said, "This is not right." She resisted Jaime's efforts, to no avail. The scene was unequivocally a

rape scene and it was not merely shocking. It was thoroughly sense-
less.[59]

The reaction to the difference in how the book and film portrayed the
event demonstrated just how unsettled the idea of consent remains
among viewers.[60] Laura Hudson, writing for *Wired*, expressed frustration over the inability of some viewers to interpret the TV scene as rape.
She wrote,

> I've already seen multiple comments, both on my recap of the epi-
> sode and others, that said she wasn't fighting hard enough for it to be
> rape, that it seemed like deep down she was really into it. Seeing
> men write comments like that about a scene where a woman is
> forced into sex—particularly since I know multiple women who have
> heard the same sorts of comments about their real-life rapes—is
> absolutely terrifying.[61]

These contradictory views reflect our lack of understanding about consent that has long been part of the history of rape and rape legislation.
Scholar Nicola Gavey wrote that historically our ideas of rape have been
informed by "not only general sexism and ideas of women as male
property, but also a set of contradictory ideas about women's sexuality."[62] In this context, only certain types of rapes are considered "legitimate," while in other cases, women are perceived as "asking for it" or as
secretly desiring to be raped. Gavey wrote,

> These views of women's masochism and the inherent untrustworthi-
> ness of a woman's allegation of rape have been recycled in public
> debate against legislative changes, as well as in the courtroom. . . .
> From this point of view, women's consent is always up for ques-
> tion.[63]

Situations in which consent is considered more ambiguous include
rapes committed by acquaintances and intimate partners. Such assaults
have often been treated less seriously than those committed by strangers. This is largely as a result of our understanding and interpretation of
consent. Historically, rape was defined in such a way that many women
"lacked the right to withhold" consent (e.g., rape of African-American
women during slavery, marital rape).[64] Further, women were expected
to demonstrate their lack of consent through utmost physical resistance.
It was not until the efforts of the anti-rape movement of the
1970–1980s that laws were reformed. Despite those efforts, however, as
scholar Rose Corrigan noted, legal reforms "did not resolve deep conflicts over the line between coerced and consensual sexual contact."[65]

Stephen Schulhofer, in his book arguing for a form of affirmative consent that is essentially freedom from unwanted sex, noted that this stems from the law's failure to recognize the sexual autonomy of both parties.

> In effect, the law permits men to assume that a woman is always willing to have sex, even with a stranger, even with substantial physical force, unless the evidence shows unambiguously that she was *un*willing.[66]

As it stands, the laws on sexual assault vary by state, and there is as yet no single definition of consent. The *New York Times* pointed out,

> Some states, like New York, ask whether a reasonable person would believe that intercourse was consensual, considering all the surrounding circumstances. Meanwhile, some states follow the "no means no" rule, while others—including New Jersey—have adopted standards requiring affirmative, freely given permission by each person.[67]

The lack of consensus on "what just happened" on *Game of Thrones* is not simply a reflection of inconsistent laws. It is also due to the ways in which viewers experience and relate to sexual coercion and sexual violence itself. Even the preferred reading of the scene expressed by the creators and actors clashed with the majority of viewers' interpretations. That the Jaime/Cersei scene prompted so much indignation indicated that we have come a long way from demanding that a victim must demonstrate "utmost physical resistance" as proof of rape. It also indicated that viewers were willing to make a determination of rape regardless of Cersei's reaction to the situation. This is not surprising given research that has demonstrated that when women who were assaulted were asked about whether or not they had experienced sexual violence, many detailed experiences of forced sex consistent with the legal definition of rape, but which they themselves did not interpret or characterize as rape.[68] Such findings include those of the National College Women Sexual Victimization survey, which revealed that only about half (46.5 percent) of "completed rape incidents were acknowledged as rape," while only 2.8 percent of attempted rape incidents were acknowledged as rape.[69]

The point here is that there is fluidity among interpretations even as they pertain to one's own experiences, and these interpretations are part of our broader cultural understanding of what is considered normative heterosexual behavior. In this context, dominant discourse around what is expected of men and women during "normal heterosex" (e.g., the persistent idea that women are passive recipients of men's sexual desire) influences what is considered rape.[70] Many women describe experiences that are neither consensual nor rape but rest somewhere on a continuum of coercive sexual activity.[71] Here, the dominant script of "no means yes" and the belief that women fantasize about rape provided cultural space for viewers to interpret Cersei's protests of "no" as consent, as well as for the belief that "deep down she was really into it."[72] As Gavey observed, when the "sense of obligation and pressure is too strong," women may feel that they do not have a choice but to acquiesce.

"CHOREOGRAPHED LIKE A BALLET"

In an article on sexual harassment at San Diego Comic-Con, writer Rebecca Keegan of the *Los Angeles Times* reported an anecdote from the 2011 *Game of Thrones* panel featuring actors from the show. She wrote,

> A mix of cheers and groans rose up in the audience when actor Jason Momoa said his favorite part of his role on the HBO show is that he gets to "rape beautiful women and have them fall in love with me."[73]

Most likely, Momoa was referring to the marital rape scene in season 1 of the show in which a female character, Daenerys Targaryen (aka the "Mother of Dragons" played by Emilia Clarke), was sold into marriage to Momoa's character (warrior Khal Drago), who promptly raped her, only for her to later fall in love with him. While the scene generated a fair amount of controversy, it would pale in comparison to the outcry over the marital rape scene in the later episode, "Unbowed, Unbent, Unbroken." Here, Sansa Stark (Sophie Turner) was forced to marry the sadist Ramsey Bolton (Iwan Rheon) and was raped on her wedding night as her childhood friend, Theon (aka Reek, played by Alfie Allen), was forced to watch. The scene was heavily criticized as unnecessary and as simply a means of furthering the character development of Theon.[74]

The viewer reaction to the scene was fierce and included Senator Claire McCaskill, who tweeted,

> Ok, I'm done Game of Thrones.Water Garden, stupid.Gratuitous rape scene disgusting and unacceptable.It was a rocky ride that just ended.[75]

In a high-profile protest move, feminist-oriented popular-culture web-site *The Mary Sue* published an article declaring that they will no longer promote the show.[76] Editor-in-chief Jill Pantozzi wrote about the scene, "After the episode ended, I was gutted. I felt sick to my stomach. And then I was angry." And of the show, "There's only so many times you can be disgusted with something you love before you literally can't bring yourself to look at it anymore."

However, others were less shocked. Actress Sophie Turner (Sansa) described her impression of the marital rape scene:

> When I read that scene, I kinda loved it. . . . It was all so messed up. It's also so daunting for me to do it. I've been making [producer Bryan Cogman] feel so bad for writing that scene: "I can't believe you're doing this to me!" But I secretly loved it.[77]

In an earlier interview, the *Telegraph* reported that with regard to the filming of a rape scene, Turner was "assured by the director that the scene would be 'choreographed like a ballet' and would be 'beautiful.'"[78]

In *The Federalist*, Leslie Loftis wrote of her reaction to the scene, "It was inevitable and, as expected, it was awful, although not particularly violent. . . . I certainly had a restless night on Sunday."[79] Loftis defended the scene and struck out against those who were offended. She did this not by distancing the show from real life, but instead by suggesting that the show is *based on real life*.[80] Loftis stated that the show is "basically a crossover between historical fiction and myth"—a frequent defense of sexual violence in the show—and pointed out to critics that sometimes life is unfair.[81] She suggested that "shrinking-violet fans" want only "happy" stories. Similarly, Robby Soave, writing for *Reason*, was dismissive of the criticism of the show because he saw it simply as part of the broader culture wars fought by those who insist on "politicizing" rape. But Soave, like Loftis, misinterpreted viewer complaints about Sansa's rape as a criticism against *all* rape portrayals and consequently overstated the objections. Soave said,

> I find this implication—that rape is bad, and therefore, should not be depicted—troubling, to say the least. . . . Many of the people who are up in arms about Sansa's rapes were silent (or at least quieter) for the myriad scenes of graphic violence throughout the previous 45 episodes of *Game of Thrones*.[82]

Yet critics had not remained silent, nor was there a chorus from viewers calling for an end to rape depiction altogether. In truth, for years, there was fairly consistent criticism against the show for its treatment of women, overuse of sexposition, and incessant sexual violence—even as viewers continued to enjoy the show. The reaction to Sansa's rape was only louder because it was perceived as the latest in an ongoing pattern of how the show portrays sexual violence. The reactions along the way were far more varied and complex than simply "don't show rape."

Even those viewers who criticized the show for certain scenes of sexual violence that seem "out of character" and "unnecessary" at times viewed the show as empowering. As feminist scholar Barbara Winslow said, there is no single feminism, but feminisms, which are commonly expressed in public discourse around sexual violence.[83] As with many other shows and their portrayals of sexual violence, *Game of Thrones* presents a fairly complex version of feminism, and this is reflected by the viewer response.[84] For example, writer Caroline Siede parsed how her reaction to the show is complicated:

> But to simply write off the show as sexist bullshit would be to throw out the naked lady with the bathwater. *Game Of Thrones* remains one of the only prestige dramas to feature a large female ensemble— only *Orange Is The New Black* can rival it for sheer number of well-developed female characters.[85]

Similarly, in a rundown of powerful female characters on the show, *BuzzFeed* pointed out "9 Ways *Game Of Thrones* Is Actually Feminist," and *Entertainment Weekly* queried in their headline, "*Game of Thrones*: Feminist or Not?" and answered in the affirmative.[86] One Mic.com headline in reference to season 5 declared, "Game of Thrones Is Back—And More Feminist Than Ever Before." The accompanying article detailed how female characters in the show are "running, ruling and ruining the world," and relayed one of the more poignant exchanges of dialogue in which two characters ponder who would eventually gain the throne. The eunuch and former member of the king's small council, Varys, declared of the potential ruler, "A monarch who can intimidate the high lords and inspire the people, a ruler loved by millions with a powerful army and the right family name."

"Good luck finding him," the listener responds.

"Who," asks Varys, "said anything about him?"[87]

"IT'S THE MOST TASTEFUL RAPE SCENE IMAGINABLE"

What is important to explore beyond teasing out the meanings of sexual violence is assessing how we are affected by the portrayal. Voyeurism and the ethics of witnessing are at the heart of much of the discussion surrounding portrayals of sexual violence. Most often, this ethical dilemma is addressed by questioning whether the violence is "necessary" for the story. According to criminologist Alison Young, what is often ignored in this discussion of whether or not to include scenes of sexual violence is the affective impact of the scenes—the ways in which the viewer corporeally experiences the images and remembers and recalls the experience.

In her study of rape revenge films, Young wrote that the focus on criminological aesthetics is less about the representation itself and more about recognition of the mental and bodily connections made by the spectator. For Young, cinema is experienced as haptic, as sensation, and as engagement with crime images as a "sign that is felt, rather than recognized or perceived through cognition."[88] As cultural critic Steven Shaviro further explained, this engagement of affect is "not *what* something is, but *how* it is—or, more precisely, *how* it affects, and how it is affected by, other things."[89] Here, Shaviro is recognizing that films employ cinematic techniques (e.g., sound, close-ups, edits, etc.) specifically designed to both repulse and attract viewers. In her work, Young connected this haptic experience to larger ethical issues inherent in the consumption of images of sexual violence. She stated,

> The inclusion of a rape scene in a film should always be questioned, since it is not possible for the spectatorial relation to the crime-image of sexual assault to involve a kind of *just looking*—a looking that is interested only in the possibilities of justice in the aftermath of injury.[90]

The viewer is implicated because "looking at and doing violence thus become conjoined in and on the body of the injured woman."[91] Scholar Patricia Pisters described how the affective encounter works. She stated,

> It does not work on our sensory-motor schema that leads to action, and it does not work in the first instance on our cognitive or mental ability. Rather, it works directly on the affective nervous system that has sensors everywhere in the flesh.[92]

This phenomenon is illustrated by one survivor's recount after viewing the American version of the film *The Girl with the Dragon Tattoo* directed by David Fincher, a rape-revenge fantasy set against the backdrop of a serial killer thriller and based on the best-selling book trilogy by Swedish author Stieg Larsson.[93] She stated the following of the rape scene,

It's a funny thing about trauma, the way the body remembers. I went through several stages of feeling when I saw that rape scene, and even writing about it now I can feel my body responding: my heart rate is up and my legs are shaky. In the theater, when it was happening, I started to feel so panicky. My muscles got tense and it was hard to breathe. Tears filled my eyes. I kept squeezing my toes together and reminding myself to breathe. I found it hard to focus on the rest of the film. I tried, but I kept hearing her screams and then I'd have to squeeze my fists and toes and breathe. As soon as the credits came up, I fled to the bathroom. I was overwhelmed with nausea but didn't throw up. It was hard to pee because I was starting to dissociate and leave my body. I felt so angry too. I sent some really evil text messages to a friend who'd texted something benign. I was furious. I wanted to tear down the stalls and kill people. It was such a fierce anger.[94]

This extreme response to the film might be understandable considering that Fincher was at ease with viewers' uncomfortable reactions. Violence against women is a major theme in *The Girl with the Dragon Tattoo*, in both the books and the films (both the Swedish film trilogy and the American film). Much of the discussion of sexual violence in the film centered around the scenes in which the female heroine, Lisbeth Salander, is raped by her state-appointed guardian. Her rape revenge culminates in a gruesome scene in which Salander tasers her rapist, rapes him, and tattoos his flesh, permanently labeling him a rapist. In an interview describing the rape-revenge scene, Fincher noted the reaction to the film. He described the audience as "literally start[ing] to squirm" as Salander returns to her rapist's apartment to seek revenge.[95] One feminist blogger described how the rape of Salander both repelled and simultaneously evoked pleasure:

It certainly was the *most* thrilling scene in a very dull, joyless movie. The rape was done with glee, that verve on screen was impossible to ignore, so instead of looking away while an emotionally disturbed, malnourished woman is being forcibly sodomized, my animal parts started wriggling. Instead of cringing, I leered. . . . The rape scene in *Girl with the Dragon Tattoo* was so lovingly done, it was downright arousing. (emphasis in original)[96]

Despite the fulfillment of rape-revenge fantasy—a plot device that transforms the androgynous Salander into a feminist heroine—viewers have criticized the rape scenes in the Fincher film for being highly stylized in ways that sexualize the violence.[97] In fact, Fincher pointed out the following:

I showed the rape scene to someone who said, *"It's the most tasteful rape scene imaginable."* But still, it's effective. (emphasis added)[98]

It is this transgressive experience—finding the film simultaneously repulsive and pleasurable—that is key to understanding rape images as encounters.[99] Swedish actress Noomi Rapace (Lisbeth Salander) indicated how intensely she experienced the rape and rape-revenge scenes in the Swedish version of the film:

> But of course it was really heavy and hard, and I dreamt a lot of nightmares and it really went deep into me . . . *when I came back to rape him and to torture him, I really felt that I enjoyed it, actually, and it kind of scared me, because I didn't expect those feelings from myself.* (emphasis added)[100]

This transgressive experience of pleasure coupled with repulsion informs many of the conversations around portrayals of sexual violence both in films and television. It also intersects with viewers' personal experiences in ways that do not always correspond to the creator's intended preferred reading of the material.

"THE MOST REPULSIVE DRAMA EVER BROADCAST ON BRITISH TV"

It is not surprising that *The Fall*, a BBC2 television show set in Belfast, Ireland, about a serial killer who murders his victims, washes their bodies, paints their fingernails, and collects locks of hair and other trophies, raised questions about the portrayal of sexual violence on television. It is surprising, however, that after the second season was released on Netflix in the United States, the series was declared "the most feminist show on television" by *The Atlantic*.[101]

Much like *The Girl with the Dragon Tattoo*, the show evoked both disgust and pleasure, with the *Sunday Times* declaring it "Terrifyingly superb, morally dubious."[102] It sparked passionate commentary from two divergent viewpoints—those who declared that the show glamorized sexual violence and those who found a feminist sensibility in the show that they described as a revelation. In one scene, Detective Gibson obtained a video of the serial killer, Spector, torturing a female victim held in captivity. As she watched the tape at the precinct, in a move that implicated Gibson—as well as the audience—Spector halted the torture, turned the camera on himself, and stated, "Why the fuck

are you watching this? You sick shit! What the fuck is wrong with you?!"
Indeed.

The aesthetics of *The Fall* were problematic for some viewers who
suggested that the show was exploitative. The *Daily Mail* headline referencing the first season read simply, "Why does the BBC think violence against women is sexy?" and called the show "the most repulsive
drama ever broadcast on British TV" due to the "graphic depictions of
sexual murder, violent abuse, necrophilia, stalking, pornography and
masturbation."[103] Similarly, the *Independent* wrote of *The Fall*, "It was a
well-crafted series, but there were rather too many shots of desirable
girls before, after and during their abuse and murder."[104] The following
tweets illustrate how the show was perceived by some as a typical misogynist fantasy of sexual violence against women—an interpretation far
from writer Allan Cubitt's intent.

> I think there's some weird sexualisation of rape/serial killing in #The-
> Fall. They're definitely trying to make it sexy
>
> #TheFall BBC's flagship #rape fantasy titillates the masses—male
> gaze froth presented as gritty realism. #Misogyny
>
> I wish all the really good BBC dramas people tell me to watch wer-
> en't about rape. Can't I see a dude victimized? #HappyValley
>
> This one was rape-murder styled like a GQ shoot. #Thefall[105]

On Twitter, criminologist David Wilson referred to the show as "male
rape fantasy" and "torture porn."[106] He then penned an article for the
Daily Mail in which he said that *The Fall* "is the sickest show on tv,"
that it is "brutal misogyny turned into entertainment, murderous cruelty elevated into pleasurable viewing. . . . It is no exaggeration to describe *The Fall* as extended rape fantasy."[107]

Others, such as Amanda Rodriguez, writing for *Bitch Flicks*, a website devoted to reviewing films and television through a feminist lens,
took a more nuanced view. She strongly praised the show for its feminist sensibility, but also found the show exploitative in the way that it
films the female victims. She wrote,

> The camera lovingly caresses and lingers upon these women's terror,
> their struggles, their bound limbs, their exposed flesh, and finally
> their corpses. The excuse can be given that it's all in the name of
> "getting into the killer's head," but the camera's gaze goes too far
> into the realm of prurience, ultimately becoming gratuitous and in-
> dulging in fantasies of rendering women helpless and objectified.[108]

As for his perspective, actor Jamie Dornan, who plays Spector, addressed the "uncomfortable viewing experience"—the tension between experiencing repulsion and pleasure—and revealed that he is decidedly empathetic: "I hope the killer gets away with it."[109]

The Fall's writer, Allan Cubitt, defended the show and its focus on violence against women in an article for the *Guardian*. He maintained that he took a decidedly feminist approach to the series in writing a female lead detective who is strong, independent, competent, and owns her own sexuality even as she navigates her way through a patriarchal society. Cubitt did acknowledge that too many crime shows deal with sexual violence in problematic ways, including failing to fully humanize the victims. He said he was therefore determined to explore the psychology of the serial killer—who eroticizes and sexualizes the victims—while still granting full humanity to the victims.[110]

In addition to highlighting what he considers the careful portrayal of victims in the show, Cubitt wrote that he felt it important that the killer's motivations and behaviors be understood from the perspective of the lead detective Stella Gibson (Gillian Anderson). Cubitt described Gibson's approach to the serial killer, Spector:

> She sees nothing mysterious about what the killer is doing. It's just misogyny—age-old male violence against women. She sees such violence as endemic in patriarchal societies.[111]

In fact, those who found the show to be feminist pointed less to the portrayal of the victims than to the portrayal of the detective.[112] They found Detective Gibson's obsession with the killer less about sexual tension or personal vulnerability and more as evidencing a professional tension between a determined crime fighter and a psychopathic killer. In her quest, Gibson does not have to sacrifice her personal life to have a successful career, and she owns her sexuality by way of unashamed, no-strings-attached sexual hookups. However, the latter occurs in ways that some viewers find discomforting. Here, similar to the discussions of *Game of Thrones*, portrayals of sexual violence are framed within the broader context of norms around female sexuality. Criminologist David Wilson suggested that Gibson's casual hookups are signs of false empowerment, reflecting aspects of the more broad-based debates around feminism, agency, and empowerment.[113]

"THE YEAR OF THE TRIGGER WARNING"

On November 18, 2013, in her conversation with a Twitter follower, writer, director, show runner, producer, and all-around television powerhouse Shonda Rhimes tweeted the following: "I agree that a trigger warning would have been a very good and responsible thing. It's not something I control, not my area but."[114] A trigger warning is basically a statement at the start of the episode that alerts viewers to the fact that it contains potentially disturbing material. Rhimes is responsible for shows such as *Grey's Anatomy*, *Private Practice*, *Scandal*, and *How to Get Away with Murder*. She has been credited with shaping prime-time television dramas, particularly in her willingness to showcase diversity in race, ethnicity, and sexual orientation among cast members. The above-mentioned tweet involved the *Scandal* episode "Everything's Coming Up Mellie."

The show's plot centers around the president of the United States' on-again, off-again relationship with his mistress, Olivia Pope. Throughout the series, the president's wife, Mellie, struggles with her knowledge of her husband's extramarital relationship, her political loyalty to her husband, what she had to sacrifice for his political ambitions, and her own drive for independence. In this episode, the show flashed back several years to a scene involving Mellie and the president's father, Big Jerry, a relationship long fraught with difficulties. The *Wall Street Journal* described the scene in their TV recap:

> And instead of being able to reason with Big Jerry, he rapes her. That scene was both disturbing and disgusting. Most shows will give viewers a warning, either at the beginning of the show or even right after the commercial break, that there will be strong sexual content. I—along with lots of viewers on Twitter—was not prepared. Mellie fought with Big Jerry and tried to push him off, but he pinned her down, raped her and may have fathered Fitz's first child . . . named Jerry.[115]

While some fans embraced the plot as an attempt to make Mellie more "real" or sympathetic, others criticized it for being a "lazy plot device" or an attempt to "soften" her.[116] Most of all, there was criticism of the episode for not presenting a "trigger warning," particularly given that other scenes in the show that included murder and torture had been prefaced with warnings.[117] It was this onslaught of attention, and Rhimes's tweet, that led *Slate*'s Amanda Marcotte to declare 2013 the year that the trigger warning went mainstream.[118]

It is now commonly recognized that people suffering from posttraumatic stress disorder (PTSD) who are exposed to traumatic events, including sexual violence, can be "triggered" by any number of stimuli, including smells, sounds, certain dates that relate to the original event, locations, images and other media, and news reports.[119] PTSD may occur after exposure, either directly or indirectly, to a traumatic event such as war, interpersonal violence, sexual violence, or natural disaster.[120] According to the American Psychiatric Association's *Diagnostic and Statistical Manual of Mental Disorders*, PTSD survivors may experience intrusive symptoms such as nightmares and flashbacks and, as a result, may behaviorally avoid anything that might be distressing that is related to the trauma. Additionally, symptoms may include, but are not limited to, increased negative feelings and emotions, hypervigilance, self-destructive behaviors, difficulty sleeping, and a sense of alienation.[121]

The debate over trigger warnings is a relatively recent one and is largely centered on the expanding usage of the concept. Reporter Alison Vingiano traced trigger warnings from early PTSD recognition to *Ms.* magazine bulletin boards to fan fiction posted on *LiveJournal* to its use on Tumblr, Twitter, and Facebook. She found evidence of its first usage on a website linked to *Feministe.*[122]

Trigger warnings originated in feminist discourse as a way of alerting readers, or discussant participants, that the material presented might be upsetting or trigger a previous traumatic event. Given that many survivors of sexual violence reported that they felt retraumatized as a result of viewing or being exposed to materials that included representations of sexual violence, trigger warnings were designed with sensitivity in mind.[123] Since then, the scope of trigger warnings has expanded beyond warnings of sexual violence to include *virtually any topic whatsoever* that could potentially evoke the slightest bit of discomfort, such as "sex, pregnancy, addiction, bullying, suicide, sizeism, ableism, homophobia, transphobia, slut shaming, victim blaming, alcohol, blood, insects, small holes, and animals in wigs."[124] There is no shortage of articles debating whether trigger warnings are a well-intentioned, good sense tactic or a silly, if not absurd, effort that has gone too far.[125]

Many who oppose trigger warnings argue simply that words or discussions do not equate to real-life experiences. That point, however, is largely irrelevant because trigger warnings are not about the *portrayals themselves*, but rather about our affective response. Nonetheless, as feminist Jessica Valenti said, there is so much variability in what might serve as a trigger that it is impossible to warn of them all. She wrote,

But as someone who has had PTSD, I know that a triggering event can be so individual, so specific, that there is no anticipating it. Last year, a position in yoga class gave me a panic attack because it so closely resembled the position I was in when I had an emergency C-section.[126]

In addition to the expanding scope of trigger warnings, their use has migrated from rather informal usage on blogs, Tumblr, and other social media to more formalized uses, such as their inclusion on college course syllabi to warn students of potentially upsetting materials. Many professors have balked at this, countering that being offended by ideas is part of the college experience itself, and indeed part of maturing into an adult. Some argue further that the use of trigger warnings will result in a chilling effect and possibly threaten academic freedom.[127]

Journalist Judith Shulevitz warned that student requests for "safe spaces," or what she called the "live-action version" of trigger warnings, are "self-infantilizing." She detailed an event in which students at Brown University were so threatened by a scheduled debate about sexual assault on campus, including the airing of contested perspectives on rape culture, that they created a "safe space" for students to retreat. Shulevitz described the space as a room

equipped with cookies, coloring books, bubbles, Play-Doh, calming music, pillows, blankets and a video of frolicking puppies, as well as students and staff members trained to deal with trauma.[128]

Shulevitz contended that campus administrators are in a "double bind": colleges are ostensibly bastions of free speech, while simultaneously charged with adhering to civil rights statutes designed to ensure that students are not subjected to a hostile environment. Creating a "safe space" such as that described above opens up criticism that victim advocacy has morphed into a strange and dangerous inability for students to be confronted with ideas that do not conform to their worldview. Shulevitz argued that the demand for trigger warnings and safe spaces is no longer about behavior itself, but rather *speech about behavior*—a trend she found alarming. The inability to distinguish "real" threats from illusory ones (or "virtual" ones), debates over trigger warnings and free speech/censorship, and anti-harassment campaigns are echoes of earlier discourse around feminism and anti-rape activism and remain central elements in the current construction of rape culture.

"GOOD" RAPE REPRESENTATIONS

Our engagement with sexual violence in television and films is not necessarily distinct from our real-life experiences. Instead, one informs the
other. A post on the blog *Brilliant at Breakfast* illustrated how engagement with portrayals of sexual violence, along with our personal experiences, folds back into our understandings of sexual violence. The blog
contributor cites, among other cultural references, Elliot Rodger, who
videotaped himself describing his plans for murder before taking the
lives of six people in a misogynist rant:

> I'm not much of one for throwing around terms like "rape culture"
> and "trigger warning," . . . I didn't get all up in arms about Jaime
> Lannister raping Cersei on *Game of Thrones* because I felt it was in
> the service of the story. . . . Some might call me a tool of the patriar-
> chy, but as someone who DID have something bad happen to me in
> college and went on to live a perfectly functional life including a
> marriage of 27 years cut short only by my husband's death last fall, I
> feel qualified to say that. But it's impossible to watch Elliot Rodger's
> horrifying video attempting to justify his actions or even skim his
> 141-page manifesto/autobiography without wondering if perhaps
> those bandying about the term "rape culture" aren't on to some-
> thing. [129]

As with the aforementioned *Scandal* episode, when the PBS series
Downton Abbey depicted a rape of one of the show's most beloved and
virtuous characters, Anna Bates (JoAnne Froggatt), the show received
more than four hundred complaints. [130] Some PBS viewers felt "betrayed," "angered," and "troubled" by the episode. [131] However, it was
the actress JoAnne Froggatt's Golden Globe acceptance speech that
illustrated another way in which these portrayals of sexual violence
touched the viewers. She stated,

> After this storyline aired, I received a small number of letters from
> survivors of rape, and one woman summed up the thoughts of many
> by saying *she wasn't sure why she'd written* but she'd just felt in
> some ways she wanted to be heard. And I'd just like to say, I heard
> you, and I hope saying this so publicly means in some way you feel
> the world hears you. (emphasis added) [132]

Such reactions from viewers reveal that scenes of sexual violence in
popular culture are processed at both an intellectual and affective level.
Engaging with the scenes as representation permits analysis of whether
the portrayals accurately map onto real-life experiences. This includes

recognition that our more complex and sophisticated portrayals of rape allow for interpretations that suggest a reinforcing of rape culture while also allowing for readings of feminist empowerment. However, to stop here—at the question of whether a scene is a "good" rape representation—is to miss the intensity with which viewers engage with the material. Our responses are not solely intellectual, and viewers are most passionate when they discuss how the scenes made them *feel* rather than how they made them *think*. In this regard, we are compelled to acknowledge that we are simultaneously repulsed by and attracted to images of sexual violence. It is here that we once again must come to terms with serial killer Spector's (*The Fall*) admonition, "Why the fuck are you watching this? You sick shit! What the fuck is wrong with you?!"

4

GEEK SPACES: "PRETTY GIRLS PRETENDING TO BE GEEKS"

When the action-adventure video game *Assassin's Creed Unity* was about to be released in November 2014, the game, which is part of a series that has thus far sold over seventy-six million copies, was eagerly anticipated.[1] That climate soon changed, however, when fans learned that the Ubisoft game, which includes a co-op feature that allows other assassins to play simultaneously along with the main character on the mission, would not feature an option for a female assassin. Ubisoft's game developer, James Therien, tried to explain the rationale for this when the game premiered at the Electronic Entertainment Expo:

> It was on our feature list until not too long ago, but it's a question of focus and production. . . . A female character means that you have to redo a lot of animation, a lot of costumes [inaudible]. It would have doubled the work on those things. And I mean it's something the team really wanted, but we had to make a decision. . . . It's unfortunate, but it's a reality of game development.[2]

The reaction to the notion that creating a female character would have "doubled the work" was swift on social media, inspiring a #WomenAreTooHardToAnimate hashtag and a tweet from a former Ubisoft animator, who stated, "In my educated opinion, I would estimate this to be a day or two's work. Not a replacement of 8000 animations."[3] Various outlets, including *The Verge*, the Associated Press, and the *Daily Beast*, reported on the backlash.[4]

Others, however, weighed in to support Ubisoft's rationale, suggesting that there were technical, as opposed to sexist, reasons for omitting the female avatar. Gary Cutlack, writing for *TechRadar*, opined that the Internet commentators who were upset about the lack of female characters took things "too far" for "dramatic effect."[5] Ubisoft responded to the criticism, pointing to its multicultural team of developers. The game creator said it intends that diversity to also be reflected in the company's games and characters.[6]

Some pop-culture journalists sought to provide context for the controversy, including Tauriq Moosa of the *Daily Beast*. Moosa, who saw the Ubisoft flap as indicative of a much larger problem, wrote that "it speaks to this wider culture, as we've seen constantly in 'geek' spaces: videogames, comics, films, sci-fi/fantasy novels, and so on."[7] Moosa's point was that these largely white, male-dominated industries produce content that too often woefully underrepresents minority characters. In particular, when they represent female characters, regardless of their race or ethnicity, the characters are often hypersexualized and portrayed as victims as opposed to heroes, warriors, or crime fighters. One tweet summarized the frustration of many gamers:

> Unless you are killing her, buying her or selling her, @Ubisoft can't animate a woman you can actually play #womenaretoohardtoanimate[8]

That comment wasn't made in isolation. Over the past few years, as geek spaces—specifically gaming and comic book communities—have transitioned from relatively insular subcultures to dominant institutions in popular culture, they have become contested sites for debate involving issues of gender, misogyny, and sexual harassment. This chapter shows that conversations once relegated to insiders are now part of the larger public discourse around women in popular culture, sexual harassment, political correctness, and rape culture.[9]

In December 2012, the news website *The Daily Dot* provided a year-end summary of the many instances of "sexism, misogyny, and attacks on women" within geek spaces.[10] Such instances included the high-profile experience of a New York Comic Con attendee who dressed as Marvel's Black Cat comic book character and subsequently reported that she was sexually harassed while being filmed for an interview. Her Tumblr account of the incident gained international attention.[11] She explained that dressing up in costumes, even flattering ones, does not warrant harassment. She wrote,

> But that does not mean we have to put up with s*** that crosses the line, it does not mean we owe them a fantasy, it does not mean we

dress up to have guys drooling over us and letting us know that we turn them on.[12]

That same year, Joe Peacock, writing for CNN, described what he saw as frustration in the geek community around "pretty girls pretending to be geeks for attention."[13] Peacock described these perceived posers as an affront to the "real" geeks, who are, presumably, men. Similarly, tech writer Tara Tiger Brown pleaded for "fake geek girls" to just go away. She described them as invaders of geek spaces who attempt to "get attention," "to maximize their klout," or to simply serve as "exhibitionists." Brown said she was distressed that the term "geek" is defined so broadly. She contended that only those who "understand [their hobby or interest] deeply" or are "extremely skillful" should be considered true geeks.[14] It is this assumption—that geek spaces are considered as *naturally* (white) male environments that are susceptible to infiltration by others—that has driven much of the hostility toward minority participants. Such assumptions also promote the idea that being a geek is something so socially desirable that legions of women find it necessary to "fake it" in order to participate.

"NOT IN THE KITCHEN ANYMORE"

Understanding how sexism became a dominant narrative in discussions around gaming culture requires a deeper look into it as a community and a hugely successful industry. In a way, it's a misnomer to refer to gaming as a subculture. The industry is a huge part of the global entertainment complex and is by no means marginal—both in terms of revenue and in terms of audience/participant reach. Total revenues for the video-gaming industry in the United States hit $23.5 billion in 2015—a 5 percent jump over the previous year—according to the Entertainment Software Association (ESA).[15] Further, according to ESA's "Essential Facts about the Computer and Video Game Industry" report, 42 percent of Americans play video games regularly. The demographics of the players may surprise those who consider gaming an immature pastime of young males—in fact, in 2015, the average age of game players was thirty-five, 44 percent of all players are female, and there are more women eighteen and older playing video games than boys age eighteen or younger.[16] A report by SuperData research shows that while females are more likely to play role-playing games, males are more likely to play first-person shooter games and massively multiplayer online games.[17] Research also shows that not all people who play identify themselves as "gamers." The very notion of a so-called gamer identity has been at the heart of popular (and academic) discussion over the years.[18]

Not only does gaming continue to surge in popularity, but so does *watching* gamers game. Described on their website as the "world's leading video platform and community for gamers," the website Twitch streams gamers playing games and broadcasts competitions, industry events, and online video shows.[19] The site is massively popular, with the *New York Times* reporting viewership rivaling those of CNN, MSNBC, and MTV.[20] *Business Insider* reported that Twitch comprises 40 percent of all live-streamed Internet content. In comparison, Major League baseball and ESPN combined reach only 13 percent.[21]

While there is a great diversity of game offerings, when broken down by genre, over 50 percent of the best-selling video games consist of action and shooter games, with *Grand Theft Auto V* and *Call of Duty* topping out the top twenty best-selling video games of 2015.[22] It is this focus on action and shooters that in part leads to the traditional perception that gaming is a primarily male-dominated space. As in other forms of popular entertainment, women and other minorities are often marginalized as characters. Many scholars have examined the intersection of gender and gaming, investigating the significance of problematic representations and underrepresentation of minorities in popular games.[23] For example, scholar Adrienne Shaw found that for many gamers, representation (or lack thereof) was not particularly problematic for them as individuals, but they did feel that it was socially important for minorities to be represented.[24]

There have been many instances in which gamers have cried foul about games they believe poorly represent woman or minority characters. Take, for example, the trailer for *Hitman: Absolution*, which premiered in 2012. It featured a male assassin violently slaughtering eight nuns who were wielding machine guns and shoulder-launch rockets. If that weren't enough, the nuns had peeled off their habits to reveal stiletto heels, bustiers, garter belts, and thigh-high fishnet stockings. The trailer elicited much criticism, including this incredulous headline published on IGN, "What the hell is with that Hitman trailer?" and this from the UK's *Mirror*, "Why the Hitman Video Game Trailer Is a Shameless Piece of Sexist Tat."[25] Keza MacDonald, writing for IGN, described why the trailer provoked such ire from fans:

> Let's be clear here: the problem is not that Agent 47 is graphically murdering a group of women, though that's pretty nasty. It's that it fetishizes the violence and sexualises the women, drawing a clear line between sex and graphic violence that makes the trailer really dis-

tressing to watch, and leaves you questioning who the hell it's designed to appeal to.[26]

Rob Fahey, writing for *Games Industry*, went further:

> The issue here, then, is the sexualisation of violence against women. It's an issue rooted in a whole morass of problems that our society struggles with. The video makes it seem as if it's "okay" for Agent 47 to kill these women not because they're assassins, but because they turn out to be dressed like prostitutes under their nuns' robes. It creates shots which emphasise the sexiness of the women even as they're being killed, and even highlights the sexiness of their corpses.[27]

Many believe that such representations of sexualized violence help foment rape culture.[28] Feminists determined to eliminate it and its root causes had long been concerned with hypersexualized portrayals. By linking sexuality to violence and objectifying women, gaming became a flashpoint for debate around the normalization of sexual violence.

Occasionally, such controversies extend beyond the insular walls of the gaming community and its niche media, in turn influencing mainstream perceptions of the industry as an all-boys club where women and other minorities are not welcome. While there may be diversity of race, gender, and sexual orientation among players, according to the Gamasutra Salary Survey of 2014, minorities remain woefully underrepresented as game programmers and engineers (5 percent), artists and animators (9 percent), and designers (13 percent).[29] Further, the self-selected survey from the International Game Developers Association also showed that women remain underrepresented in the industry. As of 2015, 75 percent of the games industry is male, and 76 percent of its members are white; women comprised 22 percent of respondents, an increase from 11 percent in 2005. Only 9 percent of the survey's respondents were East Asian, 7 percent were Latino, and 3 percent were black.[30]

The conversations around gender in gaming reached the general public when gamers began publicizing their experiences and the mainstream media covered the issue. When websites such as *Not in the Kitchen Anymore* and *Fat, Ugly or Slutty* provided evidence of the all-too-common misogynist comments faced by female gamers and other minorities, the mainstream media began to take note. In 2012, journalist James Fletcher, writing for BBC News, detailed the harassment and misogyny experienced by female gamers such as Jenny Haviner, who created the website *Not in the Kitchen Anymore* that included audio clips that she recorded while gaming online. She described the recordings as "the dated, hostile, and downright weird reactions men (and the occasional woman) display upon meeting women in-game." The audio transcripts she posted variously reveal that she was referred to as a "fuckin' slut," "stupid freakin' skunk," "a dumb c**t," and a "whore." Her site is currently on hiatus and has not been updated since May 2014.[31] Similarly, the website *Fat, Ugly or Slutty*, launched in 2011, posted submissions from those who have received "creepy, disturbing, insulting, degrading and/or just plain rude messages" from other online players.[32] Rather than attribute these comments to "young boys," who are too immature to understand the consequences of their comments, it is important to note that in 2012, the average age of gamers was thirty. The audio recordings revealed that the bulk of these comments were not coming from adolescent boys but from adult males. This point was emphasized in May 2012 in the video game podcast *Extra Credits*, which detailed gaming harassment, as did a panel that same year at PAX East titled "N00dz or GTFO! Harassment in Online Gaming."[33]

One notable instance of sexual harassment that reached mainstream media attention was the so-called Cross Assault. In February 2012, the *Street Fighter X Tekken* tournament streamed live online. During the competition, Miranda Pakozdi, a female competitor, was mercilessly harassed during game play by a team coach, Aris Bakhtanians, who later famously proclaimed that sexual harassment was so inherent in gaming culture that "if you remove that from the fighting game community, it's not the fighting game community."[34] The story was covered on the pop-culture website *Kotaku*, with a headline declaring, "This Is What a Gamer's Sexual Harassment Looks Like," as well as in the *New York Times*.[35] *Kotaku* further reported on Bakhtanians's defense of his comments:

> When asked about whether shouting "Rape that bitch!" at a match is acceptable behavior, Bakhtanians replied, "Look, man. What is unacceptable about that? There's nothing unacceptable about that. These are people, we're in America, man, this isn't North Korea. We can say what we want. People get emotional."[36]

During the incident, the video of which is available on YouTube, Bakhtanians taunted Pakozdi with comments such as "How does Miranda smell?" and he attempted to guess her bra size. She laughed at first, and then said, "That's so creepy." When she left to go to the bathroom, Bakhtanians told her,

> We got cameras in there too, right? I'm gonna hang a Mona Lisa in the bathroom with the eyes cut out. Whooooa. . . . There's already

people who have names registered as parts of your body. Hahaha. . . . How are your thighs? . . . I warmed that seat up for you. Smell that seat. . . . Take off your shirt. . . . The next time you make a mistake like that, I'm going to smell you.

The following day of competition, he suggested she wear a skirt. On day 6 of the tournament, Pakozdi forfeited and withdrew from competition—including her chances at the grand prize of $25,000. In an interview posted on YouTube after she withdrew, Pakozdi said that ultimately she had a lot of fun, but "things were kind of hard for me."[37]

The mainstream press overwhelmingly expressed disapproval of Bakhtanians's actions. However, one video-gaming forum, *The Escapist*, illustrated how *within* the gaming community there is more of a debate. In that forum, some contended that Bakhtanians was immature and his behavior inappropriate and unacceptable. Others, however, said they accept such trash talk as part of the gaming culture itself.[38] One commenter posted that trash talk is "SUPPOSED to put you ill at ease and hurt your feelings. . . . If it doesn't, then you aren't doing it right . . . chances are good that this Miranda took it way too personally."[39] Another commented that naughty language is part of the culture and is not problematic, "unless he did it in private, away from the game."[40]

Scholar Kishonna Gray, founder of the Critical Gaming Lab, a research laboratory dedicated to anti-racist, feminist research in contemporary gaming culture, echoed these findings with regard to Xbox Live, contending that sexist and racist remarks are pervasive during game play and are not necessarily considered deviant.[41] Despite the attention toward sexual harassment within the gaming community and mainstream media, gaming website *Polygon* noted in a 2014 headline that virtually nothing has changed: "Game dev harassment remains as bad as it was a year ago."[42]

"BITCHES ARE GONNA BITCH"

One afternoon, reporter Adi Robertson posted an article on the website *The Verge*, criticizing videos games such as *Watch Dogs* and *Grand Theft Auto V* for their oversexualization of women and their tendency to treat women as victims in ways that only serve to further the male protagonist's character development. Just three hours later, Robertson updated the post, telling readers that the comments section would likely be shut down due to "sockpuppet accounts . . . spamming the comments here with porn, rape threats, etc."[43] What is remarkable about the vitriol and sexual assault threats directed at Robertson that day is how *un*remarkable such actions had become. At this point, gendered harassment was the order of the day. *Badass Digest*'s Andrew Todd puts it this way:

> Layfolk who don't frequent gaming websites may not be aware (but certainly won't be surprised) that there are rampant issues with sexism, homophobia, and racism within the gaming industry.[44]

In fact, some suggest that sexism is to be expected if one has a noticeable profile in the gaming community. Brianna Wu, writing for *Polygon*, stated the problem: "If you are a woman working in the games industry, especially in a public way, you're going to experience harassment."[45] One Xbox Live gamer, Elisa Meléndez, reported that when her avatar was spotlighted on Xbox Live, she received over one thousand e-mails. She explained,

> The majority were congratulatory. The next most frequent type of message I eventually categorized as "Come-Ons or Denigration," including slurs, rape fantasies, and two pictures of male genitalia. *Adult* male genitalia, for anyone who might be tempted to dismiss such harassment as the work of a group of immature 12-year-old boys.[46]

One of the most notorious cases that illustrated the pervasiveness of misogyny and sexual harassment in the gaming community involved popular-culture critic Anita Sarkeesian. In May 2012, Sarkeesian, founder of the website Feminist Frequency, launched a Kickstarter campaign titled "Tropes vs. Women in Video Games" for the purposes of creating a web series that deconstructs and critiques representations of females in video games. By the end of the funding period, Sarkeesian had raised over $158,000 from nearly seven thousand contributors.[47]

However, the Kickstarter project sparked a firestorm of fury directed toward Sarkeesian by those who were angered by her intent to critique. She carefully documented much of the harassment and posted it on her Feminist Frequency website. Some comments posted to her YouTube page included, "Fucking downvoted and flagged for terrorism. Dumb ass nazi cunt," "show me your tits," "Tits or gtfo," "bitches are gonna bitch," and "what a stuck up bitch. I hope all them people who gave her money get raped and die of cancer."[48] In one post, Sarkeesian documented what she calls "image based harassment and visual misogyny" that was directed toward her. Here, photo-altering software was used to add degrading and sexist comments to her photos. For example, in one photo, Sarkeesian holds a sign stating, "I want female characters to be full & complete human beings." The sign was altered to say, "I want females to . . . suck my dick" and "I lick pussy for money $$$$$$$." Other photos were altered to show images of semen on her face.

The harassment was so frequent and extreme that she devoted her 2012 TEDxWomen talk exclusively to the experience of being targeted by "a massive online hate campaign."[49] In it, she explained that harassment against her included online threats of "rape, violence, sexual assault, and death"; hijacking of her Wikipedia page with "sexism, racism, and pornographic images"; a campaign to suspend her social media accounts; attempts to bring down her website by hackers; hacking into her e-mail and personal information; "pornographic images" made in her likeness that were used to portray her being raped by video game characters, and in one of the more disturbing examples, a "beat up Anita Sarkeesian" game where an image of Sarkeesian's face could be "punched" by players to transform her face into a bloody, swollen mess with black eyes.[50]

It should be noted that at this point, Sarkeesian had yet to make a video with her Kickstarter funding, though she had posted videos exploring more generally "representations of women in pop culture narratives." On August 25, 2014, Sarkeesian released one video in the series in which she showed how women are used as props in many video games to be sexually threatened or assaulted. For Sarkeesian, these nonplayable female characters provided no contribution to the plot but rather served as hypersexualized objects who endure violence for the purposes of defining the depravity and cruelty of the bad guy. Using examples from games such as *Red Dead Redemption*, *Grand Theft Auto V*, *Assassin's Creed: Brotherhood*, and *No More Heroes II*, among others, Sarkeesian presented a barrage of scenes depicting slaps, kicks, attempted rapes, slashed throats, and dismemberment. Rather than suggest that sexual violence should be prohibited from inclusion in video games, Sarkeesian suggested that the problem with the predominant portrayals is that they

> reinforce a popular misconception about gendered violence by framing it as something abnormal. As a cruelty only committed by the most transparently evil strangers. In reality however violence against women, and sexual violence in particular, is a common everyday occurrence often perpetrated by "normal men" known and trusted by those targeted.[51]

The release of this video sparked another round of threats against Sarkeesian, upon which she notified authorities and fled her house. Despite posting screenshots of threats against her, Sarkeesian was frequently accused of faking the threats.[52] Further, *Kotaku* reported in September 2014 that Sarkeesian's appearance at a Game Developer's Choice award ceremony was nearly derailed by a bomb threat, though after a sweep, no bomb was found.[53]

The rage against Sarkeesian spawned various Twitter accounts whose only purpose is to degrade her and others who would speak out against sexual harassment. For example, one account boasts a home-page photo of a brain impaled by a dildo linked to the YouTube video "It's Misogyny—/v/ the musical" with the following description:

> This video contains RAPE! If you don't like rape, or wish to not be affiliated with rape at the level of not even seeing the word rape, then, uh . . . don't read this sentence and watch the video. Sexist game dev pigs gonna sexism.[54]

The video contains no rape, only a Tim Burton–style musical parody of Sarkeesian and others who have called out video games for their misogynistic content. Another spoof account tweeted, "Everybody's a rapist, unless they ask 'would you like to engage in sexual activity with me?' which would totally kill the mood. #Yesmeansyes." and "On college campuses across the tri-state area, one in every 5 young men have become cruel, hateful lifelong gamers. #GamerGate."[55]

Though Sarkeesian had publicly discussed her experiences in 2012, it was not until a few years later that her story gained national and international attention in publications such as the *Washington Post*, *New Statesman*, *Business Insider*, *Regina Leader*, *Portland Mercury*, *Sydney Morning Herald*, and *Daily Beast*. Generally, the articles were sympathetic to Sarkeesian.[56] For example, the *New Statesman* wrote,

> Yet for pointing out obvious, incontrovertible evidence of sexist and misogynist parts of popular games, Sarkeesian gets vitriol. To be clear, this is still going on, *two years later*, every time a new video is released.[57]

Although Sarkeesian is an outlier—most people are not forced out of their homes as a result of gaming harassment—in the mass media, Sarkeesian's experiences, along with that of fellow game developers Zoe Quinn and Brianna Wu, became symbolic of what became known as the problem of misogyny in gaming.

Leigh Alexander, writing for *Gamasutra* (initially the online version of *Game Developer* magazine), explained that, "like it or not," the gaming community is mostly known among outsiders for its antifeminist harassment of women gamers and for misogynist content. Echoing Sarkeesian's proclamation that "we are witnessing a very slow and painful cultural shift," Alexander explained that the gaming community was shifting from being largely monolithic and hypermasculine into an array of creative communities that are not solely interested in the traditional fare of the past several decades.[58] It was Alexander's stinging statement that the singular image of the quintessential male white gamer was fading that created a stir.[59] She wrote,

> Traditional "gaming" is sloughing off, culturally and economically, like the carapace of a bug. . . . "Gamer" isn't just a dated demographic label that most people increasingly prefer not to use. Gamers are over. That's why they're so mad.[60]

Others expressed similar sentiments, for example, scholar and journalist Dan Golding, who characterized the reaction against women players and game developers as a desperate attempt to maintain the white, heteronormative status quo. This disruption essentially eliminates a stable "gamer" identity that has historically been that of a straight, white male.[61]

Some contend that these hostile reactions to diversity, and paranoia of the so-called social justice warrior (SJW) agenda, are a result of the perception that men are losing status in geek spaces. That anxiety is part of a broader pattern of what sociologist Michael Kimmel calls "aggrieved entitlement."[62] From school shootings to workplace violence to violence against women, Kimmel found common links where rage, fueled by aggrieved entitlement, was misdirected toward minorities rather than toward economic policies that foster inequalities. Kimmel noted that increasing gender and racial equality, coupled with decreased economic stability, has led to "a sense that those benefits to which you believed yourself entitled have been snatched away from you by unseen forces larger and more powerful."[63] This was expressed most powerfully in what became known as #GamerGate.

#GAMERGATE

During the week of August 28, 2014, *Polygon* ran a story with the headline, "An awful week to care about video games." The awful week refers to the fallout from the so-called #GamerGate[64] incident that highlighted ongoing harassment—much of it directed toward women gamers and game journalists—within the gaming community. Complaints about online harassment reached a fever pitch when deeply personal details about game developer Zoe Quinn were made public. Quinn is an indie developer who created the video game *Depression*

Quest, which is described as "an interactive fiction game where you play as someone living with depression. You are given a series of everyday life events and have to attempt to manage your illness, relationships, job, and possible treatment."[65] She was caught in a firestorm of controversy when her ex-boyfriend, Eron Gjoni, created a blog detailing her alleged infidelities. He specified that she had cheated with a gamer journalist, with the implication that she did so to garner positive reviews for her *Depression Quest* game.

By all accounts, Gjoni's website is harsh.[66] The implication that Quinn exchanged sexual favors to garner positive reviews from gamer journalists sparked a larger debate about whether the relationship between gamers and gamer journalists has become too cozy. However, the journalist Quinn was accused of having a sexual relationship with apparently never wrote about her game. Gjoni amended his original post to clarify that the timeline of Quinn's relationship with the journalist could not have influenced any reporting on her game.[67] Nevertheless, the damage to Quinn's reputation was done.

As a result of the incident, the hashtag #GamerGate was unleashed. Quinn was flooded with rape and death threats by people who united and aligned themselves under the hashtag. #GamerGate soon came to be harnessed as an admonition and threat to those so-called "social justice warriors" who would seek to voice concern over sexism and misogyny in gaming.[68] Given the documented harassment of other female gamers and developers over the past few years, Quinn reported that she was not particularly surprised by the reaction. In her interview with NPR, she stated, "I don't think I've ever released a game without getting some sort of rape threat."[69]

Quinn captured screenshots of some of the harassment and threats and shared them with readers. For example, chat logs from 4chan, an anonymous image-based website, included "she gonna get raped" and

> I feel like I would probably f*** Zoe. But not out of a loving sense of sexual attraction. More of that "hate f***" sense where you just want to assert your dominance as a male on her, a primal savagery. Then I'd probably have to sterilize myself to prevent the genome from spreading.[70]

Additionally, she reported edits on her Wikipedia page that altered her "date of death to coincide with planned public appearances (or, in one case, simply 'soon')." Further, she reported that her father received harassing phone calls including men screaming, "Your daughter's a whore."[71]

Quinn's experience was largely considered illustrative of the larger, ongoing problem of sexual harassment within gaming culture and the tech community at large.[72] The video-gaming website *The Escapist* ran an article featuring essays by female game developers expressing their reaction to #GamerGate. The essays were published anonymously out of fear of reprisals for simply speaking out on the issue. All but one of the narratives expressed concern about the rampant misogyny in gaming. The one outlier viewed the situation more optimistically:

> I think if the games industry were a cesspit filled with misogyny and hate, then I would understand the heavy focus on misogyny in games and the industry itself, but the truth is, it isn't. I really don't think that the games industry is any more sexist than any other industry.[73]

Others in the industry found the abuse too much to take. In fact, the fallout from ongoing harassment has led some women gamers and developers to abandon the industry altogether.[74] On September 1, 2014, Jenn Frank wrote an article in the *Guardian* titled "How to Attack a Woman Who Works in Video Gaming." As a result, she was accused of being an unethical journalist because she did not reveal her "relationship" with Sarkeesian and Quinn in the text of the article. In fact, she did include this information, but the editors at the *Guardian* had the paragraph removed because her relationships "did not fulfill the criteria for a 'significant connection' in line with the *Guardian*'s editorial guidelines."[75] As a result of the campaign against her and other female gamers and gamer journalists, Frank decided it was time to leave. She wrote,

> And really, my God, I don't have to do this. I've been given permission to move on to another audience. I have faith in my abilities to do something, anything else, without feeling inhibited or limited by my hobby. . . . I can finally understand and appreciate why I've watched so many games journalists walk away from all this—and, bless them, you usually never have to hear about it.[76]

Similarly, in a series of tweets, game designer and critic Mattie Brice announced in September that she would leave the industry. She stated, "I decided I'm not spending time and energy on things that don't reciprocate. The games industry never budged to make room for me."[77] In response to women leaving the industry, one #GamerGate supporter tweeted with glee, "SJWs dropping like flies before the might of #GamerGate."[78]

While it may be true that the majority of gamers do not sexually harass or revel in the exodus of women from gaming or game journalism, it is also true that gaming culture can be a hostile experience for women and other minorities. Quinn documented how #GamerGate was manufactured for the purposes of harassing women, providing conversations in 4chan detailing that the objective of GamerGate was to "cause infighting and doubt within SJW ranks."[79] According to reports, it also appears that at least a portion of those who harassed Quinn were part of a calculated campaign. For example, the #NotYourShield hashtag appeared in response to GamerGate. Initially, many mistakenly believed that women and other people of color who supported GamerGate had started this hashtag. The popular-culture website *Cinemablend* initially described #NotYourShield as being harnessed by "eclectically diverse and uniquely individual human beings" as a means of "express[ing] kinship and camaraderie" by tweeting in support of GamerGate, with many declaring that they would not be used as shields by "social justice warriors."[80] However, according to Casey Johnston, culture editor at *Ars Technica*, rather than an outgrowth of grassroots multicultural support for GamerGate, internet relay chat (IRC) logs revealed that it was users of 4chan who manufactured the hashtag and created false accounts posing as women and minorities for the purposes of supporting GamerGate and raging against Quinn and others.[81]

In another strange twist, *Vice* reported that many 4chan users had rallied behind the feminist organization The Fine Young Capitalists (TFYC) to support their effort to provide means for women to design and create games. According to *Vice*, 4chan's odd interest in TFYC began after they learned that the group had a falling-out with Quinn and became involved as a means of opposing her. 4chan users offered financial support for the TFYC project and also developed a modestly dressed female character named Vivian James who wears jeans and "a striped [green and purple] hoodie and drinks Mountain Dew Throwback." GamerGate supporters used Vivian James as evidence that those who support GamerGate are women friendly.[82] However, others quickly pointed out that the character was likely a "coded rape joke."[83] The green and purple colors represent a GIF of anal rape that went viral a few years ago in the 4chan video games board and became known as "daily dose."[84] *Know Your Meme* explained the significance of the colors,

> Images related to the gif are often not aimed at representing the GIF, but instead just contain the colors green and purple. The idea of this is to make the combination of the two colors evolve as a trigger in a person's subconscious that results in him being reminded of the gif each time he sees those colors.[85]

Further, *Vice* reported that "Gamers on Reddit (and plenty on 4chan) are already weighing in on whether they would have sex with this cartoon woman."[86]

Other hashtags in response to GamerGate included #NotAllGamers (a not-so-subtle nod to #NotAllMen), which circulated as a means of emphasizing that "not all gamers" sexually harass and threaten others within the gaming community. In a blistering critique of the attacks on the so-called SJWs, Andrew Todd, writing for *Badass Digest*, pointed out that the efforts to deflect attention by promoting #NotAllGamers ultimately ignored the larger cultural context that is permissive of abuse and harassment. Todd stated,

> The inevitable #NotAllGamers hashtag has sprung up on Twitter in the past few days, and I get where that comes from. I play video games too, and I'm not a total dick! Hooray for me. But I also think the hashtag misses the point in the same self-serving way that #Not AllMen did. This is a problem endemic to gaming, and everyone is part of that problem. There is a culture of harassment, abuse, and bigotry in the rotten core of multiplayer gaming; it has been allowed or even encouraged to fester by developers; and it has created some of the most toxic individuals on the Internet.[87]

The claim that the problem was pervasive was echoed by many and ultimately became the dominant narrative.

"I REALLY HOPE THIS IS NOT THE NEW NORMAL FOR MY LIFE"

In response to a barrage of tweets directed at her, including, "I am going to murder you both and f**k your dead corpses," game developer Brianna Wu tweeted, "I really hope this is not the new normal for my life."[88] In October 2014, she became the third high-profile female game developer to acknowledge that she had fled her home as a result of online threats. *Kotaku* posted screenshots of Wu's Twitter timeline showing threats that initially revealed her home address along with comments such as "I'm sick of you f**king feminist asshats" and "I'm going to rape your filthy ass until you bleed, then choke you to death with your husband's tiny Asian penis."[89]

Wu, who had recently attended New York Comic Con and spoke on a panel addressing representations of gender in video games, said that users of anonymous image board 8chan (which she described as users "too extreme" for 4chan) had posted rape and death threats, as well as revealed personal information about her and her family. The threats were in response to an "Oppressed Gamergater" meme she tweeted mocking GamerGate.[90] Though she had long been aware of the harassment that women in gaming have endured and discussed the topic in writing and on podcasts, she said she was nonetheless surprised at how quickly reaction to her turned toward victim blaming and accusations of lying.[91]

Invoking "gender wars," in an MSNBC video interview, she stated that there is a "literal war on women" in the gaming industry with clear messages sent that women do not belong.[92] She linked the targeted harassment faced by women gamers and developers to years of sexualized representation of women within the games themselves:

> You cannot have 30 years of portraying women as bimbos, sex objects, second bananas, damsels in distress, cleavage-y eye candy . . . eventually it normalizes this treatment of women.[93]

Although much of the media coverage involving harassment in the gaming community focused on women, men who are allies, the so-called white knights, have also been targeted. According to *GameSpot*, after sending several supportive tweets about Zoe Quinn, game developer Phil Fish was hacked. His "social security information, passwords, Polytron's PayPal account, and other sensitive data" were compromised.[94] Outraged by the onslaught, he tweeted "i'm sick of all these motherf**king death threats from these anti-feminist f**ks."[95] As a result of the harassment, he reportedly canceled games that he had in development and put up for sale rights to his game and company.[96]

Some reporters have also documented that writing about the issue made them a target. In an article suggesting that critiquing video games for sexist content is a valid endeavor, a reporter for the *Regina Leader-Post* stated, "I occasionally say things on this blog and on Twitter that make people angry, but the most hate I ever got was for a post I did on the representation of women in games."[97] Game designer and founder of Double Fine, an independent game development studio, Tim Schafer, was reportedly put on an "anti-SJW list" by GamerGate supporters for simply linking to a Sarkeesian video.[98] Similarly, at the 2014 New York Comic Con panel on gender, race, and ethnic representations in gaming, one audience member commented on the hesitancy of staff at her geek website to write any reviews of games—even positive—because the backlash can be so severe.[99]

Although the mainstream media had published articles on the harassment and misogyny around Sarkeesian's Kickstarter launch and Cross Assault, both of which occurred in 2012, coverage about the problem subsequently waned. To outsiders, those incidences must have appeared as isolated rather than as a pattern of ongoing marginalization within the gaming industry. However, when Sarkeesian canceled her talk at Utah State University due to inadequate security measures after a shooting threat, the *New York Times* took note, making GamerGate a front-page news story. The reporter described threats against Sarkeesian as "routine" at that point. [100]

Gamers, developers, journalists, and bloggers had already provided a context for these incidences of harassment and threats by writing about their own daily experiences in the industry. However, it was the experiences of Sarkeesian, Quinn, and Wu echoing through social media that grabbed the attention of a mainstream audience and what became symbolic of the problem of gendered harassment in gaming. [101] By October 2014, sexual harassment in gaming gained national attention. Articles covering harassment in gaming appeared in the *New York Times*, *San Jose Mercury News*, *New York Magazine*, the *Washington Post*, the *Daily Beast*, *Huffington Post*, *Vice*, *Forbes*, *PBS NewsHour*, *Time*, *BBC News*, *Rolling Stone*, and others. [102] By this time, the hashtag #GamerGate was tweeted over 1.2 million times and the #StopGamerGate2014 hashtag had amassed over 50,000 tweets in a twenty-four-hour period. [103]

Correspondingly, there were ongoing claims by GamerGate supporters that the so-called SJW agenda had overtaken gaming journalism. They contended that feminist-inspired concerns with reducing misogyny were pulling too much focus on issues of gender. To address whether these claims were true, author, entrepreneur, and self-described celebrity interviewer Morgan Ramsay conducted an analysis of 130,524 full-text articles collected from major video game outlets from July 11, 2013 to July 11, 2014. He found that only 0.41 percent of the total articles mentioned the keywords *feminism*, *feminist*, *sexism*, *sexist*, *misogyny*, and *misogynist*. [104] The attention toward harassment of women in gaming may have dominated how outsiders viewed the industry, but it did not fundamentally transform gaming journalism into a hub of gender studies.

While many of the mainstream articles on #GamerGate portrayed the issue as primarily about online harassment against women, it was also frequently framed in terms of a culture war. [105] Christina Hoff Sommers of the American Enterprise Institute weighed in by suggesting that it is the fault of the feminists themselves who impose "puritanical gender politics" to which GamerGate supporters merely respond. She further stated, "Today, at least in certain feminist circles, it's open season on the sexual preferences of straight males." [106] This framing of the issue in terms of a polarizing movement echoed Kyle Wagner's take on GamerGate as "a fascinating glimpse of the future of grievance politics as they will be carried out by people who grew up online."[107] Writing for *Deadspin*, Wagner pointed out similarities between the tactics of GamerGate and the "ever-present aggrieved reactionaries whose most recent manifestation is the Tea Party," where a relatively small group of people can create significant social change by agitating loudly and engaging the press in narratives that perpetuate false equivalencies.[108] Ultimately, Wagner framed GamerGate as a culture war issue that is driven by fear of losing a privileged status.

In his article for *Forbes*, Erik Kain similarly characterized the controversy as a culture war. Unlike Wagner, Kain suggested that both sides were engaged in name-calling, but Kain ultimately confirmed what many suggested about the fear of a changing male-dominated status quo. Kain wrote,

> One reader emailed to say that he has no problem with women, but video games were a nice boys club of sorts, a refuge from women where the boys could play for a while undisturbed.[109]

Similarly, Aris Bakhtanians, most notable for his involvement in the Cross Assault incident, admitted to feeling that the status quo among gaming culture is threatened. Responding on Twitter to the controversy around his statements about sexual harassment being intrinsic to fighting gaming, he apologized for his comments and stated, "When I made these statements, I was very heated as I felt that the culture of a scene I have been a part of for over 15 years was being threatened."[110]

IMITATION GAME

By 2015, GamerGate and the broader issue of harassment had been ripped from the headlines and condensed into the "Imitation Game" episode of *Law & Order: SVU* (airdate: February 11, 2015). The episode did not directly invoke the hashtag #GamerGate but rather included an amalgamation of incidents addressing the way women are treated in gaming. This included misogyny at gaming conventions, online harassment, doxing (the online leaking of personal, identifying information), and the accusation that female game developers rise in the ranks due to sexual improprieties rather than merit. The episode, which earnestly attempted to shed light on harassment, did not go over well in the gaming community. Comments were overwhelmingly negative, with most finding it "tonally weird," "ludicrous," "corny," "cheesy," "horrific . . . embarrassing," "laughable," and "the worst hour of cop drama I've ever watched."[111] More generously, *Entertainment Weekly* described the show as both "cartoonishly ham-fisted" and "surprisingly accurate," stating that "barring the more outrageous plot points (the kidnapping, the rape)—*this crap really happens.*"[112]

In short, the plot centered on a female game developer, Raina Punjabi, who became the victim of online harassment, doxing, swatting (a hoax by an anonymous caller to 911 reporting an emergency and resulting in the deployment of a SWAT team), kidnapping, and rape threats on the eve of her game's release. The perpetrators were portrayed as young men who had difficulty distinguishing "real life" from gaming.

Despite the efforts of the show to condemn misogyny and harassment of women, the episode instead contributed to the notion that women are somehow alien to gaming culture. In one scene at a gamer convention, Detective Fin Tutuola (Ice-T) educated a clueless fellow detective Amanda Rollins (Kelli Giddish) on the culture of gaming. Similarly, throughout the episode, Sergeant Olivia Benson is equally baffled. Back at the office, when talk of the case ensues, she said, "I'm not going to understand a word anyone is saying."

Many took the show to task for its use of overwrought images, including scenes of "an abduction inspired by a violent game, a captor wearing a ski mask, [and] a mysterious hacker-y broadcast." One review cited its cultural significance, saying that it contributed to public ideas about crime and justice while pointing out the ongoing difficulties of how the criminal justice system operates in the face of evolving technologies against a backdrop of misogyny.[113] Scholar Jeff Thompson similarly suggested that the episode shed light on "how the average American is likely to see issues like these." He stated,

> So, when Wednesday night's Gamergate-themed show airs, it won't necessarily say much about Gamergate, as such. But it will speak volumes about how Americans are grappling with issues, such as online threats, female harassment, doxing and the Dark Web.[114]

The show failed, however, to present these threats within the context of aggrieved entitlement. In stark contrast to the show's likely intention, it prompted remarks that served to discredit complaints of misogyny, something that Caitlin Dewey, writing for the *Washington Post*, pointed out by offering this comment taken from YouTube. She wrote,

> "You know," wrote a fairly typical YouTube commenter, "I think they are marketing this as an episode that shows these professional victims what it is like if they really WERE attacked for being a female gamer or game dev, which, of course, they [were] not."[115]

Those who contend that the threats against women in gaming are regularly fabricated and/or exaggerated have often accused Brianna Wu and others of being "professional victims." Many are quick to point out that no one has actually been murdered or violently attacked as a result of GamerGate-related threats. For example, one commenter took issue with the title of Wu's article ("I'm Brianna Wu, and I'm Risking My Life Standing Up to Gamergate") that appeared in *Bustle* (later republished in *Huffington Post*) the same week "Imitation Game" aired: "And how many people have lost their lives due to GamerGate at this point? This blog title is the definition of hyperbole."[116] The implication here is that unless the threats are carried through to fruition, they are inconsequential.

BEYOND GAMING

Over the past several years, what was once considered the relatively insular subculture of gaming exploded into a dominant mainstream force in popular culture. Part of this ongoing transition involves a shift in demographics among both consumers and producers of gaming content. As a result, there have been increasing calls for content to more broadly reflect the diversity of consumers in ways that disrupt the priority of white, male hegemonic masculinities that have long dominated the industry. By linking the changing status quo from a white male-dominated industry to that of increasing diversity (among gamers and developers) and, in turn, linking those changing dynamics to pervasive sexual harassment, the dominant narrative of "misogyny in gaming" fit the framework of rape culture outlined by earlier feminists. Most importantly, though, it was Sarkeesian's feminist-inspired criticisms that became the dominant narrative around sexual harassment to which others responded. That, along with Quinn's unapologetic response to accusations around her sexual behavior and Wu's outspokenness about sexism in the industry, converged to create the perfect storm for illustrating resistance to rape culture.

However, presenting GamerGate as a "gender war" might be counterproductive in that it may be interpreted as implying that the issue is race neutral. In her book documenting the experiences of marginalized gamers that participate in Xbox Live, scholar Kishonna Gray found that far from being condemned, harassment against minorities was an accepted, if not rewarded, activity among gamers. In response, women and other minorities have developed various strategies to cope and continue to thrive in the community.[117] Gray, and others, work to make women of color more visible, but most media accounts, both mainstream and gamer focused, present a gender dichotomy effectively ignoring the intersection of race/ethnicity, class, sexual orientation, and gender. Indeed, in the media accounts reviewed for this chapter, few discussed how the specific experiences of men and women of color in gaming intersect with gender.[118]

The ongoing controversies illustrate that gaming remains a contested site for our social understandings of sexual harassment and threats of sexual violence. For some, the significance of these dynamics may be found situated within the larger context of online harassment.[119] It is unclear, however, whether overall women are subjected to quantitatively more online harassment than men, though qualitatively there appear to be differences.[120] One report conducted by researchers investigating misogyny on Twitter in the UK noted in the affirmative, stating that "research has consistently found that women are subjected to more bullying, abuse, hateful language and threats than men when online."[121] A Pew Research Center Survey found that one in four online users had experienced some form of harassment, with women more likely to be stalked and sexually harassed, while men were more likely to be called names.[122] Another study found that celebrity male figures were more likely to receive online abuse than their female counterparts, although in contrast, female journalists were subject to about three times as much abuse as male journalists.[123] Although more research is needed on the prevalence and variability of online harassment, there are increasing efforts to understand the gendered dynamics of harassment that occur in social space that is understood as neither "online" nor "offline" but rather transcends the digital divide in ways that ultimately reproduce gender hierarchies and result in unique harms.[124]

Beyond the most prominent issues relevant to geek spaces in media accounts (e.g., demands for increased diversity in content and pervasive online harassment), GamerGate has come to represent a self-described full-fledged attack on so-called SJWs. It has extended beyond gaming to controversies around anti–sexual harassment panels at the music, film, and tech festival SXSW and ballots cast for the prestigious Hugo Awards for science fiction and fantasy works. Anger toward SJWs spread into other areas of social life, basically serving as a means to undercut critiques of restrictions on reproductive rights, issues of campus rape, police abuse of power, due process, and a plethora of other issues.[125] For example, here is how Mytheos Holt, writing for *The Federalist*, described GamerGate:

> GamerGate can be heralded as a movement that mounted *the first serious resistance to the pervasive social justice ideology* that has

crept into seemingly every area of culture and politics. (emphasis added)[126]

Here, the changing social, economic, and cultural dynamics must be understood as contributing to the sense of aggrieved entitlement on display among GamerGate supporters and others who participate in misogynistic online harassment. Part of the fallout from GamerGate is that academics have come under fire for simply studying gender and gaming and have been subsequently deemed a social and political threat. For example, writer Sheena Goodyear reported that the Canadian Games Studies conference attendees were instructed to avoid using GamerGate in any tweets during the conference. Doctoral candidate Natalie Walschots, who incidentally was deemed a "witch" by trolls in reaction to her scholarly interest in GamerGate, reported that after she appeared at a conference to discuss her work on GamerGate, Reddit users organized a campaign against her to sabotage her work. She stated to *The Mary Sue*,

> There have been calls to attend future conference panels that I am presenting on, to contact the dean of graduate studies at Concordia in an attempt to get me expelled, to buy up all the domain names associated with my name and handle to ruin my SEO for future employers.[127]

Additionally, scholars Shira Chess and Adrienne Shaw documented how their efforts to engage in a discussion around the issues of women and gaming at a Digital Games Research Association (DiGRA) conference resulted in many GamerGate supporters positing a conspiracy around their work by describing the DiGRA—which the authors report is not particularly feminist oriented—as an "SJW cult, a 'thinktank,' a government shell corporation, an institute, a pyramid scheme, and an 'enemy spawning ground.'"[128]

While the mainstream media coverage was generally supportive of the notion that there is evidence of a gendered problem within gaming and online harassment in general, one legacy of GamerGate may be how its supporters have been successful at reframing sensitivity to sexual violence itself as a social problem—that is, as a form of political correctness that is a threat to the broader culture at large and to free speech—issues that continue to resonate in broader discussions of rape culture.

5

GEEK SPACES

Feminist Interventions and SJW Drama Queens

As with the video-gaming community, comic book culture resides in a contradictory space. It features a growing number of progressive-minded creators and fans who are multiculturally inclusive, yet the industry is frequently criticized for falling short on the diversity of characters that the changing consumer demographics demand. In this chapter, I focus on a series of events that have arisen in recent years in comic book culture that illustrate how it is a vibrant space in which issues of gender, sexual harassment, and sexual violence are contested.

Fans of comics have long complained about the quality and quantity of the portrayals of women in the books. I will show how the perception of demographics within the industry, and among readership, is important for understanding the vitriolic backlash that has emerged against criticisms regarding content. I will highlight that women in the comic book community, much like women in gaming, are increasingly more likely to call out instances of harassment, create anti-harassment policies, and publicly condemn offensive images and narratives even if these discussions are messy and uncomfortable. I will also illuminate how these conversations converge with broader pop-cultural discourse in ways that both reinforce and resist assumptions about rape culture.

The fact that women have historically felt excluded from geek spaces such as that of comic books is well known. English professor Suzanne Scott wrote in her analysis of comic book culture that women have long been rendered invisible and marginalized by the industry, by male fans, and by the history documenting the medium itself—a history penned largely by men. As a result, women often feel the comic book culture too "inaccessible or inhospitable."[1]

Although women in the industry, both as consumers and producers of content, have historically been treated as interlopers, there has been a great deal of what sociologist Paul Lopes described as "gender interventions"—alternate paths women have traveled within the culture to create space for them to succeed. Throughout the past several decades, women have found underground and independent comics to be viable outlets for their writing and illustration. They have also produced autobiographical work with female-driven narratives, and fans have created fanzines that promote fellow female creators' work. Inherent in these efforts is a challenge to stereotypical portrayals of women and attempts to attract more female creators and readers.[2] Additionally, Suzanne Scott identified a more recent "transformative moment" in which there is "increased attention to the place and perception of women within comic book culture."[3]

This transitional period has not been without growing pains. In a panel at the 2015 Conference on World Affairs addressing discrimination in science and geek culture, comic writer G. Willow Wilson recounted her participation in a 2014 Marvel writer's workshop that was particularly hostile. The group had convened, ostensibly, to discuss representation of minorities in comic books. Wilson recalled that even *conversations* about racial, ethnic, and sexual minorities created an "immediate backlash" from traditional fans, which she described as men aged thirty to forty-five. She said that as soon as the discussion ensued, there was a sense that "something secret was under attack"—that is, there was the realization that one of the last places where these men could objectify women was soon to fade. They were not happy with the new social reality, she said.[4]

"THIS IS NOT SHE-THOR. THIS IS NOT LADY THOR. . . . THIS IS THOR"

Such resistance to enlarging the circle to include diverse characters has led to a palpable dearth of quality portrayals of women in books, film, and television. This point was put into stark relief at the San Diego Comic-Con of 2013, which hosted a "Women Who Kick Ass" panel, featuring actors Nicole Beharie, Natalie Dormer, Tatiana Maslany, Sarah Paulson, Katey Sagal, and Maisie Williams. All are known for their complex portrayal of powerful women in a variety of films and television shows. When asked which superhero or villain they would like to play if given the opportunity, their responses included Batman and Spider-Man, among others. None of the panel participants, however, named a female character. The omission, as Natalie Zutter writing for *Tor* pointed out, likely reflects "the profound lack of universally inspiring or realistic female heroes."[5]

Criticism of the portrayals of women in comic books, and how they are treated in the industry, are not particularly new. However, the last few years have seen a marked increase in attention to these issues in the mainstream media. Much of that coverage is devoted to how the white, male-dominated industry continues to marginalize women and other minorities. So much so that one common refrain that has emerged is that either the comic book industry must embrace diversity—as well as diversity among fans—or the industry itself will be destined to become irrelevant.[6]

More than seventy-five years since the founding of the "big two" publishers, DC and Marvel,[7] women and other minorities continue to be abysmally underrepresented both as creators and as characters in mainstream superhero books. That lack of diversity simply fails to reflect the diversity of overall comic book readership. Although one survey of DC's New 52, a major relaunching of the publisher's superhero titles in 2011, revealed that the vast majority of readers are male (93 percent), those numbers only tell part of the story.[8] Comic scholars are quick to point out that comic books encompass a range of genres besides superheroes, and that the readership dynamics are currently shifting. Surveys that include titles from independent publishers have found a larger fan base of women, and even the superhero genre appears to be expanding its readership among women.[9] According to *Publisher's Weekly*, women ages "17 to 33 were the fastest-growing group at comic book retailers nationally."[10] The digital comics reader *Comixology* offered more evidence of an expanding readership among women, reporting that although their core customer is male, twenty-seven to thirty-six years old, their newest emerging set of customers are women, seventeen to twenty-six years old, comprising about 20 percent of the readership.[11] Further, when we expand beyond "comic book readers" to a broader look at comic book culture that includes participation in comics-inspired fandom, from television shows to films to comic cons, women reach parity. In one study of self-identified comic fans based on market research on Facebook, Bret Schenker found that, "of the 24 million [comic fans], women account for 46.67%."[12]

Beyond the demographics of readership, the quantity and quality of diverse representations in mainstream comic books matter in terms of our cultural imagination—that is, do we see ourselves reflected in the books? What types of persons are represented as heroic?[13] Representation is the first step to imagining ourselves as a leading hero (or villain) and being able to fully immerse ourselves in a story. In *Comic Book Crime*, Staci Strobl and I discussed the many ways that these imaginations influence our cultural scripts about what kind of person may be perceived as heroic, what paths to justice may be pursued, and how justice may be achieved.[14] Comic fans and scholars have long echoed the sentiment that being able to "see yourself" in popular-culture representations is immensely important in shaping identities and understandings of empowerment—something that white privilege constantly obscures.[15]

Over the past few years, the San Diego and New York comic cons have held numerous panels devoted to gender and diversity in comics.[16] For fans who are not straight white males, discussion frequently centers on how rare it is to see characters on the page that "look like us" and ways to improve diversity. Often just seeing a character that is similar to one's gender, race, ethnicity, or sexual orientation is enough to feel empowered—even if that character is overtly sexualized, a villain, or otherwise morally compromised. In an interview discussing the cultural importance of female superheroes, Kathleen Hanna, the musician who is most associated with the Riot Grrrl movement of the 1990s, summarized this sentiment by stating,

> There are so few images of powerful women that women get desperate and they're like "that's powerful," and we'll just take any kind of garbage or crumb off the table that we can find and claim that as something that's powerful even when it's kind of not.[17]

In the case of mainstream American comic books, sales continue to be dominated by the superhero genre, the vast majority of which features male superheroes.[18] This lack of diverse representations has led to the mistaken notion that female-led books and superhero-inspired films do not sell. In fact, it is difficult to substantiate this argument. Since so few titles feature females as leads, how would we measure their failure or success? And, further, of the titles that do feature women, many are quite successful. In July 2014, female comic cover images comprised only about 25 to 31 percent of the total covers for Marvel and DC respectively, and female-led books made up only 12 to 16 percent of the total books published.[19] G. Willow Wilson, the writer and cocreator of the most recent incarnation of the highly popular title *Ms. Marvel*, expressed astonishment that her series made it to eight issues and counting.[20] The book is notable in that the lead, Ms. Marvel, was reimagined as Kamala Khan, a teenage Muslim, Pakistani-American. The reaction to the introduction of Kamala reverberated around the globe, ultimately trending on Twitter.[21]

In addition to the coverage of Kamala Khan among comic book–centric websites, the character was covered in such mainstream outlets as *The Atlantic*, *Wired*, *Washington Post*, *Slate*, *Daily News*, and *Islamic Monthly*. It also received mention from Stephen Colbert on the *Colbert Report*, who satirically charged that the move was further evidence of "Sharia creep" and would eventually lead to cries of "death to Captain America!" Interviews with Pakistani women published by UPI highlighted the powerful impact of Kamala Khan and the attention she garnered. Their comments reflected support, such as, "Kamala Khan will help mothers to have faith that their daughters can play an important role, as do their sons, in building the future."[22] Others were more reticent, worried that the character might "hurt" their values: "We don't want our girls so open to the world, because it is against our religion and values."[23]

Overall, the overwhelming response to the introduction of Kamala as Ms. Marvel illustrated how such characters are an exception to the rule in that there are so few female superheroes of color, and fewer still that are household names.[24]

The introduction of minority characters such as Kamala, and others that embody diversity in terms of race, ethnicity, gender, and sexual orientation, often stirs controversy, revealing how representations hold cultural importance. In July 2014, hosts on the daytime television show *The View* announced the introduction of Marvel's new female hero, Thor. The announcement elicited enthusiasm among many fans, while backlash erupted from those resistant to a change in the status quo (a male Thor was originally introduced decades ago as a Norse god).[25] Echoing a familiar refrain, Milo Yiannopoulos, contributor to the conservative website *Breitbart*, lashed out at so-called social justice warriors and claimed that by introducing a female Thor, the comic book art form has been "ruined" because of "misandry." He was similarly offended by the introduction of Miles Morales, a biracial Spider-Man in the Ultimate universe, as well as of a black Captain America, declaring that whiteness is "intrinsic" to the characters.[26] The website *PopSugar*'s headline, "Surprise, Surprise: People Are Pissed That Thor Is a Lady," summed up the reactions and provided tweets such as the following to illustrate the resistance to the move,

Oh HELL no . . .

You can't just turn Thor into a girl wtf is wrong with you Marvel?? I give up. I'm done

A black Captain America? Not a big deal at all, soldiers of all colours fought for red, white & blue. But I'm still livid over female Thor

. . . new superpowers include being judgmental, temperamental, and unreasonable[27]

The negative responses caught the attention of writers and executives at Marvel, who defended the introduction of the character.[28] In a statement on Marvel.com, writer Jason Aaron sought to ease the fears of fans who worried that the character would not be a fully fleshed-out hero in her own right. Aaron emphasized that this new Thor is not a peripheral character or "lady" version. He stated,

This is not She-Thor. This is not Lady Thor. This is not Thorita. This is THOR. This is *the* THOR of the Marvel Universe. But it's unlike any Thor we've ever seen before.[29]

The underrepresentation of female heroes in comic books extends to their film adaptations. The most iconic characters, Batman and Superman, have collectively been featured in at least fourteen films since the 1970s.[30] Additionally, over the past several decades, a slew of lesser-known characters have served as protagonists in films such as *Jonah Hex*, *Ghost Rider*, *Hellboy*, and *Guardians of the Galaxy*, none of which feature lead female heroes.[31] Even women who are established characters in their own right, such as Wonder Woman, Storm, and Black Widow, are typically relegated to supporting roles in film. Of the eighteen superheroes films DC and Marvel have announced that will premiere into 2020, only two feature women as leads—the highly anticipated *Wonder Woman* film and *Captain Marvel*, featuring Carol Danvers. In another nod toward diverse characters, one DC film is slated to star African-American actor Ray Fisher as Cyborg.[32]

BROKE BACK AND PASSIVE

Superhero comic books have the capacity to inspire readers and contribute to our cultural understandings of heroism and justice. Yet they can also serve to limit our collective imaginations, including, for example, when they portray women in hypersexualized ways. In this context, simply increasing the quantity of female characters is insufficient if the quality of those representations is still lacking. Scholars have documented the portrayals of women in comic books, ranging from the powerful Amazon warrior Wonder Woman of the 1940s to the hyper-sexualized "bad girls" of the 1990s, showing how these portrayals reflect the changing cultural norms around femininity and masculinity.[33]

Although there are notable female characters in mainstream super-hero comic books that are strong, powerful, and heroic, women are too often portrayed as peripheral to the male characters. They also often find themselves in need of saving or, in some cases, stereotyped as emotionally needy.[34] What is even more concerning is the fact that women in comics are frequently subject to violence—oftentimes brutally and sadistically victimized—in ways that only serve to advance the plots of the male characters. This well-known phenomenon, known as "fridging," was documented by comic book writer Gail Simone in 1999 and published on her website *Women in Refrigerators*.[35] The website, named after the incident in which Green Lantern's girlfriend was murdered and her body stuffed into a refrigerator, is essentially a list of women in comics that have met an untimely end. They have been variously "killed, raped, depowered, crippled, turned evil, maimed, tortured, contracted a disease or had other life-derailing tragedies."[36]

The idea that women are to be portrayed as simply sidekicks, victims, or peripheral characters that only serve the plots of male heroes may seem like a relic—a throwback to the Comics Code of the 1950s that regulated the portrayal of characters and their behavior in comics.[37] After all, we have come a long way from the fashion-conscious Wonder Woman of the late 1960s, who ultimately surrendered her uniform and superpowers and ran a mod clothing boutique. Yet readers continue to call for improvement in the quality of women characters, particularly in the best-selling mainstream comics produced by DC and Marvel.

To measure the quantity and quality of female representations, Walt Hickey, writing for *FiveThirtyEight*, used Marvel and DC Wikia databases to compile a list of characters and traits.[38] The research confirmed what even casual readers might have noticed. The vast majority of frequently appearing characters among the titles they sampled (those that appear at least ten times) is male (about 70 percent), and the few female characters that do appear are "more passive than men on the page."[39]

The significance of the quality of the portrayals is not lost on the fan base. In writing about her personal experience as a comic book fan, pop-culture writer Katie Schenkel stated that as a young girl, the hyper-sexualized female characters made her feel ill at ease, particularly when she was looking at comic book images while around a group of school-boys. She wrote,

I didn't know the term "male gaze" yet. I wouldn't learn that there was a name for it until many years later, when it would be in the back of my mind while watching so many movies and TV shows and, yes, even reading comics. But looking back, that was what I saw in that boy's scrapbook—some of my favorite characters stripped of their agency and their personality for the sake of the all-consuming male gaze. They weren't there to be characters. Merely objects.[40]

The issue that comic book portrayals of women tend to be hypersexualized and objectifying is not necessarily a new complaint, but it is an ongoing popular one. In addition to problematic narratives, fans have also heavily criticized art styles featuring exaggerated female anatomy, a trend that seemed to peak in the 1990s. The phenomenon, known as "broke back," has been described by scholar Carolyn Cocca: "A female character's back is drawn unnaturally twisted as well as arched, displaying all of her curves in front and back simultaneously." In her study of the broke-back phenomenon, Cocca noted that "almost every issue" in her sample of comic books (24 titles/144 issues) contained "sexually objectifying" portrayals. Though she found fewer objectifications among books published in the 2000s than in the 1990s, there seemed to be increased commentary among readers, confirming that women in recent years have been more vocal about their observations and criticisms of the art and content than before. Websites such as Hawkeye Initiative, for example, ridicule absurd poses and distorted anatomy by gender-swapping and juxtaposing images. Likewise, the Escher Girls Tumblr has showcased how characters are sexualized, while also pointing out that these are not necessarily problems with individual artists so much as a problem with the industry as a whole.[41]

Controversies over broke-back images reveal that fan reactions are varied; while some fans express that they are offended, others are quick to strike back against the criticisms. When Guillem March's illustration for issue #0 of DC's New 52 *Catwoman* was released, the cover was described as "back-breaking," "brokeback," "ridiculous," "racy," and "offensive," among other comments.[42] *Gammasquad*'s headline summed up the negative sentiment: "The Internet Fittingly Lambasts the Ridiculous 'Catwoman #0' Cover."[43] DC ultimately edited the image as a result of the controversy. Nonetheless, those who complained were often described as overreacting or being on a "witch hunt."[44]

A few years after releasing the controversial Catwoman cover, Marvel released an image of the variant cover for *Spider-Woman* #1 (August 2014) that received similar criticism. The cover depicted Spider-Woman in a crouched position, crawling on the top of a building with her backside tilted to the sky. The positioning was so contorted that *The*

Mary Sue interviewed three gymnasts who confirmed that it is anatomically impossible to achieve.[45] The following headlines and comments were indicative of the intense reaction to the cover:

io9: "Check Out Spider-Woman #1, Starring Spider-Woman's Ass."

Huffington Post: "Spider-Woman's New Cover Sums Up the Problematic Way Female Superheroes Are Treated."

Vox called it a "misstep" by Marvel

Slate: "It looks more like a colonoscopy than a costume."

Bustle summed up the reaction by stating, "If this is the kind of visibility those female characters are going to get, maybe they are better off not being featured at all."[46] Nonetheless, the Italian artist, Milo Manera, known for his erotic imagery, shrugged off the complaints, stating, "It seems to me that both the United States and around the world there are things much more important and serious to worry about."[47]

When asked by a reader if this type of criticism had "gone too far" and indicated a desire to "remove sexual thematics [*sic*] from comics," Marvel's senior vice president of publishing, Tom Brevoort, acknowledged the importance of the issue, stating that discussions of women in comics "seems to be bubbling up from the zeitgeist."[48]

Some, like writer Joseph Darowski, have cautioned against too readily criticizing material as offensive and misogynist. Darowski, author of *X-Men and the Mutant Metaphor: Race and Gender in the Comic Books*, wrote that one comic book creator, in a run of *The Uncanny X-Men*, responded to reader criticisms of his portrayals of women, and also religion, as coming from the "minority" of fans who are "generally unhinged."[49] Darowski noted that simply not liking a story does not mean that it is misogynist. He stated,

It is clear that his women in these stories [*The Uncanny X-Men*] are portrayed as emotionally needy, completely dependent on heterosexual pairings for meaning in their lives, and anything but independent. But that could just be poor, stereotypical writing and not misogyny.[50]

"THIS COMIC IS RIDICULOUSLY RAPEY"

Though mainstream comics have been criticized for portraying women as passive, hypersexualized, and perpetual victims of violence, there is little agreement as to the cultural significance of those representations. While it is reductionist to flatly claim that comic books "promote rape culture," it is instructive to explore how the range of reactions, from what some might view as benign, unintentional sexist imagery, to what others perceive as graphic rape narratives, reveals how our cultural understandings around sexual violence remain deeply unsettled.

There is a dearth of research focused specifically on trends of sexual violence in comic books, making it difficult to isolate whether there has been more of a presence of it over the years. However, fans have long discussed the merits of the portrayals of rape in comics. Such discourse often veers into age-old territory: whether it is necessary for art to depict sexual violence within the panels, whether a more diverse set of creators might have produced a more thoughtful comic, and whether there is a "right" way to depict sexual violence.[51] Like similar criticisms of the portrayals of rape on television, the problem is not necessarily that rape is represented at all. Rather, it is the way in which it is depicted that is perceived as problematic.

For some, the comic book adaptation of the film *Mad Max: Fury Road*, included such problematic depictions of rape. The movie, which was released in 2015 to wide critical and commercial acclaim, featured Imperator Furiosa, a female warrior who rescued and led five enslaved women called the "Five Wives" to freedom in a postapocalyptic wasteland. It was deemed a "feminist masterpiece" by *Bustle*; other outlets declared Furiosa "the hero for our age" and "the hero we deserve," among other accolades.[52] Furiosa was so inspirational that many comic artists flooded Twitter with their interpretation of the character. In June 2015, the DC imprint Vertigo released the much-anticipated comic book *Mad Max: Fury Road—Furiosa #1*, by an all-male creative team.[53] In it, a group of enslaved women are raped and forced to bear the heirs of their captor, warlord Immortan Joe. Some contended that this adaptation departed from the film by including graphic rape and other sexualized images. The backlash was fast and fierce. Within days, the feminist website *The Mary Sue* declared, "We Need to Talk about the Furiosa Comic," and eviscerated the comic for its story arc of enslaved "wives," vaginal exams, rape, and overall disrespect for women. Ana Mardoll wrote,

> First of all, this comic is ridiculously rapey, especially given that the movie attained a lot of feminist acclaim precisely because it *wasn't* rapey. It was a movie about sexual victimization without showing any rape on-screen. . . . Indeed, by showing the rape and sexual assault over and over again in this book, that will likely overwhelm the wives' valid complaints about freedom and reproductive freedom.[54]

Many took to social media to criticize the book, but it was the statements by one of the cowriters, Mark Sexton, that provoked much of the outrage.[55] A commenter on Twitter queried, "A few people are saying that you are exploiting rape in the first issue, what would you say to that?" Sexton responded in a series of tweets:

> Interesting. Could answer this any number of ways . . .
>
> Best answer is that the use of institutionalised rape by Immortan Joe is not only central to the story—
>
> but without it, the story could be viewed merely as a bunch of young spoilt girls whining about being kept in relative—
>
> luxury by an older man who's concerned with their safety. Not really much room for dramatic tension there . . . ![56]

Sexton was basically implying that rape is necessary to set up dramatic tension among the characters, even in this case, where the women were already powerless and in literal enslavement. But he is not alone in his tactic of using rape as a way to ratchet up the depravity of a villain. Prolific comic writer Mark Millar echoed the same sentiment in response to a question about sexual violence in his popular creator-owned comics: "It's the same as, like, a decapitation. It's just a horrible act to show that somebody's a bad guy."[57] For many, however, the perception is that all too often for the victims, "being raped becomes their defining characteristic."[58]

Writer and editor Teresa Jusino pressed further, questioning whether the rapes should have been depicted in the *Mad Max* comic:

> I wonder if he genuinely thinks people *wouldn't understand the concept* of women wanting freedom from a pustule-ridden, old dictator who rapes them whenever they're ovulating without *seeing* the rape happen. Because as is seemingly usually the case, both in fiction and IRL, a woman saying she's suffering isn't enough. *It has to be seen to be believed.*[59]

Although many criticized the Furiosa comic as being exploitative, it would be a mistake to assume that most representations of sexual violence in contemporary comic books are uniformly gratuitous. While some narratives reinforce rape myths—for example, those that portray rape as excessively brutal while rejecting other forms of nonviolent coercion—other narratives challenge our perceptions of sexual violence. In their study of the perpetuation of rape myths in mainstream comic books, scholars Tammy Garland, Kathryn Branch, and MacKenzie Grimes found that most rapes in comic books avoided the stereotype of stranger danger and in contrast found that rapes most commonly occurred between acquaintances or intimates. Further, they found a relatively high proportion of male rape victims (43 percent of their sample). However, in the instances in which females were portrayed as perpetrators, the study found that any physical or psychological trauma experienced by the male victims was minimized in ways that challenged interpretation of the act as rape.[60]

#CHANGETHECOVER

At times, debates over sexual violence have less to do with what is on the page than with how the narratives and images intersect with everyday, real-life experiences. As in gaming, public discourse around sexual violence in comic culture arises within the context of challenges to the white, male-dominated status quo. These changing dynamics may be interpreted as contributing to a sense of aggrieved entitlement—the sense that something deserved has been taken away. This feeling is also accompanied by a misdirected anger toward scapegoats (e.g., minorities), bolstered by righteous anger that serves as a motivator to get it back.[61] This is most explicitly observed in instances in which complaints of offensive imagery intersect with those who feel the status quo is challenged.

The reverberations of aggrieved entitlement were on full display when the variant cover image for *Batgirl* #41 (2015) by artist Rafael Albuquerque was released online. The hashtag #ChangeTheCover was launched in protest, sparking a heated debate.[62] The image was an homage to the immensely popular graphic novel *The Killing Joke* (1988). It featured the Joker, with one gun-toting arm around the teary-eyed and frightened Batgirl, while his other hand scrawled a bloody smiley face across her cheeks. The image would likely not register much of a reaction from non–comic book aficionados. However, fans would recognize it as a reference to one of the most acclaimed, and sadistic, Joker stories ever told. In it, the Joker shot Barbara Gordon and in doing so paralyzed her. During the assault, he removed her clothes and photographed her naked body in a brutal display of sexualized violence.

While some may have found Albuquerque's cover image empowering—after all, Gordon eventually became Oracle/Batgirl—others objected primarily because the image leaves Batgirl in a state of pure terror as opposed to a position of strength. Moreover, critics said, the image was far afield from the tone of the current ongoing series that is a lighter, more progressive relaunch.[63] Nonetheless, the controversy resulted in a spate of online threats of violence directed toward those advocating #ChangeTheCover. Ultimately, DC both pulled the image and denounced the harassment and threats.[64]

In response, a dueling hashtag, #SaveTheCover, quickly populated Twitter, warning of the dangers of censorship. Some attempted to equate the incident with the silencing of artistic freedom vis-à-vis "Je Suis Charlie" (i.e., "Je Suis Batgirl"). "Je Suis Charlie" was the rallying cry used by those who were outraged by the mass shooting at the satirical newspaper *Charlie Hebdo* in Paris, France, in which twelve people including cartoonists, editors, and police officers were killed.[65] Others charged that so-called SJWs were leading comics "back to the Comics Code":

> @DCComics don't give in to stupid tumblr "feminists." That's Marvel's job. Keep the Killing Joke homage cover for Batgirl 41 #Save-TheCover

> There's nothing wrong with this cover you SJW drama queens #Save-TheCover[66]

As with GamerGate, detractors claimed that the online threats were faked by SJWs in an attempt to censor the content. For example, "'Hey SJW, if you're offended, claim or fake death threats and we'll censor anything!' #SaveTheCover."[67] One tweet portrayed a modified version of the Joker/Batgirl image with Anita Sarkeesian's face superimposed on Batgirl.[68] As in gaming culture, angry fans linked so-called SJWs to the scourge of political correctness and condemned feminists for their perceived overreach on offensive speech.[69]

#FIRERICKREMENDER

Another flashpoint for the old and new guard in comic book culture was the release of *Captain America* (#22, September 2014). This particular event unfolded when a confusing narrative in the comic book led to the perception that the story contained statutory rape. Further, when a fan contested the narrative and sought to hold the writer accountable, she herself received rape threats. The *Captain America* book at issue portrayed a sex scene between a female, Jet Black (aka Jet Zola), and the male superhero Falcon. Jet Black tempted Falcon with wine and they ultimately had a night of drunken sex. Believing the female character to be underage, Jackie, a female fan, wrote a blog entry expressing "distaste" for writer Rick Remender's work on the series and encouraged others to tweet the hashtag #FireRickRemender. As a result, fans obliged.

Comic Book Resources described the confusion:

> Introduced as a child in the series' opening arc, readers have seen Jet age more than a dozen years over the past twenty-odd issues, and she states she's at least 23 in this issue, but a lot of readers felt that the age declaration coming so close to the time that writer Rick Remender decided to have her become sexually active felt—icky is an incredible understatement. This led to fans thinking that Falcon had been turned into a statutory rapist, and a viral campaign against the writer (#FireRickRemender) started. [70]

Gloria Miller, writing for examiner.com, argued that the character had quickly and confusingly aged nine years and that the scene is fraught with consent issues—for both parties. [71] Although the issue could have prompted deeper conversations about the role of consent and alcohol, instead, those supporting the hashtag were vilified. Some suggested that Jackie, who started the hashtag, did so out of a vendetta against Remender. [72] The controversy sparked podcast discussions from *iFanboy* and *TalkingComics* that defended the story line and contended that the reader simply misunderstood the story.

Responses to the criticism of Remender ranged from condescension to rage and threats of physical violence. Some on Twitter were simply dismissive of it or suggested that complaints such as these undermine legitimate reasons for outrage. For example,

> Seriously, the #firerickremender thing proves that tumblr activists are ready to jump on the slightest hint of "rape" without doing research

> This #firerickremender noise is the 2nd time in two weeks critics have forced a "rape" reading of a book they just didn't like.

The incident gained so much attention that it prompted responses from industry insiders determined to clarify that the character was, in fact, of age and that the scene was not one of sexual violence. Dan Slott, one of the more well known Marvel comics writers, tweeted a link to a Tumblr page that painstakingly detailed issue-by-issue the age transformation of the female character, Jet Black. [73] Others, such as acclaimed Marvel writer Kieron Gillen, spoke out in support of Remender and cautioned others against joining the criticism of the book. He stated of Jackie,

But—as a general rule—when a campaign was born of such clearly
malicious grounds, I would be uncomfortable with marching under
its banner, not least because it undermines any actual grievances or
points you may have.[74]

Others, such as comic book writer Ed Brubaker, implied that readers
are simply too heavily invested in the stories. He tweeted,

Seriously, people need to stop acting like fictional stories are how-to
manuals showing the exact right way to be. Oh and #firerickremend-
er.[75]

On his blog, former Marvel editor Tom Brennan framed the controversy as one of censorship, taking issue with the hashtag because of the
gravity of calling for the firing of a writer simply based on material that
made someone uncomfortable. He explained that any single story at
Marvel is a collaborative process involving multiple creators and editors
and that the actual firing of someone from their job is a very serious call
to action.[76]

Meanwhile, Jackie, the initiator of #FireRickRemender, reported
that as a result of voicing her criticisms, she has "endured rape threats,
slurs, name-calling, unwanted sexual advances, and threats to my personal safety."[77] She ultimately apologized for encouraging others to
tweet the sentiment (#FireRickRemender) but provided context for her
initial reading that squarely placed it in the broader context of rape
culture. Jackie explained,

As a survivor of sexual assault, I see it everywhere. I see it everywhere because I've been conditioned to. Because, as a person who
identifies as female, I have spent my entire life being told how to act,
dress, hold myself, and interact with others in order to keep myself
safe. Because I live in a culture where nearly all types of media traffic
in stories that excuse, glorify, or erase sexual assault. . . . I'm not
sorry, because as a female fan, I've always had to be three times as
loud to get my voice heard. I'm not sorry, because in the past few
days, I've endured rape threats, slurs, name-calling, unwanted sexual
advances, and threats to my personal safety for speaking out.[78]

What made the #FireRickRemender incident culturally significant is
that it occurred on the heels of another incident that shows how misogyny, sexual harassment, and public discourse around sexual violence
feed into the larger discourse around rape culture. A few months prior
to #FireRickRemender, in April 2014, Janelle Asselin wrote an article
for *xoJane*: "It Happened to Me: I Received Rape Threats after Criticiz-

ing a Comic Book." Asselin had reviewed *Teen Titans*, pointing out that the book is written for a teen readership (or young adults), is marketed toward teens, and includes teen characters. She noted that despite this, the cover depicted a young Wonder Girl wearing a strapless outfit and sporting what appeared to be breast implants.[79] Though Asselin criticized the art, unlike Jackie, she did not call for the firing of any individuals. As a result of her critical review, Asselin said she was inundated with misogynistic comments, received rape threats, and was accused of being a "disgruntled former employee," a "feminazi," and of having a "secret agenda." Other threats included "let's see how feminist you are when you're begging me for more," "I already ***up your bitch friends and i hope you cry like they did," and simply "can't wait to rape you." Asselin noted that ironically, some of those threats were sent to her through her online survey designed to measure the extent of sexual harassment in comics.[80]

While many in the industry were supportive of Asselin, other fans claimed that she was faking the threats to gain attention.[81] In one Twitter exchange, Asselin was accused by a fellow DC artist of being biased and unprofessional, as well as that she and her supporters were trying to "make it about sexism."[82] Yet Asselin, like many others, had simply expressed frustration with a comic book community that, while growing in gender diversity among its readership, is still contending with an undercurrent of misogyny that may rear up when a woman expresses her opinion.[83] She wrote,

> Many, many people are fed up with the fact that women can't state an opinion without getting threatened with rape. If you're not threatened with rape, you're told you're not qualified, you're not good enough, you're not welcome here.[84]

Increasingly, women like Asselin are framing these singular incidents as part of a larger problem within geeks spaces that, while comprised of many individual progressives and feminists, can be implicitly, and at times explicitly, tolerant of the mistreatment of women. Ultimately, the larger issue around these incidents is less about how people initially interpret the narratives and images and more about how the caustic reactions reveal a sense that the status quo had been challenged.

"FOR EVERY STORY YOU'RE HEARING, THERE ARE TEN THAT YOU'RE NOT"

As previously discussed, although readership demographics are shifting, many contend that the lack of diversity among the creators and editors of comic books is a contributing factor to the homogeneity of the images on the pages. Consequently, it may be one of the reasons that some women and other minorities do not feel fully welcome in comic book culture. Over the past few years, comic book historian Tim Hanley has been "gendercrunching" the numbers on the breakdown of gender among comic book creators and editors at DC and Marvel, confirming the white male dominance that has long plagued the industry. He found that from 1996 to 2011, the gender gap at DC has remained relatively stagnant overall, with women comprising about 11 percent of creators and editors in 2011, up from 10.8 percent in 1996. There has been some increase in women in editorial roles, with 22.5 percent as editors compared to 16.1 percent in 2006.[85] Similarly, Marvel shows an uptick among editors but overall remains relatively unchanged, with women comprising a total of 8.7 percent of creators and editors. As of June 2014, over 90 percent of creators were male, and 78.9 percent were white.[86] The only other publisher that comes close to DC and Marvel in terms of market share is Image comics, and it has also been criticized for its lack of diversity among creators.[87]

The dominance of white men in the industry has historically made it difficult for minorities to break in as creators. One particular incident in late 2013, involving artist Tess Fowler, brought to light how difficult it can be for women to break in, and as a by-product, how the industry continues to foster misogyny and sexual harassment. Fowler had tweeted and blogged about her experience at the San Diego Comic-Con a few years earlier, recalling that a well-known male comic book writer had feigned interest in her art and invited her to his hotel room. She declined and alleged that he retaliated against her by trashing her art on social media. Initially, Fowler did not reveal the name of the writer. It was only later, after she stated that her inbox became "filled with accounts from other women who had found themselves in my same position" with the same guy, that she identified him. Fowler explained of her decision to reveal his name that it was no longer in her mind an issue involving just her. She contended it was a "symptom of a much bigger disease," where women feel compelled to stay silent in order to get along and advance in the industry, while other men are complicit in overlooking the harm.[88] The writer she had identified responded to her accusations on his own blog, stating that although he did make a pass at her, that was the end of it, and "there was never a promise of quid pro quo, no exertion of power, no threats, and no revenge."[89]

The story was covered by various comic blogs, websites, and mentions on Twitter. The following headlines illustrate how the incident became a touchstone for the larger issue of sexual harassment within the industry:

Comics Alliance: "Sexual Harassment in Comics: The Tipping Point"

Bleeding Cool: "Tess Fowler and Modern Day Misogyny in the Comics Industry"

The Atlantic: "How to Dismantle the Comic-Books Boys' Club"

The geek-focused website Dr. Nerdlove contextualized the incident as a "casting couch" scenario under the headline "Nerds and Male Privilege." Collectively, the articles pointed out that women are too often pressured and socialized to remain silent in the face of sexism and sexual harassment.[90] Yet this incident itself revealed that women *are* speaking out, providing further evidence of feminist interventions in comic culture.[91] Rich Johnston at Bleeding Cool stated,

> People are talking about this. Really talking, at length from message board to thread to blog, there's a feeling that not only is this no longer acceptable—if it ever was—but now, with social media, that the cones of silence may be lifting and people are more willing to talk about their experiences.[92]

Yet, as with other allegations of sexual violence in society, the complainant is often at risk of being accused of lying, of attention-seeking behavior, and of being blamed for the bad behavior.[93] In this case, questioning the validity of the allegations was part of the conversation, but what was interesting here was the reliance on other men in the industry to validate the complaints of sexism. A commenter on Reddit cited one of the more pervasive problems facing women who come forward with a complaint—the idea that in order to be believed, a man must independently verify her assertions. The commenter stated,

> For the past few days I've been trying to be objective and looking at the situation as even-handed to every party possible . . . but having [a male comic artist] go out and say "I saw this happen clearly as an observer," confirms the previous statements that [the guy] has been sleazy in the past, if not currently.[94]

This point was echoed by Laura Hudson, writing for *Comics Alliance*, when she noted how fans turned to critically acclaimed writer Greg Rucka "to confirm the truth about what was happening to women, instead of asking . . . women."[95] When asked on his blog whether the allegations of how the comic book industry treats women reveal how bad it really is or whether it is simply a matter of a few isolated incidents, Rucka responded,

> No, it's not that bad. It's worse. It's endemic. For every story you're hearing, there are ten that you're not. For every instance of poor behavior you've heard of from and [sic] editor or a creator, there's another twenty stories about convention trips to strip clubs for "meetings" and the like.[96]

The lack of diverse creators within the industry has indeed at times fostered a climate conducive to gendered harassment. Yet those who follow comic book culture closely know that many editors and creators are welcoming of diversity and also highly dedicated to creating more diverse, fully realized characters. Some, like prolific comic writer Brian Michael Bendis, have taken fans to task for their resistance to diversity. Bendis blasted a male fan for complaining that "bitching women" is the reason that there are more female characters.[97] Understanding these conversations within the framework of transition from a former "all boys club" to an inclusive industry is essential to making sense of the complaints of misogyny in geek spaces—both in comic book and gaming culture.

SIN TO WIN: CONS AND SEXUAL HARASSMENT

Geek spaces are no longer isolated groups of people that comprise a small niche—they are multimillion-dollar industries that are part of our media-entertainment cultural landscape. The best example of this transformation is the massive growth of comic cons across the United States. Those conventions have exploded in popularity, expanding from small local gatherings of a few hundred in the early 1970s to the massive multimedia extravaganzas today that draw hundreds of thousands of attendees. In 2015, New York Comic Con (NYCC) drew over 167,000 attendees, more than Comic-Con International: San Diego, which previously had been deemed the largest con in North America.[98]

Scholar Henry Jenkins described the San Diego Comic-Con as "press junket, trade show, collector's mart, public forum, academic conference, and arts festival, all in one."[99] It is at these cons where embracing your inner geek is most welcome, where cosplay—dressing up as a character from a movie, book, anime, or video game—is celebrated, and fans interact face to face with creators. While the vast majority of participants attend without incident, for some it can be a place of intimidation and harassment. The following encounter, from an attendee of DC's Awesome Con, was shared with *Collective Action for Safe Spaces!*, an organization designed to raise awareness of, and prevent, sexual harassment:

> I was sitting at my convention table, selling prints and comics. I had had very little sleep and was not feeling very well. A man came up and was looking at my work; when he looked up I smiled at him politely. He exclaimed "now see, you look so much prettier when you smile! Before now I thought you were as cold and depressing as your art. You should smile more!"[100]

Beyond the unwanted verbal comments, women have also reported being groped, subjected to unwanted creeper and upskirt photographs, and threatened. To illustrate the reported accounts of harassment at the 2013 NYCC, *The Mary Sue* posted photos of female cosplayers holding signs "sharing their creeper stories." These included a woman cosplaying as Scarlet Witch, holding a sign that said, "Look at the tits on that Scarlet Witch." In another, a woman dressed as Daenerys Targaryen from *Game of Thrones* held a sign that asked, "How does it feel to be raped by your boyfriend?"[101]

In one of the more publicized accounts, in 2010, model Adrianne Curry, dressed as Princess Leia, was groped at a Star Wars convention. In a tweet the following day, Curry wrote, "I cannot believe last night happened . . . love starwars . . . but ready to leave."[102] Four years later, Curry recounted a groping incident she experienced at the San Diego Comic-Con, as well as an incident in which a man "shoved his finger down" the back of her cosplaying female friend's backside into her "butt-crack." Curry retaliated by hitting the man with her Catwoman whip and commented that the male bystanders who witnessed these events just stood by and did nothing.[103]

It's not just individual attendees that have been guilty of offensive behavior but also some of the vendors, who have set a dubious tone at the conventions. In 2009, at San Diego Comic-Con, video game publisher Electronic Arts (EA) held a "Sin to Win" contest in which men were encouraged to commit "an act of lust" by taking a photo with a booth babe to win "dinner and a SINful night with TWO hot girls, a limo service, paparazzi, and a chest full of booty."[104] "Booth babes" are women hired by some of the vendors to appear at the con, usually dressed in a sexually provocative manner. Ultimately, EA released an apology for the wording of their contest, clarifying that it was meant to be "tongue-in-cheek." One commenter on Twitter responded to their apology:

> you feminist idiot women need to relax. find something else in your life on which to expend your energy. those who say they wont buy an ea game again . . . congratulations. no one cares. EA could not care less if you idiots dont buy their games. [105]

In her online survey of San Diego Comic-Con attendees in 2014, writer Janelle Asselin found that 13 percent of respondents reported unwanted sexual comments, and "eight percent of people of all genders reported they had been groped, assaulted, or raped at a comic convention." Here is how Asselin summed up the findings:

> To put these percentages into perspective, if 13 percent of San Diego Comic-Con attendees have unwanted comments of a sexual nature made about them this week, that would be around 17,000 people. And if eight percent of SDCC attendees are groped, assaulted, or raped, that's over 10,000 attendees suffering harassment. [106]

As early as 2008, there were calls for more formal anti-harassment policies at the cons to deter misconduct. For example, Girl-Wonder.org founded the Con Anti-Harassment Project for the purpose of making conventions safer. They wrote,

> Our aims are to encourage fandom, geek community and other non-business conventions to establish, articulate and act upon anti-harassment policies, especially sexual harassment policies, and to encourage mutual respect among convention attendees, guests and staff. [107]

One researcher, Nicole Stark, found that about 60 percent of convention websites do not have an anti-harassment policy posted. She also found that only 3.47 percent specifically referenced sexual harassment and nearly 85 percent of the policies lacked specifics for reporting incidents. [108] To combat these problems, anti-harassment activism and geek spaces converged to form Geeks for CONsent, a group of women that expanded their work against street harassment to include the harassment experienced at cons. The group's website is dedicated to raise awareness, serve as a resource for those who have been harassed, and provide an anonymous outlet for stories involving harassment. The group emphasizes that cosplay is not an invitation to groping or other sexual harassment; in other words, "Cosplay =/= CONsent." The group

urged San Diego Comic-Con to edit their current anti-harassment policy from that of generally condemning "harassing or offensive behavior"
to specifically addressing sexual harassment.[109] However, as of this writing, San Diego Comic-Con has yet to do so. In 2014, the "cosplay is not
consent" refrain reached critical mass and ultimately became the tag-
line for the NYCC anti-harassment policy. NYCC's updated policy is a
zero-tolerance policy prohibiting stalking, harassment, intimidation,
disruption of panels, offensive verbal comments, bathroom policing,
physical assault, inappropriate physical contact, battery, and unwelcome
physical attention. Responses to inappropriate conduct could be as severe as expulsion but do not necessarily involve the intervention of
criminal justice agents.[110] The impact of these policies, whether they
are effective in reducing sexual harassment or are counterproductive in
ways that increase unwanted formal social control, remains to be seen.

The controversy surrounding misogyny and harassment in geek
spaces has ultimately served to reinforce, as well as undercut, feminist-
inspired assumptions about rape culture. In the past few years, there
have been notable interventions that directly challenged the status quo
of how women are represented in games and comic books, as well as
how they are treated within the industries. However, it is also true that
those who have called out problematic representations and conduct
were characterized as propagating a misguided "gender war." This, in
turn, served to undercut the feminist messaging.

Those who feel aggrieved have effectively and strategically reframed
the feminist interventions evidenced in geek spaces (e.g., women having a more prominent voice, increased diversity among creators and
consumers, the development of anti-harassment policies, etc.) as in-
fringement, as hypersensitivity, and as symptomatic of a much larger
SJW agenda. Detractors of this so-called SJW agenda say that if not
contained, it will threaten freedom of speech, and, more broadly, due
process rights within the criminal justice system. These debates continued in what might be considered the space most associated with rape
culture: college campuses.

6

RAPE CULTURE ON CAMPUS

"Real Men Don't Hurt Women"

The concept of rape culture may have garnered a sympathetic ear from the public when it burst onto the mainstream scene in 2013, but that did not last long. As attention to sexual assault on college campuses began to reach critical mass, popular media in a variety of contexts began to reinforce the notion that sexual violence rests on a continuum and that everyday forms of harassment may be viewed within a larger pattern of gender oppression (framed as symptomatic of rape culture). However, several high-profile incidents, which I will highlight in this chapter, increased scrutiny of the prevalence of sexual assault on campuses, renewed attention to false allegations, and shifted focus from how college enforcement policies fail victims to how they imperil accused young men. Taken together, these concerns culminated in a reevaluation of the very concept of rape culture itself. Conservative antifeminists emerged as the most vociferous critics against those who use rape culture as a framework for understanding sexual violence. However, other more nuanced perspectives also emerged that troubled the concept.

THE BATTLEGROUND: COLLEGE CAMPUSES

The issue of sexual assault on college campuses never fully receded from public discourse after its initial "discovery" during the 1980s when social scientists began collecting data from student surveys finding that

sexual assault was far more prevalent than indicated in official government statistics. At the time, much of the public discourse centered on
the relatively new concepts of "date/acquaintance rape," concern
around the changing definition of rape, and challenges to the emerging
statistics.[1]

By the second decade of the twenty-first century, the topic of sexual
assault on campus reemerged within the larger context of discussions of
rape culture. During this time, research indicating high rates of sexual
assault among college-aged women coupled with the work of feminist
activists who exposed deficiencies in how colleges and universities responded to complaints of sexual assault—particularly the underenforce-
ment of Title IX and the Clery Act—ignited and sustained the conversation.[2]

Activists were successful not only in raising awareness of the problem of sexual assault on campuses but also in impacting policy—the
public took notice and the federal government took action. However,
the most significant policy changes, the resulting enforcement of Title
IX and the Clery Act, have been roundly criticized, both by those concerned with the ways that enforcement negatively impacts both victims
and the accused, and by anti-anti-rape commentators, whose clear
agenda is to debunk rape culture, minimize the problem, and blame
feminists.

POISONOUS BIASES

On November 19, 2014, *Rolling Stone* published an article by journalist
Sabrina Erdely detailing Jackie's (her real name) horrific account of her
brutal gang rape at a frat party held at the University of Virginia (UVA)
in 2012. The opening paragraphs detailed the rape:

> "Shut up," she heard a man's voice say as a body barreled into her,
> tripping her backward and sending them both crashing through a low
> glass table. There was a heavy person on top of her, spreading open
> her thighs, and another person kneeling on her hair, hands pinning
> down her arms, sharp shards digging into her back, and excited male
> voices rising all around her. When yet another hand clamped over
> her mouth, Jackie bit it, and the hand became a fist that punched her
> in the face. The men surrounding her began to laugh. For a hopeful
> moment Jackie wondered if this wasn't some collegiate prank. Per-
> haps at any second someone would flick on the lights and they'd
> return to the party.

"Grab its motherfucking leg," she heard a voice say. And that's when Jackie knew she was going to be raped.[3]

The article described how, hours later, Jackie emerged from the incident and met her friends on the street who, after discussing "the social price" of reporting the crime, discouraged her from contacting the police, in part because they feared they would be excluded from future frat parties.

Jackie's story was used to highlight the abysmal response by UVA officials to complaints of sexual assault and further pointed out that the administration's response is not necessarily unique. In fact, dozens of schools in addition to UVA are under investigation by the federal government's Office for Civil Rights due to their problematic responses to complainants of sexual assault. In the article, Erdely interviewed several other victims of sexual assault who were disbelieved and/or mistreated after complaining of sexual assault at UVA and other institutions, including victims' rights advocate Liz Seccuro, who was drugged and gang-raped in 1984.[4]

In bolstering the argument that sexual assault is a major problem on college campuses, Erdely discussed frat parties as particularly problematic, the issue of involuntary incapacitation, and the rampant "no-holds-barred misogyny" on many campuses that included "a Dartmouth student's how-to-rape guide posted online this past January [and] Yale pledges chanting 'No means yes! Yes means anal!'" Erdely wrote, "Some UVA women, so sickened by the university's culture of hidden sexual violence, have taken to calling it 'UVrApe.'"[5]

As further evidence of the problem of sexual assault, Erdely reported that "one in five women is sexually assaulted in college, though only about 12 percent report it to police" and included psychologist David Lisak and Paul Miller's research, which found that "roughly nine out of 10 rapes are committed by serial offenders, who are responsible for an astonishing average of six rapes each"—claims that would later be challenged.[6]

The article brought attention to the problem of sexual assault on college campuses, investigations were launched, and the fraternity was temporarily suspended, as well as vandalized. Two days after publication, *Rolling Stone* published comments from readers that were said to "further illuminate the chilling frequency with which sexual assault on campus occurs."[7] Writer Soraya Chemaly used the concept of rape culture to explain the problem at UVA as rooted in "male dominance, violence and exploitation." She continued,

The UVA story has been catalytic, as have other similar related events elsewhere. Students are protesting, there have been public calls to shut down the Greek system on UVA's campus and people previously confounded by the expression "rape culture" are now reconsidering what it means. [8]

One NPR headline declared, "Magazine Sheds Light on Allegations of Rape Culture at UVA," and UVA music professor Bonnie Gordon penned a piece for *Slate* titled "The UVA Gang Rape Allegations Are Awful, Horrifying, and Not Shocking at All" in which she declared that "UVA has a rape culture problem."[9] One op-ed in the *Richmond Times-Dispatch* also implicated rape culture and the lack of bystander intervention for sexual assaults on campus. In her condemnation of fraternities, Melinda Skinner wrote,

> In this day and age, there may not be the categorizing of women in the same way; but a culture of rape—along with that old "boys will be boys" slap on the back by older men who have been there and done that—continues at some of the most prestigious schools in the country. [10]

But the tide quickly shifted from that of calling out rape culture to discrediting it. In one of the first pieces to question the veracity of Jackie's story, the editor-in-chief of *Worth* magazine, Richard Bradley, suggested on his blog that when read through an "editor's eyes," the story contained many red flags that made the story not impossible, but extremely unlikely to have occurred as described. On November 24, 2014, Bradley meticulously dissected the story and criticized the journalist for using so many unnamed sources and for the unlikelihood that Jackie would be gang-raped for several hours, on shards of broken glass, in pitch-black darkness, without anyone suffering serious injuries. Bradley wrote,

> Again: It's possible. You can't say it isn't. But I am reminded of the urban myth about someone waking up in a bathtub full of ice in New Orleans. This story contains a lot of apocryphal tropes. [11]

Bradley also mentioned the phrase "Grab its motherfucking leg" as being a bit too reminiscent of the film *Silence of the Lambs*. Echoing Bradley's sentiments, others began to express skepticism about the story. By December 1, Jonah Goldberg, writing for the *Los Angeles Times*, reiterated much of Bradley's skepticism, including reference to the problematic media coverage of the Tawana Brawley case that had occurred over twenty-five years prior in which Ms. Brawley, then a fifteen-year-old African-American, falsely accused as many as six white men of rape. Goldberg added, sarcastically, of the current case, "And what a convenient conversation for an expose of rape culture."[12]

Within the first few weeks of publication, others began to question some of the journalistic decisions made by Erdely and pointed out several inconsistencies with Jackie's account. Relying on Erdely's own comments about her piece, journalist Erik Wemple argued that her quest to find the "right" case to illustrate the problem of sexual assault on campuses was riddled with "poisonous biases" and a desire to produce "impact journalism."[13] The *Washington Post* uncovered several discrepancies in Jackie's account including that the fraternity held no event on the night of the alleged incident and that her friends now express doubts about her story. By December 5, 2014, *Rolling Stone* published "A Note to Our Readers" admitting that it was a mistake not to contact the alleged assaulters at Jackie's request.[14]

Media attention to the story had exploded. In fact, in her report, MSNBC's Krystal Ball found that the story received more cable news coverage *after* it became a story of a potential false allegation. She wrote,

> Of the cable news shows that covered the *Rolling Stone* allegations, 57% only covered the story after *Rolling Stone* issued its apology. In other words, most shows only found the story of a gang rape worthy of coverage when it turned into a media scandal. Of shows covering the Rolling Stone rape allegations, 31% covered the alleged rape before and after the report's retraction and 12% that reported on the story before it was retracted.[15]

Ultimately, *Rolling Stone* commissioned the Columbia University Graduate School of Journalism to investigate, and on April 5, 2015, *Rolling Stone* retracted the story.[16]

Despite red flags that should have raised skepticism, Richard Bradley noted that the editors (and readers) likely believed the story because it hewed so closely to our preconceptions of the problem of rape on college campuses—and our tendency to believe in the existence of rape culture. Bradley wrote,

> Remember: One must be most critical about stories that play into existing biases. And this story nourishes a lot of them: biases against fraternities, against men, against the South; biases about the naiveté of young women, especially Southern women; *pre-existing beliefs about the prevalence—indeed, the existence—of rape culture*; extant suspicions about the hostility of university bureaucracies to sexual

assault complaints that can produce unflattering publicity. (emphasis added)[17]

Others also questioned whether the concept of rape culture itself contributed to, if did not actually cause, the problem. *Powerline* suggested that the problems surrounding the credibility of the UVA story raised questions about the so-called rape culture on college campuses and claimed that the concept itself is "dangerous." Overall, after publication of the article, much public discourse around sexual assault on college campuses shifted from that of decrying rape culture to debunking it.[18]

By January 2015, a *Star Tribune* article linked the inability to recognize the problems in the UVA story to a moral panic around sexual assault. The headline stated, "Moral Panics Won't End Campus Rape," and the story argued that the public discourse around sexual assault on campus parallels discourse around satanic abuse cases in the 1980s.[19] Further, Heather Wilhelm, writing for the *Chicago Tribune*, called out feminists for their gullibility in believing the story and claimed that they are perpetuating rape culture in part because they do not understand "pure evil."[20]

In her critique published in *Time*, professor, social critic, and long-time feminist rabble-rouser Camille Paglia at once criticized the concept of rape culture while narrowly defining the problem of sexual assault on campuses to that of stalker-rape-murder incidents motivated by mental illness and patterned by biological essentialism. She stated,

> Despite hysterical propaganda about our "rape culture," the majority of campus incidents being carelessly described as sexual assault are not felonious rape (involving force or drugs) but oafish hookup melodramas, arising from mixed signals and imprudence on both sides.[21]

The "bad sex" hookup narrative would be repeated often as a criticism of so-called rape culture.

The *Rolling Stone* article served as a flashpoint, and it is easy to see how it served to initially exemplify rape culture and later discredit it. In fact, by the time of the article's publication, college campuses had long been a battleground over which the issue of sexual assault was waged.

DISMANTLING RAPE CULTURE THROUGH TITLE IX ENFORCEMENT

In 2009, the Center for Public Integrity (CPI) began an investigation into sexual assault on campus, and their subsequent report outlined how colleges and universities have consistently failed to respond appropriately to complaints of sexual assault. Specifically, the report detailed how enforcement mechanisms put in place by the federal government have fallen short in preventing sexual assault, responding to victims, and providing victim resources. Moreover, the mistreatment of sexual assault victims by the institutions was not some relic of the past. The report detailed instances in which women reported their victimization to the school administrators but were coerced into silence, and ultimately concluded that "a thick blanket of secrecy still envelops cases involving allegations of sexual assault on campus." According to federal law, school administrations were charged with responding to complaints and, when appropriate, enforcing some sort of sanction, but their responses had time and again been found woefully inadequate. Further, the report found that students "deemed 'responsible' for alleged sexual assaults on college campuses can face little or no consequences for their acts," while the trauma for victims is often "compounded" after they come forward to report the incident to administrators, only 10 to 25 percent of the students found responsible were permanently expelled.[22]

The CPI report documented that data collected through the Clery Act—legislation mandating the collection and dissemination of crime data on campuses and the improvement of public safety—were inadequate due to confusion about the law and the large number of campuses that reported zero incidents. And the report documented that the Department of Education's Office for Civil Rights (OCR) was stunningly ineffective in enforcing Title IX—the federal law prohibiting sex discrimination in any federally funded education program or activity.[23]

In 2010, NPR teamed with the Center for Public Integrity and produced a series of articles discussing the problem of sexual assault on campuses.[24] The following year, a "Dear Colleague Letter" was issued by the OCR reiterating the requirements of Title IX and outlining obligations that colleges and universities must meet in response to sexual violence, including education, prevention recommendations, and potential remedies. As evidence that sexual assault was a major problem, the letter cited the 2007 Campus Sexual Assault Study, which found that "one out of five undergraduate women experience an attempted or completed sexual assault during their college years," as well as findings from the Clery Act indicating that nearly 3,300 forcible sex offenses were recorded by campuses in 2009.[25]

Overall, the Dear Colleague Letter outlined that institutions are required to take "immediate and effective steps to end sexual harassment and sexual violence." School administrators and faculty members were tasked with investigating and adjudicating what might be serious, violent felonies, though the complainant may always report the case to law enforcement regardless of the institutional outcome. The Dear Colleague Letter pointed out that in contrast to the "beyond a reasonable doubt standard" used in criminal cases, institutions are required to use the "preponderance of the evidence" standard (i.e., it is more likely than not that sexual harassment or violence occurred).

The letter was intended to remedy the lackluster enforcement of Title IX. However, as scholar Emily Suran pointed out, Title IX is more powerful as a rhetorical tool than a legal remedy. Historically, the federal government has been reluctant to use the greatest enforcement power that it has, which is to pull funding from institutions that do not comply. In fact, though there have been investigations, Title IX has remained virtually unenforced since its inception. The *New York Times* reported in 2011,

> The Office for Civil Rights certainly has the power to enforce the law: any school that is found to be violating Title IX risks losing its federal funds. But that punishment has never been used since Congress passed the law in 1972. [26]

Nonetheless, the letter was widely considered a "game changer," with one activist hailing it as "a lifelong dream." [27] In her law review article detailing how the unprecedented activism around sexual assault on campus shifted the cultural landscape around Title IX, Suran credited social media as a valuable tool for providing a forum for survivors and activists. Here is how Suran described the significance of Title IX:

> As a piece of legal machinery, Title IX is relatively ineffective. But as a social conceit, Title IX has immense perceived power. Title IX gave people the legal hook with which they could grapple for change. The law might not be able change a culture, but people can. [28]

By 2013, activist groups such as End Rape on Campus, Know Your IX, and ED ACT NOW organized and prompted a national conversation— with the specific focus of dismantling rape culture, in part through reforming the ways that institutions respond to complaints. By transforming sexual harassment into sex discrimination and channeling public outrage about sexual assaults on campus into recognition of a widespread social problem, Suran declared that for survivors, Title IX has effectively become an extralegal solution. [29]

The publicity and activism around the Dear Colleague Letter likely contributed to increases in Title IX reported complaints. Since 2000, reports increased from 4,987 to 9,989 in 2014. As of March 1, 2016, there were 208 sexual violence cases under investigation at 167 postsecondary institutions. The high number of complaints is generally interpreted as either supporting the notion that there is a serious problem with sexual assault on campus, or at minimum that there is no actual increase in sexual assault but rather increased awareness and willingness to report.[30]

Despite raised awareness and increasing numbers of complaints, schools could hardly be accused of meting out overly harsh punishments for students that were found responsible. In fact, in their report, the *Huffington Post* found that less than a third of students adjudicated responsible were expelled by their institution. Tyler Kingkade wrote that according to data from nearly three dozen colleges and universities,

> a conservative estimate of the cases shows 13 percent of students found responsible for sexual assault were expelled; at most, 30 percent were expelled. In addition, between 29 to 68 percent were suspended.[31]

In 2015, journalist Jon Krakauer wrote a scathing indictment of how the University of Montana, local law enforcement, and the District Attorney's Office failed victims of sexual assault in Missoula, Montana. Specifically, in his analysis of cases, Krakauer noted how rape myths and stereotypes coupled with lack of training and resources resulted in gross injustices for victims of sexual assault. Krakauer was careful to note that "the deficiencies at the heart of the Missoula imbroglio were not unique to western Montana."[32] In contrast to many skeptics who charge that sexual assault cases are often incidents of he said/she said that are too fuzzy to result in conviction, Krakauer found that "seemingly strong" cases were too often rejected for prosecution.[33] For example, he found that from January 2008 to April 2012, the police department referred 114 cases of sexual assault of adult women for prosecution, but only 14 cases resulted in charges filed. Krakauer's research is in line with other findings demonstrating that the criminal justice system has long failed victims of sexual assault.[34]

Notably, Krakauer acknowledged that responses by academic institutions to complaints of sexual assault vary dramatically, and as a result, some schools have implemented much more efficient and fair means of adjudication than others. However, he cautioned against sole reliance on the criminal justice system as a solution to the problem and instead advocated in favor of the federal policies outlined in the Dear Colleague Letter and recommendations by the White House Task Force. As for Missoula, Krakauer argued that reforms such as oversight of the county attorney's office and implementation of best practices for law enforcement and prosecutors have improved the process and increased chances of conviction.[35]

Nonetheless, in general, reaction to the requirements outlined in the Dear Colleague Letter and the subsequent enforcement of Title IX was mixed at best. The letter was praised by many activists and survivors and led to increased actions by schools across the country to address the issue. Simultaneously, the letter was heavily criticized for using the oft-maligned "one in five" statistic, for saddling administrators and faculty with alleged criminal cases that arguably are more appropriately addressed by the criminal justice system, and for implementing the relatively low standard of proof for a finding of "responsible."

THE NUMBERS

In 2014, in an effort to address growing concerns of sexual assault on college campuses, President Barack Obama established the White House Task Force on Protecting Students from Sexual Assault. In his weekly audio address on January 25, 2014, President Obama stated,

> Perhaps most important, we need to keep saying to anyone out there who has ever been assaulted: you are not alone. We have your back. I've got your back.[36]

The purpose of the task force is to help prevent sexual assaults and provide support for victims. President Obama placed some of the responsibility on young people of all genders to "show women the respect they deserve." He continued, "I want every young man in America to know that real men don't hurt women."[37]

By the end of 2014, the issue of sexual violence on college campuses had so penetrated public consciousness that the parody website Reductress.com published an article titled "The Six Best Colleges for Not Getting Raped" and stated, "The trend we're seeing for 2015 is a high demand for not being raped."[38] Further, activists and victims declared that a "watershed" moment had occurred when President Barack Obama became "the first American president to utter the phrase 'sexual violence'" and convened a task force to address the issue.[39] Politicians such as Senators Kirsten Gillibrand and Claire McCaskill became fierce advocates promoting legislation that addressed sexual violence against women.[40] However, despite the initial enthusiasm, efforts to combat rape on college campuses have become, to put it mildly, a legal and ethical quagmire.

In 2014, the White House Task Force issued their report, *Not Alone*, and in the introduction wrote, "One in five women is sexually assaulted while in college." The statistic was based on the National Institute of

Justice's Campus Sexual Assault Study (CSA) and has been widely cited by activists and journalists.[41] However, the "one in five" statistic was met with skepticism by some outlets, most notably because it was presented in the report as if the numbers were representative of colleges and universities nationwide, yet the study was limited to two universities.[42] As a result, the task force report simultaneously raised awareness of sexual assault on campus and, unintentionally, raised skepticism about its prevalence.

For example, in one article, the *Washington Post* fact-checked the CSA study and initially concluded a "verdict pending," stating they needed "more information" before they could make a decision about the validity of the statistics. Though the study was methodologically rigorous, was approved by more than one institutional review board, and utilized a variety of descriptive, bivariate, and multivariate analyses, the *Washington Post* pointed out some of the study's limitations that would continue to be echoed by skeptics and used to discredit the study (as well as the concept of rape culture): that it was limited to two universities, that the response rate was relatively low, and that (like all social science research) "the results depend on how questions are phrased and answers interpreted."[43]

Misunderstandings and misrepresentation of the study stirred controversy. In response, two coauthors of the study, Christopher Krebs and Christine Lindquist, wrote an article in *Time* clarifying their findings that the "one in five" statistic included acts of sexual battery *and* rape. The authors noted that if the results were limited to *only* rape (defined as unwanted sexual penetration), the calculated prevalence was one in seven. They emphasized that it is "inappropriate to use the 1-in-5 number in the way it's being used today, *as a baseline* or *the only statistic* when discussing our country's problem with rape and sexual assault" (emphasis added).[44] While many skeptics seized on the aforementioned quote, they failed to mention that the authors also continued:

> *Our results are not inconsistent with other studies that surveyed undergraduate students about their sexual-assault experiences,* and surveying students directly about their sexual-assault experiences using behaviorally specific language remains the most scientifically valid way to measure the prevalence of sexual assault. (emphasis added)[45]

After conducting their own nationwide online poll, the *Washington Post* eventually offered an update to their initial article that ultimately "confirmed the 1 in 5 statistic."[46]

One of the more controversial reactions to the statistics came from conservative columnist George Will, who wrote that he found the rate to be implausible and implied that being a victim of sexual assault on campus is a way to "make victimhood a coveted status that confers privileges," and followed with dismissive remarks about a rape at Swarthmore College. Many readers, including sexual assault survivor Lisa Sendrow who stated in her interview with CNN that "rape culture needs to change," met Will's article with outrage. However, Will and the *Washington Post* were not the only skeptics. The *Washington Examiner* stated simply in a headline, "No, 1 in 5 Women Have Not Been Raped on College Campuses."[47] But this headline was wildly misleading; neither the White House Task Force report nor the CSA study reported that one in five women had been raped, but that one in five women had been sexually assaulted. It is this contention around what is "rape" and what is "sexual assault" that drives much of the debate around statistics of sexual assault on college campuses.

Those seeking to minimize the problem of sexual assault on campus also seized on the Bureau of Justice Statistics (BJS) report that used data from the National Crime Victimization Survey (NCVS), finding that "the rate of *rape and sexual assault* was 1.2 times higher for nonstudents (7.6 per 1,000) than for students (6.1 per 1,000)."[48] For example, John Hinderaker, writing for *Powerline*, used the BJS report as evidence of "how far 'rape culture' dogma departs from reality." Sierra Rayne's response to the BJS report in the *American Thinker* was to simply disregard the data by stating, "We will never, ever know the real rate of sexual assaults in any demographic group, never mind among the populace as a whole." The report was described as "unverifiable," riddled with "uncertainty," and containing either "under- or over-estimates." Further, the *Chronicle of Higher Education* weighed in by stating that the BJS data "challenges conventional wisdom about the heightened danger on college campuses" and noted that other reports that implement different methodologies have reached different conclusions.[49] Relying primarily on the discredited UVA story and the BJS report, journalist Cathy Young argued that narratives of rape have been received by the public and the press uncritically and that they have been used by activists to push the idea that there is a rape crisis on college campuses. She wrote,

> Will 2015 see a pushback against the anti-"rape culture" movement on campus? If so, good. This is a movement that has capitalized on laudable sympathy for victims of sexual assault to promote gender warfare, misinformation and moral panic.[50]

Similarly, in her article published on Slate.com on December 7, 2014, Emily Yoffe argued that the misuse of statistics on the prevalence of rape coupled with what she described as rigorous but misguided enforcement of Title IX by the Office for Civil Rights created an environment unfair to the accused.[51]

As a result of the ongoing backlash against the "one in five" statistic, politicians and activists moved away from using specific numbers to define the problem. For example, Senator Kirsten Gillibrand removed the "one in five" statistic from her website and avoided mention of the statistic at the premiere of a *Vice News* campus rape mini-documentary, leading the *Daily Caller* to declare that both Senator Gillibrand and Senator Claire McCaskill failed to present "a hard number on the rate for sexual assault on campus."[52]

Similarly, in an interview with Bill Maher on *Real Time with Bill Maher*, Annie E. Clark, survivor, activist, and cofounder of End Rape on Campus, resisted reliance on the one in five statistic:

> The best statistics that we have from the Department of Justice are between 1 in 4 and 1 in 5 women are sexually assaulted on campus and that number is very high and it has been disputed, however, if we're to even say that statistic is wrong and it was 1 in 20 or 1 in 100 imagine if 1 in 100 students were shot or 1 in 100 students had their Apple laptop stolen on campus, what would be saying about that? So, it's not even an issue of the numbers, it's about the issue itself.[53]

Getting to the "truth" of just how many sexual assaults occur on college campuses is a daunting task, and researchers readily acknowledge that there are varying methodologies, definitions of sexual assault, units of analysis, and time frames that impact the results.[54] However, over the decades, measurements of sexual assault have evolved into what is considered best practices, and behaviorally specific language has emerged as the most valid way to measure sexual assault in surveys.[55] Given the vast differences in the many colleges and universities across the country (e.g., community colleges, for-profit colleges, commuter colleges, historically black colleges and universities, women's colleges, Ivy League universities, etc.), it makes little sense to assume that there is a given national statistic that accurately assesses the rates on campus. As Cantor et al. stated, the one in five number may not be an accurate "global rate," but despite ongoing skepticism, studies consistently find that sexual assault remains a significant problem among college-age women.[56] For example, the release of the Campus Climate Validation (Pilot) Study in January 2016 spanned nine institutions of higher learning ranging in size, region, and status and included responses from twenty-three thousand students. The prevalence rates of completed sexual assault (i.e., that included sexual battery and rape) across the schools *during the 2014–2015 school year* for females ranged from 4.2 to 20 percent and for males from 1.4 to 5.7 percent. The prevalence rates of completed sexual assault *since entering college* for females ranged from 12 to 38 percent and for males from 3.7 percent to 11.8 percent.[57]

In another study of twenty-seven universities in the United States, the Association of American Universities (AAU) Campus Climate Survey on Sexual Assault and Sexual Misconduct found that since enrollment, 11.7 percent of students experienced nonconsensual sexual contact by physical force, threats of physical force, or incapacitation since enrollment. Among females, "the incidence of sexual assault and sexual misconduct due to physical force, threats of physical force, or incapacitation" was 23.1 percent, with 10.8 percent reporting that they experienced penetration.[58]

A prior study, the National College Women Sexual Victimization Study, found that 2.8 percent of college women experienced either completed or attempted rape within the 6.9-month period since the start of the academic year under study. During that time period, the researchers found that 11 percent of women experienced unwanted sexual conduct, 13.1 percent reported being stalked, and 77 percent experienced "at least one form of non contact sexual abuse."[59] As the study's authors have noted, to focus only on the incidence and prevalence of *rape* overlooks the extent to which women are subject to other (criminal and noncriminal) forms of sexual victimization, including sexual coercion, unwanted sexual contact, and noncontact sexual abuses. These may include, among other behaviors, grabbing, fondling, verbal coercion, misuse of authority, taunting, indecent exposure, and voyeurism. In fact, in their literature review, the researchers concluded that "little has changed since the 1950s with respect to the extent of these types of victimizations committed against college women."[60] Overall, they concluded,

> There is little doubt that sexual victimization is sufficiently pervasive that college women will repeatedly encounter sexist and harassing comments, will likely receive an obscene phone call, will have a good chance of being stalked and of enduring some type of coerced sexual contact, and will be at some risk—especially over the course of a college career—of experiencing an incident in which someone she knows will attempt to use force, against her will, in the pursuit of sexual intercourse.[61]

Importantly, the researchers "found no evidence of political correctness run amok—of respondents applying the label of rape indiscriminately." Therefore, the authors argue, this is not a situation of carelessly labeling everything "rape" but instead is recognition that patterns of behavior rest on a continuum of sexual violence against women—a view that is an integral component of a feminist understanding of rape culture, but a perspective that irks, and at times infuriates, those who demand a clear demarcation between a narrow definition of "forcible rape" and other forms of sexual assault.[62]

ADVOCACY AND "EPIDEMIC"—*THE HUNTING GROUND*: "A HORROR MOVIE"

One of the most publicized efforts to raise awareness of the problem of sexual assault on college campuses and the failure of administrators to respond adequately to victim complaints was the release of director Kirby Dick's documentary film *The Hunting Ground* (produced by Amy Ziering).[63] On January 23, 2015, the film premiered at the Sundance Film Festival with Senators Kirsten Gillibrand and Barbara Boxer in attendance and was designed for maximum impact on policy. Sundance positioned the film as "a piercing, monumental exposé of rape culture on campuses, poised to light a fire under a national debate." Similarly, the *New York Times* echoed the sentiment in their headline that declared, "'The Hunting Ground,' a Film about Rape Culture at Colleges." So confident that the film would have an impact on the way that college administrators respond to sexual assault complaints, the *New York Times* quoted Senator Barbara Boxer at the Sundance premiere: "Believe me, there will be fallout."[64]

Indeed, many commentaries on the film were favorable, and some deemed the film revelatory. Alexander Nazaryan, writing for *Newsweek*, declared the film "a horror movie, as frightening as any film I have seen since *The Shining*." One *Entertainment Weekly* headline read, "'The Hunting Ground' exposes an 'epidemic' of rape in American colleges." Kelsey Miller, writing for *Refinery 29*, characterized the film this way: "In the last few years, rape culture has been a constant presence in news headlines but never before has the reality been depicted so explicitly." According to *Vanity Fair*, the "extraordinary buzz" that the film elicited propelled it to wide release just a month after the Sundance premiere.[65]

Describing the extent to which the film captured the zeitgeist around the issue of sexual assault on college campuses, in her interview with *Vanity Fair*, producer Amy Ziering stated,

> "We'd thought that [the situation] would be analogous to *The Invisible War*," with a bit of media traction on the military assault issue before the film's release. . . . "But it turned out we were chasing a tiger."[66]

However, despite initial praise for the film, by the time of the film's wider release, skepticism was mounting around the so-called epidemic of sexual assault on college campuses, and within six months, the film was described by the *Washington Examiner* as a "continuing collapse" of propaganda.[67] By the time CNN announced that they would air the documentary in November 2015, one of the accused referenced in the film had threatened a lawsuit against the network, another accused's lawyers penned a scathing press release condemning the film, and CNN convened a postscreening panel to discuss the controversies swirling around the film.[68]

The Hunting Ground focused primarily on two female students at the University of North Carolina at Chapel Hill, Annie E. Clark and Andrea Pino, and their efforts to compel administrators to address the needs of victims by encouraging the filing of Title IX complaints. Both recounted their experiences of being raped and detailed how they transformed their victimization into activism with the goal of helping other students who shared similar experiences. The film contained numerous interviews with other victims and bolstered their narratives with statistics illustrating the scope of the problem. Among other criticisms, it was this tactic of focusing on the voices of victims that raised concern among skeptics, who insisted that the documentary should have included perspectives from those accused as well as administrators.

The film addressed the reluctance of victims to report, the stigma surrounding male victimization, the intersection of sports and sexual assault, and the fraternity culture that condones sexual assault. Overall, through the use of victim narratives, the film rebuked colleges and universities for their lack of enforcement. In an interview with *Democracy Now!*, producer Amy Ziering explained the title of the film:

> It's [rape is] actually a calculated, premeditated act. It is not a hookup gone bad. It's not he said/she said. . . . it's a hunting ground, it's a place where people are not safe, not because there's a preponderance of perpetrators, but because there's nothing in place to prosecute those people, and there's no incentive to do so.[69]

The film relied heavily on the research of Dr. David Lisak, including his research finding that the majority of men not prosecuted for rape (i.e., undetected offenders) were repeat offenders, suggesting that the problem of rape on college campuses is primarily that of serial predators. Critics would later challenge these claims by pointing to research investigating the trajectory of rapists across high school and college, finding that rapists form a more heterogeneous group and that "most men in college who commit rape do so during limited time frames."[70]

THE FALLOUT

Notwithstanding the increased scrutiny of sexual assault on college campuses, prior to the film's release, the dominant narrative in media and popular culture was that sexual assault on college campuses was a major problem. However, coverage began to take a more critical stance. In media interviews, the creators were questioned about how the material was presented, including whether the film was "balanced" appropriately. In this regard, the *Rolling Stone* debacle cast a long shadow, as *Variety* attested in its review: "The absence of testimony from the accused is an understandable omission (though as the *Rolling Stone* article's rollback indicates, that can be a problem)."[71]

Moreover, days after the film's official release, Emily Yoffe published her oft-cited, searing takedown of the film on *Slate*. In sum, Yoffe argued that the filmmakers were biased in their presentation and that administrative responses to complaints of sexual assault, as mandated by the federal government, have lurched too far in favor of the victim at the expense of the accused—a complaint that continues to resonate with many critics of Title IX enforcement. She wrote,

> But a rush to the opposite extreme—to privileging the claims of accusers without due diligence or due process or any recognition that sex can be murky territory—has already had real and devastating consequences at universities across the country.[72]

In further attempts to discredit the film and debunk the so-called rape culture on college campuses, the credibility of at least two victims appearing in the film has been questioned by various outlets. Erica Kinsman (Florida State University), who identified her assailant as Jameis Winston (Heisman award–winning athlete), detailed her experiences in the film and how she was mistreated and neglected by school administrators because of what she believed was the high social status of the accused. The film criticized the police department and the school for their lack of an adequate response to Kinsman's complaint. Despite DNA evidence linking Winston to the accused, no charges were brought against Winston due to insufficient evidence.[73]

Others pushed back against the film and the tactics of the filmmakers, including Florida State University president John Thrasher, who claimed that the creators delayed reaching out for comment and withheld details about how the film would criticize actions by the school. Although director Kirby Dick disputes that account, such allegations further portray the filmmakers as one sided.[74] Ultimately, Kinsman was awarded $950,000 in a federal lawsuit against the school; the Title IX investigation is still ongoing.[75]

However, it was not school administrators who gained the most traction toward discrediting the film. Yoffe followed up her earlier article with further criticism of the film, this time with details on the criminal trial and conviction of another accused, Brandon Winston. Kamilah Willingham, a former Harvard Law student featured in the film, alleged that she was raped by Winston (who was not named in the film, but whose name later became a matter of public record). The school initially suspended Winston but then later reinstated him.[76] Yoffe reported that Winston was ultimately brought to trial—on criminal charges involving a third party (not Willingham, but a female victim, "KF," that was present with both Willingham and the accused). He was charged with two felony counts of

> indecent assault and battery—that is, unwanted sexual touching, not rape. In March, he was cleared of all felony charges and found guilty of a single count of misdemeanor nonsexual touching.[77]

Yoffe suggested that because the filmmakers were serving as activists rather than truth tellers, the film distorted what happened on the night of the incident. This in part contributed to a narrative shift from a focus on victims of sexual assault to the plight of the accused. Yoffe wrote,

> It's a story of an ambiguous sexual encounter among young adults that almost destroyed the life of the accused, a young black man with no previous record of criminal behavior. It's a story that demonstrates how deeply the filmmakers' politics colored their presentation of the facts—and how deeply flawed their influential film is as a result.[78]

In their press release supporting their client Brandon Winston, the law firm Zalkind, Duncan, and Bernstein condemned the film as "a dangerous and disingenuous piece of propaganda." The press release stated, "It is disturbing to us that the filmmakers and CNN see Mr. Winston, a young black man accused of sexual assault, and refuse to believe he is anything but guilty."[79]

In addition to the press release in support of Brandon Winston, by the time of the film's scheduled screening on CNN (November 2015), Jameis Winston's attorneys threatened to sue the network, claiming that the film was "false and defamatory." Moreover, that same month, nineteen Harvard Law professors, which the *New York Times* described as having "among them prominent black and feminist legal scholars," penned a letter denouncing the film, citing Yoffe's piece as instructive and stating that "justice has been served in the end, but at enormous costs to this young man."[80] What had begun as an effort to expose rape culture on college campuses had shifted into debates around the murkiness of consent; increasing concerns of false allegations, including the broader implications of race; and problematic enforcement of Title IX.

Together, increased skepticism about the scope of the problem, attempts to discredit victim narratives that were reframed as he said/she said incidents, and increased attention to the plight of the accused problematized rape culture as a useful concept in understanding sexual violence. Meghan Daum's article in the *Los Angeles Times* illustrated this transition and the tendency to link concerns of anti-rape campus activists to larger issues of "grievance culture." Daum concluded that the film should be considered advocacy rather than journalism, but nonetheless should be seen because it "shines a light on . . . rape culture."[81]

While acknowledging that rape culture is "real," Daum continued with an oft-repeated criticism of campus anti-rape activism, that "violent rape is not the same as psychologically coercive sex, which in turn is not the same as regrettable sex, which is not the same as fielding an unwanted touch or kiss at a party." Daum cautioned that conflating these encounters is part of the so-called grievance culture and undercuts claims made by anti-rape activists.[82] Others such as Naomi Schaefer Riley, writing for the *New York Post*, echoed the sentiments of many skeptics by suggesting that the so-called rapes on college campuses were more likely "a preponderance of sexual encounters fueled by bad judgment and free-flowing alcohol" and concluded that only a shift from liberal permissiveness that condones drunkenness and sexual promiscuity to conservative policies at colleges (e.g., restricting dorm visits of the opposite sex and the implementation of classes on chivalry "instead of ones about the 'rape culture'") will reduce rates of sexual violence.[83] However, there was another case in particular that raised awareness around campus sexual assault while also stirring controversy around issues of "bad sex," consent, and the plight of the accused.

"CECI N'EST PAS UN VIOL"

In May 2014, journalist Amanda Hess declared Columbia University "ground zero for the national political struggle over campus sexual assault." The handling of sexual assault cases by Columbia University gained attention when, according to the *New York Times*, twenty-three students signed on to three separate complaints with the Department of Education's Office of Civil Rights.[84]

Earlier in 2014, anti-rape activism on campus at Columbia was critically questioned when it was revealed that anonymous actors were publicly posting "rape lists" around campus that included the names of accused offenders, including those deemed "responsible" by campus officials. While some argued that such a tactic is a legitimate means of public shaming, many found it abhorrent. For some, the issues coming to the fore at Columbia were symptomatic of the larger problem among campuses across the country.[85]

In what became one of the more controversial instances of campus anti-rape activism, Columbia student Emma Sulkowicz launched her senior thesis performance art piece "Carry That Weight" in which she carried a fifty-pound mattress around campus.[86] In an interview with the *New York Times*, Sulkowicz explained that her art was a protest against the handling of sexual assault complaints on campus and that she intended to carry the mattress until she graduated or until the "man she accuses of attacking her is no longer on campus, whether he leaves or is expelled or graduates." Here is how the *New York Times* described her account of the assault:

> On the evening of the first day of classes of her sophomore year, Ms. Sulkowicz said, she was anally raped in her dorm room by a fellow student with whom she had had consensual sex twice before, according to the police report. In the aftermath, Ms. Sulkowicz suffered in silence, then filed a complaint with the university. This led to a hearing before a panel that found him not responsible, according to a campus newspaper report in *The Columbia Spectator*, a decision that was upheld upon appeal.[87]

Initially, Sulkowicz's case became one of the most prominent examples of how complaints are generally mishandled. Media reports indicated the performance art inspired students at as many as one hundred other schools to carry mattresses or pillows in solidarity with the cause.[88]

Sulkowicz indeed carried the mattress at her commencement the following spring. However, by that time, Sulkowicz and her performance piece had been heavily criticized and her credibility questioned.

According to *New York* magazine, In the aftermath of the ceremony, Sulkowicz was subjected to online trolling (@fakerape, #rapehoax), and posters appeared on campus with a photo of Sulkowicz declaring her a "Pretty Little Liar." Scholar Camille Paglia weighed in stating that Sulkowicz basically performed a parody of "the worst aspects of . . . grievance-oriented feminism" and that her behavior was an example of "perpetually lugging around your bad memories—never evolving or moving on!"[89]

While carrying a mattress on campus might strike some as a simple stunt, many activists hailed Sulkowicz's move as a brilliant contribution to the anti-rape movement.[90] Author Rebecca Solnit wrote,

> Sulkowicz's genius was to make her burden tangible, and in so doing make it something others could share. . . . In Sulkowicz's case, you could actually carry that mattress.[91]

Sulkowicz's project gained the attention of politicians as well as activists. In January 2015, Sulkowicz was invited to the State of the Union Address as a guest of Senator Kirsten Gillibrand, cosponsored by Senator Claire McCaskill, of the pending Campus Accountability and Safety Act, S.590, that would, among other provisions, require a memorandum of understanding between colleges and local law enforcement as well as a biannual survey measuring incidents of sexual violence and harassment.[92] By this time, the Sulkowicz case was referenced by anti-rape activists as yet another example that proved the existence of rape culture, while it was simultaneously held up by skeptics as another case of ambiguous consent—a he said/she said incident demonstrating the perils of hookup culture.

The accused, Paul Nungesser, continues to maintain his innocence and has since filed a lawsuit against Columbia University.[93] According to reports, Sulkowicz initially did not report the incident until she learned that two other fellow students had claimed they were victimized. According to the *Columbia Spectator*,

> two classmates told her that Paul [Nungesser] had been abusive to them too—one who had been in a long-term relationship with him, the other alleging he groped her.[94]

The *New York Times* reported that there were three accusations against Nungesser, each of which was either dismissed or overturned on appeal. In the first public statement made by Nungesser to the *New York Times* in December 2014, he declared that he was innocent and stated that the three complaints were "the result of collusion."[95] Nungesser described his experiences with Sulkowicz as bullying, and the *New York Times Magazine* detailed that

> he was called a rapist on a list anonymously scrawled in campus bathrooms. Columbia's undergraduate newspaper published his name when Sulkowicz went to the police. . . . Nungesser's friends fell away. He found himself shunned on campus.[96]

The narrative that initially focused on the problems faced by victims of sexual assault was now more frequently directed toward reactions to the accused and the process of adjudication itself, specifically the subsequent concerns about aggressive enforcement of Title IX.[97]

Journalist Judith Shulevitz used the Sulkowicz case to illustrate why the general public distrusts the adjudication procedures at colleges and universities, deeming them a "shadow justice system."[98] However, this was not the first time that concerns around college policies designed to address sexual assault on campus were expressed. Writing for the *New York Times*, Professor Jed Rubenfeld wrote that colleges and universities scrambling to address the demands of the federal government have implemented policies employing a standard lower than beyond a reasonable doubt, and there is concern that professors and administrators are not equipped to adjudicate serious crimes such as rape. Similarly, twenty-eight members of the Harvard Law School faculty issued a statement rejecting Harvard's 2014 sexual harassment policy. Among their concerns were that the scope of the offenses is too broad, the procedures are impartial or "stacked against the accused," and there is a lack of adequate representation.[99] These concerns around enforcement continue to resonate as schools are adjusting to demands of the federal government while balancing the needs of complainants with due process rights of the accused.

Frequently, concerns about due process were framed as a problem of how "bad sex" was being transformed into "the crime of rape" via campus policies that overreach in defining consent. Notably, Rubenfeld wrote that such policies supported by many feminist activists—defining consent as the presence of the affirmative, "positive," "specific," and "unambiguous"—are overly broad and misguided while leaving unaddressed the significance of the role of alcohol. In her op-ed for the *New York Times*, Judith Shulevitz wrote that calls for affirmative consent lead to "the criminalization of what we think of as ordinary sex and of sex previously considered unsavory but not illegal." Cathy Young's article for the *Daily Beast*, in which she interviewed Nungesser, similarly framed the Sulkowicz incident as one of regretted sex by suggesting that her continuing, friendly correspondence on Facebook with Nungesser after the incident indicated that the accused is innocent. As for the other allegations leveled against Nungesser, Young speculated about their motives, stating that one of the women was reportedly "suffering from serious depression," and again pointed out that friendly conversations transpired between Nungesser and the complainants after the alleged incidents occurred.[100]

Given Young's numerous attempts to discredit "rape culture" and her dogged determination to uncover inconsistencies in victim accounts of rape, her piece could be read as a rape-apologist attack riddled with victim-blaming rhetoric.[101] It may also be read as a cautionary tale about the extent to which cases that initiated as consensual but were later alleged by one party to be coercive are virtually impossible to adjudicate to a satisfying conclusion. Part of this predicament is the way that consent is legally defined and culturally understood.[102]

As for Sulkowicz, her latest art project was a website titled "Ceci N'est Pas Un Viol," or "This Is Not a Rape," which included an eight-minute video followed by a "comments" section.[103] The *Daily Caller* described the video:

> The "artistic" tape shows Sulkowicz having sex in a Columbia dorm room with an unknown man, who suddenly becomes violent and starts to hit her, choke her, and otherwise subject her to what looks like a rape.[104]

The explicit video was posted on her website along with a description of the project. Not surprisingly, due to the graphic nature of the project, many dismissed it as porn and "perverted." The *Federalist* headline read, "Oops, I guess I just raped Emma Sulkowicz." Further, the *Daily Beast* suggested that Sulkowicz is inviting criticism because she "turn[ed] a personal experience into a public spectacle and declare[d] it art." One headline in the *Libertarian Republic* simply declared Sulkowicz a "typical tyrannical leftist," while *Breitbart* declared her a "narcissistic sociopath."[105] However, it is worth quoting an excerpt from Sulkowicz's website:

> Ceci N'est Pas Un Viol is not about one night in August, 2012. It's about your decisions, starting now. It's only a reenactment if you disregard my words. It's about you, not him. . . .
> . . . If you watch this video without my consent, then I hope you reflect on your reasons for objectifying me and participating in my rape, for, in that case, you were the one who couldn't resist the urge to make Ceci N'est Pas Un Viol about what you wanted to make it about: rape.
> Please, don't participate in my rape. Watch kindly.[106]

Perhaps to dismiss the piece as simply public spectacle, porn, or attention-seeking behavior is to miss the point. Artist Hannah Rubin pointed out the significance of the comments section to the webpage and how the piece is designed to implicate the viewer by revealing that the *reactions to the piece are part of the project itself* and say more about the viewers (and consequently the proliferation of so-called rape culture) than the piece itself. Rubin observed,

> The story of Sulkowicz's rape isn't an easy one—it's ripe with conflict and contradiction. It pushes hard on our traditional views of rape as a purely violent, evil encounter that occurs in the dark. They knew each other, they had had consensual sex prior, she continued to communicate with him afterwards . . . and yet, and yet . . . he hit her, he slapped her, she said no, and he did not listen. We watch the tape, we watch it happen, and still, the majority of the comments still find her to be the guilty party. [107]

Together, controversies swirling around the *Rolling Stone* article, *The Hunting Ground*, and the Sulkowicz case amplified the debates around sexual assault on campuses and led to a reconsideration of the concept of rape culture itself.

RAINN AND RAPE CULTURE

Perhaps the most stunning rebuke of the concept of rape culture came not from journalists focused on discrediting victim accounts, antifeminists, or men's rights activists, but from what is billed as the largest and most recognized anti-sexual violence organization, Rape, Abuse and Incest National Network (RAINN). On February 28, 2014, RAINN penned a letter to the White House Task Force to Protect Students from Sexual Assault offering comments and recommendations for reducing sexual violence on campuses. The letter made clear the organization's opposition to the concept:

> In the last few years, there has been an unfortunate trend towards blaming "rape culture" for the extensive problem of sexual violence on campuses. While it is helpful to point out the systemic barriers to addressing the problem, it is important to not lose sight of a simple fact: Rape is caused not by cultural factors but by the conscious decisions, of a small percentage of the community, to commit a violent crime. [108]

Ultimately, RAINN discredited use of the concept by stating that prevention messaging has been so successful that the dominant cultural understanding among young adults is basically that rape is wrong—bolstered by the fact that only a small percentage of young male college students actually commit rape. From RAINN's perspective, changing attitudes is of lower priority than risk reduction. However, in their prevention recommendations, they do not abandon the notion of changing attitudes altogether. They offered a three-tiered approach to the problem that included risk reduction and education around issues of consent along with bystander intervention education—an approach focused specifically on messaging designed to change norms among bystanders. The letter also voiced objections to policies that placed enforcement in the hands of college and university internal boards rather than with law enforcement.[109]

The reaction to RAINN's stance brought to the fore the fact that feminists themselves were not monolithic with their embrace of the concept. Several articles pointed out that holding offenders accountable *and* accepting that cultural factors contribute to permissive attitudes about sexual violence, victim blaming, and dismal rates of conviction and prosecution are not mutually exclusive. Others—given the history of the mistreatment of sexual assault victims by the criminal justice system—objected to the notion that the criminal justice system is the best avenue of recourse for victims.[110]

Meanwhile, the most vociferous critics of the notion of rape culture used RAINN's statement to further an explicit antifeminist agenda. On March 20, 2014, writing for *Time*, Caroline Kitchens used RAINN's condemnation of the use of the term "rape culture" to bring attention to what she considered the "real" problem: "hostile environments for innocent males."[111] A week after Kitchens's article appeared, political analyst Zerlina Maxwell published a counter-article in *Time* relaying her own experiences of victimization. Maxwell flatly rejected Kitchens's argument by launching the hashtag #RapeCultureIsWhen that spurred tweets from women detailing their everyday experiences, including,

> Rape culture is when women who come forward are questioned about what they were wearing.

> Rape culture is when survivors who come forward are asked, "Were you drinking?"

> Rape culture is when people say, "she was asking for it."[112]

The popularity of #RapeCultureIsWhen has been described as a means of feminists' "reclaim[ing] the conversation" and acknowledging that rape culture exists.[113] Nonetheless, by the end of 2014, the narrative around rape culture had shifted dramatically, with many declaring it a fiction.

FALSE ALLEGATIONS AND THE "EMOTIONAL DARK SIDE OF PROMISCUITY"

Collectively, the discrediting (and/or attempted discrediting) of various high-profile victim accounts of rape led journalist Radley Balko to query, "Given that there are so many legitimate incidents to choose from, why have so many high-profile cases ultimately fallen apart?" Notably, Balko cautioned against the mantra of "believe every accuser" by implying that victims who come forward publicly are doing so to "generate publicity" and suggested that the accounts offered by those who come forward should be scrutinized more closely than those who are reluctant. Balko stated,

> This isn't an argument that college students (and anti-rape activists in particular) never get raped. Nor is it an argument that accusations should never be believed. Nor is it an argument that rape victims should be ashamed to come forward. It's only to say that generally speaking, an alleged victim eager to generate publicity about what happened to her may require more verification than an alleged victim who is reluctant to come forward. All else being equal, reluctant witnesses are more persuasive than eager ones. (Of course, all else is rarely equal.)[114]

Balko's contention that refusing to remain silent somehow renders victims less "persuasive" is incomprehensible. He joined the chorus of others who cast doubt on victim accounts by reframing the issue as one of due process concerns and false allegations, ultimately urging us to avoid "believing every accuser."[115]

In contrast, it might be argued that "believing" credible statements by those who file criminal complaints—at least initially, if only in order to move forward with a proper investigation—may be preferable to a default position of disbelief or the stubborn refusal to acknowledge evidence of suppression and misclassification of rape cases.[116] At the very least, police departments should not classify "*all* rape cases as 'unfounded' *as a default*," as was the case with the police department in Norfolk, Virginia.[117] It should also be acknowledged that reliance on an extremely narrow definition of rape results in cases being incorrectly dismissed, as the Marshall Project reported. They found that Philadelphia police reopened many cases after a citizens' review effort led to the discovery that "more than 1,800 crimes had been incorrectly dismissed, including 681 rapes. Thirty-three men connected to the re-opened cases were convicted."[118] Perhaps rather than urging disbelief, it is reasonable that officers may instead "demonstrate respect, impartiality, empathy and . . . maintain an open mind" when faced with a complainant.[119]

As Balko articulated, the looming fear for many is the potential for false allegations. This fear was expressed by A. J. Delgado in the *National Review*, where she not only argued that there is no rape epidemic but added the empirically unsupported assertion that women *routinely* make false accusations. As for evidence, Delgado recounted the story of how she talked a friend out of making a false claim of rape after a drunken night of partying that ended in consensual sex—and shame—for her friend. Delgado wrote,

> To the extent some in our society remain skeptical of rape claims, women themselves bear a share of the blame. After all, for every legitimate, actual rape claim there may be another that was not: a girl who cried rape.[120]

Initially, it may seem that those fearful of false allegations are on to something. One study published in the *Cambridge Law Journal* found that over the past few decades false reports of rape ranged anywhere from 1.5 to 90 percent, a range that is virtually useless for gaining any understanding of false allegations. Other scholars have similarly acknowledged that varying methodologies result in conflicting estimates of false allegations from "very common" to "quite rare."[121] Those findings likely lead many observers to conclude that we are simply unable to offer any reasonable estimate of false allegations. In contrast, other researchers have concluded that false allegation rates range generally from 2 to 10 percent and that it is no longer accurate to claim, as Balko did, that they are "all over the map." For example, in a study that examined reports at the Los Angeles Police Department in 2008, scholars Cassia Spohn, Clair White, and Katharine Tellis found a false report rate of 4.5 percent.[122]

Part of the problem is defining what exactly is a false allegation. For example, lack of arrest and/or conviction does not equate to a "false" allegation. In their study, scholars Lisak et al. stated, "To classify a case as a false allegation, a thorough investigation must yield evidence that a crime did not occur."[123] Legal scholar Candida Saunders reported that criminal justice professionals are more likely to say that rape allegations are "false" than are researchers. The reason for this, according to Saunders, is that police and prosecutors reported that it is not necessarily uncommon for complainants to make false statements, that is, concealments and/or distortions, when reporting. Part of this tendency may be related to trauma or due to victims altering details because they do not believe that their accounts will be considered credible. It is rare, however, for "a complainant to allege rape when, in fact, no rape occurred."[124] Further, scholar Liz Kelly reported that among police officers in the UK,

> despite a focus for more than a decade on victim care, a culture of suspicion remains, accentuated by a tendency to conflate false allegations with retractions and withdrawals, as if in all such cases no sexual assault occurred.[125]

As criminologist Joanne Belknap stated in her work on rape victims, the far more significant problem is underreporting—not false allegations.[126] Moreover, much of the discussion of false allegations in popular media focuses on cases of ambiguous consent that are often described by skeptics as he said/she said or labeled as instances of "regrettable sex." However, research has found that allegations that have been proven false tend to differ from the more common allegations involving acquaintance/date rape. For example, Spohn et al. found that false reports to the Los Angeles Police Department tended to have characteristics that hewed closely to the concept of "real rape" described by Susan Estrich in her book *Real Rape* (e.g., aggravated rape committed by "a stranger, multiple assailants, or a suspect wielding a weapon, or that she suffered from collateral injuries").[127] Given these findings, it is less likely that false allegations involve murky "he said/she said" scenarios that have so frequently captured media attention in discussions of rape on college campuses.

In the discourse of rape culture, false allegations are used by some as a pretext for demonizing women for not being "prepared" for the double standard that awaits them if they choose to engage in premarital sex. For example, like Delgado, Robert Tracinski writing for the *The Federalist* stated that claims of rape are too frequently sexual regrets, and he ridiculed the notion that women may later perceive their encounters as coercive. For Tracinski, coercive sex is "blunt, it is physical, it is perceptual." He wrote,

> Dubious claims about "rape culture" are an attempt to create an all-purpose scapegoat for the emotional dark side of promiscuity. . . .

But it's clear that some young women are not psychologically prepared for this. [128]

From this perspective, not only is the prevention of rape placed on the shoulders of women, but so is the existence and perpetuation of the campus hookup culture. Further, Tracinski's statement that sexual violence is not subject to later "reinterpretation" runs counter to the many experiences that women have shared about how they cope with sexual violence. For example, research has shown that reporting is often delayed (if the victim reports at all), and that those in close relationships with the perpetrator are more likely to delay reporting, particularly among younger victims. Further, many women may not initially consider their experience rape even though they describe behaviors that fall under the legal definition of rape. [129]

"THIS IS BIGGER THAN ANY OF US"

The discursive shift from dismantling rape culture on college campuses to discrediting the concept itself was no more apparent than in the depictions of campus sexual assault in popular culture. For example, *Law & Order: SVU* tackled the issue of campus rape in their episode "Girl Dishonored" that aired in April 2013. [130] *Jezebel* described the episode as an amalgamation of over a dozen real-life incidents of sexual assault, including the Steubenville, Ohio, case and incidents from various campuses that failed to hold offenders accountable. In an effort to portray victim sensitivity, the episode included an homage to Project Unbreakable's website portraying photos of survivors holding signs that include quotes made by perpetrators and others in response to their assaults. Writer Katie J. M. Baker wrote,

> The episode's standard disclaimer—"The following story is fictional and does not depict any actual person or event"—is utter bullshit, given that SVU writers stole lines straight out of survivors' mouths. [131]

Similarly, Alexandra Brodsky, survivor and founding codirector of Know Your IX, wrote of the episode,

> Maybe, for once, instead of pretending that SVU is fiction, they could embrace reality, make a difference, and say, "The following story is NOT FICTITIOUS, it is based on the real lives of brave, young

women from across the country. They're still fighting to be heard and you can help."[132]

Brodsky further explained that one of the major problems with the "Girl Dishonored" episode was its "optimistic tone" and satisfying ending where the "rapists are brought to trial and [the victim] decides to return to school." Brodsky continued by emphasizing that, alternatively, "the ending should have more accurately reflected the continuous battle against colleges that Survivors face."[133]

Though the episode itself did not make direct reference to "rape culture," the *Huffington Post* declared in their headline that it "Shines a Light on the Rape Culture at College Campuses."[134] In fact, *Law & Order: SVU* has generally been praised by scholars as privileging feminist sensibilities by countering rape myths and avoiding victim blaming. In their 2006 analysis, Lisa Cuklanz and Sujata Moorti pointed out that generally the show "highlights the power in gender relations, including within the family, and provides evidence of 'rape culture' as a potential factor in the commission of the crime."[135]

However, by 2015, the treatment of campus sexual assault by *Law & Order: SVU* in the episode "Devastating Story" shifted from its "optimistic tone" of "Girl Dishonored" to a cautionary tale—one that exposed anti-rape advocates who, in their quest to end rape culture, were as damaging to anti-rape activism as the offenders themselves (airdate April 2015). The episode contained echoes of the *Rolling Stone* UVA story, the perils of irresponsible journalism, the irrevocable consequences of false allegations, and warnings about what happens when advocacy efforts trump the "truth." Here, the concept of rape culture shifted from an object of concern to itself being problematic. The clear villain in this episode was a feminist female college professor who was so determined to "end rape culture" that she encouraged a student to embellish her report of rape to include a gang rape (as opposed to the victim's actual experience of being raped by a single offender). At the urging of her professor, the victim, Heather Manning, quickly became "the face of a movement" to end campus sexual assault. She appeared on various media outlets, and it was during these interviews that well-meaning but naive reporters were easily misled by their readiness to uncritically believe the victim's account. In one incredulous exchange, when questioned by the detectives about the specifics of the crime (i.e., the detectives queried, "Was she raped?"), the professor told the detectives,

It doesn't matter what happened to her.
What matters is it happens every day. . . .

... This isn't about you or these boys or this case.
This is bigger than any of us.
This is about eliminating rape culture once and for all. [136]

Here, the show presented the stereotype of a feminist professor/advocate that is so zealous in fighting for her cause that she stubbornly rejected all objective facts relevant to the case. In their recap of the episode, the *Daily News* described the plot as involving a false allegation where the victim was "egged on by her professor to come forward with the gang rape story." The piece pointed out the obvious parallels between the *Law & Order: SVU* plot and that of Jackie's discredited story as published in *Rolling Stone*, but omitted from their summary the detail that the fictional complainant actually *was raped* by one offender. [137]

Further, *TV Fanatic* summarized how the episode was as much about the debate around the concept of rape culture as about rape itself. The article stated that the episode "highlights the pitfalls of such 'false' accusations, and the damage tampering with criminal evidence can do when it comes to truly attacking 'rape culture.'" [138] Correspondingly, reader comments on the recap post quickly evolved from discussion of the episode into a debate about the merits of the concept of rape culture. For example, one reader wrote,

> Rape culture is a myth, and it is largely perpetuated by feminism. Seriously, aside from the prison community, in what part of our society do people openly talk about the desire to rape, or their plans to rape, or anything related to rape, as if it's an [*sic*] socially acceptable behavior? [139]

Here, it was not the *perpetuation* of rape culture itself that was the problem, but the *acknowledgment and unquestioning "belief in"* rape culture that misled the detectives. The result was the inability to prosecute, leaving a "dangerous predator" at large on campus and the lingering assumption that allegations are either false or exaggerated.

The episode ended when Detective Benson basically echoed the words of Richard Bradley, who initially questioned the *Rolling Stone* story, by confirming that personal belief in the existence of rape culture prevented her from viewing the case objectively. She stated,

> You know, it was the perfect story.
> It confirmed all of my preconceived notions.
> And that alone should have made me approach it with more skepticism. . . .

. . . They thought this would be the case that would change rape
culture and it did.
It set the clock back 30 years. [140]

The ending further left Detective Benson in the regrettable position of
asking the school administration to take action against a known rapist
because the criminal justice system was powerless to do so. Here, unlike the optimistic conclusion in the earlier episode, the victim's embel-
lishment at the urging of her professor precluded the possibility of any
criminal charges for the perpetrator.

REAPPROPRIATING RAPE CULTURE

Since the end of 2012, the concept of rape culture entered public consciousness and, with robust student activism around Title IX, the release of the White House Task Force on Protecting Students from
Sexual Assault report, and the release of *The Hunting Ground*, became
inextricably linked with campus sexual assault. However, those same
instances of activism led to increasing scrutiny of the concept. "Rape
culture" was no longer an adequate explanation for gendered violence,
but instead its recognition was framed as part of the problem.

This transformation, however, must be understood within the larger
cultural context of how rape culture has been negotiated. The concerns
of hypersensitivity, condemnation of so-called political correctness,
mockery of trigger warnings, and claims of censorship that dominated
popular culture discourse dovetailed with attacks on the credibility of
high-profile victims, scrutiny of statistics, indignation over calls for campus "safe spaces," concerns of due process, and attempts to reframe the
problem as one of false allegations. Although campuses have been a
dominant space through which these debates have evolved, popular
culture has also contributed to our basic understanding of what rape
culture is and where the groundwork was set for the term to be reap-
propriated and used against itself.

This is illustrated in a case that occurred at Vanderbilt University in
2015. Two former football players were charged with raping and so-
domizing an unconscious female student. One defendant was charged
with "urinating on the victim while using racial slurs" and recording the
rape on a cell phone. According to reports, all involved were intoxicated, and the victim had no recollection of the incident until school officials investigating another crime on campus viewed security videos. The
AP reported,

> They [school officials] were shocked to see players carrying an un-
> conscious woman into an elevator and down a hallway, taking com-
> promising pictures of her and then dragging her into the room.[141]

In an ironic twist, the defense attorney of one of the defendants offered
rape culture itself as a defense. In this case, popular culture, "peer
pressure," and "campus culture" were blamed for the crime.[142] *Bitch
Media* reported that in a public statement,

> the defense attorney pinned blame on "social media, that came in the
> way of television shows that glamorize and promote sexual activity"
> for creating a "culture of sex and drinking."[143]

Further, according to Reuters,

> Batey's attorney said the football player from Nashville was influ-
> enced by a campus culture of sexual freedom, promiscuity and exces-
> sive alcohol consumption that contrasted with the manner of his
> upbringing.[144]

Ultimately, the two men were convicted in January 2015 on "multiple
counts of rape and aggravated sexual battery" but were released from
incarceration in June of the same year after the judge declared a mistri-
al upon learning that the jury foreperson "was himself a victim of sexual
abuse."[145]

7

RECONCILING PANIC AND POLICY

In this book, I set out to explore how the social meanings of sexual violence are contested through popular mediums, with a particular focus on how the concept of "rape culture" entered the collective imagination. It was not an attempt to unmask rape culture, but rather an effort to trace how the concept became a popular, albeit contested, framework for understanding sexual violence. The phrase originated in the 1970s as second-wave feminists argued that the privileging of patriarchy, with its reinforcement of gendered sex roles and oppressive behavior, contributes to the implicit and explicit encouragement of sexual violence. The concept provided a foundation for understanding that sexual violence rests on a continuum of behavior, that rape myths continue to proliferate, and that changes in criminal law do not necessarily translate into justice. Decades later, dislodged from its academic roots, it reemerged as a broad framework for understanding attitudes and behaviors that intersected with a range of everyday experiences, from street harassment to gang rape.

I realized relatively early in the process that a traditional content analysis of news articles focused on "rape culture" would be insufficient to grasp how the concept had permeated public discussions about sexual violence. High-profile cases such as the one in Steubenville, Ohio, helped propel it into popular discourse. However, the debate over rape culture, and whether it even exists, was played out in facets of society not easily captured by traditional news articles. Considering that emotions and public sentiment around crime and social control are fueled at the intersection of mass media, social media, and popular culture, I chose to focus on conversations that resonated in public discussions through those avenues.[1] While some might dismiss a low-culture analysis, I argue that rape culture cannot be fully understood apart from these prime arenas where our collective imagination is informed. As such, our understanding of sexual violence is constantly in flux. It oftentimes reflects early ideological debates; at other times, it demonstrates the entrenchment of long-standing stereotypes and victim blaming. It is within this constantly shifting landscape that our treatment of victims, response to perpetrators, and policy making occur.

Overall, there remains disagreement on whether the term "rape culture" is a useful concept for understanding sexual violence. Those who utilize it must navigate the landscape of ideological differences both among those who share their cause as well as among those who reject it. Or, as scholar Chris Atmore declared,

> there is no longer any easy counterposition of "them" to "us," and all kinds of political interests get served through making claims and counterclaims about sexual violence.[2]

London-based freelance writer Rhiannon Lucy-Cosslett wrote that she, and others who tell their victimization stories in ways that do not conform to a victim narrative (that is, if a victim expresses regrets or acknowledges ways in which she could have, or should have, done something differently), often gets "shouted down, ridiculed, and abused" by other feminists. Ultimately, Lucy-Cosslett acknowledged that we live in a rape culture but found that the concept may be more divisive than helpful. She explained that when she wrote an article about an attack she had suffered, she regretfully engaged in victim blaming. She wrote,

> I still fundamentally believe in what I was trying, so inarticulately, to get at—which is that feminist debate about rape has become so anger-filled and simplistic that at times it seems to decry the very existence of common-sense safety advice. But I realise also that I had internalised many of the prevailing societal attitudes towards female victims and was using them against myself and other women.[3]

Even among feminists, ideological differences do arise in ways that are divisive. Michelle Goldberg, writing for *The Nation*, pointed out that "tone policing" and other forms of "trashing" directed toward feminists not only come from the ranks of the neoconservative right wing or men's rights advocates, but also emerges when feminists face off against each other, in ways that, as Goldberg suggested, are potentially destructive to the movement itself.[4] Nonetheless, in popular media, the most vociferous resistance to the concept emerged in ways that reinforce victim blaming and reignited familiar feminist backlashes from the past.

Feminists who first articulated the concept of rape culture drew attention to the ways that mediated sexual violence frequently objectifies and oppresses women. We have seen how the way in which sexual violence is represented continues to be of concern in popular culture, specifically when women and people of color are marginalized as characters and only a narrow range of situations are presented. Simultaneously, we have found that reactions to images of sexual violence are varied and have as much to do with affect and emotional intensity as does intellectual interpretation. Popular culture serves as a site for not only processing whether or not there are "good" representations, but also for revealing our intense connection to portrayals that reflect our lived experiences. It is this process of everyday engagement that contributes largely to our understandings of sexual violence. More nuanced portrayals of sexual violence allow space for multiple interpretations of oppression, as well as empowerment, reflecting the extent to which we view expressions of sexuality as linked to political empowerment. The significance here is not to settle on a correct interpretation, but to recognize that the process itself is valuable and informs our collective imagination.

Popular culture continues to be relevant, as certain niche venues have proven rich environments for exploring issues of sexual violence, for example, geek spaces such as gaming and comic culture. The GamerGate controversy revealed how gendered harassment thrived and how feminist interventions operated as resistance. Such experiences can be attributed to various social factors. Sociologist Michael Kimmel observed how the changing demographic, social, and economic landscape in American society has contributed to a sense of aggrieved entitlement in which angry white males may lash out against scapegoats (e.g., minorities) rather than direct their anger toward those individuals and institutions responsible for economic inequalities.[5] In this context, male privilege is contested and masculinity itself is perceived as under threat. This is seen most acutely in the microcosm of geek spaces where gendered harassment is linked to the long-standing lack of diversity in industries such as gaming and comic books. The subsequent changing demographics that challenge the status quo result in a sense of aggrieved entitlement that too frequently manifests as sexual harassment and threats of rape and death.

While this phenomenon as it occurs in geek spaces has been conceptualized as primarily an online harassment issue, the observed discourse more broadly contributes to larger ideological debates around feminism, social justice, academia, censorship, free speech, and due process. Objections to the rise of political correctness that have reemerged in various aspects of social life, up to and including the 2016 campaign for the president of the United States, would be virtually nonexistent without the ability to link those charges of political correctness to so-called trivial examples of everyday gendered harassment.[6] For example, complaints of popular culture representations and microaggressions, as well as threats of rape and death, are deemed inconsequential as long as overall rape rates remain relatively low. Similarly, calls for trigger warnings on television shows are characterized as absurd when compared to concerns of soldiers suffering from PTSD that return home from a war zone. Further, it is no surprise that use of the term "social justice warrior" (SJW) as a pejorative ramped up over the past few years and fed into more mainstream discussions as a result of increasing attention toward GamerGate and men's rights activists in general.[7] In effect, the label "SJW" condemns those who "bitch" about representations—both in terms of content and in terms of diversity within the industries themselves—as a threat to society at large. Further, male allies who support feminist interventions in geek spaces are deemed, disparagingly, as "white knights," while academics that study the issue are similarly viewed as social threats.

For detractors, minimizing and discrediting so-called rape culture in the context of geek spaces and campus culture has itself become de rigueur. However, this is not so with regard to international instances of sexual violence. As shown with the much-publicized New Delhi rape case that occurred in late 2012, the concept of rape culture is generally accepted uncritically in the United States when directed toward other cultures. Despite the myriad efforts to discredit the concept when applied domestically, it continues to be invoked when discussing instances of sexual violence occurring in Europe when perpetrated by refugees, immigrants, or by those of Middle Eastern descent.[8]

One of the key issues of concern among those opposed to the concept of rape culture is the contention that because violence against women is worse in other locales, particularly in the context of practices such as genital mutilation, honor killings, and acid attacks, it is difficult to conceive of the contemporary twenty-first-century United States as a culture of rape. In her article for the *American Thinker*, Carol Brown said that feminists who suggest that the United States is a rape culture should move to a "Muslim-majority country—perhaps Iran or Syria— where you can experience first-hand the war on women."[9] Similarly, Ian Tuttle, writing for the *National Review*, used the Rotherham, UK, child sexual exploitation scandal—in which an estimated 1,400 children were sexually exploited—to suggest that the minimal coverage in feminist-focused media outlets and blogs is a sign that feminists lack a "moral seriousness" with regard to sexual violence.[10] Tuttle wrote, "Is it possible, then, that after years of tying 'rape' to Disney films and fantasy video games, these feminists are at a loss for words when confronted with the real thing?" Tuttle continued by stating that rape culture is only of interest to feminists when it does not involve actual rape.[11]

Conservative editor and commentator Rich Lowry echoed that senti- ment and opined that, unlike in the United States, Rotherham is a "terrifyingly real and endemic rape culture" empowered by multicultu- ralism. He suggested that feminists are not interested in the incident because it does not create for a "fashionable hashtag."[12] These critics are implying that as long as women (and children) in the United States are not subjected to unspeakable horrors, then what would be consid- ered more minor forms of sexual violence are inconsequential and, therefore, that the characterization of the United States as a "rape cul- ture" is a misnomer.

Other backlash to the concept surfaced in the debates around sexual assault on campuses, leading some detractors to declare that rape cul- ture was a fiction, akin to the moral panic around satanic child ritual sexual abuse scandals that arose in the 1980s. It was primarily in this context that the concept of rape culture shifted from a framework for explaining and understanding the problem to *the problem itself*. Ironi- cally, efforts by the federal government, journalists, and activists to raise awareness of sexual assault on college campuses also inadvertently in- creased scrutiny toward victim accounts, ignited debates around con- sent and victim blaming, renewed concerns around false allegations, and resulted in challenges to enforcement policies that were seen as infringing on the due process rights of the accused.

Echoing other conservative and libertarian pundits, Glenn Reynolds described the so-called campus rape epidemic as a "current moral pan- ic" that "seems more like political agitprop and mass hysteria than any- thing else."[13] In fact, understanding social reaction to sexuality as a moral panic is not new. Scholars have documented how media hype around pornography, sexual orientation, child sexual abuse, sex offend- ers, and other issues related to sexuality constitute moral panics.[14] How- ever, what rings disingenuous about casting rape culture as a moral panic is that detractors often couch their concern under a shroud of misogyny. For example, Reynolds longs for the "old days" when rape was unambiguously defined as "forcible penetration at the hands of a stranger" and charges that the real perpetrators to be feared are women who rape men.[15] Here, moral panic is invoked as a means of silencing and denigrating women rather than illuminating legitimate concerns about how public sentiment around rape culture might impact public policy.

Moreover, suggesting that rape culture constitutes a moral panic implies that there is a grand consensus on sexual violence. However, I found instead that the discourse reveals that there is very *little* consensus with regard to our understandings of sexual violence. This is, unsurprisingly, rooted in our patterns of normative heterosexual behavior that, as Nicola Gavey noted, are "patterned or scripted in ways that permit far too much ambiguity."[16] As a result, definitions of sexual violence remain contested, debate continues about the nature and scope of the problem, and there remains wide disagreement on the best means of prevention and enforcement.

This is perhaps not surprising given how scholars Angela McRobbie and Sarah Thornton explained the contemporary media landscape. The public is quite savvy to media manipulation and quick to recognize overreaction. Due to increased fragmentation of media, marginalized scapegoats (e.g., youth subcultures, sex offenders, etc.) are more likely than ever to have a powerful voice in shaping counternarratives. They wrote,

> The kinds of issues and political debates which were once included on the agendas of moral panic theorists as sites of social anxiety, and even crisis, could now be redefined as part of an endless debate about who "we" are and "what" our national culture is.[17]

Further, as sociologist Nancy Whittier pointed out, by implying that concern of sexual violence is akin to a moral panic, the assumption is that claims of victimization are wildly exaggerated and that existing sanctions are "not only sufficient but excessive."[18] For example, in her article lambasting political correctness and warning of the dangers of false allegations, journalist Judith Levine wrote, "There is no dearth of seriousness about sexual violence in America: we have the harshest sex crime laws outside Iran."[19] Similarly, in her article in the *National Review*, Mona Charen blamed feminists themselves for the campus rape problem and expressed that our culture already forcefully condemns rapists. She wrote,

> Of course the culture must teach men not to rape. Western culture has been doing so for thousands of years. Next to murder, rape is the most harshly punished crime.[20]

Such claims vastly oversimplify both the cultural and legal responses to sexual violence. For sure, during the twentieth century in the United States, cultural attitudes shifted and legal reforms were implemented. However, scholars have noted that these changes have not necessarily translated into justice. As scholar Rose Corrigan noted in her work on rape crisis centers, victims are still likely to face overwhelming resistance, reluctance, and even outright contempt from legal and medical systems targeted by the feminist anti-rape movement of the 1970s.[21]

In their 2005 article on rape reform, legal scholars Ilene Seidman and Susan Vickers declared, "Rape is the least reported, least indicted, and least convicted non-property felony in America."[22] Low rates of reporting and case attrition remain of concern among researchers. For example, based on their review of the data, researchers Kimberly Lonsway and Joanne Archambault summarized, "About 5% to 20% of all rapes are reported to law enforcement, 7% to 27% of these reports are prosecuted, and 3% to 26% yield a conviction."[23] The phenomenon of arrest and conviction rates not keeping pace with reported rape has been described as the sexual assault "justice gap."[24] As other scholars have noted, Lonsway and Archambault stated that one possible explanation as to why the attrition rate remains high: "because the laws have changed but attitudes have not."[25] In their book detailing the sexual assault justice gap in various countries, Barbara Krahé and Jennifer Tempkin similarly recognized that legal reform alone is insufficient to address the injustices that occur with regard to the experiences of rape victims in the criminal justice system; there must also be an effort to change attitudes and perceptions.[26]

Criminal case processing, though, is a complex phenomenon, and research findings have been mixed. Some researchers have found victim behavior, such as failing to appear and being uncooperative, as important factors in determining prosecutors' perceptions of convictability.[27] Others, such as scholar Lisa Frohmann, found that in addition to legally relevant variables, prosecutors base their charging decisions on "assumptions about relationships, gender, and sexuality" with "the typification of normal heterosexual relations play[ing] an important role in assessing these cases."[28] In other words, it is impossible to separate case outcomes from the cultural context in which they occur. Prosecutors make decisions about the rejection of cases and convictability based on legally relevant variables, but also on cultural assumptions they hold, or that they believe jurors hold, about victim behavior and credibility. Behaviors that deviate from "normal heterosexual relations" are more likely to result in a case rejection (e.g., continuing a relationship after alleging a rape has occurred, delayed reporting, and suspicions of ulterior motives for filing complaint).[29] This book's analysis of the emergence of "rape culture" is an attempt to show how various cultural assumptions about sexual violence flow through popular media. It suggests that our failure of policy is a reflection of our cultural ambivalence around what constitutes sexual violence.

But what of the assertion that, of those convicted, we already punish sex offenders quite harshly in the United States? Does the calling out of a "rape culture" inherently demand a harsh criminal justice intervention? While it is true that contemporary sex offender legislation implemented in the 1990s in the United States (e.g., sex offender registration, residency restrictions, and community notification laws) has rightly been described as excessively punitive as well as counterproductive, it is also true that these forms of legislation coexist alongside a criminal justice response to sexual violence that has long been described as shockingly inadequate.[30]

Instead of dismissing the issue, as some reactionary critics do, one alternative is to view sexual violence on a continuum (e.g., behaviors ranging from catcalling to sexual harassment to groping to rape), while simultaneously acknowledging that rape falls at the far end of the spectrum. It follows that not all behaviors that rest on the continuum require a criminal justice response.[31] In fact, within feminism, there has historically been notable resistance to reliance on the criminal justice system as a means of attaining justice. As scholar Susan Caringella pointed out, "contrary to public perception, so-called feminist rape reforms did not reach for higher levels of punishment in rape cases overall."[32] Many involved in the anti-rape movement in the 1970s were less concerned with harsh punishments than with legal reform that engages and empowers the victim in the process. For example, in *Rape: The First Sourcebook for Women* published in 1974, the editors remarked,

> We do not want to make rape laws more punitive, be we do want the courts to recognize the rights of women to a fair and equitable trial as a first step in eliminating sexism in our legal system. The laws as they stand now reflect only suspicion and mistrust of the victim.[33]

In fact, research has shown that while victims of sexual violence are interested in offender accountability, they are also interested in validation and fairness. They are not particularly punitive and instead often advocate for non-retributive responses. In her study of rape reform, Rose Corrigan found that contemporary rape crisis center advocates "rarely talk about criminal penalties for rape as a part of their agenda related to victim services."[34]

Despite these findings, there is an underlying assumption among those who cast rape culture as a moral panic that feminists have an undue influence on public policy. In this context, it has been suggested that feminists have contributed to the punitive state by promoting increased surveillance, policing, prosecution, and punishment to address violence against women—a phenomenon known as carceral feminism.

For example, scholar Kristin Bumiller outlined how anti-rape activism efforts intersected with the growth of neoliberalism and that reliance on increased punitive power in response to sexual violence has only increased women's dependency on the state.[35] Scholar Lise Gotell countered that the carceral feminism critique vastly overstates the power of the feminist movement in shaping public policy and cautions against an "absolute rejection of criminalization strategies."[36]

Rather than viewing misguided sex offender legislation as definitive evidence that sexual violence in American society is sufficiently morally condemned and effectively punished, sex offender legislation should instead be recognized, as Corrigan noted, as conflicting directly with feminist-inspired rape reform goals. As Corrigan pointed out, support for sex offender registration and community notification laws is driven by a retributive sentiment based on unfounded fears of stranger-predators. It is not driven by the recognition that attitudes and perceptions around sexual violence are rooted in a patriarchal society or that society provides sexual scripts that reflect power imbalances privileging male domination and encouraging female subordination in ways that do a disservice both to male and female victims. In this way, the laws themselves contribute to our collective imagination by defining sexual violence as stranger-danger incidents perpetrated by predators. They also minimize more common types of sexual violence that deviate from our construction of "real rape," such as acquaintance rape and incest, as well as incidents that involve nonfemale victims.[37] As a result, current patterns of enforcement contrast with the assumption that we "already" punish effectively. Instead, what remains unattended is reform that addresses the difficult balance between the needs of victims while avoiding draconian policies that do little to increase public safety.

Overall, the discourse around rape culture has produced little emphasis on calls for increased punitive criminal justice policies. This could be due to the continuing recognition that the criminal justice system has historically failed victims of sexual violence and that existing rape reform has been largely ineffective. Or perhaps it might be more generally attributed to the growing bipartisan movement away from the punitive turn in criminal justice.[38] Whatever the impetus, there has been a demand for cultural awareness, a change in attitudes, and an overall cultural shift aimed at altering existing attitudes and behaviors toward sexual violence that tend to silence victims. There is also a move toward finding solutions that lie outside the scope of criminal justice.

One area where enforcement policies are undergoing significant transition is on college campuses. Though sexual assault at universities has been subject to much debate over the past several decades, recent controversies unfolded at a rapid pace. By early 2015, the media narrative began shifting away from presenting sexual assault on campuses as a crisis to presenting the proposed policy solutions as problematic. Despite the efforts of activists to argue that victims had long been ignored and/or mistreated by school administrators, many high-profile cases and efforts to raise consciousness were met with scrutiny. As a result, the narrative often echoed that the *real* problem was inflated statistics, the inevitability of false allegations, and the ensnarement of innocent young men into flawed school disciplinary procedures (and/or a flawed criminal justice system). The discourse around sexual assault in this context reveals ongoing tension between victim reliance on the criminal justice system (and its history of failing victims of sexual assault) and/or social control that relies on school administrators (who arguably may not be the most knowledgeable about or best positioned to address rape and sexual assault). Although the government provided guidelines for schools receiving federal funding, the implementation of the policies, institutional definitions of sexual assault, disputes about consent, and trajectory of enforcement remain varied and continue to unfold. As such, the debate over Title IX enforcement and school disciplinary procedures is far from over. Nonetheless, after his multiyear investigation into responses to complaints of sexual assault in Missoula, Montana, journalist Jon Krakauer concluded,

> The oft-repeated claim that university adjudications categorically deny the constitutional right of due process to perpetrators is specious. Campus disciplinary proceedings cannot, and should not, be held to the same restrictive standards as criminal proceedings, because they don't result in incarceration or require the rapist to register as a sex offender. [39]

Here, the effort to move accountability outside the realm of the criminal justice system is not without controversy, and fierce debates continue, particularly around the issue of expanding carceral power in the form of civil and administrative policies. [40] While school disciplinary procedures might be one area that could afford less reliance on the criminal justice system through alternative avenues such as restorative justice, this can only be accomplished if there is a fundamental move away from institutionalizing traditional judicial processes toward more innovative approaches. [41] In this way, simply calling for administrative procedures to mirror the criminal justice system is likely to be dissatisfying to both victims and those accused. Furthermore, we will not achieve a move toward restorative approaches when inundated with questionable narratives promoting the notion that the vast majority of campus rapists are serial predators or the assumption that overzealous feminist professors and activists harbor disdain for due process and push their "agenda" without regard to the truth.

As feminists have demonstrated in their quest for cultural awareness and rape reform, there are no easy solutions to the problem of sexual violence. "Rape culture," which first emerged from the halls of academia, is now ubiquitous in popular discourse, showing up in news reports, social media outlets, and television crime dramas. There's no putting the genie back in the bottle; there's no erasing the concept. It is clear that our perceptions of, and responses to, sexual violence are influenced by the ever-present buzz of these forms of media in our lives. We do a disservice if we dismiss this engagement as lowbrow and irrelevant. Navigating through the terrain of rape culture requires an understanding of how our collective imagination is informed and indelibly shaped by this media-cultural sphere.

APPENDIX

METHODOLOGY

The collection of data involving academic and newspaper sources containing the concept of "rape culture" emerged from a project with my colleague Emily Horowitz. We conducted searches in academic and newspaper databases to track the frequency of the concept in both contexts. The search spanned from January 1, 1980, to April 2014 whenever possible, as some journals were not in publication as early as 1980.

For academic articles, we conducted a full-text search for the phrase "rape culture" in ProQuest, which included eighty-one databases spanning 1970 to April 2014. We excluded non-English-language articles as well as articles on agriculture and pollution. The earliest article in our search appeared in 1989. It is likely that the phrase appeared in articles prior to 1989, but there may be technical or scanning limitations that undercounted those articles.

For dissertations, we searched ProQuest for the keyword "rape culture" from 1979 to March 2014. We used WorldCat to search for "rape culture" designated as a "keyword" for books published between 1970 and early 2014. We included only those works published in English and excluded textbooks.

For newspapers and magazines, we used two methods to find instances of articles that referenced "rape culture." Due to the sheer number of mass media publications now archived in library databases (we used ProQuest), searching the frequency of the term "rape culture" in all full-text articles across all newspapers became unwieldy. As a result, we used two methods in our effort to decrease the number of hits for "rape culture" while still using a reliable and meaningful method to extract the frequency of this term in mainstream publications.

First, we looked at all articles that included the term "rape culture" in the ten highest-circulation U.S. newspapers. Newspapers in this category included those identified by the Alliance for Audited Media as having the highest circulation in the United States. This group of newspapers included the following publications: *Wall Street Journal*, *USA Today*, *New York Times*, *Los Angeles Times*, *San Jose Mercury News*, *New York Post*, *Washington Post*, *Denver Post*, *Chicago Tribune*, and *Daily News*. We reviewed all articles in these top-ten high-circulation newspapers individually to ensure that the articles referred to the feminist concept of "rape culture."[1] Next, we looked at articles in all *other* mainstream newspapers cataloged in ProQuest in English with the term "rape culture" in the title of the article. We excluded two sources cataloged in the ProQuest newspaper database: *University Wire* and *Off Our Backs*. We excluded *University Wire* because it appeared to artificially boost our numbers because the same story would appear multiple times. We also excluded articles from *Off Our Backs* because this is an overtly feminist publication, and we wanted to keep the focus on the frequency of the term in mainstream, nonfeminist/nonacademic publications. We then reviewed each article with "rape culture" in the headline to ensure that the articles referred to the feminist concept of "rape culture." The lower-circulation newspapers included in our study are listed below.

LOWER-CIRCULATION NEWSPAPERS

Asian News International

Battle Creek Enquirer

Bennington Banner

Birmingham Mail

Boston Globe

Businessline

Calgary Herald

Charleston Gazette

Cincinnati Enquirer

Cowichan Valley Citizen

CTV National News-CTV Television

Daily Gulf Times

Daily Mail

Daily Press

Daily Star

Denver Post

Derby Evening Telegraph

Des Moines Register

Edmonton Journal

Eugene Weekly

Evansville Courier & Press (2007–current)

The Examiner

Florida Times Union

Fort Collins Coloradoan

Fuse Magazine

The Gazette

Globe and Mail

Guardian

Hartford Courant

Herald Sun with Chapel Hill Herald

Here

Herizons

Hindustan Times

Imphal Free Press

Journal-Gazette

Journal News

Kashmir Times

Madison Capital Times

Manawatu Standard

Memphis Flyer

Milwaukee Journal

Mint

The Nation

National Post

Nelson Mail

Oakland Tribune

Omaha World-Herald

Ottawa Citizen

Pantagraph

Peace River Block Daily News

The People

Philadelphia Daily News

Plain Dealer

Post-Standard

Press-Citizen

Prince George Citizen

Punjab Newsline

San Francisco Chronicle (pre-1997 full-text)

San Jose Mercury News

Santa Fe Reporter

St. Louis Post-Dispatch

St. Petersburg Times

Star-Phoenix

Star Tribune

Sunday Herald

Sunday Independent

Targeted News Service

Telegraph.co.uk

Telegraph-Herald

Times-Colonist

Times of India (online)

Times-Transcript

Toronto Star

The Tyee

US Fed News Service, Including US State News

USA Today

Vancouver Sun

Voice Male

Whitehorse Star

Women in Higher Education

RESOURCES

Alexander, M. (2012). *The new Jim Crow: Mass incarceration in the age of colorblindness*. New York: New Press.

Amnesty International. (2010, March 8). Rape victims worldwide denied justice and dignity. Retrieved February 17, 2015, from http://www.amnesty.org/en/news-and-updates/report/rape-victims-worldwide-denied-justice-and-dignity-2010-03-08.

Angiolini, R. H. D. E. (2015). *Report of the independent review into the investigation and prosecution of rape in London*. London, UK: Metropolitan Police and Crown Prosecution Service.

Atluri, T. (2013). The young and the restless. Gender, "youth," and the Delhi gang rape case of 2012. *Sikh Formations*, 9(3), 361–379.

Atmore, C. (1000). Victims, backlash, and radical feminist theory (or, the morning after they stole feminism's fire). In S. Lamb (Ed.), *New versions of victims: Feminists struggle with the concept*. New York: New York University Press.

Austin, S., Solic, P., Swenson, H., & Jeter-Bennett, G. (2014). Anita Hill roundtable. *Frontiers: A Journal of Women Studies*, 35(3), 65–74.

Bailey, F. Y., & Hale, D. (Eds.). (1997). *Popular culture, crime, and justice*. Belmont, CA: Wadsworth.

Bartlett, J., Norrie, R., Patel, S., Rumpel, R., & Wibberley, S. (2014, May). Misogyny on Twitter. London, UK: Demos. Retrieved December 12, 2015, from http://www.demos.co.uk/files/MISOGYNY_ON_TWITTER.pdf?1399567516.

Baumgardner, J. (2011). *F 'em!: Goo goo, Gaga, and some thoughts on balls*. Berkeley, CA: Free Press.

Baumgardner, J., & Richards, A. (2010). *Manifesta: Young women, feminism, and the future* (10th anniversary ed.). New York: Free Press.

Baxandall, R., & Gordon, L. (2000). *Dear sisters: Dispatches from the women's liberation movement*. New York: Basic Books.

Beckett, K., & Murakawa, N. (2012). Mapping the shadow carceral state: Toward an institutionally capacious approach to punishment. *Theoretical Criminology*, 16(2), 221–244.

Belair-Gagnon, V., Mishra, S., & Agur, C. (2014). Reconstructing the Indian public sphere: Newswork and social media in the Delhi gang rape case. *Journalism*, 15(8), 1059–1075.

Belknap, J. (2010). Rape: Too hard to report and too easy to discredit victims. *Violence against Women*, 16(12), 1335–1344.

Benedict, H. (1992). *Virgin or vamp: How the press covers sex crimes*. New York: Oxford University Press.

Bernstein, E. (2012). Carceral politics as gender justice? The "traffic in women" and neoliberal circuits of crime, sex, and rights. *Theory and Society*, 41(3), 233–259.

Bevacqua, M. (2000). *Rape on the public agenda: Feminism and the politics of sexual assault*. Boston, MA: Northeastern University Press.

Bicanic, I. A. E., Hehenkamp, L. M., van de Putte, E. M., van Wijk, A. J., & de Jongh, A. (2015). Predictors of delayed disclosure of rape in female adolescents and young adults. *European Journal of Psychotraumatology*, 6, 23645–23649.

Black, G. (1996). *Hollywood censored: Morality codes, Catholics, and the movies*. Cambridge, UK: Cambridge University Press.

Breiding, M., Smith, S., Basile, K., Walters, M., Chen, J., & Merrick, M. (2014). *Prevalence and characteristics of sexual violence, stalking, and intimate partner violence victimization—national intimate partner and sexual violence survey, United States, 2011.* Atlanta, GA: Centers for Disease Control and Prevention. Retrieved February 15, 2016, from http://www.cdc.gov/mmwr/pdf/ss/ss6308.pdf.

Brown, J. (2011). *Dangerous curves: Action heroines, gender, fetishism, and popular culture.* Jackson: University Press of Mississippi.

Brownmiller, S. (1975). *Against our will: Men, women and rape.* New York: Penguin.

Buchwald, E., Fletcher, P. R., & Roth, M. (2005). *Transforming a rape culture* (2nd ed.). Minneapolis, MN: Milkweed Editions.

Bumiller, K. (2008). *In an abusive state: How neoliberalism appropriated the feminist movement against sexual violence.* Durham, NC: Duke University Press.

Campbell, B., & Manning, J. (2014). Microaggression and moral cultures. *Comparative Sociology, 13,* 692–726.

Cantor, D., Fisher, B., Chibnall, S., Townsend, R., Lee, H., Bruce, C., & Thomas, G. (2015). *Report on the AAU Campus Climate Survey on Sexual Assault and Sexual Misconduct.* Rockville, MD: Association of American Universities.

Carey, K., Durney, S., Shepardson, R., & Carey, M. (2015). Incapacitated and forcible rape of college women: Prevalence across the first year. *Journal of Adolescent Health, 56*(6), 678–680.

Caringella, S. (2009). *Addressing rape reform in law and practice.* New York: Columbia University Press.

Carr, J. (2013). The SlutWalk movement: A study in transnational feminist activism. *Journal of Feminist Scholarship, 4,* 24–38.

Carter, C., & Weaver, K. (2003). *Violence and the media.* Philadelphia, PA: Open University Press.

Cassell, J., & Jenkins, H. (1998). *From Barbie to Mortal Kombat: Gender and computer games.* Cambridge, MA: MIT Press.

Cheit, R. (2014). *The witch-hunt narrative: Politics, psychology, and the sexual abuse of children.* New York: Oxford University Press.

Chess, S., & Shaw, A. (2015). A conspiracy of fishes, or, how we learned to stop worrying about #gamergate and embrace hegemonic masculinity. *Journal of Broadcasting & Electronic Media, 59*(1), 208–220.

Christie, N. (1986). "Ideal victim." In *From crime policy to victim policy,* ed. E. Fattah (pp. 17–30). London, UK: Macmillan.

Chunn, D., Boyd, S., & Lessard, H. (Eds.). (2007). *Reaction and resistance: Feminism, law, and social change.* Vancouver, Canada: UBC Press.

Clark, H. (2015). A fair way to go: Justice for victim-survivors of sexual violence. In A. Powell, N. Henry, & A. Flynn (Eds.), *Rape justice: Beyond the criminal law* (pp. 18–35). Hampshire, UK: Palgrave Macmillan.

Clear, T., & Frost, N. A. (2014). *The punishment imperative: The rise and fall of mass incarceration in America.* New York: New York University Press.

Cocca, C. (2014). The "broke back test": A quantitative and qualitative analysis of portrayals of women in mainstream superhero comics, 1993–2013. *Journal of Graphic Novels and Comics, 5*(4), 411–428.

Coleman, G. (2014). *Hacker, hoaxer, whistleblower, spy: The many faces of anonymous.* New York: Verso.

Connell, N., & Wilson, C. (Eds.). (1974). *Rape: The first sourcebook for women by New York radical feminists.* New York: Plume.

Coronel, S., Coll, S., & Kravitz, D. (2015, April 5). Rolling Stone and UVA: The Columbia University Graduate School of Journalism report. *Columbia Journalism Review.* Retrieved May 8, 2015, from http://www.cjr.org/investigation/rolling_stone_investigation.php.

Corrigan, R. (2013). *Up against a wall: Rape reform and the failure of success.* New York: New York University Press.

Cuklanz, L. (1999). *Rape on prime time: Television, masculinity, and sexual violence.* Philadelphia: University of Pennsylvania Press.

Cuklanz, L. M., & Moorti, S. (2006). Television's 'new' feminism: Prime-time representations of women and victimization. *Critical Studies in Media Communication, 23*(4), 302–321.

Daly, K. (1995). Review of *Transforming a Rape Culture,* by Emilie Buchwald, Pamela R. Fletcher, and Martha Roth. *Signs, 20,* 760–766.

Daly, K. (2015). Sexual violence and justice: How and why context matters. In A. Powell, N. Henry, & A. Flynn (Eds.), *Rape justice: Beyond the criminal law* (pp. 36–52). Hampshire, UK: Palgrave Macmillan.

Daly, K., & Bouhours, B. (2010). Rape and attrition in the legal process: A comparative analysis of five countries. *Crime and Justice, 39*(1), 565–650.

Darehshori, S. (2013). *Capitol offense: Police mishandling of sexual assault cases in the District of Columbia* (pp. 1–210). Human Rights Watch.

Darowski, J. (2014). *X-Men and the mutant metaphor: Race and gender in the comic books.* Lanham, MD: Rowman & Littlefield.

Deflem, M. (Ed.). (2010). *Popular culture, crime and social control.* Bingley, UK: Emerald Group.

Delgado, R., & Stefancic, J. (2001). *Critical race theory.* New York: New York University Press.

Drache, D., & Velagic, J. (2013). A report on sexual violence journalism in four leading Indian English language publications before and after the Delhi bus rape. *ICA Pre-Conference Workshop on South Asian Communication Scholarship*, 1–25.

Durham, M. G. (2014). Scene of the crime. *Feminist Media Studies*, *15*(2), 175–191.

Edwards, S., Bradshaw, K., & Hinsz, V. (2014). Denying rape but endorsing forceful intercourse: Exploring differences among responders. *Violence and Gender*, *1*(4), 188–193.

Estrich, S. (1988). *Real rape.* Cambridge, MA: Harvard University Press.

Eterno, J., & Silverman, E. (2012). *The crime numbers game: Management by manipulation.* Boca Raton, FL: CRC Press.

Fahs, B., Dudy, M., & Stage, S. (Eds.). (2013). *The moral panics of sexuality.* New York: Palgrave Macmillan.

Ferguson, C. (2010). Media violence effects and violent crime: Good science or moral panic? In *Violent Crime: Clinical and Social Implications* (pp. 1–20). Thousand Oaks, CA: Sage.

Ferrell, J., Hayward, K., & Young, J. (2008). *Cultural criminology: An invitation.* Thousand Oaks, CA: Sage.

Field, R. (2004). Rape culture. In M. Smith (Ed.), *Encyclopedia of Rape.* Westport, CT: Greenwood Press.

Fingeroth, D. (2004). *Superman on the couch: What superheroes really tell us about ourselves and our society.* New York: Continuum.

Fisher, B., Cullen, F., & Turner, M. (2000). *The sexual victimization of college women.* Washington, DC: National Institute of Justice. Retrieved February 20, 2016, from https://www.ncjrs.gov/pdffiles1/nij/182369.pdf.

Fisher, B. S., Daigle, L., & Cullen, F. (2010). *Unsafe in the ivory tower: The sexual victimization of college women.* Thousand Oaks, CA: Sage.

Foss, K. (2010). Choice or chance? Gender, victimization, and responsibility in CSI: Crime Scene Investigation. *Journal of Research on Women and Gender*, *1*(1), 98–115.

Freedman, E. (2013). *Redefining rape: Sexual violence in the era of suffrage and segregation.* Cambridge, MA: Harvard University Press.

Friedman, J., & Valenti, J. (2008). *Yes means yes!: Visions of female sexual power and a world without rape.* Berkeley, CA: Seal Press.

Frohmann, L. (1991). Discrediting victims' allegations of sexual assault: Prosecutorial accounts of case rejections. *Social Problems*, *38*(2), 213–226.

Ganguly, M., Kashyap, A., & Thapa, T. (2014). *Silenced and forgotten: Survivors of Nepal's conflict-era sexual violence*. Human Rights Watch. Retrieved February 15, 2016, from http://www.hrw.org/sites/default/files/reports/nepal0914_ForUpload_0.pdf.

Garcia-Moreno, C., Pallitto, C., Devries, K., Stockl, H., Watts, C., Abrahams, N., & Petzold, M. (2013). *Global and regional estimates of violence against women: Prevalence and health effects of intimate partner violence and non-partner sexual violence* (No. 978 92 4 156462 5) (P. Howes, Ed.). World Health Organization.

Garcia-Moreno, C., Zimmerman, C., Morris-Gehring, A., Heise, L., Amin, A., Abrahams, N., et al. (2014). Violence against women and girls. *The Lancet*, *385* (9978), 1–11.

Garland, D. (2008). On the concept of moral panic. *Crime, Media, Culture*, *4*(1), 9–30.

Garland, T. S., Branch, K. A., & Grimes, M. (2015). Blurring the lines: Reinforcing rape myths in comic books. *Feminist Criminology*, *11*(1), 48–68.

Garrett, G. (2008). *Holy superheroes! Exploring the sacred in comics, graphic novels, and film.* Louisville, KY: Westminster John Knox Press.

Gavey, N. (2005). *Just sex? The cultural scaffolding of rape.* New York: Routledge.

Gilbert, N. (1998). Realities and mythologies of rape. *Society*, *35*(2), 356–362.

Goode, E., & Nachman, B.-Y. (2009). *Moral panics: The social construction of deviance* (2nd ed.). West Sussex, UK: Blackwell Publishing.

Gotell, L. (2015). Reassessing the place of criminal law reform in the struggle against sexual violence: A critique of the critique of carceral feminism. In A. Powell, N. Henry, & A. Flynn (Eds.), *Rape justice: Beyond the criminal law* (pp. 53–71). Hampshire, UK: Palgrave Macmillan.

Gray, K. (2014). *Race, gender, and deviance in Xbox live: Theoretical perspectives from the virtual margins.* New York: Routledge.

Gregg, M., & Seigworth, G. (2010). *The affect theory reader.* Durham, NC: Duke University Press.

Griffin, S. (1971). Rape: The all-American crime. *Ramparts Magazine*, 26–35.

Hajdu, D. (2008). *The ten cent plague: The great comic-book scare and how it changed America*. New York: Picador.

Harding, K. (2014). *Asking for it: The alarming rise of rape culture—and what we can do about it*. Boston, MA: Da Capo Lifelong Books.

Harper, T. (2014). *The culture of digital fighting games: Performance and practice*. New York: Routledge.

Heberle, R. (1996). Deconstructive strategies and the movement against sexual violence. *Hypatia , 11*(4), 63–76.

Henry, N., & Powell, A. (2015). Embodied harms: Gender, shame, and technology-facilitated sexual violence. *Violence against Women , 21*(6), 758–779.

Herdt, G. (2009). *Moral panics, sex panics: Fear and the fight over sexual rights*. New York: New York University Press.

Herman, D. (1979). The rape culture. In *Women: A feminist perspective* (2nd ed., pp. 41–53). Palo Alto, CA: Mayfield.

Hohl, K., & Stanko, E. A. (2015). Complaints of rape and the criminal justice system: Fresh evidence on the attrition problem in England and Wales. *European Journal of Criminology , 12*(3), 324–341.

Horeck, T. (2004). *Public rape: Representing violation in fiction and film*. London, UK: Routledge.

Horowitz, E. (2014). *Protecting our kids? How sex offender laws are failing us*. New York: Praeger.

Hust, S. J. T., Marett, E. G., Lei, M., Ren, C., & Ran, W. (2015). Law & Order, CSI, and NCIS: The association between exposure to crime drama franchises, rape myth acceptance, and sexual consent negotiation among college students. *Journal of Health Communication , 20*(12), 1–13.

Ivory, J. (2006). Still a man's game: Gender representation in online reviews of video games. *Mass Communication and Society , 9*(1), 103–114.

Jay, A. (2014, August 21). Independent inquiry into child sexual exploitation in Rotherham (1997–2013). Rotherham Metropolitan Borough Council. Retrieved March 22, 2015, from   http://www.rotherham.gov.uk/downloads/file/1407/independent_inquiry_cse_in_rotherham.

Jayachandran, J. (2014). Outrage, debate or silence: An analysis of reader comments and online rape. In N.-C. Schneider & F.-M. Titzmann (Eds.), *Studying youth, media and gender in post-liberalisation India: Focus on and beyond the "Delhi gang rape."* Berlin, Germany: Frank & Timme.

Jenkins, H. (2012, June 1). Superpowered fans. *Boom: A Journal of California, 2*(2), 22–36.

Jenkins, P. (2001). *Beyond tolerance: Child pornography online*. New York: New York University Press.

Jewkes, Y. (2011). *Media & crime*. London, UK: Sage, 2011.

Johnson, H., Fisher, B. S., & Jaquier, V. (2015). *Critical issues on violence against women: International perspectives and promising strategies*. New York: Routledge.

Karp, D. R. (2004). *Restorative justice on the college campus: Promoting student growth and responsibility, and reawakening the spirit of campus community*. Springfield, IL: Charles C. Thomas.

Kaveney, R. (2008). *Superheroes! Capes and crusaders in comics and films*. New York: I. B. Tauris.

Kelly, L. (2010). The (in)credible words of women: False allegations in European rape research. *Violence against Women , 16*(12), 1345–1355.

Kilpatrick, D., & Ruggiero, K. (2004). *Making sense of rape in America: Where do the numbers come from and what do they mean?* Charleston, SC: National Crime Victims Research and Treatment Center, Medical University of South Carolina.

Kimmel, M. (2015). *Angry white men: American masculinity at the end of an era*. New York: Nation Books.

Kimmel, M. (2008). *Guyland: The perilous world where boys become men*. New York: HarperCollins.

King, D., & Smith, C. L. (2012). *Men who hate women and women who kick their asses: Stieg Larsson's millennium trilogy in feminist perspective*. Nashville, TN: Vanderbilt University Press.

Kjaerum, M. (2014). *Violence against women: An EU-wide survey*. European Union Agency for Fundamental Rights, Luxembourg.

Koss, M. P. (1992). The under detection of rape: Methodological choices influence incidence estimates. *Journal of Social Issues , 48*(1), 61–75.

Koss, M. P. (2011). Hidden, unacknowledged, acquaintance, and date rape: Looking back, looking forward. *Psychology of Women Quarterly , 35*(2), 348–354.

Koss, M., Gidycz, C., & Wisniewski, N. (1985). Hidden rape: Incidence and prevalence of sexual aggression and victimization in a national sample of students in higher education (pp. 1–31). Presented at the Annual Convention of the American Psychological Association, Los Angeles, CA.

Krahé, B., & Tempkin, J. (2008). *Sexual assault and the justice gap: A question of attitude.* Portland, OR: Hart Publishing.

Krakauer, J. (2015). *Missoula: Rape and the justice system in a college town.* New York: Doubleday.

Krebs, C., Lindquist, C., Berzofsky, M., Shook-Sa, B., Peterson, K., Planty, M., & Stroop, J. (2016, January 19). *Campus climate survey validation study final technical report.* Washington, DC: Bureau of Justice. Retrieved February 16, 2016, from http://www.bjs.gov/content/pub/pdf/ccsvsftr.pdf.

Krebs, C. P., Lindquist, C. H., Warner, T. D., Fisher, B., & Martin, S. (2007). *The campus sexual assault study (CSA) final report: January 2005 through December 2007.* Washington, DC: National Institute of Justice.

Krug, E., Dahlberg, L., Mercy, J., Zwi, A., & Lozano, R. (Eds.). (2002). *World report on violence and health.* World Health Organization, Geneva.

Kruttschnitt, C., Kalsbeek, W., & House, C. (2014). *Estimating the incidence of rape and sexual assault: Panel on measuring rape and sexual assault in Bureau of Justice Statistics household surveys.* Washington, DC: National Academies Press.

Lancaster, R. (2011). *Sex panic and the punitive state.* Berkeley: University of California Press.

Lisak, D., Gardinier, L., Nicksa, S. C., & Cote, A. (2010). False allegations of sexual assault: An analysis of ten years of reported cases. *Violence against Women , 16*(12), 1318–1334.

Lisak, D., & Miller, P. (2009). Repeat rape and multiple offending among undetected rapists. *Violence and Victims , 17*(1), 73–84.

Lombardi, K., & Jones, K. (2010). *Sexual assault on campus: A frustrating search for justice.* Washington, DC: Center for Public Integrity. Retrieved May 16, 2016 from http://www.cloudfront-files-1.publicintegrity.org/documents/pdfs/Sexual%20Assault%20on%20Campus.pdf.

Lonsway, K. (1994) Rape myths: In review. *Psychology of Women Quarterly, 18*(2), 133–164.

Lonsway, K. (2010). Trying to move the elephant in the living room: Responding to the challenge of false rape reports. *Violence against Women, 16*(12), 1356–1371.

Lonsway, K., & Archambault, J. (2012). The "justice gap" for sexual assault cases: Future directions for research and reform. *Violence against Women, 18*(2), 145–168.

Lopes, P. (2006). Culture and stigma: Popular culture and the case of comic books. *Sociological Forum , 21*(3), 387–414.

Madrid, M. (2009). *The supergirls: Fashion, feminism, fantasy, and the history of comic book heroines.* Ashland, OR: Exterminating Angel Press.

Mantilla, K. (2015). *Gendertrolling: How misogyny went viral.* Santa Barbara, CA: Praeger.

Matthews, N. (2005). *Confronting rape: The feminist anti-rape movement and the state.* New York: Taylor & Francis.

McCormack, C., & Prostran, N. (2012). Asking for it. *International Feminist Journal of Politics , 14*(3), 410–414.

McGlynn, C. (2011). Feminism, rape and the search for justice. *Oxford Journal of Legal Studies , 31*(4), 825–842.

McRobbie, A., & Thornton, S. L. (1995). Rethinking "moral panic" for multi-mediated social worlds. *British Journal of Sociology, 46*(4), 559–574.

Miriam, K. (2012). Feminism, neoliberalism, and SlutWalk. *Feminist Studies, 38,* 262–266.

Morris, T. (2005). *Superheroes and philosophy: Truth, justice, and the Socratic way.* Peru, IL: Open Court.

Muldoon, S. D., Taylor, S. C., & Norma, C. (2015). The survivor master narrative in sexual assault. *Violence against Women, 22*(5), 565–587.

Nathan, D., & Snedeker, M. (2001). *Satan's silence: Ritual abuse and the making of a modern American witch hunt.* Lincoln, NE: Choice Press.

Nguyen, T. (2013). From SlutWalks to SuicideGirls: Feminist resistance in the third wave and postfeminist era. *WSQ: Women's Studies Quarterly , 41*(3), 157–172.

Nyberg, A. K. (1998). *Seal of approval: The history of the comics code.* Jackson: University Press of Mississippi.

O'Keefe, T. (2014). My body is my manifesto: SlutWalk, FEMEN and femmenist protest. *Feminist Review , 107*(107), 1–19.

O'Toole, M. E., Van Brunt, B., & Sokolow, B. A. (2015). Sexual assault on college and university campuses: Roundtable discussion. *Violence and Gender, 2*(1), 2–9.

Phillips, N. D., & Strobl, S. (2013). *Comic book crime: Truth, justice, and the American way.* New York: New York University Press.

Pierce, C., Carew, J., Pierce-Gonzalez, D., & Wills, D. (1978). An experiment in racism: TV commercials. *Television and Education , 44,* 62–82.

Pisters, P. (2003). *The matrix of visual culture: Working with Deleuze in film theory*. Stanford, CA: Stanford University Press.

Pittaro, M. (2007). Cyber stalking: An analysis of online harassment and intimidation. *International Journal of Cyber Criminology*, *1*(2), 180–197.

Planty, M., Langton, L., Krebs, C., Berzofsky, M., & Smiely-McDonald, H. (2013, March). *Female victims of sexual violence, 1994–2010*. Washington, DC: Bureau of Justice Statistics. Retrieved February 14, 2016, from http://www.bjs.gov/content/pub/pdf/fvsv9410.pdf.

Potter, J. (1999). *On media violence*. Thousand Oaks, CA: Sage.

Potter, J. (2003). *The 11 myths of media violence*. Thousand Oaks, CA: Sage.

Powell, A. (2015). Seeking rape justice: Formal and informal responses to sexual violence through technosocial counter-publics. *Theoretical Criminology*, *19*(4), 571–588, 1362480615576271.

Powell, A., & Henry, N. (2016). Policing technology-facilitated sexual violence against adult victims: Police and service sector perspectives. *Policing and Society*, 1439463.2016.1154964.

Powell, A., Henry, N., & Flynn, A. (Eds.). (2015). *Rape justice: Beyond the criminal law*. Hampshire, UK: Palgrave Macmillan.

Presdee, M. (2001). *Cultural criminology and the carnival of crime*. London, UK: Routledge.

Projansky, S. (2001). *Watching rape: Film and television in postfeminist culture*. New York: New York University Press.

Puri, J. (2006). Stakes and states: Sexual discourses from New Delhi. *Feminist Review*, *83*, 139–148.

Pustz, M. (1999). *Comic book culture: Fanboys and true believers*. Jackson: University Press of Mississippi.

Raphael, J. (2013). Rape is rape: How denial, distortion, and victim blaming are fueling a hidden acquaintance rape crisis. Chicago, IL: Chicago Review Press.

Reger, J. (2014). Micro-cohorts, feminist discourse, and the emergence of the Toronto SlutWalk. *Feminist Formations*, *26*(1), 49–69.

Richie, B. (2012). *Arrested justice: Black women, violence, and America's prison nation*. New York: New York University Press.

Robbins, T. (2002, September). Gender differences in comics. *Image & Narrative*, *4*.

Rumney, P. (2006). False allegations of rape. *Cambridge Law Journal*, *65*(1), 128.

Russell, D. (1998). Wife rape and the law. In M. E. Odem & J. Clay-Warner (Eds.), *Confronting rape and sexual assault* (pp. 71–81). Wilmington, DE: SR Books.

Russell-Brown, K. (2004). *Underground codes: Race, crime, and related fires*. New York: New York University Press.

Russell-Brown, K. (2009). *The color of crime* (2nd ed.). New York: New York University Press.

Sable, M. R., Danis, F., Mauzy, D. L., & Gallagher, S. K. (2006). Barriers to reporting sexual assault for women and men: Perspectives of college students. *Journal of American College Health*, *55*(3), 157–162.

Salter, M. (2013). Justice and revenge in online counter-publics: Emerging responses to sexual violence in the age of social media. *Crime, Media, Culture*, *9*(3), 225–242.

Saunders, C. L. (2012). The truth, the half-truth, and nothing like the truth: Reconceptualizing false allegations of rape. *British Journal of Criminology*, *52*(6), 1152–1171.

Schechter, H. (2005). *Savage pastimes: A cultural history of violent entertainment*. New York: St. Martin's.

Schulhofer, S. (1998). *Unwanted sex: The culture of intimidation and the failure of law*. Cambridge, MA: Harvard University Press.

Schwartz, M. D., & DeKeseredy, W. S. (1997). *Sexual assault on the college campus: The role of male peer support*. Thousand Oaks, CA: Sage.

Scott, S. (2013). Fangirls in refrigerators: The politics of (in)visibility in comic book culture. *Transformative Works and Cultures*, *13*.

Seidman, I., & Vickers, S. (2005). The second wave: An agenda for the next thirty years of rape law reform. *Suffolk University Law Reform*, *38*, 467–491.

Shaw, A. (2012). Do you identify as a gamer? Gender, race, sexuality, and gamer identity, *New Media & Society*, *14*(1), 28–44.

Shaw, A. (2014). *Gaming at the edge: Sexuality and gender at the margins of gamer culture*. Minneapolis, MN: University of Minnesota Press.

Sinozich, S., & Langton, L. (2014). *Rape and sexual assault victimization among college-age females, 1995–2013* (No. NCJ 248471). Washington, DC: Bureau of Justice Statistics.

Snipes, D. J., Calton, J. M., Green, B. A., Perrin, P. B., & Benotsch, E. G. (2015). Rape and Posttraumatic Stress Disorder (PTSD): Examining the mediating role of explicit sex-power beliefs for men versus women. *Journal of Interpersonal Violence*, 0886260515592618.

Sommers, C. H. (1994). *Who stole feminism? How women have betrayed women*. New York: Touchstone.

Spohn, C., & Holleran, D. (2001). Prosecuting sexual assault: A comparison of charging decisions in sexual assault cases involving strangers, acquaintances, and intimate partners. *Justice Quarterly*, 18(3), 651–688.

Spohn, C., & Tellis, K. (2012). The criminal justice system's response to sexual violence. *Violence against Women*, 18(2), 169–192.

Spohn, C., White, C., & Tellis, K. (2014). Unfounding sexual assault: Examining the decision to unfound and identifying false reports. *Law Society Review*, 48(1), 161–192.

Stuller, J. (2010). *Ink-stained amazons and cinematic warriors: Superwomen in modern mythology*. New York: I. B. Tauris.

Surette, R. (2010). *Media, crime, and criminal justice: Images, realities and policies* (4th ed.). Belmont, CA: Wadsworth.

Swartout, K. M., Koss, M. P., White, J. W., Thompson, M. P., Abbey, A., & Bellis, A. L. (2015). Trajectory analysis of the campus serial rapist assumption. *JAMA Pediatrics*, 169(12), 1148–1154.

Trend, D. (2007). *The myth of media violence: A critical introduction*. Malden, MA: Blackwell.

Van de Voorde, C. (2014). *Blurred lines: A critical interpretive ethnography of "rape culture," victim blaming, and women's rights in late modern India*. Paper presented at the meeting of the American Society of Criminology, San Francisco, CA.

Warshaw, R. (1994). *I never called it rape: The Ms. report on recognizing, fighting, and surviving date and acquaintance rape*. New York: Harper Perennial.

West, C., & Zimmerman, D. H. (1987). Doing gender. *Gender & Society*, 1(2), 125–151.

White House. (2014). *Not alone: The first report of the White House Task Force to Protect Students from Sexual Assault*. White House Task Force. Washington, DC.

Whittier, N. (2009). *The politics of child sexual abuse: Emotion, social movements, and the state*. New York: Oxford University Press.

Whittier, N. (2015). Where are the children? Theorizing the missing piece in gendered sexual violence. *Gender & Society* 30(1), 95–108.

Young, A. (2010). *The scene of violence: Cinema, crime, affect*. New York: Routledge.

Young, J. (2009). Moral panic: Its origins in resistance, ressentiment and the translation of fantasy into reality. *British Journal of Criminology*, 49, 4–16.

Yung, C. R. (2014). How to lie with rape statistics: America's hidden rape crisis. *Iowa Law Review*, 99, 1196–1256.

NOTES

1. RAPE CULTURE

1. Ralph Ellis and Sara Sidner, "Rampage in College Town Began with Stabbings," CNN.com, May 27, 2014, http://www.cnn.com/2014/05/24/justice/california-shooting-deaths/index.html; Ian Lovett and Adam Nagourney, "Video Rant, Then Deadly Rampage in California Town," *New York Times*, May 24, 2014, http://www.nytimes.com/2014/05/25/us/california-drive-by-shooting.html; Staff, "The Virgin Gunman's Chilling Video Rant in Full," *Daily Mail Online*, 2014, http://www.dailymail.co.uk/news/article-2638543/Mountains-skulls-rivers-blood-Elliot-Rodgers-chilling-video-rant-shot-movie.html.

2. Ann Hornaday, "In a Final Videotaped Message, a Sad Reflection of the Sexist Stories We So Often See on Screen," *Washington Post*, 2014, http://www.washingtonpost.com/lifestyle/style/in-a-final-videotaped-message-a-sad-reflection-of-the-sexist-stories-we-so-often-see-on-screen/2014/05/25/dec7e7ea-e40d-11e3-afc6-a1dd9407abcf_story.html.

3. Christopher Rosen, "Seth Rogen & Judd Apatow Denounce Washington Post Critic for Elliot Rodger Connection [UPDATE]," *Huffington Post*, 2014, http://www.huffingtonpost.com/2014/05/27/seth-rogen-washington-post-elliot-rodger_n_5396541.html?view=print&comm_ref=false.

4. Frank Bruni, "Full Screed Ahead," *New York Times*, 2014.

5. Hornaday, "In a Final Videotaped Message, a Sad Reflection of the Sexist Stories We So Often See on Screen."

6. Jess Zimmerman, "Not All Men: A Brief History of Every Dude's Favorite Argument," Time.com, April 28, 2014.

7. BBC News, "#YesAllWomen: California Rampage Sparks Twitter Response," BBC News, May 26, 2014, http://www.bbc.com/news/world-27565815; Rev. Dr. Susan Brooks Thistlethwaite, "Yes, There Is a War on Women and #YesAllWomen," *Huffington Post*, 2014, http://www.

huffingtonpost.com/rev-dr-susan-brooks-thistlethwaite/yes-there-is-a-war-on-wom_b_5397167.html?view=print&comm_ref=false.

8. Jessica Valenti, "#YesAllWomen Reveals the Constant Barrage of Sexism That Women Face," *Guardian*, 2014.

9. Reuters, "Miss Nevada Wins Miss USA Beauty Pageant," June 9, 2014, http://www.reuters.com/article/2014/06/09/us-usa-missusapageant-idUSKBN0EK08520140609; "Miss Nevada Interview Response," YouTube, June 9, 2014.

10. According to Krug et al., sexual violence is defined as, "any sexual act, attempt to obtain a sexual act, unwanted sexual comments or advances, or acts to traffic, or otherwise directed, against a person's sexuality using coercion, by any person regardless of their relationship to the victim, in any setting, including but not limited to home and work." E. Krug, L. Dahlberg, J. Mercy, A. Zwi, and R. Lozano, eds., *World Report on Violence and Health* (Geneva: World Health Organization, 2002).

11. Soopermexican, "Miss USA Winner Sparks Feminist Fury: Encourages Women to Avoid Being Victims through Self-Defense," June 2014, http://www.ijreview.com/2014/06/145792-feminists-spew-scorn-miss-usa-pageant-winner-self-defense-stance.

12. Ibid.

13. Katie Pavlich, "Feminists Freak Out over Miss Nevada Suggestion Women Learn Self Defense to Avoid Rape," June 9, 2014, http://townhall.com/tipsheet/katiepavlich/2014/06/09/feminists-freak-out-over-miss-nevada-suggestion-women-learn-self-defense-n1849213.

14. Rachel Burger, "3 Reasons Why Miss Nevada Is Not Perpetuating Rape Culture | Thoughts on Liberty," June 12, 2014, http://thoughtsonliberty.com/3-reasons-why-miss-nevada-is-not-perpetuating-rape-culture.

15. It is acknowledged that this democratizing function is somewhat limited in that not all individuals have access to participation. Rebecca Solnit, "Listen Up, Women Are Telling Their Story Now," *Guardian*, December 30, 2014, http://www.theguardian.com/news/2014/dec/30/-sp-rebecca-solnit-listen-up-women-are-telling-their-story-now; Kira Cochrane, "The Fourth Wave of Feminism: Meet the Rebel Women," *Guardian*, December 10, 2013, http://www.theguardian.com/world/2013/dec/10/fourth-wave-feminism-rebel-women.

16. Jeff Ferrell, Keith Hayward, and Jock Young, *Cultural Criminology: An Invitation* (Thousand Oaks, CA: Sage, 2008).

17. Alyssa Rosenberg, "The Culture Wars Are Back, and This Time, Everyone Can Win," *Washington Post*, October 8, 2014, http://www.washingtonpost.com/news/act-four/wp/2014/10/08/the-culture-wars-are-back-and-this-time-everyone-can-win.

18. Rosalyn Baxandall and Linda Gordon, *Dear Sisters: Dispatches from the Women's Liberation Movement* (New York: Basic Books, 2000); Maria Bevacqua, *Rape on the Public Agenda: Feminism and the Politics of Sexual Assault* (Boston, MA: Northeastern University Press, 2000); Nancy Matthews, *Con-*

fronting Rape: The Feminist Anti-Rape Movement and the State (New York: Taylor & Francis, 2005).

19. Susan Estrich, *Real Rape* (Cambridge, MA: Harvard University Press, 1988); Barbara Krahé and Jennifer Tempkin, *Sexual Assault and the Justice Gap: A Question of Attitude* (Portland, OR: Hart, 2008); Diana Russell, "Wife Rape and the Law," in *Confronting Rape and Sexual Assault*, ed. Mary E Odem and Jody Clay-Warner (Wilmington, DE: SR Books, 1998), 71–81.

20. Staff, "Women of the Year: Great Changes, New Chances, Tough Choices," Time.com, January 5, 1975, http://content.time.com/time/magazine/article/0,9171,947597,00.html.

21. Susan Brownmiller, *Against Our Will—Men, Women and Rape* (New York: Penguin, 1975), 5.

22. Bevacqua, *Rape on the Public Agenda: Feminism and the Politics of Sexual Assault*.

23. Nicola Gavey, *Just Sex? The Cultural Scaffolding of Rape* (New York: Routledge, 2005), 31; Noreen Connell and Cassandra Wilson, ed., *Rape: The First Sourcebook for Women by New York Radical Feminists* (New York: Plume, 1974).

24. For a historical analysis of the anti-rape movement, including how radical and liberal feminists approached the problem as well as the impact of race and class on the movement, see Maria Bevacqua's *Rape on the Public Agenda* and Nancy Matthews's *Confronting Rape: The Feminist Anti-Rape Movement and the State*.

25. Mike Presdee, *Cultural Criminology and the Carnival of Crime* (London, UK: Routledge, 2001), 11.

26. Matthews, *Confronting Rape: The Feminist Anti-Rape Movement and the State*, xii.

27. Ibid., 13.

28. Bevacqua, *Rape on the Public Agenda: Feminism and the Politics of Sexual Assault*, 195.

29. Ibid.; Susan Caringella, *Addressing Rape Reform in Law and Practice* (New York: Columbia University Press, 2009); Rose Corrigan, *Up Against a Wall: Rape Reform and the Failure of Success* (New York: New York University Press, 2013); Kathleen Daly and Brigitte Bouhours, "Rape and Attrition in the Legal Process: A Comparative Analysis of Five Countries," *Crime and Justice* 39, no. 1 (2010): 565–650; Beth Richie, *Arrested Justice: Black Women, Violence, and America's Prison Nation* (New York: New York University Press, 2012); Stephen Schulhofer, *Unwanted Sex: The Culture of Intimidation and the Failure of Law* (Cambridge, MA: Harvard University Press, 1998); Ilene Seidman and Susan Vickers, "The Second Wave: An Agenda for the Next Thirty Years of Rape Law Reform," *Suffolk University Law Reform* 38 (2005): 467–91.

30. Schulhofer, *Unwanted Sex: The Culture of Intimidation and the Failure of Law*, 39.

31. Renee Heberle, "Deconstructive Strategies and the Movement against Sexual Violence," *Hypatia* 11, no. 4 (1996): 63–76, 73.

32. Susan Griffin, "Rape: The All-American Crime," *Ramparts Magazine*, September 1971, 26–35.

33. Ibid., 27.

34. Joetta Carr, "The SlutWalk Movement: A Study in Transnational Feminist Activism," *Journal of Feminist Scholarship* 4 (2013): 24–38.

35. Margaret Lazarus and Renner Wunderlich, *Rape Culture* (USA: Cambridge Documentary Films, 1975/1983); Margaret Lazarus, "Rape Culture?," UserPages.UMBC.edu, March 15, 2000, http://userpages.umbc.edu/~korenman/wmst/rapeculture2.html.

36. *Rape Culture*, Cambridge Documentary Films, accessed May 4, 2014, http://www.cambridgedocumentaryfilms.org/filmsPages/rapeculture.html.

37. Ibid.

38. Dianne Herman, "The Rape Culture," in *Women: A Feminist Perspective*, 2nd ed. (Palo Alto, CA: Mayfield, 1979), 45.

39. Connell and Wilson, *Rape: The First Sourcebook for Women by New York Radical Feminists*.

40. Herman, "The Rape Culture," 43.

41. Gavey, *Just Sex? The Cultural Scaffolding of Rape*, 33.

42. Emilie Buchwald, Pamela R. Fletcher, and Martha Roth, *Transforming a Rape Culture* (Minneapolis, MN: Milkweed Editions, 2005), xiv.

43. Robin Field, "Rape Culture," in *Encyclopedia of Rape*, ed. M. Smith (Westport, CT: Greenwood, 2004).

44. Ibid.

45. Jaclyn Friedman and Jessica Valenti, *Yes Means Yes! Visions of Female Sexual Power and a World without Rape* (Berkeley, CA: Seal Press, 2008), 198.

46. Ibid.

47. Kathleen Daly, review of *Transforming a Rape Culture*, by Emilie Buchwald, Pamela R. Fletcher, and Martha Roth, *Signs* 20 (1995): 761.

48. Nickie D. Phillips, "Blurred Lines: The Concept of Rape Culture in Contemporary Society" (paper presented at the Academy of Criminal Justice Sciences Conference, Philadelphia, PA, 2014); Nickie D. Phillips and Emily Horowitz, "The Steubenville Rape Case: Sexual Assault, Social Media, and Vigilante Justice" (paper presented at the Society for the Study of Social Problems Conference, New York, 2013).

49. Ibid.

50. Heather MacDonald, "What Campus Rape Crisis?" *Los Angeles Times*, February 24, 2008, http://articles.latimes.com/2008/feb/24/opinion/op-mac_donald24; Katie Roiphe, "Date Rape's Other Victim," *New York Times*, June 13, 1993, http://www.nytimes.com/1993/06/13/magazine/date-rape-s-other-victim.html.

51. Phillips and Horowitz, "The Steubenville Rape Case: Sexual Assault, Social Media, and Vigilante Justice"; Phillips, "Blurred Lines: The Concept of Rape Culture in Contemporary Society"; Nickie D. Phillips, "Violent Attractions and Popular Culture" (paper presented at the International Crime, Media, and Popular Culture Studies Conference, Terre Haute, IN, 2014).

52. Google, "About Trends Graphs—Trends Help," Support.Google.com, 2014, https://support.google.com/trends/answer/4355164?hl=en.

53. *Social justice warrior* (SJW) is a derogatory term directed against those on the Internet who publicly call out misogyny and sexualized violence against women. According to the *Urban Dictionary*, the assumption is that the SJWs are insincere in their beliefs and only support positions in which they gain social status within their circles. Or, in other words, *SJW* is "a term that bigots use to insult people who don't like their bigotry." *Urban Dictionary*, "Social Justice Warrior," UrbanDictionary.com, September 30, 2014, http://www.urbandictionary.com/define.php?term=social%20justice%20warrior.

54. *Urban Dictionary*, "Rape Culture," UrbanDictionary.com, 2014, http://www.urbandictionary.com/define.php?term=Rape+Culture.

55. Libby Brooks, "We Must All Counter the Mood Music of Rape Culture," Guardian.co.uk, January 7, 2013, http://www.theguardian.com/commentisfree/2013/jan/07/rape-culture-libby-brooks.

56. Curtis Rush, "Cop Apologizes for 'Sluts' Remark at Law School," *The Star*, February 18, 2011, http://www.thestar.com/news/gta/2011/02/18/cop_apologizes_for_sluts_remark_at_law_school.html.

57. Ibid.

58. "Slut shaming" refers to derogatory comments or actions toward women who exhibit agency in their sexual behavior, including behaviors such as unapologetic premarital sex, non-monogamous sex, and dressing in what might be considered less-than-modest ways.

59. R. Contreras, "Cop's Rape Comment Sparks Wave of 'SlutWalks,'" NBCNew.com, May 6, 2011, accessed January 2, 2015, http://www.nbcnews.com/id/42927752/ns/us_news-life/t/cops-rape-comment-sparks-wave-slutwalks; E. Nussbaum, "How the Blogosphere Has Transformed the Feminist Conversation," NYMag.com, October 30, 2011, accessed January 2, 2015, http://nymag.com/news/features/feminist-blogs-2011-11/#print; Slut-Walk, "FAQs | SlutWalk Toronto," Slutwalktoronto.com, 2011, http://www.slutwalktoronto.com/about/faqs; Laura Stampler, "SlutWalks: Coming to a City Near You," *Huffington Post*, April 20, 2011, http://www.huffingtonpost.com/2011/04/20/slutwalk-united-states-city_n_851725.html.

60. Stampler, "SlutWalks: Coming to a City Near You."

61. Ray Filar, "SlutWalking Is Rooted in Riot Grrl Attitude | Ray Filar," Guardian.co.uk, May 9, 2011, http://www.theguardian.com/commentisfree/2011/may/09/slutwalk-feminist-activism.

62. Sierra Austin, Peggy Solic, Haley Swenson, and Gisell Jeter-Bennett, "Anita Hill Roundtable," *Frontiers: A Journal of Women Studies* 35, no. 3 (January 2014): 65–74.

63. Jennifer Baumgardner and Amy Richards, *Manifesta: Young Women, Feminism, and the Future*, 10th ed. (New York: Free Press, 2010).

64. Ibid.

65. Jennifer Baumgardner, *F ' Em!: Goo Goo, Gaga, and Some Thoughts on Balls* (Berkeley, CA: Free Press, 2011); Kira Cochrane, "The Fourth Wave of

Feminism: Meet the Rebel Women," *Guardian*, December 10, 2013, http://www.theguardian.com/world/2013/dec/10/fourth-wave-feminism-rebel-women.

66. Baumgardner, *F ' Em!: Goo Goo, Gaga, and Some Thoughts on Balls*.

67. Tara Murtha, "SlutWalk Philly Changes Protest Name to 'a March to End Rape Culture,'" *RH Reality Check*, September 26, 2013, http://rhrealitycheck.org/article/2013/09/26/slutwalk-philly-changes-protest-name-to-a-march-to-end-rape-culture.

68. Carr, "The SlutWalk Movement: A Study in Transnational Feminist Activism"; Theresa O'Keefe, "My Body Is My Manifesto: SlutWalk, FEMEN and Femmenist Protest," *Feminist Review* 107, no. 107 (June 6, 2014): 1–19; Clare McCormack and Nevena Prostran, "Asking for It," *International Feminist Journal of Politics* 14, no. 3 (September 2012): 410–14; Kathy Miriam, "Feminism, Neoliberalism, and SlutWalk," *Feminist Studies*, 38, no. 1 (2012); Tram Nguyen, "From SlutWalks to SuicideGirls: Feminist Resistance in the Third Wave and Postfeminist Era," *WSQ: Women's Studies Quarterly* 41, no. 3 (Fall/Winter 2013):157–72; Kayley Whalen, "SlutWalk and Sexual Empowerment," *American Humanist*, July 2011, http://americanhumanist.org/news/details/2011-07-slutwalk-and-sexual-empowerment.

69. O'Keefe, "My Body Is My Manifesto: SlutWalk, FEMEN and Femmenist Protest," 15.

70. Miriam, *Feminism, Neoliberalism, and SlutWalk*, 262.

71. Ibid., 263.

72. Ibid.

73. Nguyen, "From SlutWalks to SuicideGirls: Feminist Resistance in the Third Wave and Postfeminist Era," 160.

74. Miriam, *Feminism, Neoliberalism, and SlutWalk*; Nguyen, "From SlutWalks to SuicideGirls: Feminist Resistance in the Third Wave and Postfeminist Era"; Jo Reger, "Micro-Cohorts, Feminist Discourse, and the Emergence of the Toronto SlutWalk," *Feminist Formations* 26, no. 1 (2014): 49–69.

75. Nguyen, "From SlutWalks to SuicideGirls: Feminist Resistance in the Third Wave and Postfeminist Era."

76. Walter Moseley and Rae Gomes, "Ten Things to End Rape Culture," *The Nation*, February 4, 2013, http://www.thenation.com/article/172643/ten-things-end-rape-culture.

77. Sarah Ogden Trotta, "Five Ways Rape Culture Exists Unnoticed and Goes Unchecked in Our Everyday Life," *Everyday Feminism*, January 28, 2013, http://everydayfeminism.com/2013/01/five-ways-rape-culture-exists-unnoticed.

78. Buchwald, Fletcher, and Roth, *Transforming a Rape Culture*; Julia Kacmarek, "Rape Culture Is . . . ," *Huffington Post*, June 1, 2013. http://www.huffingtonpost.com/julia-kacmarek/rape-culture-is_b_3368577.html.

79. Friedman and Valenti, *Yes Means Yes! Visions of Female Sexual Power and a World without Rape*; Kate Harding, *Asking for It: The Alarming Rise of Rape Culture—and What We Can Do about It* (Boston, MA: Da Capo Lifelong Books, 2014).

80. Melissa McEwan, "Shakesville: Rape Culture 101," Shakesville.com, October 9, 2009, http://www.shakesville.com/2009/10/rape-culture-101.html.

81. Chloe Angyal, "Remember, 'Rape Culture' Is Just a Myth," *Feministing*, September 20, 2013, http://feministing.com/2013/09/20/remember-rape-culture-is-just-a-myth.

82. Sociological Images. "Rape Culture (Trigger Warning)," *Pinterest*, accessed November 28, 2014, https://www.pinterest.com/socimages/rape-culture-trigger-warning.

83. Chester Pierce, Jean Carew, Diane Pierce-Gonzalez, and Deborah Wills, "Pierce, an Experiment in Racism: TV Commercials," *Television and Education* 44 (1978): 62–82.

84. Ibid.

85. Richard Delgado and Jean Stefancic, *Critical Race Theory* (New York: New York University Press, 2001).

86. Katheryn Russell-Brown, *The Color of Crime*, 2nd ed. (New York: New York University Press, 2009).

87. Michelle Alexander, *The New Jim Crow: Mass Incarceration in the Age of Colorblindness* (New York: New Press, 2012); Katheryn Russell Brown, *Underground Codes: Race, Crime, and Related Fires* (New York: New York University Press, 2004).

88. microaggressions, "Microaggressions: Power, Privilege, and Everyday Life," Microaggressions.com, accessed April 3, 2015, http://www.microaggressions.com.

89. Tanzina Vega, "Students See Many Slights as Racial 'Microaggressions,'" *New York Times*, March 21, 2014, http://www.nytimes.com/2014/03/22/us/as-diversity-increases-slights-get-subtler-but-still-sting.html.

90. Jonathan Chait, "Not a Very P.C. Thing to Say," *New York Magazine*, January 27, 2015, http://nymag.com/daily/intelligencer/2015/01/not-a-very-pc-thing-to-say.html.

91. Paul Rowan Brian, "Unmasking the Mustachioed Menace of Microaggression," *The Federalist*, December 16, 2013, http://thefederalist.com/2013/12/16/unmasking-mustachioed-menace-microaggression.

92. Bradley Campbell and Jason Manning, "Microaggression and Moral Cultures," *Comparative Sociology* 13 (2014): 692–726.

93. Chris Hernandez, "'Microaggressions' and 'Trigger Warnings,' Meet Real Trauma," *The Federalist*, March 24, 2015, http://thefederalist.com/2015/03/24/microaggressions-and-trigger-warnings-meet-real-trauma.

94. Alec Torres, "You Could Be a Racist and Not Even Know It," *National Review*, February 3, 2014, http://www.nationalreview.com/corner/370227/you-could-be-a-racist-and-not-even-know-it-alec-torres.

95. Correspondent, "USA: Don't Tell Me to Smile—Stop Street Harassment," Stopstreetharassment.org, August 16, 2013, http://www.stopstreetharassment.org/2013/08/nosmile.

96. Tatyana Fazlalizadeh, "About—Stop Telling Women to Smile," Stoptellingwomentosmile.com, 2013, http://stoptellingwomentosmile.com/About; Alicia Maule, "'Stop Telling Women to Smile': Feminist Artist Goes Global,"

MSNBC, March 16, 2015, http://www.msnbc.com/msnbc/stop-telling-women-smile-feminist-artist-goes-global; Sarah Shearman, "Stop Telling Women to 'Smile': New York Street Art Says It How It Is," *Telegraph*, February 24, 2014, http://www.telegraph.co.uk/women/womens-life/10653324/Stop-telling-wom-en-to-smile-New-York-street-art-says-it-how-it-is.html; Tara Culp-Ressler, "'Stop Telling Women to Smile' Project Tackles Gender-Based Harassment with Street Art," *Think Progress*, September 12, 2013, http://thinkprogress.org/health/2013/09/12/2614421/stop-telling-women-smile.

97. Ana Cecilia Alvarez, "'Stop Telling Women to Smile:' Tatyana Fazlalizadeh's Viral Street Art," *Daily Beast*, August 1, 2013, http://www.thedailybeast.com/witw/articles/2013/08/01/tatyana-fazlalizadeh-s-street-art-project-stop-telling-women-to-smile.html.

98. Holly Yan, "Woman in New York Street Harassment Video: 'My Story Is Not Unique,'" CNN, October 30, 2014, http://www.cnn.com/2014/10/30/living/hollaback-10-hours-walking-in-nyc/index.html; Hermione Hoby, "The Woman in 10 Hours Walking in NYC: 'I Got People Wanting to Slit My Throat,'" *Guardian*, December 17, 2014, http://www.theguardian.com/lifeandstyle/2014/dec/17/the-woman-in-10-hours-walking-in-nyc-i-got-people-wanting-to-slit-my-throat; Corinne Lestch, "'Catcall' Video Actress Receiving Rape Threats," *Daily News*, October 29, 2014, http://www.nydailynews.com/new-york/aspiring-actress-catcall-video-receiving-rape-threats-exec-article-1.1991391; Hanna Rosin, "The Problem with That Catcalling Video: They Edited Out the White Guys," *Slate*, October 29, 2014, http://www.slate.com/blogs/xx_factor/2014/10/29/catcalling_video_hollaback_s_look_at_street_harassment_in_nyc_edited_out.html.

99. Kelsey McKinney, "The Woman Who Made a Video about Catcalling Is Already Getting Rape Threats," Vox.com, October 29, 2014, http://www.vox.com/2014/10/29/7088867/catcall-video-hollaback-rape-threats.

100. Ibid.

101. Sebastien Malo, "Jewish Woman in 108-Catcall Video Gets Rape Threats—Breaking News," *Forward*, October 30, 2014, http://forward.com/news/breaking-news/208238/jewish-woman-in-108-catcall-video-gets-rape-threat.

102. Harry Readhead, "'100 Catcalls' Video: Director Admits 'Editing Out White People,'" Metro.co.uk, October 30, 2014, http://metro.co.uk/2014/10/30/100-catcalls-video-director-admits-editing-out-white-people-4928473.

103. Hollaback, "Statement about Recent Street Harassment PSA," Ihollaback.org, October 30, 2014. http://www.ihollaback.org/blog/2014/10/30/statement-about-recent-street-harassment-psa.

104. Sally Kohn, "2015: Make It a Year of Solutions," CNN, December 31, 2014, http://www.cnn.com/2014/12/31/opinion/kohn-2015-solutions/index.html; Mark Seal, "The One Accuser Who May Finally Bring Bill Cosby Down for Good," *Vanity Fair*, July 6, 2016, http://www.vanityfair.com/news/2016/07/bill-cosby-andrea-constand-sexual-assault-trial.

105. Ann Friedman, "2014: The Year Everyone (Finally) Started Talking about Sexual Assault," *NYMag*, December 14, 2014, http://thecutso-

cial.nymag.com/thecut/2014/12/2014-the-year-we-listened-to-abuse-survivors.html.

106. White House, "Not Alone: The First Report of the White House Task Force to Protect Students from Sexual Assault," White House Task Force, Washington, DC, April 2014.

107. Ultimately, the Columbia University Graduate School of Journalism issued a scathing report detailing *Rolling Stone*'s failed journalism. Sheila Coronel, Steve Coll, and Derek Kravitz, "Rolling Stone and UVA: The Columbia University Graduate School of Journalism Report," *Columbia Journalism Review*, April 5, 2015, http://www.cjr.org/investigation/rolling_stone_ investigation.php.

108. Sabrina Erdely, "A Rape on Campus: A Brutal Assault and Struggle for Justice at UVA," *Rollingstone.com*, November 19, 2014, http://www.rollingstone.com/culture/features/a-rape-on-campus-20141119.

109. Jim Byset, "2014: Rape Culture on the Ropes," *A Voice for Men*, December 31, 2014, http://www.avoiceformen.com/mens-rights/false-rape-culture/2014-rape-culture-on-the-ropes.

110. Caroline Kitchens, "It's Time to End 'Rape Culture' Hysteria," Time.com, March 20, 2014, http://time.com/30545/its-time-to-end-rape-culture-hysteria.

111. Mona Charen, "Who Really Created the 'Rape Culture'?," *National Review*, May 9, 2014, http://www.nationalreview.com/article/377565/who-really-created-rape-culture-mona-charen; Kitchens, "It's Time to End 'Rape Culture' Hysteria."

112. Jay Ambrose, "Jay Ambrose Commentary: Campus Rape Is a Problem, but It's Been Exaggerated," *Columbus Dispatch*, August 8, 2014, http://www.dispatch.com/content/stories/editorials/2014/08/08/campus-rape-is-a-problem-but-its-been-exaggerated.html.

113. David Garland, "On the Concept of Moral Panic," *Crime, Media, Culture* 4, no. 1 (April 1, 2008): 9–30; Erich Goode and Ben-Yahuda Nachman, *Moral Panics: The Social Construction of Deviance*, 2nd ed. (West Sussex, UK: Blackwell, 2009); Angela McRobbie and Sarah L. Thornton, "Rethinking 'Moral Panic' for Multi-Mediated Social Worlds," *British Journal of Sociology* 46, no. 4 (December 1, 1995): 559–74.

114. Sommers has been railing against the concept of rape culture since at least the mid-1990s. Christina Hoff Sommers, "Researching the 'Rape Culture' of America," D.UMN.edu, 1995, http://www.d.umn.edu/cla/faculty/jhamlin/3925/Readings/RapeCultureSummers.pdf;Christina Hoff Sommers, "Rape Culture Panic Is Not the Answer," YouTube, May 19, 2014, http://www.youtube.com/watch?v=FKgrYVtYSCk. On linking rape complaints to false memory syndrome, see also Joanne Belknap, "Rape: Too Hard to Report and Too Easy to Discredit Victims," *Violence against Women* 16, no. 12 (December 1, 2010): 1335–44.

115. Christina Hoff Summers, "Rape Culture Is a 'Panic Where Paranoia, Censorship, and False Accusations Flourish,'" Time.com, May 15, 2014, http://time.com/100091/campus-sexual-assault-christina-hoff-sommers.

116. Judith Levine, "Feminism Can Handle the Truth," Bostonreview.net, December 6, 2014, http://bostonreview.net/blog/judith-levine-uva-rape-denial-ism-rolling-stone-hoax-feminism.

117. Matt Walsh, "Rape Culture Doesn't Exist and There Is No Rape Epidemic," *The Blaze*, December 9, 2014, http://www.theblaze.com/contributions/rape-culture-doesnt-exist-and-there-is-no-rape-epidemic; Barbara Kay, "Barbara Kay: Rape Culture Proofiness Feeds Moral Panic over Non-Existent Epidemic," *National Post*, January 19, 2015, http://news.nationalpost.com/2015/01/19/barbara-kay-rape-culture-proofiness-feeds-moral-panic-over-non-existent-epidemic.

118. Chris Atmore, "Victims, Backlash, and Radical Feminist Theory (or, the Morning after They Stole Feminism's Fire)," in *New Versions of Victims: Feminists Struggle with the Concept*, ed. Sharon Lamb (New York: New York University Press, 1999); Christina Hoff Sommers, *Who Stole Feminism? How Women Have Betrayed Women* (New York: Touchstone, 1994); Gavey, *Just Sex? The Cultural Scaffolding of Rape*; Neil Gilbert, "Realities and Mythologies of Rape," *Society* 35, no. 2 (1998): 356–62; Jody Raphael, *Rape Is Rape* (Chicago, IL: Chicago Review Press, 2013).

119. Maria Bevacqua, *Rape on the Public Agenda: Feminism and the Politics of Sexual Assault* (Boston, MA: Northeastern University Press, 2000), 183.

120. Meenakshi Ganguly, Aruna Kashyap, and Tejshree Thapa, "Silenced and Forgotten: Survivors of Nepal's Conflict-Era Sexual Violence," Human Rights Watch, September 2014, http://www.hrw.org/sites/default/files/reports/nepal0914_ForUpload_0.pdf; Claudia Garcia-Moreno et al., "Global and Regional Estimates of Violence against Women: Prevalence and Health Effects of Intimate Partner Violence and Non-Partner Sexual Violence," ed. Penny Howes, *World Health Organization*, 2013; Charu Lata Hogg, "'We Will Teach You a Lesson,'" HRW.org, February 2013; Amnesty International, "Rape Victims Worldwide Denied Justice and Dignity," Amnesty International, March 8, 2010, http://www.amnesty.org/en/news-and-updates/report/rape-victims-worldwide-denied-justice-and-dignity-2010-03-08; Morten Kjaerum, *Violence against Women: An EU-Wide Survey*, European Union Agency for Fundamental Rights, Luxembourg, Belgium, 2014; Samer Muscati and Tirana Hassan, "'Here, Rape Is Normal': A Five-Point Plan to Curtail Sexual Violence in Somalia," HRW.org, February 2014; UNIFEM, "The Facts: Violence against Women & Millennium Developmental Goals," Endvawnow.org, 2010, http://www.endvawnow.org/uploads/browser/files/EVAW_FactSheet_KM_2010EN.pdf.

121. Ibid.

122. Hogg, "'We Will Teach You a Lesson'"; Muscati and Hassan, "'Here, Rape Is Normal': A Five-Point Plan to Curtail Sexual Violence in Somalia"; Ganguly, Kashyap, and Thapa, "Silenced and Forgotten: Survivors of Nepal's Conflict-Era Sexual Violence."

123. Garcia-Moreno et al., "Global and Regional Estimates of Violence against Women: Prevalence and Health Effects of Intimate Partner Violence

and Non-Partner Sexual Violence"; Claudia Garcia-Moreno et al., "Violence against Women and Girls," *Lancet* 385, no. 9978 (November 21, 2014): 1–11.

124. Garcia-Moreno et al., "Global and Regional Estimates of Violence against Women: Prevalence and Health Effects of Intimate Partner Violence and Non-Partner Sexual Violence," 20.

125. Dean Kilpatrick and Kenneth Ruggiero, "Making Sense of Rape in America: Where Do the Numbers Come From and What Do They Mean?," National Crime Victims Research and Treatment Center, Medical University of South Carolina, Charleston, VA, 2004.

126. Atmore, "Victims, Backlash, and Radical Feminist Theory (or, the Morning After They Stole Feminism's Fire)"; Mary Koss, Christine Gidycz, and Nadine Wisniewski, "Hidden Rape: Incidence and Prevalence of Sexual Aggression and Victimization in a National Sample of Students in Higher Education" (paper presented at the Annual Convention of the American Psychological Association, Los Angeles, CA, 1985), 1–31; Raphael, *Rape Is Rape*; Gavey, *Just Sex? The Cultural Scaffolding of Rape*.

127. Kilpatrick and Ruggiero, "Making Sense of Rape in America: Where Do the Numbers Come From and What Do They Mean?"; Candace Kruttschnitt, William Kalsbeek, and Carole House, "Estimating the Incidence of Rape and Sexual Assault," Panel on Measuring Rape and Sexual Assault in Bureau of Justice Statistics Household Surveys, Washington, DC, National Academies Press, 2014.

128. Kilpatrick and Ruggiero, "Making Sense of Rape in America: Where Do the Numbers Come From and What Do They Mean?" For a history on the evolution of the legal definition of rape, see E. Freedman, *Redefining Rape* (Cambridge, MA: Harvard University Press, 2013). For a comparison of methodology around the study of sexual violence among official statistics, see Kruttschnitt, Kalsbeek, and House, "Estimating the Incidence of Rape and Sexual Assault," and Bonnie S. Fisher, Leah Daigle, and Francis Cullen, *Unsafe in the Ivory Tower: The Sexual Victimization of College Women* (Thousand Oaks, CA: Sage, 2010).

129. Kruttschnitt, Kalsbeek, and House, "Estimating the Incidence of Rape and Sexual Assault"; Garcia-Moreno et al., "Global and Regional Estimates of Violence against Women: Prevalence and Health Effects of Intimate Partner Violence and Non-Partner Sexual Violence"; Holly Johnson, Bonnie S. Fisher, and Veronique Jaquier, *Critical Issues on Violence against Women: International Perspectives and Promising Strategies* (New York: Routledge, 2015); Raphael, *Rape Is Rape*.

130. The study's definition of sexual violence "includes completed, attempted, or threatened rape or sexual assault." The report used the following definitions: "Rape is the unlawful penetration of a person against the will of the victim, with use or threatened use of force, or attempting such an act. Rape includes psychological coercion and physical force, and forced sexual intercourse means vaginal, anal, or oral penetration by the offender. Rape also includes incidents where penetration is from a foreign object (e.g., a bottle), victimizations against male and female victims, and both heterosexual and

homosexual rape. Attempted rape includes verbal threats of rape. Sexual assault is defined across a wide range of victimizations, separate from rape or attempted rape. These crimes include attacks or attempted attacks generally involving unwanted sexual contact between a victim and offender. Sexual assault may or may not involve force and includes grabbing or fondling. Sexual assault also includes verbal threats." Michael Planty, Lynn Langton, Christopher Krebs, Marcus Berzofsky, and Hope Smiley-McDonald, "Female Victims of Sexual Violence, 1994–2010," Bureau of Justice Statistics, March 2013, http://www.bjs.gov/content/pub/pdf/fvsv9410.pdf.

131. Their report, *Estimating the Incidence of Rape and Sexual Assault*, published in 2014, points out four major obstacles that impact the accuracy of the NCVS:

> (1) a sample design that is inefficient for measuring these low-incidence events, (2) the context of "crime" that defines the survey, (3) a lack of privacy for respondents in completing the survey, and (4) the use of words with ambiguous meaning for key measures in the questionnaire.

Kruttschnitt, Kalsbeek, and House, "Estimating the Incidence of Rape and Sexual Assault," 161.

132. FBI, "Crime in the United States," FBI.gov, 2014, https://www.fbi.gov/about-us/cjis/ucr/crime-in-the-u.s/2014/crime-in-the-u.s.-2014/tables/table-1/table_1_crime_in_the_united_states_by_volume_and_rate_per_100000_inhabitants_1995-2014.xls.

133. Kruttschnitt, Kalsbeek, and House, "Estimating the Incidence of Rape and Sexual Assault."

134. RAINN, "FBI Changes Its Definition of Rape," RAINN.org, January 2012, https://rainn.org/news-room/fbi-changes-rape-definition.

135. John Eterno and Eli Silverman, *The Crime Numbers Game: Management by Manipulation* (Boca Raton, FL: CRC Press, 2012); Raphael, *Rape Is Rape*.

136. Graham Rayman, "NYPD Forced to Apologize Publicly to Rape Victim for Downgrading Her Attack," *Village Voice*, May 10, 2010, http://www.villagevoice.com/news/nypd-forced-to-apologize-publicly-to-rape-victim-for-downgrading-her-attack-6723133.

137. Eterno and Silverman, *The Crime Numbers Game: Management by Manipulation*; Graham Rayman, "The NYPD Tapes Confirmed," *Village Voice*, March 7, 2012, http://www.villagevoice.com/2012-03-07/news/the-nypd-tapes-confirmed.

138. John Eterno and Eli Silverman, "Unveiling Compstat," Unveiling-NYPDCompstat.Blogspot.com, March 1, 2010. http://unveilingnypdcompstat.blogspot.com/2010_03_01_archive.html; Sara Darehshori, "Capitol Offense: Police Mishandling of Sexual Assault Cases in the District of Columbia," Human Rights Watch, January 2013.

139. Raphael, *Rape Is Rape*.

140. Matthew Breiding, Sharon Smith, Kathleen Basile, Mikel Walters, Jieru Chen, and Melissa Merrick, "Prevalence and Characteristics of Sexual Violence, Stalking, and Intimate Partner Violence Victimization—National Intimate Partner and Sexual Violence Survey, United States, 2011," CDC.gov (Atlanta, GA, September 5, 2014).

141. Ibid. The report specified sexual violence as

> rape (completed or attempted forced penetration or alcohol- or drug-facilitated penetration) and sexual violence other than rape, including being made to penetrate a perpetrator, sexual coercion (nonphysically pressured unwanted penetration), unwanted sexual contact (e.g., kissing or fondling), and noncontact unwanted sexual experiences (e.g., being flashed or forced to view sexually explicit media).

Breiding et al., "Prevalence and Characteristics of Sexual Violence, Stalking, and Intimate Partner Violence Victimization—National Intimate Partner and Sexual Violence Survey, United States, 2011."

142. Alexandrea Boguhm, "Conservative Media Jump on Sexual Assault Truther Bandwagon, Cry Foul on White House Report," Media Matters for America, April 30, 2014, http://mediamatters.org/research/2014/04/30/conservative-media-jump-on-sexual-assault-truth/199098; Glenn Reynolds, "A Rape Epidemic—by Women?" USAToday.com, September 23, 2014, http://www.usatoday.com/story/opinion/2014/09/22/rape-cdc-numbers-misleading-definition-date-forced-sexual-assault-column/16007089; Staff, "CDC Finds That 1 in 5 Women Are Raped; Men's Rights Activists Cry 'Rape Hysteria,'" Ravishly.com, September 9, 2014, http://www.ravishly.com/2014/09/09/cdc-rape-statistics-mens-rights-activists-false-accusations; Yuval Levental, "An Inquiry into the CDC's 1 in 5 Rape Figure," A Voice for Men, September 23, 2014, http://www.avoiceformen.com/mens-rights/false-rape-culture/an-inquiry-into-the-cdcs-1-in-5-rape-figure.

143. Cathy Young, "The CDC's Rape Numbers Are Misleading," Time.com, September 17, 2014, http://time.com/3393442/cdc-rape-numbers.

144. Caroline Heldman and Baillee Brown, "The Second Wave of Backlash against Anti-Rape Activism," MSmagazine.com, August 19, 2014.

145. Raphael, *Rape Is Rape*; Gavey, *Just Sex? The Cultural Scaffolding of Rape*; Bevacqua, *Rape on the Public Agenda: Feminism and the Politics of Sexual Assault*; Martin D. Schwartz and Walter S. DeKeseredy, *Sexual Assault on the College Campus: The Role of Male Peer Support* (Thousand Oaks, CA: Sage, 1997).

2. THE MAINSTREAMING OF RAPE CULTURE

1. Tara Culp-Ressler, "Thousands Protest Rape Culture in New Zealand, Saying It's Become 'a National Health Crisis,'" *Think Progress*, November 18,

2013, http://thinkprogress.org/health/2013/11/18/2957101/rape-culture-protest-zealand; Sophie Ryan, "Roast Busters Case: 'Where Was the Respect?'—Police—National—NZ Herald News," *New Zealand Herald*, October 29, 2014, http://www.nzherald.co.nz/nz/news/article.cfm?c_id=1&objectid=11350007; Ian Steward and Kelly Dennett, "Roast Busters: Horrific New Zealand Gang Rape Case Leads to Zero Charges," *Daily Life*, October 30, 2014, http://www.dailylife.com.au/news-and-views/news-features/roast-busters-horrific-new-zealand-gang-rape-case-leads-to-zero-charges-20141030-3j64i.html; Annie Lu, "Roast Busters Scandal Investigation: No Charges Filed," *International Business Times*, October 30, 2014, http://au.ibtimes.com/articles/571200/20141030/roast-busters-charges-auckland-new-zealand-gang.htm; Brendan Manning, "Roast Busters: Protests Today Aim to 'Bust Rape Culture'—National—NZ Herald News," *New Zealand Herald*, November 16, 2013, http://www.nzherald.co.nz/nz/news/article.cfm?c_id=1&objectid=11158233; Hilary Whiteman, "New Zealand Outrage Over 'Roast Busters' Online Boasts of Teen Rape—CNN.com," CNN, November 6, 2013, http://www.cnn.com/2013/11/05/world/asia/new-zealand-roast-busters-teen-sex/index.html; "'Teen Rape Club' Prompts Worldwide Outrage," *Huffington Post*, November 6, 2013, http://www.huffingtonpost.com/2013/11/06/roast-busters-new-zealand-teen-rape-club_n_4221597.html.

2. Culp-Ressler, "Thousands Protest Rape Culture in New Zealand, Saying It's Become 'a National Health Crisis'"; Katie Kenny, "Anger over Rape Culture," Stuff.co.nz, November 16, 2013, http://www.stuff.co.nz/national/crime/9408076/Thousands-march-in-Roast-Busters-protests; Post, "'Teen Rape Club' Prompts Worldwide Outrage."

3. Manning, "Roast Busters: Protests Today Aim to 'Bust Rape Culture'—National—NZ Herald News."

4. Sam Boyer, "Roast Busters: Women Chain Themselves to Police Station in Protest," *New Zealand Herald*, November 6, 2014, http://www.nzherald.co.nz/nz/news/article.cfm?c_id=1&objectid=11354347.

5. Ibid.; Lu, "Roast Busters Scandal Investigation: No Charges Filed"; Steward and Dennett, "Roast Busters: Horrific New Zealand Gang Rape Case Leads to Zero Charges."

6. V. Belair-Gagnon, S. Mishra, and C. Agur, "Reconstructing the Indian Public Sphere: Newswork and Social Media in the Delhi Gang Rape Case," *Journalism* 15, no. 8 (October 9, 2014): 1059–75.

7. Lauren Wolfe, "End Culture of Rape in 2013," CNN, January 3, 2013, http://www.cnn.com/2013/01/01/opinion/wolfe-end-rape-in-2013/index.html.

8. Heather Timmons and Sruthi Gottipati, "Victim of Gang Rape in India Dies at Hospital in Singapore," *New York Times*, December 28, 2012, http://www.nytimes.com/2012/12/29/world/asia/condition-worsens-for-victim-of-gang-rape-in-india.html.

9. Leslee Udwin, *India's Daughter*, documentary, vol. 62 (UK/India, 2015).

10. Nils Christie, "Ideal Victim," in *From Crime Policy to Victim Policy*, ed. Ezzat A. Fattah (London, UK: Macmillan, 1986), 17–30.

11. Jason Burke, "Delhi Rape: How India's Other Half Lives | World News," Guardian.co.uk, September 10, 2013, http://www.theguardian.com/world/2013/sep/10/delhi-gang-rape-india-women.

12. Daniel Drache and Jennifer Velagic, "A Report on Sexual Violence Journalism in Four Leading Indian English Language Publications before and after the Delhi Bus Rape" (paper presented at ICA Pre-Conference Workshop on South Asian Communication Scholarship, June 10, 2013), 1–25.

13. Reuters, "Last of Suspects in Mumbai Brutal Gang Rape of Photojournalist Arrested," *New York Daily News*, August 25, 2013, http://www.nydailynews.com/news/world/suspects-mumbai-brutal-gang-rape-photojournalist-arrested-article-1.1436483; Leeza Mangaldas, "Misogyny in India: We Are All Guilty," CNN, January 3, 2013, http://www.cnn.com/2012/12/30/world/asia/misogyny-india/index.html; Isha Sharma, "The Video That Brings Out the 'Indian Rape Culture,'" *Times of India*, September 29, 2013, http://timesofindia.indiatimes.com/life-style/people/The-video-that-brings-out-the-Indian-Rape-Culture/articleshow/23214251.cms.

14. Sally Kohn, "Is India the Rape Capital of the World?" *More*, April 8, 2013, http://www.more.com/news/india-rape-capital-world.

15. Olga Khazan and Rama Lakshmi, "10 Reasons Why India Has a Sexual Violence Problem," December 29, 2012, http://www.washingtonpost.com/blogs/worldviews/wp/2012/12/29/india-rape-victim-dies-sexual-violence-proble; Jyoti Puri, "Stakes and States: Sexual Discourses from New Delhi," *Feminist Review* 83 (July 5, 2006): 139–48.

16. Karuna Madan, "Change of Mindset Can End Rape Culture in India," Gulfnews.com, June 13, 2014, http://gulfnews.com/news/world/india/change-of-mindset-can-end-rape-culture-in-india-1.1346695.

17. Timmons and Gottipati, "Victim of Gang Rape in India Dies at Hospital in Singapore."

18. Jason Burke, "India to Name and Shame Sex Offenders as Rape Protests Grow," Guardian.co.uk, December 28, 2012, http://www.theguardian.com/world/2012/dec/28/india-name-shame-sex-offenders.

19. Meenakshi Gigi Durham, "Scene of the Crime," *Feminist Media Studies* 15, no. 2 (May 14, 2014): 185.

20. Ibid., 184.

21. Sumnima Udas, "Covering the Rape Case That Changed India—CNN.com," CNN, December 15, 2013, http://www.cnn.com/2013/12/04/world/asia/india-rape-problem-udas/index.html.

22. Madan, "Change of Mindset Can End Rape Culture in India."

23. Christopher Zara, "Delhi Rape Reports Skyrocket in 2015 amid 'India's Daughter' Premiere: Report," *International Business Times*, March 7, 2015, http://www.ibtimes.com/delhi-rape-reports-skyrocket-2015-amid-indias-daughter-premiere-report-1839794.

24. Mark Magnier, "India Gang Rape Called 'Tipping Point' That Set Off Protests," *Los Angeles Times*, January 14, 2013, http://articles.latimes.com/2013/jan/14/world/la-fg-india-rape-20130115; Timmons and Gottipati, "Victim of Gang Rape in India Dies at Hospital in Singapore."

25. John Xenakis, "World View: Gang Rape Victim Sparks Nationwide Protests in India," Breitbart.com, December 29, 2012, http://www.breitbart.com/national-security/2012/12/29/29-dec-12-world-view-gang-raped-victim-sparks-nationwide-protests-in-india.

26. Cecile Van de Voorde, "Blurred Lines: A Critical Interpretive Ethnography of 'Rape Culture,' Victim Blaming, and Women's Rights in Late Modern India" (American Society of Criminology, San Francisco, CA, 2014); Shenali Waduge, "Rape in India: Why Are There No Mass Protests for Raped Dalit Women?," *Eurasia Review*, December 28, 2012, http://www.eurasiareview.com/28122012-rape-in-india-why-are-there-no-mass-protests-for-raped-dalit-women-oped.

27. Mandakini Gahlot, "Despite Tougher Laws, India Can't Shake Rape Culture," USAToday.com, June 14, 2014, http://www.usatoday.com/story/news/world/2014/06/14/india-rape/10003071.

28. Kohn, "Is India the Rape Capital of the World?"

29. Tara Atluri, "The Young and the Restless: Gender, 'Youth,' and the Delhi Gang Rape Case of 2012," *Sikh Formations* 9, no. 3 (December 2013): 361–79.

30. Jesna Jayachandran, "Outrage, Debate or Silence: An Analysis of Reader Comments and Online Rape," in *Studying Youth, Media and Gender in Post-Liberalisation India: Focus on and Beyond the "Delhi Gang Rape,"* ed. Nadja-Christina Schneider and Fritzi-Marie Titzmann (Berlin: Frank & Timme, 2014), 54.

31. Larisa Epatko, "Banned Documentary Examines Brutal Delhi Gang Rape," PBS, March 11, 2015, http://www.pbs.org/newshour/rundown/documentary-india-gang-rape; Reuters, "Interview with Mukesh Singh, India Gang-Rapist, Gets Documentary Banned," CBCNews, March 4, 2015, http://www.cbc.ca/1.2981178.

32. Udwin, *India's Daughter*.

33. Ibid.

34. Laura Bates, "The Protests Sparked by Gang-Rape in India Aren't the Beginning and They Won't Be the End," *Independent*, January 9, 2013, http://www.independent.co.uk/voices/comment/the-protests-sparked-by-gangrape-in-india-arent-the-beginning-and-they-wont-be-the-end-8440901.html; Udwin, *India's Daughter*.

35. Nilanjana Roy, "Viewpoints: Has Delhi Rape Case Changed India?," BBC News, September 10, 2013, http://www.bbc.com/news/world-asia-india-24012424.

36. Ruchira Gupta, "Victims Blamed in India's Rape Culture," CNN, August 28, 2013, http://www.cnn.com/2013/08/27/opinion/gupta-india-rape-culture/index.html.

37. Burke, "India to Name and Shame Sex Offenders as Rape Protests Grow"; Rashmee Roshan Lall, "Gang Rape Verdict Exposes the Uneven Nature of Indian Justice," *The National*, September 16, 2013, http://www.thenational.ae/gang-rape-verdict-exposes-the-uneven-nature-of-indian-justice.

38. AFP, "Rape 'Sometimes Right,' Says Indian Minister Babulal Gaur," *Sydney Morning Herald*, June 6, 2014, http://www.smh.com.au/world/rape-sometimes-right-says-indian-minister-babulal-gaur-20140605-zrzat.html.

39. Gahlot, "Despite Tougher Laws, India Can't Shake Rape Culture."

40. Gupta, "Victims Blamed in India's Rape Culture."

41. Atluri, "The Young and the Restless: Gender, 'Youth,' and the Delhi Gang Rape Case of 2012."

42. Ibid., 374.

43. Ibid., 371.

44. Durham, "Scene of the Crime," 175.

45. Ibid., 185.

46. Ibid., 185.

47. Helen Benedict, "Covering Rape Responsibly," *Women under Siege*, February 1, 2013, http://www.womenundersiegeproject.org/blog/entry/covering-rape-responsibly.

48. Kohn, "Is India the Rape Capital of the World?"; Jean Mackenzie, "Steubenville vs. Delhi: A Tale of Two Coverages," *Salon*, March 20, 2013, http://www.salon.com/2013/03/20/steubenville_vs_delhi_a_tale_of_two_coverages_partner.

49. Shannon Corregan, "Rape Culture Isn't Just India's Problem," *Times Colonist*, January 25, 2013, http://www.canada.com/story.html?id=72ddb22f-fd93-463d-b2ee-cea4b0475d33.

50. Afsun Qureshi, "Afsun Qureshi: How India's Rape Culture Came to Canada," *National Post*, January 3, 2013, http://news.nationalpost.com/2013/01/03/afsun-qureshi-how-indias-rape-culture-came-to-canada.

51. Ibid.

52. J. S. Verma, Seth Leila, and Gopal Subramanium, "Justice Verma Committee Report: Report of the Committee on Amendments to Criminal Law," Prsindia.org, January 23, 2013, 414, http://www.prsindia.org/parliamenttrack/report-summaries/justice-verma-committee-report-summary-2628.

53. Kristin Bumiller, *In an Abusive State: How Neoliberalism Appropriated the Feminist Movement against Sexual Violence* (Durham, NC: Duke University Press, 2008); Victoria Law, "Against Carceral Feminism," Jacobinmag.com, October 17, 2014, https://www.jacobinmag.com/2014/10/against-carceral-feminism; Clare McGlynn, "Feminism, Rape and the Search for Justice," *Oxford Journal of Legal Studies* 31, no. 4 (December 1, 2011): 825–42; Anastasia Powell, "Seeking Rape Justice: Formal and Informal Responses to Sexual Violence through Technosocial Counter-Publics," *Theoretical Criminology*, March 19, 2015, 1–18.

54. Staff, "New Anti-Rape Law Comes into Force," *Times of India*, April 3, 2013, http://timesofindia.indiatimes.com/india/New-anti-rape-law-comes-into-force/articleshow/19359543.cms.

55. "2 Teens to Plead Not Guilty in Steubenville Death Threat Case," CBS Pittsburgh, March 27, 2013, http://pittsburgh.cbslocal.com/2013/03/27/2-teens-to-plead-not-guilty-in-steubenville-death-threat-case; Laura Collins, "Teen Girls 'Who Made Death Threats to Steubenville Rape Victim' Are Held

in Custody 'to Protect Victim from Immediate Harm,'" *Daily Mail*, May 27, 2015, http://www.dailymail.co.uk/news/article-2295853/Teen-girls-death-threats-Steubenville-rape-victim-held-custody-protect-victim-immediate-harm.html.

56. Yvonne Jewkes, *Media & Crime* (London, UK: Sage, 2011).

57. Amy Goodman, "Hacker Group Anonymous Leaks Chilling Video in Case of Alleged Steubenville Rape, Cover-Up," DemocracyNow.org, January 7, 2013, http://www.democracynow.org/2013/1/7/hacker_group_anonymous_leaks_chilling_video.

58. Ariel Levy, "Trial by Twitter," *New Yorker*, August 5, 2013, http://www.newyorker.com/magazine/2013/08/05/trial-by-twitter.

59. Michael Pearson, "Phone Records the Focus in Steubenville Rape Trial," Fox8, March 14, 2013, http://fox8.com/2013/03/14/another-marathon-day-in-steubenville-rape-trial.

60. Laura Collins, "Teenage Boy Ordered by Judge to Tell Court of the Moment He Filmed 'Vomiting, Drunk Girl, 16, Being Touched Intimately on Backseat of Car by Ohio Footballer Accused of Raping Her,'" *Daily Mail*, March 15, 2013, http://www.dailymail.co.uk/news/article-2293965/Teenage-boy-forced-tell-court-moment-filmed-vomiting-drunk-girl-16-touched-inti-mately-Ohio-footballer-accused-raping-her.html; Michael O'Keefe, "Team-mate of Steubenville Football Players Testifies He Taped Sex Act," *New York Daily News*, March 15, 2013, http://www.nydailynews.com/news/national/teammate-steubenville-football-players-testifies-taped-sex-act-article-1.1290358.

61. Chelsea Carter, Poppy Harlow, and Brian Vitagliano, "Steubenville Rape Trial Focuses on Text Messages, Cell Phone Pictures," CNN, March 14, 2013,

62. Goodman, "Hacker Group Anonymous Leaks Chilling Video in Case of Alleged Steubenville Rape, Cover-Up."

63. Alexander Abad-Santos, "Everything You Need to Know about Steuben-ville High's Football 'Rape Crew,'" *The Atlantic*, January 3, 2013, http://www.theatlanticwire.com/national/2013/01/steubenville-high-football-rape-crew/60554.

64. Kate Harding, *Asking for It: The Alarming Rise of Rape Culture—and What We Can Do About It* (Boston, MA: Da Capo Lifelong Books, 2014).

65. Alexandria Goddard, "Big Red Players Accused of Rape & Kidnapping," Prinniefied.com, August 23, 2012, http://prinniefied.com/wp/2012/08/23/steu-benville-high-school-gang-rape-case-firs.

66. Levy, "Trial by Twitter."

67. Juliet Macur and Nate Schweber, "Rape Case Unfolds Online and Di-vides Steubenville—NYTimes.com," NYTimes.com, December 16, 2012, http://www.nytimes.com/2012/12/17/sports/high-school-football-rape-case-un-folds-online-and-divides-steubenville-ohio.html?pagewanted=all&_r=1&.

68. David Muir and Elizabeth Vargas, "Video: Steubenville: After the Par-ty's Over," ABCNews.Go.com, March 22, 2013, http://abcnews.go.com/2020/video/steubenville-partys-18795344.

69. Dan Wetzel, "Steubenville Suspect's Text Messages Paint Disturbing Picture of Night of Alleged Rape," Sports.Yahoo.com, March 15, 2013, http://sports.yahoo.com/news/highschool--steubenville-suspects--text-messages-paint-disturbing-picture-of-night-of-alleged-rape--according-to-prosecutors-053236470.html.

70. Michael Pearson, "Defense Battles Social Media Blizzard in Ohio Rape Case," CNN, January 4, 2013, http://www.cnn.com/2013/01/04/justice/ohio-rape-online-video/index.html.

71. Michael Kimmel, *Guyland: The Perilous World Where Boys Become Men* (New York: HarperCollins, 2008), 45.

72. Ibid., 59.

73. Ibid.

74. Juliet Macur, "In Steubenville Rape Case, a Lesson for Adults," *New York Times*, November 26, 2013, http://www.nytimes.com/2013/11/27/sports/in-steubenville-rape-case-a-lesson-for-adults.html.

75. Baker, "Why Is No One Talking about the Second Steubenville Rape Case?"

76. Goodman, "Hacker Group Anonymous Leaks Chilling Video in Case of Alleged Steubenville Rape, Cover-Up"; Kristen Gwynne, "How Anonymous Hacking Exposed Steubenville High School Rape Case," Alternet.org, January 4, 2013, http://www.alternet.org/how-anonymous-hacking-exposed-steubenville-high-school-rape-case; Tom Ley, "'She Is So Raped Right Now': Partygoer Jokes about the Steubenville Accuser the Night of the Alleged Rape," *Deadspin*, January 2, 2013, http://deadspin.com/5972527/she-is-so-raped-right-now-former-student-jokes-about-the-steubenville-accuser-the-night-of-the-alleged-rape.

77. Nickie Phillips and Emily Horowitz, "The Steubenville Rape Case: Sexual Assault, Social Media, and Vigilante Justice" (paper presented at the Society for the Study of Social Problems, New York, 2014).

78. Irin Carmon, "Rape in the Age of Social Media," *Salon*, January 10, 2013, http://www.salon.com/2013/01/10/rape_in_the_age_of_social_media.

79. Nickie D. Phillips and Emily Horowitz, "The Steubenville Rape Case: Sexual Assault, Social Media, and Vigilante Justice" (paper presented at the Society for the Study of Social Problems Conference, New York, 2013).

80. Ibid.

81. Bob Garfield and Amanda Marcotte, "Rape Culture and the Steubenville Trial," Onthemedia.org, March 22, 2013, http://www.onthemedia.org/story/277667-rape-culture-and-steubenville-trial/transcript/?utm_source=sharedUrl&utm_medium=metatag&utm_campaign=sharedUrl; Nicholas Kristoff, "Is Delhi So Different from Steubenville?" *New York Times*, January 12, 2013, http://www.nytimes.com/2013/01/13/opinion/sunday/is-delhi-so-different-from-steubenville.html; Ariel Levy, "Trial by Twitter," *New Yorker*, August 5, 2013, http://www.newyorker.com/magazine/2013/08/05/trial-by-twitter; Sarah Sobieraj, "Steubenville: 'Digital Residue' of Sexual Assault Lifts Veil on Rape Culture," *Cognoscenti*, March 12, 2013, http://cognoscenti.wbur.org/2013/03/12/steubenville-sarah-sobieraj.

82. Vaidehi Joshi, "We Stand with Jada: When Rape Is an Ongoing Viral Trend, We Have a Big Problem," Bustle.com, July 17, 2014, http://www.bustle.com/articles/31841-we-stand-with-jada-when-rape-is-an-ongoing-viral-trend-we-have-a-big-problem.

83. Ann Friedman, "When Rape Goes Viral," *Newsweek*, July 24, 2013, http://www.newsweek.com/2013/07/24/when-rape-goes-viral-237742.html.

84. ChannelZeroYT, "#OccupySteubenville February 2, 2013 Info Release," YouTube, January 25, 2013, http://www.youtube.com/watch?v=Sh-qCcxY6hw.

85. Phillips and Horowitz, "The Steubenville Rape Case: Sexual Assault, Social Media, and Vigilante Justice."

86. Connor Simpson, "The Steubenville Victim Tells Her Story," *The Wire*, March 16, 2013, http://www.theatlanticwire.com/national/2013/03/steuben-ville-victim-testimony/63192.

87. RAINN, "FBI Changes Its Definition of Rape," RAINN.org, January 2012, https://rainn.org/news-room/fbi-changes-rape-definition.

88. Levy, "Trial by Twitter."

89. Muir and Vargas, "Video: Steubenville: After the Party's Over."

90. "Ohio Rape Trial Verdict Announced," *Huffington Post*, March 17, 2013, http://www.huffingtonpost.com/2013/03/17/steubenville-rape-trial-ver-dict_n_2895541.html.

91. Nathan Jurgenson, "The IRL Fetish," TheNewInquiry.com, June 28, 2012, http://thenewinquiry.com/essays/the-irl-fetish/.

92. Wetzel, "Steubenville Suspect's Text Messages Paint Disturbing Picture of Night of Alleged Rape."

93. Powell, "Seeking Rape Justice: Formal and Informal Responses to Sexual Violence through Technosocial Counter-Publics"; Friedman, "When Rape Goes Viral."

94. Phillips and Horowitz, "The Steubenville Rape Case: Sexual Assault, Social Media, and Vigilante Justice."

95. Josh Harkinson. "Exclusive: Meet the Woman Who Kicked Off Anonymous' Anti-Rape Operations," *Mother Jones*, May 13, 2013, http://www.motherjones.com/politics/2013/05/anonymous-rape-steubenville-reh-taeh-parsons-oprollredroll-opjustice4rehtaeh.

96. Michael Salter, "Justice and Revenge in Online Counter-Publics: Emerging Responses to Sexual Violence in the Age of Social Media," *Crime, Media, Culture* 9, no. 3 (December 1, 2013): 8.

97. Abigail Pesta, "'Thanks for Ruining My Life,'" *Newsweek*, December 10, 2012, http://www.newsweek.com/thanks-ruining-my-life-63423.

98. Jason Riley, "The Courier-Journal Local News Section," *Courier-Journal*, January 15, 2013, http://archive.courier-journal.com/article/20130115/NEWS01/301150050/Savannah-Dietrich-case-prompts-bill-would-allow-juve-nile-victims-talk; Jason Riley and Andrew Wolfson, "Savannah Dietrich Abuse Case: Teens Who Assaulted 16-Year-Old Thought It Would Be 'Funny,'" KSDK.com, August 31, 2012, http://www.ksdk.com/news/article/335973/28/Sa-vannah-Dietrich-abuse-case-Teens-who-assaulted-16-year-old-thought-it-would-be-funny.

99. Ibid.

100. Marissa Alter, "Bill Passed to Allow Juvenile Case Victims to Speak Publicly," WLKY.com, March 28, 2013, http://www.wlky.com/news/local-news/louisville-news/Bill-passed-to-allow-juvenile-case-victims-to-speak publicly/19510166; Jason Riley, "The Courier-Journal Local News Section," *Courier-Journal*, January 15, 2013, http://archive.courier-journal.com/article/20130115/NEWS01/301150050/Savannah-Dietrich-case-prompts-bill-would-allow-juvenile-victims-talk.

101. "BBC Trending: Is #JadaPose a Social Media Low?," BBC News, July 14, 2014, http://www.bbc.com/news/blogs-trending-28239914; Ryan Broderick, "Houston Teenagers Turned a Photo of a 16-Year-Old Girl's Alleged Sexual Assault into a 'Meme,'" *BuzzFeed*, July 10, 2014, http://www.buzzfeed.com/ryanhatesthis/houston-teenagers-turned-a-photo-of-a-16-year-old-girls-alle; Claire Cohen, "Mocking of Teen Rape Victim Prompts Major Internet Backlash," *Telegraph*, July 15, 2014, http://www.telegraph.co.uk/women/womens-life/10968068/Teen-rape-victim-viral-photos-Jadapose-prompts-major-internet-backlash.html; Ronan Farrow, "Jada's Mom: 'I Couldn't Believe That That Was My Child,'" MSNBC, July 11, 2014, http://www.msnbc.com/ronan-farrow-daily/watch/i-couldn-t-believe-that-that-was-my-child-302322755919.

102. Aaron Reiss, "When Tweeting Goes Bad: Mocking #Jadapose Hashtag Spreads on Twitter," *Houston Press*, July 9, 2014, http://www.houstonpress.com/news/when-tweeting-goes-bad-mocking-jadapose-hashtag-spreads-on-twitter-6713405.

103. Shelby Ivy Christie, "#StandWithJada Twitter Campaign to Fight Mockery of Teen's Sexual Assault Is Picking Up Steam," *Global Grind*, July 15, 2014, http://globalgrind.com/2014/07/15/standwithjada-twitter-campaign-fight-mockery-teens-sexual-assault-video; Lilly Workneh, "Social Media Stands in Support of 16-Year-Old Rape Victim with #IamJada," *The Grio*, July 15, 2014, http://thegrio.com/2014/07/15/social-media-stands-in-support-of-16-year-old-rape-victim-with-iamjada.

104. Meghan Daum, "When Cellphones and Social Media Become the Enemy," *Los Angeles Times*, July 16, 2014, http://www.latimes.com/opinion/op-ed/la-oe-daum-jada-rape-culture-20140717-column.html.

105. Laura Bates, "#JadaPose: The Online Ridiculing of a Teen Victim Is Part of a Sickening Trend," *Guardian*, July 17, 2014, http://www.theguardian.com/lifeandstyle/womens-blog/2014/jul/17/jadapose-online-ridiculing-rape-victims-sickening-trend.

106. "In Defense of Jada: The Danger of Being a Black Girl in a Rape Culture," July 12, 2014.

107. Lynette Holloway, "Mom of Victim in 'Viral' Rape Video Speaks Out," *The Root*, July 12, 2014, http://www.theroot.com/articles/culture/2014/07/mom_of_victim_in_viral_rape_video_speaks_out.html.

108. Staff, "16-Year-Old Girl Says Her Rape Went Viral: 'I'm Just Angry,'" KHOU, July 11, 2014, http://www.khou.com/story/local/2015/06/16/12664610.

109. Katie J. M. Baker, "We Wouldn't Know about the Steubenville Rape Case if It Wasn't for the Blogger Who 'Complicated' Things," *Jezebel*, Decem-

ber 17, 2012, http://jezebel.com/5969076/we-wouldnt-know-about-the-steu-benville-rape-case-if-it-wasnt-for-the-blogger-who-complicated-things; Harkinson, "Exclusive: Meet the Woman Who Kicked Off Anonymous' Anti-Rape Operations"; David Kushner, "Anonymous vs. Steubenville," Rolling-Stone.com, November 27, 2013, http://www.rollingstone.com/culture/news/anonymous-vs-steubenville-20131127; Justin Peters, "Stop Comparing the Steubenville Hacker to the Steubenville Rapists. It's Misleading and Wrong," *Slate*, June 12, 2013, http://www.slate.com/blogs/crime/2013/06/12/de-ric_lostutter_kyanonymous_stop_comparing_the_steubenville_hacker_to_the.html; Theodore Hamm, "No Country for Dickheads Deric Lostutter with Theodore Hamm," July 15, 2013, http://www.brooklynrail.org/2013/07/express/nocountryfor-dickheadsderic-lostutter-with-theodore-hamm.

110. Alexander Abad-Santos, "Inside the Anonymous Hacking File on the Steubenville 'Rape Crew,'" *The Atlantic*, January 2, 2013, http://www.theatlanticwire.com/national/2013/01/inside-anonymous-hacking-file-steubenville-rape-crew/60502.

111. Harkinson, "Exclusive: Leader of Anonymous Steubenville Op on Being Raided by the FBI."

112. Powell, "Seeking Rape Justice: Formal and Informal Responses to Sexual Violence through Technosocial Counter-Publics."

113. Lee Stranahan. "Steubenville: The Real Story," StranahanInEx-ile.Wordpress.com, January 14, 2013, https://stranahaninexile.wordpress.com; Lee Stranahan, "Anonymous Sensationalizes Steubenville Rape Case," *Breitbart*, January 10, 2013, http://www.breitbart.com/big-government/2013/01/10/anonymous-sensationalizes-steubenville-rape-case; Cathy Young, "Anonymous Is No Hero," *Real Clear Politics*, June 9, 2013, http://www.realclearpolitics.com/articles/2130/06/09/anonymous_is_no_hero_118733.html.

114. Emily Bazelon, "The Online Avengers," *New York Times*, January 15, 2015, http://www.nytimes.com/2014/01/19/magazine/the-online-aveng-ers.html.

115. Julia Prodis Sulek, "Audrie Pott: Boys Admit Sexually Assaulting Saratoga Teen Who Committed Suicide," *San Jose Mercury News*, January 14, 2014, http://www.mercurynews.com/crime-courts/ci_24913018/audrie-pott-boys-ad-mit-sexually-assaulting-saratoga-teen.

116. Tara Culp-Ressler, "Maryville Rape Survivor Fights Victim-Blaming: 'This Is Why I Am Not Shutting Up,'" *Think Progress*, October 21, 2013, http://thinkprogress.org/health/2013/10/21/2808231/maryville-rape-survivor-victim-blaming.

117. Daisy Coleman. "I'm Daisy Coleman, the Teenager at the Center of the Maryville Rape Media Storm, and This Is What Really Happened," xo-Jane.com, October 18, 2013, http://www.xojane.com/it-happened-to-me/daisy-coleman-maryville-rape.

118. Gabriella Coleman, *Hacker, Hoaxer, Whistleblower, Spy: The Many Faces of Anonymous* (New York: Verso, 2014).

119. Dylan Stableford, "#Steubenville Verdict: The Reaction on Twitter," News.Yahoo.com, March 17, 2013, http://news.yahoo.com/blogs/lookout/steubenville-verdict-twitter-163715978.html.

120. Lisa Wade, "Responses to the Steubenville Verdict Reveal Rape Culture," TheSocietyPages.org, March 19, 2013, http://thesocietypages.org/socimages/2013/03/19/this-is-rape-culture-responses-to-the-steubenville-verdict.

121. Annie Rose Strasser and Tara Culp-Ressler, "How the Media Took Sides in the Steubenville Rape Case," *Think Progress*, March 18, 2013, http://thinkprogress.org/health/2013/03/18/1732701/media-steubenville.

122. Vlae Kershner, "Update: Steubenville Rapist's Lying Text," *SFGate*, March 19, 2013, http://blog.sfgate.com/hottopics/2013/03/19/update-steubenville-rapist%e2%80%99s-lying-text.

123. Caitlin Donohue, "There Was No Rape Episode on 'Leave It to Beaver' [UPDATED] | SF Politics," SFBG.com, March 19, 2013, http://www.sfbg.com/politics/2013/03/19/there-was-no-rape-episode-leave-it-beaver; Brock Keeling, "Downplaying Rape: SFGate Compares Steubenville Rapist to Lovable Eddie Haskell [UPDATE]," sfist.com, March 19, 2013, http://sfist.com/2013/03/19/downplaying_rape_sfgate_compares_co.php; Vlae Kershner, "Update: Steubenville Rapist's Lying Text," *SFGate*, March 19, 2013, http://blog.sfgate.com/hottopics/2013/03/19/update-steubenville-rapist%e2%80%99s-lying-text.

124. Ibid.

125. "CNN Transcript Guilty Verdict in Steubenville Rape Trial," Transcripts.CNN.com, March 17, 2013, http://transcripts.cnn.com/TRANSCRIPTS/1303/17/rs.01.html.

126. Ibid.

127. Michelle Dean, "Why the Steubenville Rapists Won't Be 'Labeled' for Life," *NYMag*, March 21, 2013, http://nymag.com/thecut/2013/03/steubenville-rapists-wont-be-labeled-for-life.html; editorial, "Convicted Steubenville Sex Offender Does Not Belong on High School Football Team: Editorial," Cleveland.com, August 14, 2014, http://www.cleveland.com/opinion/index.ssf/2014/08/convicted_steubenville_sex_offender_does_not_belong_on_high_school_football_team_editorial.html; Emily Horowitz, *Protecting Our Kids? How Sex Offender Laws Are Failing Us* (New York: Praeger, 2014); Jenny Kutner, "Convicted Steubenville Rapist Trent Mays Released from Juvenile Detention," *Salon*, January 7, 2015, http://www.salon.com/2015/01/07/convicted_steubenville_rapist_trent_mays_released_from_juvenile_detention; Sara Morrison, "Steubenville Rapist Ma'lik Richmond Has Been Released," *The Wire*, January 5, 2014, http://www.thewire.com/national/2014/01/steubenville-rapist-malik-richmond-has-been-released/356707; David Moye, "Steubenville Rapist Returns to School Football Team," *Huffington Post*, August 11, 2014, http://www.huffingtonpost.com/2014/08/11/malik-richmond_n_5669903.html; staff, "Steubenville Rape Case Update: Trent Mays, Convicted of Raping Teen, Ordered to Register as Sex Offender," CBSNews.com, June 14, 2013, http://www.cbsnews.com/news/steubenville-rape-case-update-trent-mays-convicted-of-raping-teen-ordered-to-register-as-sex-offender; Andrew Welsh-Huggins,

"Steubenville Rapist Keeps Sex Offender Status," *Huffington Post*, June 20, 2014, http://www.huffingtonpost.com/2014/06/20/malik-richmond_n_5516790.html.

128. In November 2013, the Ohio attorney general, Mike DeWine, announced the indictments of four adults with charges ranging from tampering with evidence, obstruction of justice, failure to report child abuse, and making false statements. These charges were related to both the Jane Doe case as well as the earlier April 2012 case. This was in addition to the indictment of the Steubenville high school director of technology for "obstructing justice, evidence tampering, obstructing official business and perjury" in October that year. Madison Gray, "School Official Arrested in Apparent Cover Up of Steubenville Rape Case," Time.com, October 8, 2013, http://nation.time.com/2013/10/08/school-official-arrested-in-apparent-cover-up-of-steubenville-rape-case.

129. "4 More Charged in Steubenville Rape Case," CNN, November 26, 2013, http://www.cnn.com/2013/11/25/justice/ohio-steubenville-rape-case/index.html; Tracy Connor, "Steubenville Case: Four More Charged, Including Superintendent, Volunteer Coach—NBC News," NBC News, November 25, 2013, http://www.nbcnews.com/news/other/steubenville-case-four-more-charged-including-superintendent-volunteer-coach-f2D11653644.

130. Gary Trust, "Robin Thicke's 'Blurred Lines' Is Billboard's Song of the Summer," *Billboard*, September 5, 2013, http://www.billboard.com/articles/news/5687036/robin-thickes-blurred-lines-is-billboards-song-of-the-summer.

131. Julie Gerstein, "Robin #Thicke's New Video Is Full of Nipples, Lambs & Pharrell (NSFW)," *The Frisky*, March 27, 2013, http://www.thefrisky.com/2013-03-27/robin-thickes-new-video-is-full-of-nipples-lambs-pharrell-nsfw.

132. Auckland Law Review, "Robin Thicke—Blurred Lines [Feminist Parody] 'Defined Lines,'" YouTube, August 30, 2013, http://www.youtube.com/watch?v=tC1XtnLRLPM; Matilda Battersby and Jess Denham, "Feminist Parody of Robin Thicke's 'Blurred Lines' Removed from YouTube for Being 'Inappropriate,'" September 3, 2013, http://www.independent.co.uk/arts-entertainment/music/news/feminist-parody-of-robin-thickes-blurred-lines-removed-from-youtube-for-being-inappropriate-8795998.html; Tricia Romano, "'Blurred Lines,' Robin Thicke's Summer Anthem, Is Kind of Rapey," *Newsweek*, June 17, 2013, http://www.thedailybeast.com/articles/2013/06/17/blurred-lines-robin-thicke-s-summer-anthem-is-kind-of-rapey.html; Doug Barry, "'Blurred Lines' Gender-Swapped Parody Briefly Removed by YouTube," *Jezebel*, September 2, 2013, http://jezebel.com/blurred-lines-gender-swapped-parody-briefly-removed-b-1239286796; Solange Castellar, "Feminist Blurred Lines Parody Deemed 'Too Hot' for Youtube #Notfuckingplastic," *Bust*, September 5, 2015, http://bust.com/feminist-blurred-lines-parody-deemed-too-hot-for-youtube-notfuckingplastic.html; Amanda Marcotte, "Why the Mod Carousel Parody of 'Blurred Lines' Works So Well," RawStory.com, July 24, 2013, http://www.rawstory.com/rs/2013/07/why-the-mod-carousel-parody-of-blurred-lines-works-so-well; Bryan J. Lowder, "We Take It Back: This Is the 'Blurred Lines' Parody We Needed," *Slate*, July 23, 2013, http://www.slate.com/blogs/browbeat/2013/07/23/_blurred_lines_gender_swapped_

parody_from_mod_carousel_the_best_robin_thicke.html; Lindy West, "The Gender-Swapped 'Blurred Lines' Video Is Suddenly Age-Restricted; Lindy West, "The Gender-Swapped 'Blurred Lines' Video Is Suddenly Age-Restricted," *Jezebel*, July 24, 2013, http://jezebel.com/why-is-the-gender-swapped-blurred-lines-video-suddenl-896571665; Gerstein, "Robin #Thicke's New Video Is Full of Nipples, Lambs & Pharrell (NSFW)"; Veronica Linares, "Robin Thicke's 'Blurred Lines' Dubbed 'Rapey' by Critics," UPI, June 18, 2013, http://www.upi.com/Entertainment_News/2013/06/18/Robin-Thickes-Blurred-Lines-dubbed-rapey-by-critics/9741371566710.

133. Eric Ducker, "Q&A: Veteran Music Video Director Diane Martel on Her Controversial Videos for Robin Thicke and Miley Cyrus," *Grantland*, June 26, 2013, http://grantland.com/hollywood-prospectus/qa-veteran-music-video-director-diane-martel-on-her-controversial-videos-for-robin-thicke-and-miley-cyrus.

134. Stelios Phili, "Robin Thicke on That Banned Video, Collaborating with 2 Chainz and Kendrick Lamar, and His New Film: The Q: GQ," *GQ*, September 2, 2013, http://www.gq.com/blogs/the-feed/2013/05/robin-thicke-interview-blurred-lines-music-video-collaborating-with-2-chainz-and-kendrick-lamar-mercy.html; Callie Beusman, "'Blurred Lines' Director Meant the Video to Be 'Subtly Ridiculing,'" *Jezebel*, June 26, 2013, http://jezebel.com/blurred-lines-director-meant-the-video-to-be-subtly-589343435.

135. Ducker, "Q&A: Veteran Music Video Director Diane Martel on Her Controversial Videos for Robin Thicke and Miley Cyrus."

136. Phili, "Robin Thicke on That Banned Video, Collaborating with 2 Chainz and Kendrick Lamar, and His New Film: The Q: GQ."

137. Hilary Lewis, "Robin Thicke to Critics Who Say 'Blurred Lines' Condones Rape: 'That's Ridiculous,'" *Hollywood Reporter*, July 10, 2013, http://www.hollywoodreporter.com/earshot/robin-thicke-blurred-lines-rape-583092.

138. Jimmy Johnson, "Robin Thicke's Blurred Vision: A Critique of a Rape Anthem in Two Parts," Truthout.org, August 4, 2013, http://www.truthout.org/opinion/item/17847-robin-thickes-blurred-vision-a-critique-of-a-rape-anthem-in-two-parts.

139. "VH1 on Twitter," VH1, June 30, 2014, https://twitter.com/VH1/status/483725228850569216; Michelle Broder Van Dyke, "Robin Thicke and VH1 Laugh Off Questions about Misogyny," *BuzzFeed*, July 1, 2014, http://www.buzzfeed.com/mbvd/robin-thicke-and-vh1-laugh-off-questions-about-misogyny; Michelle Broder Van Dyke, "Robin Thicke's Planned Q&A Session on Twitter Flooded with Queries about Misogyny," *BuzzFeed*, June 30, 2014, http://www.buzzfeed.com/mbvd/robin-thickes-asked-about-misogyny.

140. Daniel D'Addario, "Miley, Macklemore and the Fake-Sex-Positive VMAs," *Salon*, August 26, 2013, http://www.salon.com/2013/08/26/miley_macklemore_and_the_fake_sex_positive_vmas.

141. Ibid.

142. Gabrielle Chung, "Watch Miley Cyrus and Robin Thicke's Awkwardly Inappropriate VMAs Performance," August 25, 2013, http://www.celebuzz.com/2013-08-25/watch-miley-cyrus-and-robin-thickes-awkwardly-

inappropriate-vmas-performance; Richard Cohen, "Richard Cohen: Miley
Cyrus, Steubenville and Culture Run Amok," *Washington Post*, September 2,
2013, http://www.washingtonpost.com/opinions/richard-cohen-miley-cyrus-
steubenville-and-culture-run-amok/2013/09/02/1cecafa6-11af-11e3-bdf6-
e4fc677d94a1_story.html; MSNBC, "MSNBC'S Mika Brzezinski Has Best
Possible Reaction to Miley Cyrus' VMA Performance," YouTube, August 26,
2013, http://www.youtube.com/watch?v=cLc9V3KTA0g.

143. Ibid.

144. Cohen, "Richard Cohen: Miley Cyrus, Steubenville and Culture Run
Amok."

145. Alexandra Petri, "Deep Thoughts about Miley Cyrus's VMA Performance," *Washington Post*, August 27, 2013, http://www.washingtonpost.com/
blogs/compost/wp/2013/08/27/deep-thoughts-about-miley-cyruss-vma-perfor-
mance; Jody Rosen, "Rosen: The 2013 VMAs Were Dominated by Miley's
Minstrel Show," *Vulture*, August 26, 2013, http://www.vulture.com/2013/08/
jody-rosen-miley-cyrus-vmas-minstrel.html; NinjaCate, "Solidarity Is for Miley
Cyrus: The Racial Implications of Her VMA Performance," *Jezebel*, August 26,
2013, http://groupthink.jezebel.com/solidarity-is-for-miley-cyrus-
1203666732?action_type_map=["og.likes"]&fb_action_types=og.likes&
fb_source=other_multiline&action_object_map=[155252038013239]&ac-
tion_ref_map=[]&fb_action_ids=907524606455; Dodai Stewart, "On Miley
Cyrus, Ratchet Culture and Accessorizing with Black People," *Jezebel*, June 20,
2013, http://jezebel.com/on-miley-cyrus-ratchet-culture-and-accessorizing-
with-514381016; Clinton Yates, "Miley Cyrus and the Issues of Slut-Shaming
and Racial Condescension," *Washington Post*, August 26, 2013, http://
www.washingtonpost.com/entertainment/music/miley-cyrus-and-the-issues-of-
slut-shaming-and-racial-condescension/2013/08/26/f3aee436-0e68-11e3-bdf6-
e4fc677d94a1_story.html.

146. Soraya Chemaly, "Miley Cyrus Joins the Boys' Club," Alternet.org, August 26, 2013, http://www.alternet.org/media/miley-cyrus-joins-boys-club.

147. Alyssa Rosenberg, "Miley Cyrus' Performance at the VMAs and How
Ratchet Culture Became the New Implied Bisexuality," August 26, 2013, http:/
/thinkprogress.org/alyssa/2013/08/26/2527091/miley-cyrus-vmas-britney-
spears-bisexual.

148. Sezin Koehler, "From the Mouths of Rapists: The Lyrics of Robin
Thicke's Blurred Lines » Sociological Images," TheSocietyPages.org, September 17, 2013, http://thesocietypages.org/socimages/2013/09/17/from-the-
mouths-of-rapists-the-lyrics-of-robin-thickes-blurred-lines-and-real-life-rape;
Katie J. M. Baker, "Yikes: 'Blurred Lines' Lyrics Aren't So Catchy When Rapists Read Them," *Jezebel*, September 17, 2013, http://jezebel.com/yikes-
blurred-lines-lyrics-arent-so-catchy-when-rap-1335658624.

149. Jessica Best, "Police Launch 'No Blurred Lines' Campaign against Rape
in Reference to Controversial Robin Thicke Hit," *Mirror*, September 23, 2014,
http://www.mirror.co.uk/news/uk-news/police-launch-no-blurred-lines-
4313316.

150. Gregory Kane, "Gregory Kane: Time to End the Rape Culture," *Washington Examiner*, April 21, 2013, http://www.washingtonexaminer.com/gregory-kane-time-to-end-the-rape-culture/article/2527748.

151. Desire Thompson, "Rick Ross Explains Controversial 'U.O.N.E.O.' Line: 'It Was a Misunderstanding,'" Vibe.com, March 28, 2015, http://www.vibe.com/article/rick-ross-explains-controversial-uoneo-line-it-was-misunderstanding; Chris Martins, "Rick Ross' Belated Apology for 'U.O.N.E.O.' Could Cost Him Millions," *Spin*, April 17, 2013, http://www.spin.com/articles/rick-ross-reebok-rape-fallout-millions-uoneo; Sean Michaels, "Rick Ross Bungles 'Date Rape Lyric' Apology as Furore Grows," Guardian.co.uk, April 5, 2013, http://www.theguardian.com/music/2013/apr/05/rick-ross-bungles-apology-date-rape.

152. Adam Lee, "Richard Dawkins Has Lost It: Ignorant Sexism Gives Atheists a Bad Name," Guardian.co.uk, September 18, 2014, http://www.theguardian.com/commentisfree/2014/sep/18/richard-dawkins-sexist-atheists-bad-name; Tim Teeman, "Atheist King Richard Dawkins' Rape Fantasy," *Newsweek*, July 31, 2014, http://www.thedailybeast.com/articles/2014/07/31/atheist-king-richard-dawkins-s-rape-fantasy.html

153. Anonymous, "I Was Raped When I Was Drunk. I Was 14. Do You Believe Me, Richard Dawkins?," *New Statesman*, September 19, 2014, http://www.newstatesman.com/voices/2014/09/i-was-raped-when-i-was-drunk-i-was-14-do-you-believe-me-richard-dawkins.

154. Nadeska Alexis, "Cee Lo Tried to Have a Discussion about Rape and Consent on Twitter and It Went Horribly Wrong," MTV, September 2, 2014, http://www.mtv.com/news/1918097/cee-lo-discuss-rape-twitter-backlash; Richard Dawkins, "@RichardDawkins," Twitter.com, September 12, 2014, https://twitter.com/search?q=from%3Aricharddawkins%20since%3A2014-08-01%20until%3A2014-09-30&src=typd; Richard Dawkins, "Richard Dawkins on Twitter," Twitter.com, July 28, 2014, https://twitter.com/RichardDawkins/status/494012678432894976; Nina Ricafort, "Is CeeLo Green Perpetuating Rape Culture?," *Live Mag UK*, September 8, 2014, http://www.livemaguk.com/ceelo-green-rape-comments-twitter; CeeLo Green, "Biography | Cee Lo Green | Official Website," Ceelogreen.com, accessed January 17, 2015, http://www.ceelogreen.com/about.htm; Elizabeth Plank, "CeeLo Green's Disgusting Comments Prove Rape Culture Is Alive and Well," Mic.com, September 2, 2014, http://mic.com/articles/97800/ceelo-green-s-disgusting-comments-prove-rape-culture-is-alive-and-well; Rachel Zarrell, "CeeLo Green's Reality Show Canceled a Day after Tweeting It's Only Rape if the Person Is Conscious," *BuzzFeed*, September 1, 2014, http://www.buzzfeed.com/rachelzarrell/cee-lo-green-says-its-only-rape-if-the-person-is-conscious; August Brown, "Cee Lo Green Temporarily Deletes Twitter Account after Rape Comments," September 2, 2014; David Edwards, "CeeLo Green Defends Alleged Drink-Spiking: It's Only 'Really' Rape When She's Conscious," RawStory.com, September 2, 2014, http://www.rawstory.com/rs/2014/09/ceelo-green-defends-alleged-drink-spiking-its-only-really-rape-when-shes-conscious.

155. Darian Lusk, "Who Is Hannibal Buress, and Why Did He Call Bill Cosby a 'Rapist'?," CBSNews.com, November 18, 2014, http://www.cbsnews.com/news/who-is-hannibal-buress-and-why-did-he-call-bill-cosby-a-rapist; Anna Silman, "Hannibal Buress Called Bill Cosby a Rapist," *Vulture*, October 20, 2014, http://www.vulture.com/2014/10/hannibal-buress-called-bill-cosby-a-rapist.html.

156. Matt Giles and Nate Jones. "Timeline: Abuse Charges against Bill Cosby," *Vulture*, March 3, 2015, http://www.vulture.com/2014/09/timeline-of-the-abuse-charges-against-cosby.html; Kate Pickert, "A Timeline Guide to Guide to the Bill Cosby Rape Allegations," Time.com, November 18, 2014, http://time.com/3592547/bill-cosby-rape-allegations-timeline.

157. Mark Seal, "The One Accuser Who May Finally Bring Bill Cosby Down for Good," *Vanity Fair*, July 6, 2016, http://www.vanityfair.com/news/2016/07/bill-cosby-andrea-constand-sexual-assault-trial.

158. Alan Scherstuhl, "Here's the 1969 Bill Cosby Routine about Wanting to Drug Women's Drinks," *Village Voice*, November 17, 2014, http://www.villagevoice.com/news/heres-the-1969-bill-cosby-routine-about-wanting-to-drug-womens-drinks-6721448.

159. Marc Lamont Hill, "Cosby Controversy: 6 Signs of Rape Culture," CNN, November 20, 2014, http://www.cnn.com/2014/11/20/opinion/hill-bill-cosby-case-rape-culture/index.html.

160. Staff, "CNN's Don Lemon to Cosby Rape Accuser: 'You Know, There Are Ways Not to Perform Oral Sex if You Didn't Want to Do It.'" *Media Matters for America*, November 18, 2014, http://mediamatters.org/video/2014/11/18/cnns-don-lemon-to-cosby-rape-accuser-you-know-t/201625.

161. Barbara Bowman, "Bill Cosby Raped Me: Why Did It Take 30 Years for People to Believe My Story?," *Washington Post*, November 13, 2014, https://www.washingtonpost.com/posteverything/wp/2014/11/13/bill-cosby-raped-me-why-did-it-take-30-years-for-people-to-believe-my-story.

162. Editorial, "Finally, Vindication Arrives for Bill Cosby's Accusers," *Washington Post*, July 8, 2015, https://www.washingtonpost.com/opinions/a-vindication-of-cosbys-accusers/2015/07/08/1a4456b4-24e5-11e5-b72c-2b7d516e1e0e_story.html; staff, "Bill Cosby Said in 2005 That He Got Sedative to Give Women for Sex," Pix.com, July 6, 2015, http://pix11.com/2015/07/06/documents-cosby-admitted-in-2005-to-getting-quaaludes-to-give-to-women-he-sought-sex-with; Pamela Engel, "The Backstory behind the Shocking Bill Cosby Rape Allegations," *Business Insider*, November 20, 2014, http://www.businessinsider.com/the-women-who-have-accused-bill-cosby-of-rape-2014-11; Matt Giles and Nate Jones, "Timeline: Abuse Charges against Bill Cosby," *Vulture*, March 3, 2015, http://www.vulture.com/2014/09/timeline-of-the-abuse-charges-against-cosby.html.

163. Wesley Morris and Rembert Brown, "The Bill Cosby Issue: Processing the Fall of an Icon," *Grantland*, November 21, 2014, http://grantland.com/hollywood-prospectus/bill-cosby-rape-allegations-the-fall-of-an-icon; Rebecca Traister, "Why America Took So Long to Wake Up to the Truth about Bill

Cosby," *New Republic*, November 19, 2014, https://newrepublic.com/article/120338/bill-cosby-rape-allegations-why-america-took-so-long-wake.

164. Brittney Cooper, "The Terrible Truth about Bill Cosby," October 29, 2014, http://www.alternet.org/terrible-truth-about-bill-cosby.

165. Jenée Desmond-Harris, "Bill Cosby's Disturbing Love of Power, from Race Rants to Drugging Women," Vox.com, July 8, 2015, http://www.vox.com/2014/11/21/7259069/bill-cosby-rape-allegations; Hadley Freeman, "How Bill Cosby's Image Shielded Him from Claims of Rape," *Guardian*, November 19, 2014, http://www.theguardian.com/commentisfree/2014/nov/19/bill-cosby-image-shielded-claims-rape-lectured-black-america.

166. Ta-Nehisi Coates. "This Is How We Lost to the White Man," *The Atlantic*, May 2008, http://www.theatlantic.com/magazine/archive/2008/05/-this-is-how-we-lost-to-the-white-man/306774.

167. Rebecca Traister, "Why America Took So Long to Wake Up to the Truth about Bill Cosby," *New Republic*, November 14, 2014, https://newrepublic.com/article/120338/bill-cosby-rape-allegations-why-america-took-so-long-wake.

168. Beverly Johnson, "Bill Cosby Drugged Me. This Is My Story," VanityFair.com, December 2014, http://www.vanityfair.com/culture/2014/12/bill-cosby-beverly-johnson-story.

169. Estelle Freedman, "Redefining Rape," *Chronicle of Higher Education*, September 16, 2013, 1–7.

170. Helen Benedict, *Virgin or Vamp: How the Press Covers Sex Crimes* (New York: Oxford University Press, 1992), 26.

171. Ibid. See Beth Richie's *Arrested Justice* for analysis of how disadvantaged black women are at risk for abuse, including sexual assault. Beth Richie, *Arrested Justice: Black Women, Violence, and America's Prison Nation* (New York: New York University Press, 2012).

172. Ta-Nehisi Coates, "Bill Cosby and His Enablers," *The Atlantic*, January 12, 2016, http://www.theatlantic.com/politics/archive/2016/01/bill-cosby-and-his-enablers/422448.

173. RAINN, "Cosby Allegations Lead to Spike in Hotline Use," RAINN.org, November 24, 2014, https://rainn.org/news-room/cosby-allegations-lead-to-hotline-spike.

174. Jason Cherkis, "Jackie Fox of the Runaways Opens Up about Her Traumatic Rape," *Huffington Post*, July 9, 2015, http://highline.huffingtonpost.com/articles/en/the-lost-girls.

175. Ibid.

176. Jackie Fuchs, "'Being a Passive Bystander Is Not a Crime,'" *Huffington Post*, July 13, 2015, http://www.huffingtonpost.com/jackie-fuchs/lets-stop-blaming-passive-bystanders-_b_7785482.html.

177. Kimberly Lonsway, "Rape Myths: In Review," *Psychology of Women Quarterly* 18, no. 2 (1994): 133–64.

178. Jackie Fuchs, "'Being a Passive Bystander Is Not a Crime,'" *Huffington Post*, July 13, 2015. http://www.huffingtonpost.com/jackie-fuchs/lets-stop-blaming-passive-bystanders-_b_7785482.html.

179. Puente, "Number of Cosby Accusers Passes 50."

180. Leanne Aguilera, "Whoopi Goldberg Defends Bill Cosby after Quaaludes Admission: 'He's Innocent until Proven Guilty,'" ETOnline.com, July 7, 2015, http://www.etonline.com/news/167476_whoopi_goldberg_defends_bill_cosby_after_quaaludes_admission_he_innocent_until_proven_guilty.

181. Gabrielle Bluestone, "Jill Scott Finally Admits She Was Wrong about Bill Cosby," *Gawker*, July 7, 2015, http://gawker.com/jill-scott-finally-admits-she-was-wrong-to-defend-bill-1716218337.

182. Ibid.; Emma Wilkinson, "'Completely Disgusted': Bill Cosby Has Lost Jill Scott's Support," NBC News, July 7, 2015, http://www.nbcnews.com/story-line/bill-cosby-scandal/bill-cosby-has-lost-jill-scotts-support-n387931.

183. Margaret Lyons, "The Sitcom Season in Rape Jokes," *Vulture*, January 20, 2012, http://www.vulture.com/2012/01/rape-jokes-sitcoms-broke-girls.html; Raúl Pérez and Viveca S. Greene, "Debating Rape Jokes vs. Rape Culture: Framing and Counter-Framing Misogynistic Comedy," *Social Semiotics* 26, no. 3 (2016): 1–18.

184. Tricia Romano, "Rainn Wilson, '2 Broke Girls,' and the Rise of the Rape Joke," *Newsweek*, February 22, 2012, http://www.thedailybeast.com/articles/2012/02/22/rainn-wilson-2-broke-girls-and-the-rise-of-the-rape-joke.html.

185. Comedians such as Chris Rock and Jerry Seinfeld lashed out against the so-called political correctness that seemingly pervades college campuses, with Seinfeld stating he no longer performs at college campuses because of students' close scrutiny of comic material and their ignorance. Dana Rose Falcone, "Jerry Seinfeld: PC College Students 'Don't Know What the Hell They're Talking About,'" *Entertainment Weekly*, June 8, 2015, http://www.ew.com/article/2015/06/08/jerry-seinfeld-politically-correct-college-campuses; Dean Obeidallah, "Jerry Seinfeld Doesn't Get Political Correctness," CNN.com, June 11, 2015, http://www.cnn.com/2015/06/10/opinions/obeidallah-jerry-seinfeld/index.html.

186. Anushay Hossain, "Why Amy Schumer Is Your New Feminist Best Friend," *Huffington Post*, May 29, 2015, http://www.huffingtonpost.com/anushay-hossain/why-amy-schumer-is-your-new-feminist-best-friend_b_7293376.html; Anna Klassen, "Amy Schumer Is a Feminist Icon & Here's 5 Undeniable Reasons Why," Bustle.com, April 16, 2015, http://www.bustle.com/articles/76598-amy-schumer-is-a-feminist-icon-heres-5-undeniable-reasons-why; Melena Ryzik, "The Sneaky Power of Amy Schumer, in 'Trainwreck' and Elsewhere," *New York Times*, July 8, 2015, http://www.nytimes.com/2015/07/12/movies/the-sneaky-power-of-amy-schumer-in-trainwreck-and-elsewhere.html; Anna Silman, "15 Feminist Amy Schumer Sketches That Will Make You Stand Up and Cheer," *Salon*, May 3, 2015, http:/www.salon.com/2015/05/03/15_feminist_amy_schumer_sketches_that_will_make_you_stand_up_and_cheer.

187. Amy Schumer, "Inside Amy Schumer—Court of Public Opinion: The Trial of Bill Cosby," YouTube, May 26, 2015, http://www.youtube.com/watch?v=1sq4gVZ4cBc.

188. Ryan Broderick, Heben Nigatu, and Jessica Testa, "What Is Rape Culture?," *BuzzFeed*, February 5, 2014, http://www.buzzfeed.com/ryanhatesthis/what-is-rape-culture.

3. "HEY TV, STOP RAPING WOMEN"

1. Roxanne Gay, "'Game of Thrones' Glamorizes Rape: That Was Not Consent, and Rape Is Not a Narrative Device," *Salon*, 2014, http://www.salon.com/2014/04/21/game_of_thrones_and_the_glamorization_of_rape.

2. Madeleine Davies, "The Game of Thrones Rape Scene Was Unnecessary and Despicable," *Jezebel*, 2014, http://jezebel.com/the-game-of-thrones-rape-scene-was-unnecessary-and-desp-1565671570.

3. Sarah Hughes, "Rape on TV: A Justified Look at Violence against Women or a Crude Plot Device?," *Guardian*, December 13, 2014, http://www.theguardian.com/tv-and-radio/2014/dec/13/tv-rape-portrayal-storm.

4. Mary McNamara, "TV's Alleged 'Rape Glut' May Just Be a More Reflective Reality," *Los Angeles Times*, June 12, 2015, http://www.latimes.com/entertainment/tv/la-ca-st-critics-notebook-rape-on-tv-20150614-column.html; Chris Osterndorf, "TV's Rape Problem Is Bigger Than 'Game of Thrones,'" *Salon*, April 22, 2014, http://www.salon.com/2014/04/22/tvs_rape_problem_is_bigger_than_game_of_thrones_partner; Sonia Saraiya, "The Truth about TV's Rape Obsession: How We Struggle with the Broken Myths of Masculinity, on Screen and Off," *Salon*, June 25, 2015, http://www.salon.com/2015/06/25/the_truth_about_tvs_rape_obsession_how_we_struggle_with_the_broken_myths_of_masculinity_on_screen_and_off; Amy Zimmerman, "TV's Rape Obsession: What 'Outlander' Got Right and 'Game of Thrones' Gets Very Wrong," *Daily Beast*, June 2, 2015, http://www.thedailybeast.com/articles/2015/06/02/tv-s-rape-obsession-what-outlander-got-right-and-game-of-thrones-gets-very-wrong.html.

5. Henry Jenkins, "The Value of Media Literacy Education in the 21st Century: A Conversation with Tessa Jolls (Part Three)," HenryJenkins.org, September 17, 2014, http://henryjenkins.org/2014/09/the-value-of-media-literacy-education-in-the-21st-century-a-conversation-with-tessa-jolls-part-three.html.

6. Cynthia Carter and Kay Weaver, *Violence and the Media* (Philadelphia, PA: Open University Press, 2003); Christopher Ferguson, "Media Violence Effects and Violent Crime: Good Science or Moral Panic?," in *Violent Crime: Clinical and Social Implications* (Thousand Oaks, CA: Sage, 2010), 1–20; David Hajdu, *The Ten Cent Plague: The Great Comic-Book Scare and How It Changed America* (New York: Picador, 2008); James Potter, *On Media Violence* (Thousand Oaks, CA: Sage, 1999); James Potter, *The 11 Myths of Media Violence* (Thousand Oaks, CA: Sage, 2003); David Trend, *The Myth of Media Violence: A Critical Introduction* (Malden, MA: Blackwell, 2007).

7. The Motion Picture Production Code (Hollywood films), the Comics Code Authority (comic books), and the Parents Music Resource Center (music

industry) were efforts to crack down on morally questionable entertainment. Gregory Black, *Hollywood Censored: Morality Codes, Catholics, and the Movies* (Cambridge, UK: Cambridge University Press, 1996); Amy Kiste Nyberg, *Seal of Approval: The History of the Comics Code* (Jackson: University Press of Mississippi, 1998); Zach Schonfeld, "An Oral History of the PMRC's War on Explicit Lyrics," *Newsweek*, September 19, 2015, http://www.newsweek.com/2015/10/09/oral-history-tipper-gores-war-explicit-rock-lyrics-dee-snider-373103.html.

8. Harold Schechter, *Savage Pastimes: A Cultural History of Violent Entertainment* (New York: St. Martin's, 2005).

9. Margaret Lyons, "How Much Rape Is Too Much Rape on My Favorite Shows? Your Pressing TV Questions, Answered," *Vulture*, May 27, 2015, http://www.vulture.com/2015/05/stay-tuned-rape-tv-game-of-thrones.html; Margaret Lyons, "Maxing Out on Murder: Good Luck Finding a Decent TV Drama without Rape or Killing," *Vulture*, April 17, 2013, http://www.vulture.com/2013/04/maxing-out-on-murder-shows.html; Jane Martinson, "Rape on Television: The Questions We Should All Be Asking," *Guardian*, June 17, 2013, http://www.theguardian.com/lifeandstyle/the-womens-blog-with-jane-martinson/2013/jun/17/rape-on-television-white-queen; Hollie McKay, "TV Now Exploiting Rape for Ratings?," FoxNews.com, June 2, 2015, http://www.foxnews.com/entertainment/2015/06/02/tv-now-exploiting-rape-for-ratings; Saraiya, "The Truth about TV's Rape Obsession: How We Struggle with the Broken Myths of Masculinity, on Screen and Off."

10. Alyssa Rosenberg, "From Washington to Westeros, How Rape Plays Out on TV," *Washington Post*, April 4, 2014.

11. Tiffany Jenkins, "Is There Too Much Rape on Stage and TV?," *Independent*, August 28, 2013, http://www.independent.co.uk/arts-entertainment/theatre-dance/features/is-there-too-much-rape-on-stage-and-tv-8788256.html.

12. Chris Richards, "It's as if Robin Thicke Figured Out How to Transpose an Anthony Weiner Selfie into R&B," WashingtonPost.com, June 29, 2014, http://www.washingtonpost.com/entertainment/music/robin-thicke-ignites-discussion-with-paula-but-these-songs-arent-worth-talking-about/2014/06/29/ce1f8b3a-ffc1-11e3-8572-4b1b969b6322_story.html.

13. Michael Deacon, "The Fall May Be 'Repulsive'—but It's Right to Show the Graphic Murder of Women," *Telegraph*, November 13, 2014, http://www.telegraph.co.uk/culture/tvandradio/11228749/the-fall-bbc-2-murder-women-gillian-anderson.html; McKay, "TV Now Exploiting Rape for Ratings?"

14. Rebecca Reid, "If Rape Scenes on Stage and Screen Aren't Horrific Then They Aren't Doing Their Job," *Telegraph*, June 30, 2015, http://www.telegraph.co.uk/women/womens-life/11708465/William-Tell-gang-rape-scene-at-Royal-Opera-House-should-be-horrific.html.

15. Karen Valby, "Hey TV: Stop Raping Women," *Entertainment Weekly*, February 27, 2014, http://www.ew.com/article/2014/02/27/tv-rape-scenes-downton-abbey-house-of-cards-scandal.

16. Lisa Cuklanz, *Rape on Prime Time: Television, Masculinity, and Sexual Violence* (Philadelphia, PA: University of Pennsylvania Press, 1999); Katherine

Foss, "Choice or Chance? Gender, Victimization, and Responsibility in CSI: Crime Scene Investigation," *Journal of Research on Women and Gender* 1, no. 1 (2010); Tanya Horeck, *Public Rape: Representing Violation in Fiction and Film* (London, UK: Routledge, 2004); Stacey J. T. Hust et al., "Law & Order, CSI, and NCIS: The Association between Exposure to Crime Drama Franchises, Rape Myth Acceptance, and Sexual Consent Negotiation among College Students," *Journal of Health Communication*, September 29, 2015, 1–13.

17. Victoria McNally, "An Expert Explains Why 'Game of Thrones' Can't 'Just Throw' Their Rape Story Line in One Episode," MTV, May 18, 2015, http://www.mtv.com/news/2163324/game-of-thrones-rape-portrayal.

18. Lauren Duca, "Middlebrow: 'Downton Abbey' and the Problem of Rape as a Plot Point," *Huffington Post*, March 25, 2014, http://www.huffingtonpost.com/2014/02/26/middlebrow-downton-abbey_n_4858325.html.

19. Jada Yuan, "Orange Is the New Black Is the Only TV Show That Understands Rape," *Vulture*, July 6, 2015, http://www.vulture.com/2015/07/orange-is-the-new-black-is-the-only-tv-show-that-understands-rape.html.

20. Natasha Vargas-Cooper, "What Makes a Good Rape Scene," FeministFilm.Tumblr.com, December 26, 2011, http://feministfilm.tumblr.com/post/14822373493/what-makes-a-good-rape-scene-by-natasha.

21. Cuklanz, *Rape on Prime Time: Television, Masculinity, and Sexual Violence*; Susan Estrich, *Real Rape* (Cambridge, MA: Harvard University Press, 1988).

22. Candace West and Don H. Zimmerman, "Doing Gender," *Gender & Society* 1, no. 2 (June 1, 1987): 125–51.

23. Cuklanz, *Rape on Prime Time: Television, Masculinity, and Sexual Violence*.

24. Ibid., 5.

25. Ibid., 156.

26. Eliana Dockterman, "Comic-Con Women Protest Sexual Harassment," *Time*, July 28, 2014, http://time.com/3045797/women-comic-con-sexual-harrassment-petition; Rosenberg, "From Washington to Westeros, How Rape Plays Out on TV."

27. Cuklanz, *Rape on Prime Time: Television, Masculinity, and Sexual Violence*.

28. Foss, "Choice or Chance? Gender, Victimization, and Responsibility in CSI: Crime Scene Investigation."

29. Carrie Nelson, "'Transparent' Recap 1x3: 'Rollin,'" *Observer*, October 3, 2014, http://observer.com/2014/10/transparent-recap-1x3-rollin; Jenelle Riley, "Amazon, 'Transparent' Make History at Golden Globes," *Variety*, January 11, 2015, http://variety.com/2015/tv/news/amazon-transparent-make-history-at-golden-globes-1201400485.

30. Nelson, "'Transparent' Recap 1x3: 'Rollin.'"

31. Sarah Projansky, *Watching Rape: Film and Television in Postfeminist Culture* (New York: New York University Press, 2001), 232.

32. Ibid., 95.

33. Emily Nussbaum, "Emily Nussbaum on the Rape Episode of 'Private Practice'," *NYMag*, November 15, 2010, http://nymag.com/arts/tv/reviews/69621.

34. Leigh Alexander, "What Did They Do to You? Our Women Heroes Problem," Gamasutra.com, June 11, 2014, http://www.gamasutra.com/view/news/219074/What_did_they_do_to_you_Our_women_heroes_problem.php.

35. McNamara, "Is There a 'Right' Way to Depict Rape on TV?"

36. Chauncey DeVega, "Michonne or Maggie? Race, Gender, and Rape on the Walking Dead TV Series," Alternet.org, November 26, 2012, http://www.alternet.org/speakeasy/chaunceydevega/michonne-or-maggie-race-gender-and-rape-walking-dead-tv-series.

37. "Comic-Con Women Protest Sexual Harassment"; Jace Hall, "Keeping It Real: Rape in Video Games," JaceHallShow.com, May 1, 2013, http://www.jacehallshow.com/keeping-it-real/20130501/rape-in-video-games-rape-gaming-stop.

38. Walbert Castillo, "Military Sexual Assault Reform Bill Falls Short," CNN.com, June 16, 2015, http://www.cnn.com/2015/06/16/politics/military-sexual-assault-bill/index.html; Laura Bassett, "Military Rape Cases Will Stay in the Chain of Command," *Huffington Post*, June 16, 2015, http://www.huffingtonpost.com/2015/06/16/gillibrand-military-sexual-assault_n_7597386.html.

39. Nina Strochlic, "House of Cards Star's Real Battle against Rape," *Daily Beast*, March 7, 2014, http://www.thedailybeast.com/articles/2014/03/07/house-of-cards-star-s-real-battle-against-rape.html.

40. Stuart Jeffries, "House of Cards Recap: Season Two, Episode Four—'Your Wife's on the Line,'" *Guardian*, February 21, 2014, http://www.theguardian.com/tv-and-radio/tvandradioblog/2014/feb/21/house-of-cards-season-two-episode-four; Conor Friedersdorf, "Feminism, Depravity, and Power in House of Cards," *The Atlantic*, February 20, 2014, http://www.theatlantic.com/politics/archive/2014/02/feminism-and-power-in-em-house-of-cards-em/283960; Ralph Keyes, *The Quote Verifier: Who Said What, Where, and When* (New York: St. Martin's, 2006); Erin Whitney, "How Claire Underwood Changed the TV Antihero Forever," *Huffington Post*, March 5, 2014, http://www.huffingtonpost.com/2014/03/05/house-of-cards-tv-antihero-archetype_n_4899440.html.

41. Valby, "Hey TV: Stop Raping Women."

42. Kelsea Stahler, "'House of Cards' Season 2 Tackles Rape Scene Like No Other Thriller Has," Bustle.com, February 14, 2014, http://www.bustle.com/articles/15595-house-of-cards-season-2-tackles-rape-scene-like-no-other-thriller-has.

43. Meghann McCluskey, "Rape Culture Critical Analysis: Netflix's House of Cards: Colorado Coalition against Sexual Assault," CCASA.org, March 14, 2014, http://www.ccasa.org/rape-culture-critical-analysis-netflixs-house-of-cards.

44. Diane Gordon, "Esme Bianco on Being at the Forefront of Game of Thrones' Sexposition Revolution," *Vulture*, February 9, 2015, http://

www.vulture.com/2015/02/game-of-thrones-esme-bianco-sexposition-revolu-tion.html; Michael Hann, "How 'Sexposition' Fleshes Out the Story," *Guardian*, March 11, 2012, http://www.theguardian.com/tv-and-radio/2012/mar/11/sexposition-story-tv-drama; Margaret Lyons, "'Game of Thrones' Great Moments in Sexposition," *Vulture*, June 13, 2011, http://www.vulture.com/2011/06/game_of_thrones_sexposition.html; Myles McNutt, "Game of Thrones—'You Win or You Die,'" *Cultural Learnings*, May 29, 2011, http://cultural-learnings.com/2011/05/29/game-of-thrones-you-win-or-you-die.

45. Laurie Penny, "Laurie Penny on Game of Thrones and the Good Ruler Complex," *New Statesman*, June 4, 2012, http://www.newstatesman.com/blogs/tv-and-radio/2012/06/game-thrones-and-good-ruler-complex.

46. Gay, "'Game of Thrones' Glamorizes Rape: That Was Not Consent, and Rape Is Not a Narrative Device"; Danielle Henderson, "Game of Thrones: Too Much Racism and Sexism—So I Stopped Watching," *Guardian*, April 29, 2014, http://www.theguardian.com/tv-and-radio/2014/apr/29/game-of-thrones-racism-sexism-rape; Bethany Jones, "Game of Thrones, Sex and HBO: Where Did TV's Sexual Pioneer Go Wrong?," *Jezebel*, June 5, 2014, http://jeze-bel.com/game-of-thrones-sex-and-hbo-where-did-tvs-sexual-pion-1586508636; Erik Kain, "Does 'Game of Thrones' Have a Misogyny Problem? [Updated]," *Forbes*, April 21, 2014, http://www.forbes.com/sites/erikkain/2014/04/21/does-game-of-thrones-have-a-misogyny-problem.

47. Andi Zeisler, "Does It Matter Whether Game of Thrones Is Feminist?," BitchMagazine.org, June 7, 2013, http://bitchmagazine.org/post/does-it-mat-ter-whether-game-of-thrones-is-feminist.

48. red3blog, "@Red3blog on Twitter," Twitter.com, April 21, 2014, https://twitter.com/red3blog/status/458280758852194304; KMeehlhause, "Kellie Meehlhause on Twitter," Twitter.com, May 27, 2014, https://twitter.com/KMeehlhause/status/471383141744005120; AverageCharles, "Charles Gerian on Twitter," Twitter.com, February 24, 2014, https://twitter.com/Average-Charles/status/478362301385695232.

49. Aaron Crouch, "'Game of Thrones' Director on Controversial Scene: Jaime 'Traumatized,' Cersei 'a Wreck' (Q&A)," *Hollywood Reporter*, April 20, 2014, http://www.hollywoodreporter.com/live-feed/game-thrones-director-controversial-scene-697733.

50. Ibid.

51. Alan Sepinwall, "Review: 'Game of Thrones'—'Breaker of Chains,'" *Hit-Fix*, April 20, 2014, http://www.hitfix.com/whats-alan-watching/review-game-of-thrones-breaker-of-chains-uncle-deadly.

52. Ibid.

53. James Hibberd, "'Game of Thrones' Stars Get Candid about THAT Scene: 'It Wasn't Rape,'" *Entertainment Weekly*, April 7, 2015, http://www.ew.com/article/2015/04/07/jaime-cersei-controversy-sex; Tyler Johnson, "Lena Headey on Game of Thrones Rape Scene: It Felt Great!," *Hollywood Gossip*, April 29, 2014, http://www.thehollywoodgossip.com/2014/04/lena-hea-dey-talks-game-of-thrones-rape-scene-it-wasnt-right-but.

54. Marlow Stern, "Game of Thrones' Most WTF Sex Scene: Nikolaj Coster-Waldau on Jaime Lannister's Darkest Hour," *Daily Beast*, April 20, 2014, http://www.thedailybeast.com/articles/2014/04/20/game-of-thrones-most-wtf-sex-scene-nikolaj-coster-waldau-on-jaime-lannister-s-darkest-hour.html.

55. Gay, "'Game of Thrones' Glamorizes Rape: That Was Not Consent, and Rape Is Not a Narrative Device"; Davies, "The Game of Thrones Rape Scene Was Unnecessary and Despicable."

56. Scott Meslow, "The Sexual Politics of Game of Thrones Just Got Enormously Worse," *The Week*, April 20, 2014, http://theweek.com/articles/447693/sexual-politics-game-thrones-just-got-enormously-worse.

57. In fact, the commentary around the scene became so unrelenting that the book's author, George R. R. Martin, felt obligated to respond. On his blog, Martin stated of the scene, "The whole dynamic is different in the show. . . . The scene was always intended to be disturbing . . . but I do regret if it has disturbed people for the wrong reasons." G. R. R. Martin, "Author, Author!," April 21, 2014, accessed July 10, 2015, http://grrm.livejournal.com/367116.html.

58. Robert Chan, "Wait, Was That in the Book?! The Original Text of That Jaime and Cersei Scene from 'Game of Thrones,'" News.Yahoo.com, April 23, 2014, https://www.yahoo.com/tv/bp/the-original-text-of-the-jaime-and-cersei-lannister-scene-from-game-of-thrones-174712598.html.

59. Gay, "'Game of Thrones' Glamorizes Rape: That Was Not Consent, and Rape Is Not a Narrative Device."

60. Ibid.

61. Laura Hudson, "That Game of Thrones Scene Wasn't a 'Turn-on,' It Was Rape," Wired.com, April 21, 2014, http://www.wired.com/2014/04/game-of-thrones-rape.

62. Nicola Gavey, *Just Sex? The Cultural Scaffolding of Rape* (New York: Routledge, 2005), 19.

63. Ibid., 22.

64. Estelle Freedman, "Redefining Rape," *Chronicle of Higher Education*, September 16, 2013, 1–7.

65. Rose Corrigan, *Up Against a Wall: Rape Reform and the Failure of Success* (New York: New York University Press, 2013), 75.

66. Stephen Schulhofer, *Unwanted Sex: The Culture of Intimidation and the Failure of Law* (Cambridge, MA: Harvard University Press, 1998), 276.

67. Ian Urbina, "The Challenge of Defining Rape," NYTimes.com, October 11, 2014, http://www.nytimes.com/2014/10/12/sunday-review/being-clear-about-rape.html?_r=0.

68. Gavey, *Just Sex? The Cultural Scaffolding of Rape*.

69. Bonnie S. Fisher, Leah Daigle, and Francis Cullen, *Unsafe in the Ivory Tower: The Sexual Victimization of College Women* (Thousand Oaks, CA: Sage, 2010), 132.

70. Ibid.

71. Ibid., 136.

72. Hudson, "That Game of Thrones Scene Wasn't a 'Turn-on,' It Was Rape."

73. Rebecca Keegan, "Comic-Con 2014: Outcry, Action against Harassment Grows," *Hero Complex*, July 24, 2014, http://herocomplex.latimes.com/fans/comic-con-2014-outcry-action-against-harassment-grows.

74. From the perspective of Sansa, the scene was viewed as unnecessary because she had already been subjected to an enormous amount of pain and suffering on her journey, and this was viewed as egregious. From the perspective of the rapist, it was argued the scene was unnecessary because the show had already demonstrated Ramsey as evil and sadistic through scenes in which he had tortured and castrated his prisoner, Theon. L. Hill, "'Game of Thrones' Recap: Another Brutal Wedding, Another Vicious Rape," *Salon*, May 18, 2015, accessed July 28, 2015, http://www.salon.com/2015/05/18/game_of_thrones_recap_the_honor_of_your_presence_is_requested_at_another_brutal_wedding; T. Ley, "Game of Thrones Is Gross, Exploitative, and Totally Out of Ideas," May 18, 2015, accessed July 28, 2015, http://theconcourse.deadspin.com/game-of-thrones-is-gross-exploitative-and-totally-out-1705235364; Joanna Robinson, "Game of Thrones Absolutely Did Not Need to Go There with Sansa Stark," VanityFair.com, May 27, 2015, http://www.vanityfair.com/hollywood/2015/05/game-of-thrones-rape-sansa-stark.

75. Claire McCaskill, "Ok I'm done . . . ," Twitter.com, May 19, 2015, https://twitter.com/clairecmc/status/600636817239605249.

76. Jill Pantozzi, "We Will No Longer Be Promoting HBO's Game of Thrones," *The Mary Sue*, May 18, 2015, http://www.themarysue.com/we-will-no-longer-be-promoting-hbos-game-of-thrones.

77. James Hibberd, "'Game of Thrones': Sophie Turner Reveals She 'Loved' That Horrifying Scene," *Entertainment Weekly*, May 17, 2015, http://www.ew.com/article/2015/05/17/game-thrones-sansa-wedding.

78. Tim Walker, "Game of Thrones Star Sophie Turner Films Rape Scene in Front of Parents," *Telegraph*, March 6, 2014, http://www.telegraph.co.uk/culture/tvandradio/game-of-thrones/10679012/Game-of-Thrones-star-Sophie-Turner-films-rape-scene-in-front-of-parents.html.

79. Leslie Loftis, "'Game of Thrones' Fans Need to Understand Sansa's Rape," *The Federalist*, May 22, 2015, http://thefederalist.com/2015/05/22/game-of-thrones-fans-shouldnt-leave-because-of-sansa-starks-rape.

80. Similarly, the author of the book series, George R. R. Martin, is frequently quoted as defending the sexual violence in his books by suggesting that its inclusion reveals a larger truth. Predictably, the notion that somehow sexual violence is necessary for historical accuracy, in a series that features dragons, white walkers (zombies), and other mythical creatures, generated some backlash. David Itzkoff, "For 'Game of Thrones,' Rising Unease over Rape's Recurring Role," *New York Times*, May 2, 2014, accessed July 8, 2015, http://www.nytimes.com/2014/05/03/arts/television/for-game-of-thrones-rising-unease-over-rapes-recurring-role.html.

81. Loftis, "'Game of Thrones' Fans Need to Understand Sansa's Rape."

82. Robby Soave, "Yes, Game of Thrones Is a Show about Rape: I Still Hated That Scene," *Reason*, May 20, 2015, http://social.reason.com/blog/2015/05/20/yes-game-of-thrones-is-a-show-about-rape.

83. Barbara Winslow, personal conversation, February 3, 2015.

84. Emily Tess Katz, "Why Talking about 'Game of Thrones' Rape Is Important for Feminism," *Huffington Post*, May 22, 2015, http://www.huffingtonpost.com/2015/05/22/game-of-thrones-rape-scenes_n_7410386.html; Zeisler, "Does It Matter Whether Game of Thrones Is Feminist?"; Meghan Murphy, "Just Because You Like It, Doesn't Make It Feminist: On Game of Thrones' Imagined Feminism," *Feminist Current*, April 26, 2013, http://feministcurrent.com/7578/just-because-you-like-it-doesnt-make-it-feminist; Suzanne Samin, "Last Night's Episode of 'Game of Thrones' Was More Proof of the Show's Disturbingly Un-Feminist Path," xoJane.com, May 18, 2015, http://www.xojane.com/issues/sansa-stark-marital-rape.

85. Caroline Siede, "The Naked Hypocrisy of Game of Thrones' Nudity," Boingboing.Net, May 12, 2015, http://boingboing.net/2015/05/12/the-naked-hypocrisy-of-game-of.html.

86. Jennifer Armstrong, "'Game of Thrones': Feminist or Not?," *Entertainment Weekly*, April 18, 2011, http://www.ew.com/article/2011/04/18/game-of-thrones-feminist-or-not; Kate Aurther, "9 Ways 'Game of Thrones' Is Actually Feminist," *BuzzFeed*, April 17, 2013, http://www.buzzfeed.com/kateaurthur/9-ways-game-of-thrones-is-actually-feminist; Kate Maltby, "Why Feminists Like Me Are Addicted to Game of Thrones," *Spectator*, June 16, 2015, http://specc.ie/1IIcQZu.

87. Scott Bixby, "There's Something Very Different about This Season of 'Game of Thrones,'" Mic.com, April 10, 2015, http://mic.com/articles/115172/game-of-thrones-is-back-and-more-feminist-than-ever-before.

88. Alison Young, *The Scene of Violence: Cinema, Crime, Affect* (New York: Routledge, 2010), 9.

89. Steven Shaviro, 2007, 8, as quoted in Melissa Gregg and Gregory Seigworth, *The Affect Theory Reader* (Durham, NC: Duke University Press, 2010).

90. Young, *The Scene of Violence*, 70.

91. Ibid., 72.

92. Patricia Pisters, *The Matrix of Visual Culture: Working with Deleuze in Film Theory* (Stanford, CA: Stanford University Press, 2003), 70.

93. *The Girl with the Dragon Tattoo*—the Swedish version originally titled *Men Who Hate Women*—is the first of Stieg Larsson's *Millennium* trilogy. The book was first published in 2005 and sold over sixty million copies in fifty countries (http://www.stieglarsson.com). *The Girl Who Played with Fire* and *The Girl Who Kicked the Hornets' Nest* followed in 2006 and 2007, respectively. The books spawned a Swedish film trilogy, with the first installment reaching the highest-grossing film ever in Sweden and Europe's top moneymaker in 2009. Susan Donalson James, "Rape Victims Applaud Power of Stieg Larsson Films to Educate," ABCNews.com, August 27, 2010, http://abcnews.go.com/Health/MindMoodResourceCenter/stieg-larssons-film-girl-dragon-tattoo-teaches-college/story?id=11490699&page=1#.T-N4mWNXNhs.

For a collection of feminist perspectives on the themes of sexual violence in the films and books, see D. King and C. L. Smith, eds., *Men Who Hate Women and Women Who Kick Their Asses: Stieg Larsson's Millennium Trilogy in Feminist Perspective* (Nashville, TN: Vanderbilt University Press, 2012).

94. Liz Spikol, "Rape Scene in the Girl with the Dragon Tattoo," Blog.PhillyWeekly.com, January 4, 2012, http://blog.phillyweekly.com/trouble/2012/01/04/rape-scene-in-the-girl-with-the-dragon-tattoo-major-spoilers.

95. Rodrigo Perez, "Interview: David Fincher Talks Violence, Unpleasant Revenge & the Odd, Perverse Relationship That Drew Him to 'The Girl with the Dragon Tattoo,'" *Indiewire*, December 21, 2011, http://blogs.indiewire.com/theplaylist/david-fincher-talks-violence-unpleasant-revenge-the-odd-perverse-relationship-that-drew-him-to-the-girl-with-the-dragon-tattoo.

96. Vargas-Cooper, "What Makes a Good Rape Scene."

97. Catherine Traywick, "David Fincher's Girl with the Dragon Tattoo Comes to Life," MsMagazine.com, November 26, 2011, http://msmagazine.com/blog/2011/12/26/david-fincher-brings-the-girl-with-the-dragon-tattoo-to-life; Maria Aspan, "The Better Part of Valor: Should David Fincher Have Skipped the Dragon Tattoo Rape Scene?," Maspan.Tumblr.com, January 4, 2012, http://maspan.tumblr.com/post/15325639376/david-fincher-dragon-tattoo-rape; Catherine Traywick, "The Rape of 'The Girl with the Dragon Tattoo,'" MsMagazine.com, April 14, 2010, http://msmagazine.com/blog/2010/04/14/the-rape-of-the-girl-with-the-dragon-tattoo.

98. Declan Cashin, "Inside the World of Dragon Tattoo Director David Fincher," *Independent*, December 16, 2011, http://www.independent.ie/entertainment/movies/inside-the-world-of-dragon-tattoo-director-david-fincher-26803583.html.

99. This tweet by one viewer exemplifies this mixed reaction: "thx to #MOUTHTAPEDSHUT for #DragonTattoo screening(+poster). Mind=Blown. Im left feeling dirty & raw in the best possible way, thx Fincher!" Amir Swarko, "Thx to #MOUTHTAPEDSHUT," @amirest, Twitter.com, December 13, 2011, http://twitter.com/Amirest/status/146562161689374720.

100. Noomi Rapace, "The Girl with the Dragon Tattoo—Exclusive: Noomi Rapace and Niels Arden Oplev Interview," YouTube, September 24, 2010, http://www.youtube.com/watch?v=vAD-6EQLqto.

101. Amy Sullivan, "'The Fall': The Most Feminist Show on Television," *The Atlantic*, January 23, 2015, http://www.theatlantic.com/entertainment/archive/2015/01/the-fall-the-most-feminist-show-on-television/384751. The show debuted in 2013 in the UK and was declared BBC2's "highest-rated drama series in 10 years." The second season of the show was released in the United States in January 2015. Sarah Dempster, "The Fall Is One of the Best BBC Dramas in Years," *Guardian*, May 11, 2013, http://www.theguardian.com/tv-and-radio/2013/may/11/the-fall-gillian-anderson.

102. Hughes, "Rape on TV: A Justified Look at Violence against Women or a Crude Plot Device?"

103. "Why Does the BBC Think Violence against Women Is Sexy?," June 9, 2013.

104. Jenkins, "Is There Too Much Rape on Stage and TV?"

105. Janice Turner, "Janice Turner on Twitter," @VictoriaPeckham, Twitter.com, May 13, 2013, https://twitter.com/VictoriaPeckham/status/334062689070510080; Fozziebare, "Fozziebare on Twitter," Twitter.com, July 13, 2015, https://twitter.com/Fozziebare/status/509132728831586304; John Goodfellow, "John Goodfellow on Twitter," @yorkbassman, Twitter.com, November 28, 2014, https://twitter.com/yorkbassman/status/538375133216669696; Aaron Abernethy, "Aaron Abernethy on Twitter," @theronster, Twitter.com, November 13, 2014, https://twitter.com/theronster/status/533018616157847552.

106. David Wilson, "Prof David Wilson on Twitter," Twitter.com, November 20, 2014, https://twitter.com/ProfDavidWilson/status/535542388698406914.

107. David Wilson, "Top Criminologist Says BBC Thriller the Fall Is the Sickest Show on TV," *Daily Mail*, November 23, 2014, http://www.dailymail.co.uk/tvshowbiz/article-2846810/Top-criminologist-says-BBC-thriller-Fall-sickest-TV.html.

108. Amanda Rodriguez, "Gillian Anderson, Feminism, and BBC's 'The Fall,'" Btchflcks.com, January 8, 2014, http://www.btchflcks.com/2014/01/gillian-anderson-feminism-and-bbcs-the-fall.html#.VaQPBpNVikq.

109. Chris Harvey, "Jamie Dornan on the Fall: 'I Hope the Killer Gets Away with It,'" *Telegraph*, November 3, 2014, http://www.telegraph.co.uk/culture/tvandradio/11205248/jamie-dornan-gillian-anderson-the-fall-interview.html.

110. Allan Cubitt, "The Fall's Writer Allan Cubitt on Women and Violence in TV Drama," *Guardian*, June 7, 2013, http://www.theguardian.com/tv-and-radio/2013/jun/07/the-fall-allan-cubitt-women-violence.

111. Ibid.

112. Sullivan, "'The Fall': The Most Feminist Show on Television."

113. Wilson, "Top Criminologist Says BBC Thriller the Fall Is the Sickest Show on TV."

114. Shonda Rhimes, "I Agree That a Trigger Warning . . . ," @shondarhimes, Twitter.com, November 18, 2013, https://twitter.com/shondarhimes/status/402575982302740480.

115. Cicely Dyson, "'Scandal' Recap, Season 3, Episode 7, 'Everything's Coming Up Mellie,'" *Wall Street Journal*, November 14, 2013, http://blogs.wsj.com/speakeasy/2013/11/14/scandal-season-3-episode-8-vermont-is-for-lovers-too-tv-recap.

116. Margaret Lyons, "Scandal's Rape Isn't about Likability," *Vulture*, November 15, 2013, http://www.vulture.com/2013/11/scandal-mellie-rape-bigger.html; Erin Strecker, "'Scandal': We Need to Talk about That [SPOILER]," *Entertainment Weekly*, November 15, 2013, http://www.ew.com/article/2013/11/15/scandal-mellie-rape; Michael Arceneaux, "How You Like Her Now? Recapping Scandal, 'Everything's Coming Up Mellie' (Season 3, Episode 7)," *Complex*, November 15, 2013, http://www.complex.com/pop-culture/2013/11/scandal-recapeverythings-coming-up-mellie; Katie Atkinson, "Scandal Recap: Understanding Mellie," *Entertainment Weekly*, November 14, 2013, http://www.ew.com/recap/scandal-recap-mellie-everythings-coming-up/3; Sonia Sa-

raiya, "Scandal: 'Everything's Coming Up Mellie,'" *A.V. Club*, November 14, 2013, http://www.avclub.com/tvclub/everythings-coming-up-mellie-105604; Dyson, "'Scandal' Recap, Season 3, Episode 7, 'Everything's Coming Up Mellie'"; Hughes, "Rape on TV: A Justified Look at Violence against Women or a Crude Plot Device?"

117. "Scandal: The Sexual Assault Scene Was TERRIBLE," *Gradient Lair*, November 15, 2013, http://www.gradientlair.com/post/67050277590/scandal-abc-terrible-sexual-assault-jerry-mellie; Jamie Nesbitt Golden, "We Can Now Add 'Scandal' to the Long List of TV Shows That Lazily Rely on a Rape Scene to Make a Hated Character More Sympathetic," xoJane.com, November 15, 2013, http://www.xojane.com/entertainment/scandal-mellie-rape.

118. Amanda Marcotte, "The Year of the Trigger Warning," *Slate*, December 30, 2013, http://www.slate.com/blogs/xx_factor/2013/12/30/trigger_warnings_from_the_feminist_blogosphere_to_shonda_rhimes_in_2013.html.

119. While some research has focused on the traumatic effects of rape, other scholars reject the term "trauma" and instead prefer to describe the survivor's reaction to their experience as "identity shock," or what they consider "normal reactions to abnormal if not abhorrent behaviors by fellow citizens that suddenly threaten survivors' largely routine sense of social safety." S. D. Muldoon, S. C. Taylor, and C. Norma, "The Survivor Master Narrative in Sexual Assault," *Violence against Women*, December 30, 2015, 1–23, 2.

120. D. J. Snipes et al., "Rape and Posttraumatic Stress Disorder (PTSD): Examining the Mediating Role of Explicit Sex-Power Beliefs for Men versus Women," *Journal of Interpersonal Violence*, July 3, 2015, 1–18; Iva A. E. Bicanic et al., "Predictors of Delayed Disclosure of Rape in Female Adolescents and Young Adults," *European Journal of Psychotraumatology* 6 (May 11, 2015): 23645–49.

121. *Diagnostic and Statistical Manual of Mental Disorders*, 2013.

122. Alison Vingiano, "How the 'Trigger Warning' Took Over the Internet," *BuzzFeed*, May 5, 2014, http://www.buzzfeed.com/alisonvingiano/how-the-trigger-warning-took-over-the-internet.

123. Bailey Loverin, "Trigger Warnings Avert Trauma: Opposing View," USAToday.com, April 21, 2014, http://www.usatoday.com/story/opinion/2014/04/21/trigger-warnings-ptsd-bailey-loverin-editorials-debates/7985479.

124. Jenny Jarvie, "TRIGGER WARNING: This Is an Article about the Insidious Spread of Trigger Warnings," *New Republic*, March 3, 2014, http://www.newrepublic.com/article/116842/trigger-warnings-have-spread-blogs-college-classes-thats-bad.

125. AAUP, "On Trigger Warnings," AAUP.org, August 2014, http://www.aaup.org/report/trigger-warnings; Heather MacDonald, "Neo-Victorianism on Campus," *Weekly Standard*, October 20, 2014, http://www.weeklystandard.com/articles/neo-victorianism-campus_810871.html; Elizabeth Freeman et al., "Essay by Faculty Members about Why They Will Not Use Trigger Warnings," InsideHigherEd.com, May 29, 2014, https://www.insidehighered.com/views/2014/05/29/essay-faculty-members-about-why-they-will-not-use-trigger-warnings#sthash.1umm5li5.pqnKjO8F.dpbs; Jo-

nah Goldberg, "The Peculiar Madness of 'Trigger Warnings,'" *Los Angeles Times*, May 19, 2014, http://www.latimes.com/opinion/op-ed/la-oe-goldberg-trigger-warnings-20140520-column.html; Editorial Board, "Warning, This Editorial May Upset You: Our View," USAToday.com, April 21, 2014, http://www.usatoday.com/story/opinion/2014/04/21/trigger-warnings-college-campuses-editorials-debates/7985381; Editorial, "Demanding to Be Regarded as Vulnerable Infants," *Macleans*, May 21, 2014, http://www.macleans.ca/i; Jennifer Medina, "Warning: The Literary Canon Could Make Students Squirm," *New York Times*, May 17, 2014, http://www.nytimes.com/2014/05/18/us/warning-the-literary-canon-could-make-students-squirm.html; Tracy Moore, "We Don't Have to Use Trigger Warnings, but We Can Learn from Them," *Jezebel*, May 20, 2014, http://jezebel.com/we-dont-have-to-use-trigger-warnings-but-we-can-learn-1578653191; Judith Shulevitz, "In College and Hiding From Scary Ideas," *New York Times*, March 21, 2015, http://www.nytimes.com/2015/03/22/opinion/sunday/judith-shulevitz-hiding-from-scary-ideas.html; Jill Filipovic, "We've Gone Too Far with 'Trigger Warnings,'" *Guardian*, March 5, 2014, http://www.theguardian.com/commentisfree/2014/mar/05/trigger-warnings-can-be-counterproductive; Alexandra Brodsky, "Trigger Warning: School," *Feministing*, March 6, 2014, http://feministing.com/2014/03/06/trigger-warning-school; Jessica Valenti, "Feminists Talk Trigger Warnings: A Round-Up," *The Nation*, March 6, 2014, http://www.thenation.com/blog/178725/feminists-talk-trigger-warnings-round; Avi Strauss, "Trigger Warnings: Insulating Thought and Opinion from Challenges," *The Commentator*, March 22, 2015, http://yucommentator.org/2015/03/trigger-warnings-insulating-thought-and-opinion-from-challenges; Avens O'Brien, "What's the Problem with Trigger Warnings?," *Libertarian Republic*, March 24, 2015; Chris Hernandez, "'Microaggressions' and 'Trigger Warnings,' Meet Real Trauma," *The Federalist*, March 24, 2015, http://thefederalist.com/2015/03/24/microaggressions-and-trigger-warnings-meet-real-trauma; Choire Sicha, "When 'Trigger Warning' Lost All Its Meaning," *The Awl*, May 30, 2012, http://www.theawl.com/2012/05/when-trigger-warning-lost-all-its-meaning; Florence Waters, "Trigger Warnings: More Harm Than Good?," *Telegraph*, October 4, 2014, http://www.telegraph.co.uk/culture/books/11106670/Trigger-warnings-more-harm-than-good.html; Barbara King, "Grappling with Trigger Warnings and Trauma on Campus," NPR, August 21, 2014, http://www.npr.org/blogs/13.7/2014/08/21/342096499/grappling-with-trigger-warnings-and-trauma-on-campus; Ponta Abadi, "Trigger-Warning Debate Ignores Survivors' Voices," MsMagazine.com, May 20, 2014, http://msmagazine.com/blog/2014/05/29/the-trigger-warning-debate-ignores-survivors-voices; Editorial Board, "Warning: College Students, This Editorial May Upset You," *Los Angeles Times*, March 31, 2014, http://www.latimes.com/opinion/editorials/la-ed-trigger-warnings-20140331-story.html.

126. Valenti, "Feminists Talk Trigger Warnings: A Round-Up."

127. Wendy Kaminer, "The Progressive Ideas behind the Lack of Free Speech on Campus," *Washington Post*, February 20, 2015, http://www.washingtonpost.com/opinions/the-progressive-ideas-behind-the-lack-of-free-

speech-on-campus/2015/02/20/93086efe-b0e7-11e4-886b-c22184f27c35_
story.html; AAUP, "On Trigger Warnings"; Medina, "Warning: The Literary
Canon Could Make Students Squirm."

128. Judith Shulevitz, "In College and Hiding from Scary Ideas," *New York
Times*, March 21, 2015, http://www.nytimes.com/2015/03/22/opinion/sunday/
judith-shulevitz-hiding-from-scary-ideas.html.

129. Jill, "Brilliant at Breakfast: Where No One Cashes in on Unpaid Writers," BrilliantatBreakfast.Blogspot.com, April 25, 2014, http://brilliantatbreak-
fast.blogspot.com/2014/05/and-its-only-going-to-get-worse.html.

130. John Plunkett, "Downton Abbey Rape Scene Will Not Face Investigation Despite Complaints," *Guardian*, November 4, 2014, http://www.
theguardian.com/media/2013/nov/04/downton-abbey-rape-scene-no-
investigation-itv.

131. Jess Denham, "Joanne Froggatt: Downton Abbey Star Wins Golden
Globe for Role in Rape Storyline," *Independent*, January 21, 2015, http://
www.independent.co.uk/arts-entertainment/tv/news/golden-globes-2015-
downton-abbey-star-joanne-froggatt-wins-for-role-in-rape-storyline-
0071414.html; Michael Getler, "A Downton Downer and Other Things," PBS,
January 13, 2014, http://www.pbs.org/ombudsman/2014/01/the_mailbag_a_
downton_downer_and_other_things.html; Dave Itzkoff, "Watching 'Downton
Abbey': A Shocking Crime," *New York Times*, January 12, 2014, http://arts-
beat.blogs.nytimes.com/2014/01/12/watching-downton-abbey-a-shocking-
crime; Emily Orley, "'Downton Abbey' Finally Went Too Far," *BuzzFeed*,
February 10, 2014, http://www.buzzfeed.com/emilyorley/downton-abbey-rape-
storyline-finally-went-too-far; June Thomas, "Downton Abbey Continues Its
Sadistic Streak against Women," *Slate*, January 12, 2015, http://www.slate.com/
blogs/xx_factor/2014/01/12/downton_abbey_rape_why_is_the_show_so_
horrible_to_anna_and_other_women.html.

132. Claire Cohen, "Golden Globes 2015: Joanne Froggatt's Rape Survivor
Tribute Was Brilliantly Bold," *Telegraph*, January 12, 2015, http://www.
telegraph.co.uk/women/womens-life/11339721/Golden-Globes-2015-Joanne-
Froggatts-rape-survivor-tribute-was-bold.html.

4. GEEK SPACES: "PRETTY GIRLS PRETENDING TO BE GEEKS"

1. Ubisoft, "Facts & Figures | About Ubisoft | Ubisoft Group," Ubisoft,
2014, https://www.ubisoftgroup.com/en-US/about_ubisoft/facts_and_figures.
aspx.

2. Steven Burns, "No Female Leads in Assassin's Creed Unity 'Unfortu-
nate but a Reality of Game Development.'" VideoGamer.com, June 11, 2014.
http://www.videogamer.com/pc/assassins_creed_unity/news/no_female_leads_
in_assassins_creed_unity_unfortunate_but_a_reality_of_game_development_
ubi.html.

3. Jonathan Cooper, "In my educated opinion, I would estimate this to be a day or two's work. Not a replacement of 8000 animations," June 11, 2014, Twitter.com, https://twitter.com/GameAnim/status/476638349097058304.

4. Rich McCormick, "Adding Female Characters to New 'Assassin's Creed' Would 'Double the Work,' Says Ubisoft," *The Verge*, 2014, http://www.theverge.com/2014/6/11/5799386/no-female-characters-in-assassins-creed-unity-too-much-work; Associated Press, "Lack of Leading Ladies Haunts Video Games—CBS Dallas / Fort Worth," 2014; Tauriq Moosa, "Video Games Need More Than Damsels and Dames," *Daily Beast*, 2014, http://www.thedailybeast.com/articles/2014/06/18/video-games-need-more-than-damsels-and-dames.print.html#; Jonathan Ore, "Ubisoft Grilled after Female Assassin's Creed Characters Cut for Production Reasons—Your Community," CBCNews, 2014, http://www.cbc.ca/newsblogs/yourcommunity/2014/06/ubi-soft-grilled-after-female-assassins-creed-characters-cut-for-production-rea-sons.html.

5. Dennis Scimeca, "The Real Reason Women Were Left Out of 'Assassins Creed Unity,'" *Daily Dot*, 2014, http://www.dailydot.com/opinion/reason-women-left-out-assassins-creed; Gary Cutlack, "Internet United over Lack of Female Characters in Assassin's Creed Unity," *TechRadar*, 2014, http://www.techradar.com/news/gaming/internet-united-over-lack-of-female-charac-ters-in-assassin-s-creed-unity-1253288.

6. Evan Narcisse, "Ubisoft Responds to Assassin's Creed Female Charac-ter Controversy," *Kotaku*, 2014, http://kotaku.com/ubisoft-responds-to-assas-sins-creed-female-character-co-1589413130.

7. Moosa, "Video Games Need More Than Damsels and Dames."

8. JJovana on Twitter, "Unless You Are Killing Her, Buying Her or Selling Her, @Ubisoft Cant Animate a Woman You Can Actually Play. #Womenare-toohardtoanimate," @JJovana, 2014, https://twitter.com/JJovana/status/477162264743530496.

9. Arthur Chu, "Your Princess Is in Another Castle: Misogyny, Entitle-ment, and Nerds," *Daily Beast*, May 27, 2014, http://www.thedailybeast.com/articles/2014/05/27/your-princess-is-in-another-castle-misogyny-entitlement-and-nerds.html; Kate Harding, *Asking for It: The Alarming Rise of Rape Cul-ture—and What We Can Do about It* (Boston, MA: Da Capo Lifelong Books, 2014).

10. Aja Romano, "Rape, Harassment, and Misogyny in Geek Culture: 2012 in Review," *Daily Dot*, December 18, 2012, http://www.dailydot.com/society/rape-misogyny-female-geek-gamers-culture.

11. Aja Romano, "Black Cat Cosplayer Sexually Harassed at Comic Con Becomes Tumblr Hero," *Daily Dot*, October 16, 2012, http://www.dailydot.com/news/black-cat-cosplayer-nycc-harassment-tumblr; Alyssa Rosenberg, "Convention Etiquette 101: How to Avoid Crossing the Line at Comic-Con," Wired.com, July 15, 2013, http://www.wired.com/2013/07/convention-eti-quette-comic-con; staff, "'We Don't Owe Them a Fantasy': Woman Who Dressed in Racy Costume for Comic Con Speaks Out about Sexual Harass-ment," *Daily Mail*, October 20, 2012, http://www.dailymail.co.uk/news/article-

2220586/Comic-Con-Mandy-Caruso-dressed-racy-costume-recalls-sexual-ha-rassment-fans.html.

12. Mandy Caruso, "The Grind Haus, at Comic Con Today, I Went as Black Cat. This Is a . . . ," Beautilation.Tumblr.com, 2012, http://beautilation.tumblr.com/post/33538802648.

13. As a disclaimer, Peacock wrote, "And be it known that I am good friends with several stunningly beautiful women who cosplay as stunningly beautiful characters from comics, sci-fi, fantasy and other genres of fandom." Joe Peacock, "Booth Babes Need Not Apply," CNN, July 24, 2012, http://geekout.blogs.cnn.com/2012/07/24/booth-babes-need-not-apply.

14. Tara Tiger Brown, "Dear Fake Geek Girls: Please Go Away," *Forbes*, March 26, 2012, http://www.forbes.com/sites/tarabrown/2012/03/26/dear-fake-geek-girls-please-go-away.

15. ESA, "U.S. Video Game Industry Generates $23.5 Billion in Revenue for 2015," Theesa.com, February 16, 2016, http://www.theesa.com/article/u-s-video-game-industry-generates-23-5-billion-in-revenue-for-2015.

16. ESA, "Essential Facts about the Computer and Video Game Industry," Theesa.com, 2015, http://www.theesa.com/wp-content/uploads/2015/04/ESA-Essential-Facts-2015.pdf.

17. Andy Chalk, "Researchers Find That Female PC Gamers Outnumber Males," *PC Gamer*, October 28, 2014, http://www.pcgamer.com//researchers-find-that-female-pc-gamers-outnumber-males; Jessica Conditt, "Report: Men Play More MMOs, FPSes; Women Rule Mobile, RPG | Joystiq," Joystiq.com, October 28, 2014, http://www.joystiq.com/2014/10/27/report-men-play-more-mmos-fpscs-women-rule-mobile-rpg; Heather Newman, "Women Game Much More Than You Realize, Research Firm Shows," *Venture Beat*, October 28, 2014, http://venturebeat.com/2014/10/28/women-game-much-more-than-you-realize-research-firm-shows.

18. Monica Anderson, "Views on Gaming Differ by Race, Ethnicity," *Pew Research Center*, December 17, 2015, http://www.pewresearch.org/fact-tank/2015/12/17/views-on-gaming-differ-by-race-ethnicity; Justine Cassell and Henry Jenkins, *From Barbie to Mortal Kombat: Gender and Computer Games* (Cambridge, MA: MIT Press, 1998); Adrienne Shaw, "Do You Identify as a Gamer? Gender, Race, Sexuality, and Gamer Identity," *New Media & Society* 14, no. 1 (February 24, 2012): 28–44.

19. "Twitch—About," Twitch.tv, accessed September 26, 2014, http://www.twitch.tv/p/about.

20. Gregor Aisch and Tom Giratikanon, "Charting the Rise of Twitch," *New York Times*, August 27, 2014, http://www.nytimes.com/interactive/2014/08/26/technology/charting-the-rise-of-twitch.html.

21. Ibid. In 2014, Amazon bought Twitch for $917 million in cash. Eugene Kim, "Amazon Buys Twitch for $970 Million in Cash," *Business Insider*, August 25, 2014, http://www.businessinsider.com/amazon-buys-twitch-2014-8.

22. Chris Morris, "Here Are the Best Selling Video Games of 2015," *Fortune*, January 14, 2016, http://fortune.com/2016/01/14/here-are-the-best-selling-video-games-of-2015.

23. Karen Dill and Kathryn Thill, "Video Game Characters and the Socialization of Gender Roles: Young People's Perceptions Mirror Sexist Media Depictions," *Sex Roles* 57, no. 11 (December 1, 2007): 851–64.; Kishonna L. Gray, *Race, Gender, and Deviance in Xbox Live: Theoretical Perspectives from the Virtual Margins* (New York: Routledge, 2014); Todd Harper, *The Culture of Digital Fighting Games: Performance and Practice* (New York: Routledge, 2014); James Ivory, "Still a Man's Game: Gender Representation in Online Reviews of Video Games," *Mass Communication and Society* 9, no. 1 (2006): 103–14; Adrienne Shaw, *Gaming at the Edge: Sexuality and Gender at the Margins of Gamer Culture* (Minneapolis: University of Minnesota Press, 2014).

24. Angela, "Thoughts of a Feminist Gamer, Opinions on Diversity in the Realms of Gaming and Geekery," AngelWitchPaganHeart.Wordpress.com, December 15, 2015, https://angelwitchpaganheart.wordpress.com/2015/12/15/thoughts-of-a-feminist-gamer-opinions-on-diversity-in-the-realms-of-gaming-and-geekery; Shaw, *Gaming at the Edge: Sexuality and Gender at the Margins of Gamer Culture*.

25. Grant Howitt, "Naughty Nuns Mislead in the Hitman: Absolution Trailer," *Guardian*, June 1, 2012; Keza MacDonald, "Opinion: What the Hell Is with That Hitman Trailer?," IGN, May 30, 2012, http://www.ign.com/articles/2012/05/30/opinion-what-the-hell-is-with-that-hitman-trailer; Dan Silver, "Why the Hitman Video Game Trailer Is a Shameless Piece of Sexist Tat Designed to Get the Internet Worked into a Lather," *Mirror*, May 31, 2012, http://www.mirror.co.uk/news/technology-science/technology/hitman-why-the-video-game-trailer-is-a-shameless-855466.

26. MacDonald, "Opinion: What the Hell Is with That Hitman Trailer?"

27. Rob Fahey, "Can't We Discuss This Like Adults?," *Games Industry*, May 31, 2012, http://www.gamesindustry.biz/articles/2012-05-31-cant-we-discuss-this-like-adults.

28. Ultimately, MacDonald later reported that Tore Blysted, the game director, was caught off guard by the criticisms and apologized for offending people. Blysted explained that the trailer was only one possible scenario from one level of the game and that stylistically, the game is designed to be reminiscent of film directors Quentin Tarantino and Robert Rodriquez's grind-house style. Keza MacDonald, "IO Apologetic over Hitman Trailer Controversy," IGN, June 6, 2012, http://www.ign.com/articles/2012/06/07/io-apologetic-over-hitman-trailer-controversy.

29. Gamasutra, "Gamasutra Salary Survey 2014," GameSetWatch.com, July 2014, http://www.gamesetwatch.com/2014/09/05/GAMA14_ACG_SalarySurvey_F.pdf.

30. Johanna Weststar and Marie-Josee Legualt, "IGDA Developer Satisfaction Survey: Summary Report 2015," C.YMCDN.com, September 2, 2015, https://c.ymcdn.com/sites/www.igda.org/resource/collection/CB31CE86-F8EE-4AE3-B46A-148490336605/IGDA%20DSS%202015-SummaryReport_Final_Sept15.pdf.

31. Jenny Haviner, "Not in the Kitchen Anymore," accessed September 8, 2014, http://www.notinthekitchenanymore.com.

32. The site's last post was October 9, 2013, with a follow-up post addressing the hiatus on June 21, 2015. "About | Fat, Ugly or Slutty," FatUglyOrSlutty.com, 2011, http://fatuglyorslutty.com/about; Amy O'Leary, "In Virtual Play, Sexual Harassment Is All Too Real," *New York Times*, August 1, 2012, http://www.nytimes.com/2012/08/02/us/sexual-harassment-in-online-gaming-stirs-anger.html.

33. Extra Credits, "Extra Credits: Harassment," YouTube, May 20, 2012, http://www.youtube.com/watch?v=Dt9GwmOWoqo; James Fletcher, "Sexual Harassment in the World of Video Gaming," BBC News, June 3, 2012, http://www.bbc.co.uk/news/magazine-18280000; Eric Patterson, "[PAX East] Exposing the Harassment Female Gamers Receive Online," EGM, April 9, 2012, http://www.egmnow.com/articles/news/pax-east-exposing-the-harassment-female-gamers-receive-online.

34. Keza MacDonald, "Are Gamers Really Sexist?," Guardian.co.uk, March 6, 2012, http://www.theguardian.com/technology/gamesblog/2012/mar/06/are-gamers-really-sexist.

35. Fletcher, "Sexual Harassment in the World of Video Gaming"; O'Leary, "In Virtual Play, Sexual Harassment Is All Too Real"; MacDonald, "Are Gamers Really Sexist?"; Jason Schreier, "This Is What a Gamer's Sexual Harassment Looks Like," *Kotaku*, February 29, 2012, http://kotaku.com/5889415/this-is-what-a-gamers-sexual-harassment-looks-like; Marcos Valdez, "Cross Assault Sexual Harassment Controversy Overshadows On-Screen Combat," *Venture Beat*, February 29, 2012, http://venturebeat.com/2012/02/29/cross-assault-sexual-harassment-controversy-overshadows-on-screen-combat.

36. Kirk Hamilton, "Competitive Gamer's Inflammatory Comments Spark Sexual Harassment Debate [Update]," February 28, 2012, http://kotaku.com/5889066/competitive-gamers-inflammatory-comments-spark-sexual-harassment-debate.

37. "Cross Assault—Day 6—Elimination & Interview," YouTube, February 27, 2012, http://www.youtube.com/watch?v=X6Ii-5KknyY.

38. "The Escapist: Forums: Gaming Discussion: Cross Assault? More Like Sexual Assault," n.d.

39. Ibid.

40. Ibid.

41. Gray, *Race, Gender, and Deviance in Xbox Live: Theoretical Perspectives From the Virtual Margins*.

42. Brian Crecente, "Game Dev Harassment Remains as Bad as It Was a Year Ago," *Polygon*, August 19, 2014, http://www.polygon.com/2014/8/19/6002893/plague-of-game-dev-harassment-one-year-later.

43. Adi Robertson, "Stop Ruining My Escapist Fantasies, Sarkeesian Haters," *The Verge*, August 28, 2014, http://www.theverge.com/2014/8/28/6078517/stop-ruining-my-escapist-fantasies-sarkeesian-haters.

44. Andrew Todd, "Video Games, Misogyny, and Terrorism: a Guide to Assholes," *Badass Digest*, August 26, 2014, http://badassdigest.com/2014/08/26/video-games-misogyny-and-terrorism-a-guide-to-assholes.

45. Brianna Wu, "No Skin Thick Enough: The Daily Harassment of Women in the Game Industry," *Polygon*, July 22, 2014, http://www.polygon.com/2014/7/22/5926193/women-gaming-harassment.

46. Elisa Meléndez, "What It's Like for a Girl Gamer," *Slate*, August 13, 2012, http://www.slate.com/articles/double_x/doublex/2012/08/sexual_harassment_in_the_gaming_world_a_real_life_problem_for_female_gamers_.html.

47. Anita Sarkeesian, "Tropes vs. Women in Video Games," *Feminist Frequency*, May 17, 2012, https://www.kickstarter.com/projects/566429325/tropes-vs-women-in-video-games.

48. Anita Sarkeesian, "Harassment, Misogyny and Silencing on YouTube | Feminist Frequency," *Feminist Frequency*, 2012, http://www.feministfrequency.com/2012/06/harassment-misogyny-and-silencing-on-youtube.

49. Anita Sarkeesian, "Anita Sarkeesian at TEDxWomen 2012," YouTube, December 4, 2012, http://www.youtube.com/watch?v=GZAxwsg9J9Q.

50. Michael Tresca, "Critic of Sarkeesian's Kickstarter Virtually Punches Her in the Face," July 9, 2012, http://www.examiner.com/article/critic-of-sarkeesian-s-kickstarter-virtually-punches-her-the-face.

51. Anita Sarkeesian, "Women as Background Decoration (Part 2)," FeministFrequency.com, August 25, 2014, http://www.feministfrequency.com/2014/08/women-as-background-decoration-part-2.

52. Twitchy Staff, "Gamers 'Calling Bullsh°T' on Interview with Feminist Social Justice Warrior," Twitchy.com, November 19, 2014, http://twitchy.com/2014/11/19/gamers-calling-bullsht-on-interview-with-feminist-social-justice-warrior.

53. Stephen Totillo, "Bomb Threat Targeted Anita Sarkeesian, Gaming Awards Last March," Kotaku, September 17, 2014, http://kotaku.com/bomb-threat-targeted-Anita-Savkesian-gaming-awards-la-1636032301.

54. anitasarcasmian, "Anita Sarcasmian (@Anitasarcasmian) | Twitter," Twitter.com, 2014, https://twitter.com/anitasarcasmian.

55. fakefemfreq, "Everybody's a rapist, unless they ask 'would you like to engage in sexual activity with me?' which would totally kill the mood. #gamergate," *Twitter.com*, September 29, 2014, https://twitter.com/fakefemfreq/status/516672580653436929; fakefemfreq, "On college campuses across the tri-state area, one in every 5 young men have become cruel, hateful lifelong gamers. #gamergate," Twitter.com, September 24, 2014, https://twitter.com/fakefemfreq/status/514670694660333568.

56. Soraya Nadia McDonald, "Gaming Vlogger Anita Sarkeesian Is Forced from Home After Receiving Harrowing Death Threats," *Washington Post*, August 29, 2014, http://www.washingtonpost.com/news/morning-mix/wp/2014/08/29/gaming-vlogger-anita-sarkeesian-is-forced-from-home-after-receiving-harrowing-death-threats; Ian Steadman, "Tropes vs Anita Sarkeesian: On Pass-

ing Off Anti-Feminist Nonsense as Critique," *New Statesman*, August 27, 2014, http://www.newstatesman.com/future-proof/2014/08/tropes-vs-anita-sar-keesian-passing-anti-feminist-nonsense-critique; James DexX Dominguez, "Feminist Game Critic Driven from Home by Disturbing Online Threats," *Sydney Morning Herald*, August 29, 2014, http://www.smh.com.au/digital-life/games/feminist-game-critic-driven-from-home-by-disturbing-online-threats-20140829-109t2y.html; Tauriq Moosa, "Fanboys, White Knights, and the Hair-ball of Online Misogyny," *Daily Beast*, August 28, 2014, http://www.thedailybeast.com/articles/2014/08/28/fanboys-white-knights-and-the-hairball-of-online-misogyny.html; Mark Melynchuk, "Anita Sarkeesian's Videos on Women in Gaming Are Worthwhile, Says White Knight Reporter," *Regina Leader-Post*, August 26, 2014, http://leaderpost.com/entertainment/anita-sarkeesians-videos-on-women-in-gaming-are-worthwhile-says-white-knight-reporter; Anna Minard, "Anita Sarkeesian Threatened with Rape and Murder for Daring to Keep Critiquing Video Games," *Portland Mercury Blog-town*, August 28, 2014, http://blogtown.portlandmercury.com/BlogtownPDX/archives/2014/08/28/anita-sarkeesian-threatened-with-rape-and-murder-for-daring-to-keep-critiquing-video-games; Julie Bort, "After Exposing Sexism in the Video Game Industry, This Woman Received Rape Threats on Twitter," *Business Insider*, August 27, 2014, http://www.businessinsider.com/game-industry-critic-faces-rape-threats-2014-8.

57. Steadman, "Tropes vs Anita Sarkeesian: On Passing Off Anti-Feminist Nonsense as Critique."

58. Leigh Alexander, "Gamasutra—'Gamers' Don't Have to Be Your Audience. 'Gamers' Are Over," Gamasutra.com, August 28, 2014, http://www.gamasutra.com/view/news/224400/Gamers_dont_have_to_be_your_audience_Gamers_are_over.php.

59. The debate in the gamer-focused media around the issue of whether "gamers are over" was fierce, with Reddit users compiling a list of thirty-four articles published between August 28 and September 10, 2014, addressing the debate around whether so-called gamers and the gamer identity are eroding. SuperflyD, "Is There a List of All the 'Gamers Are Dead' Articles?—/R/Kotak-uInAction." Reddit.com, September 2014, http://www.reddit.com/r/KotakuInAction/comments/2gsslk/is_there_a_list_of_all_the_gamers_are_dead.

60. Leigh Alexander, "Gamasutra—'Gamers' Don't Have to Be Your Audience. 'Gamers' Are Over," Gamasutra.com, August 28, 2014, http://www.gamasutra.com/view/news/224400/Gamers_dont_have_to_be_your_audience_Gamers_are_over.ph.

61. Dan Golding, "The End of Gamers," Dangolding.Tumblr.com, August 28, 2014, http://dangolding.tumblr.com/post/95985875943/the-end-of-gamers; Anita Sarkeesian, "Anita Sarkeesian, Feminist Frequency—XOXO Festival (2014)," YouTube, October 7, 2014, http://www.youtube.com/watch?v=ah8mhDW6Shs; Kyle Wagner, "The Future of the Culture Wars Is Here, and It's Gamergate," *Deadspin*, October 14, 2014, http://deadspin.com/the-future-of-the-culture-wars-is-here-and-its-gamerga-1646145844.

62. Michael Kimmel, *Angry White Men: American Masculinity at the End of an Era* (New York: Nation Books, 2015).

63. Ibid.

64. The hashtag was started by actor Adam Baldwin who tweeted #Gamer-Gate along with YouTube clips exposing so-called ethical problems with gamer journalism. Adam Baldwin, "Adam Baldwin on Twitter: '#GamerGate: Pt. 1: Https://T.Co/VMIwtoFlhD Pt. 2: Https://T.Co/bLrgB8JGwQ,'" Twitter.com, August 27, 2014, https://twitter.com/AdamBaldwin/status/504801169638567936; Stephen Totillo, "Another Woman in Gaming Flees Home Following Death Threats," *Kotaku*, October 11, 2014, http://kota-ku.com/another-woman-in-gaming-flees-home-following-death-thre-1645280338; Chris Plante, "An Awful Week to Care about Video Games," *Polygon*, August 28, 2014, http://www.polygon.com/2014/8/28/6078391/video-games-awful-week.

65. In 2015, Quinn launched an anti-harassment task force, Crash Override, http://www.crashoverridenetwork.com; Zoe Quinn, "Depression Quest: An Interactive (Non)Fiction about Living with Depression," Depression-Quest.com, accessed September 26, 2014, http://www.depressionquest.com.

66. Eron Gjoni, "TL;DR:," *The Zoe Post*, August 16, 2014, http://thezoe-post.wordpress.com/2014/08/16/tldr.

67. Ibid.

68. Andy Baio, "72 Hours of #Gamergate—the Message—Medium," *Medium*, October 27, 2014, https://medium.com/message/72-hours-of-gamergate-e00513f7cf5d; Chris Remo, Jake Rodkin, and Sean Vanaman, "Idle Thumbs: Ridonkulous Rift," IdleThumbs.net, August 27, 2014, https://www.idlethumbs.net/idlethumbs/episodes/ridonkulous-rift; Taylor Wofford, "Is GamerGate about Media Ethics or Harassing Women? Harassment, the Data Shows," *Newsweek*, October 25, 2014, http://www.newsweek.com/gamer-gate-about-media-ethics-or-harassing-women-harassment-data-show-279736.

69. Nate Rott, "#Gamergate Controversy Fuels Debate on Women and Video Games," NPR, September 24, 2014, http://www.npr.org/blogs/alltech-considered/2014/09/24/349835297/-gamergate-controversy-fuels-debate-on-women-and-video-games.

70. David Futrelle, "Zoe Quinn's Screenshots of 4chan's Dirty Tricks Were Just the Appetizer. Here's the First Course of the Dinner, Directly from the IRC Log," WeHuntedtheMammoth.com, September 8, 2014, http://wehun-tedthemammoth.com/2014/09/08/zoe-quinns-screenshots-of-4chans-dirty-tricks-were-just-the-appetizer-heres-the-first-course-of-the-dinner-directly-from-the-irc-log.

71. Zoe Quinn, "5 Things I Learned as the Internet's Most Hated Person," *Cracked*, September 16, 2014, http://www.cracked.com/blog/5-things-i-learned-as-internets-most-hated-person.

72. Karla Mantilla, *Gendertrolling: How Misogyny Went Viral* (Santa Barbara, CA: Praeger, 2015).

73. Anonymous, "Female Game Developers Share Their Views on #Gamer-Gate," EscapistMagazine.com, September 24, 2014, http://

www.escapistmagazine.com/articles/view/video-games/features/12306-Female-Game-Developers-Make-Statements-on-GamerGate.

74. Brianna Wu, "I'm Brianna Wu, and I'm Risking My Life Standing Up to Gamergate," *Huffington Post*, February 11, 2015, http:// www.huffingtonpost.com/bustle/im-brianna-wu-and-im-risking-my-life-stand-ing-up-to-gamergate_b_6661530.html.

75. Jenn Frank, "On Leaving," InfiniteLives.net, September 11, 2014, http:/ /infinitelives.net/2014/09/11/on-leaving.

76. Ibid.

77. Mattie Brice, "Lewdomattiebrice on Twitter: 'I Decided I'm Not Spending Time and Energy on Things That Don't Reciprocate. the Games Industry Never Budged to Make Room for Me,'" Twitter.com, September 4, 2014, https://twitter.com/xMattieBrice/status/507685120963145728.

78. David Futrelle, "You'll Never Guess What Misogynistic Gamebros Did to These Two Women in Gaming! (HINT: Drove Them Out.)," WeHunted-TheMammoth.com, September 5, 2014, http://wehuntedthemammoth.com/ 2014/09/05/youll-never-guess-what-misogynistic-gamebros-did-to-these-two-women-in-gaming-hint-drove-them-out, https://twitter.com/AlrightAnon/stat-us/507395891838590976.

79. Aja Romano, "Zoe Quinn Claims 4chan Was behind GamerGate the Whole Time," *Daily Dot*, September 6, 2014, http://www.dailydot.com/geek/ zoe-quinn-outs-4chan-behind-gamergate.

80. William Usher, "You Won't Believe Why This Hashtag Is Popular in Gaming," *Cinemablend*, September 10, 2014.

81. Leo Reyna, "#GamerGate Revealed as Misogynist and Racist Move-ment from 4chan," Examiner.com, September 6, 2014, http:// www.examiner.com/article/gamergate-revealed-as-misogynist-and-racist-movement-from-4chan.

82. Mytheos Holt, "GamerGate's Anniversary and the Rise of the Video-Cons," *The Federalist*, August 15, 2015, http://thefederalist.com/2015/08/15/ gamergates-anniversary-and-the-rise-of-the-videocons; Cathy Young, "Blame GamerGate's Bad Rep on Smears and Shoddy Journalism," Observer.com, October 13, 2015, http://observer.com/2015/10/blame-gamergates-bad-rep-on-smears-and-shoddy-journalism.

83. Allegra Ringo, "Meet the Female Gamer Mascot Born of Anti-Feminist Internet Drama," *Vice*, August 28, 2014, http://www.vice.com/read/meet-the-female-gamer-mascot-created-by-anti-feminists-828?utm_source=vicetwitterus.

84. Dr Nerdlove, "What We Talk about When We Talk about GamerGate," DoctorNerdlove.com, October 24, 2014, http://www.doctornerdlove.com/ 2014/10/when-we-talk-about-gamergate.

85. Know Your Meme, "Daily Dose/Piccolo Dick," *Know Your Meme* (Phil-adelphia, PA, 2014), http://knowyourmeme.com/memes/daily-dose-piccolo-dick; Nerdlove, "What We Talk about When We Talk about GamerGate."

86. Erik Kain, "GamerGate: A Closer Look at the Controversy Sweeping Video Games," *Forbes*, September 4, 2014, http://www.forbes.com/sites/erik-

kain/2014/09/04/gamergate-a-closer-look-at-the-controversy-sweeping-video-games; Fine Young Capitalists, "The Fine Young Capitalists," TheFineYoung-Capitalists.com, 2014, http://www.thefineyoungcapitalists.com/Voting; Ringo, "Meet the Female Gamer Mascot Born of Anti-Feminist Internet Drama."

87. Todd, "Video Games, Misogyny, and Terrorism: A Guide to Assholes."

88. Brianna Wu, "I Really Hope This Is Not the New Normal for My Life," Twitter.com, October 14, 2014, https://twitter.com/Spacekatgal/status/522221951830720512.

89. Totillo, "Another Woman in Gaming Flees Home Following Death Threats."

90. David Futrelle, "Yet Another Woman in Gaming Has Been Driven from Her Home by Death Threats," WeHuntedTheMammoth.com, October 11, 2014, http://wehuntedthemammoth.com/2014/10/11/yet-another-woman-in-gaming-has-been-driven-from-her-home-by-death-threats.

91. NYCC, October 12, 2014, "The Mary Sue Presents—All on the Table," NYCC14.MapYourShow.com, October 12, 2014, http://nycc14.mapyourshow.com/6_0/sessions/session-details.cfm?ScheduleID=341.

92. YouTube, "MSNBC the Reid Report on #GamerGate," YouTube, October 13, 2014, http://www.youtube.com/watch?v=MlnY17pgYwg.

93. Brianna Wu et al., "Isometric #18: Rainbows and Sunshine," 5by5.tv, September 8, 2014, http://5by5.tv/isometric/18.

94. Josh Wirtanen, "GeekParty—Phil Fish Goes on Epic Twitter Crusade to Defend Zoe Quinn," GeekParty.com, August 17, 2014, http://geekparty.com/phil-fish-goes-on-epic-twitter-crusade-to-defend-zoe-quinn; Aja Romano, "4chan Hacks and Doxes Zoe Quinn's Biggest Supporter," August 22, 2014, http://www.dailydot.com/geek/4chan-hacks-phil-fish-over-his-defense-of-zoe-quinn; Emmaunel Maiberg, "Phil Fish Selling Rights to Fez after Being Hacked," *GameSpot*, August 23, 2014, http://www.gamespot.com/articles/phil-fish-selling-rights-to-fez-after-being-hacked/1100-6421882; Jim Vorel, "Fez Creator Phil Fish and Polytron Corporation Hacked, Doxxed," August 22, 2014, http://www.pastemagazine.com/articles/2014/08/fez-creator-phil-fish-and-polytron-corporation-hac-1.html.

95. Phil Fish, "Im Sick of All These Motherfucking Death Threats from These Anti-Feminist Fucks," Twitter.com, September 12, 2012, https://twitter.com/PHIL_FISH/status/510505343060029440.

96. Maiberg, "Phil Fish Selling Rights to Fez after Being Hacked."

97. "Anita Sarkeesian's Videos on Women in Gaming Are Worthwhile, Says White Knight Reporter"; Jesse Singal, "Gamergate Should Stop Lying to Journalists—and Itself," *NYMag*, October 20, 2014, http://nymag.com/scienceofus/2014/10/gamergate-should-stop-lying-to-itself.html.

98. Victoria McNally, "[UPDATED] A Disheartening Account of the Harassment Going on in Gaming Right Now (and How Adam Baldwin Is Involved)," *The Mary Sue*, August 28, 2014, http://www.themarysue.com/video-game-harassment-zoe-quinn-anita-sarkeesian.

99. NYCC, "The Mary Sue Presents—All on the Table."

100. Ibid. Notably, the *New York Times* reported that Sarkeesian was told "the campus police could not prevent people with weapons from entering her talk." Nick Wingfield, "Feminist Critics of Video Games Facing Threats in 'GamerGate' Campaign," *New York Times*, October 15, 2014, http://www.nytimes.com/2014/10/16/technology/gamergate-women-video-game-threats-anita-sarkeesian.html.

101. Fletcher, "Sexual Harassment in the World of Video Gaming."

102. Charlie Brooker, "Gamergate: The Internet Is the Toughest Game in Town—if You're Playing as a Woman," *Guardian*, October 20, 2014, http://www.theguardian.com/commentisfree/2014/oct/20/gamergate-internet-tough-est-game-woman-enemies; Arthur Chu, "Of Gamers, Gates, and Disco Demolition: The Roots of Reactionary Rage," *Newsweek*, October 16, 2014, http://www.thedailybeast.com/articles/2014/10/16/of-gamers-gates-and-disco-demolition-the-roots-of-reactionary-rage.html; Sean Collins, "Anita Sarkeesian on GamerGate: 'We Have a Problem and We're Going to Fix This,'" RollingStone.com, October 17, 2014, http://www.rollingstone.com/culture/features/anita-sarkeesian-gamergate-interview-20141017; Caitlin Dewey, "Inside Gamergate's (Successful) Attack on the Media," *Washington Post*, October 20, 2014, http://www.washingtonpost.com/news/the-intersect/wp/2014/10/20/inside-gamergates-successful attack-on-the-media; Mike Diver, "Does Someone Have to Actually Die before GamerGate Calms Down?," *Vice*, October 14, 2014, http://www.vice.com/read/calm-down-gamergate-283; Drew Harwell, "Gamergate Scandal May Scare Away Female Video Gamers," *Washington Post*, October 24, 2014, http://www.standard.net/Entertainment/2014/10/24/Gamergate-scandal-may-scare-away-female-video-gamers; Gwen Ifill, "#Gamergate Leads to Death Threats against Women," PBS, October 16, 2014, http://www.pbs.org/newshour/bb/gamergate-leads-death-threats-women-gaming-industry; Erik Kain, "#GamerGate Is Not a Hate Group, It's a Consumer Movement," *Forbes*, October 9, 2014, http://www.forbes.com/sites/erikkain/2014/10/09/gamergate-is-not-a-hate-group-its-a-consumer-movement; Erik Kain, "It's Time for Video Game Journalists to Engage with #GamerGate," *Forbes*, October 6, 2014, http://www.forbes.com/sites/erikkain/2014/10/06/its-time-for-video-game-journalists-to-engage-with-gamergate; Erik Kain, "Why It Makes Sense for Intel to Pull Ads from Gamasutra over #GamerGate and Why It's Still the Wrong Move," *Forbes*, October 4, 2014, http://www.forbes.com/sites/erikkain/2014/10/04/why-it-makes-sense-for-intel-to-pull-ads-from-gamasutra-over-gamergate-and-why-its-still-the-wrong-move; David Lee, "Big Firms 'Must Condemn GamerGate,'" BBC News, October 29, 2015, http://www.bbc.com/news/technology-29821050; HuffPost Live, "What Is #Gamergate?," *Huffington Post*, October 15, 2014, http://www.huffingtonpost.com/2014/10/15/gamergate_n_5989616.html; "Slam the Door on the Hate from 'Gamergate,'" *Los Angeles Times*, October 18, 2014, http://herocomplex.latimes.com/games/slam-the-door-on-the-hate-from-gamergate; Barbara Ortutay, "Four in 10 Adults Have Been Harassed Online, Majority Have Seen It, Study Finds," *San Jose Mercury News*, October 22, 2014, http://www.mercurynews.com/business/ci_26777096/four-10-adults-have-been-ha-

rassed-online-majority; Kevin Rawlinson and Leo Kelion, "'Gaming Press Must Tackle Misogyny,'" BBC News, October 14, 2014, http://www.bbc.com/news/technology-29616197; Susan Rohwer, "It's Time to Silence 'Gamergate,' End the Misogyny in Gaming Culture," *Los Angeles Times*, October 17, 2014, http://www.latimes.com/opinion/opinion-la/la-ol-anita-sarkeesian-gamergate-20141017-story.html; Singal, "Gamergate Should Stop Lying to Journalists—and Itself"; Rebecca Solnit, "Listen Up, Women Are Telling Their Story Now," *Guardian*, December 30, 2014, http://www.theguardian.com/news/2014/dec/30/-sp-rebecca-solnit-listen-up-women-are-telling-their-story-now; Chris Sullentrop, "The Disheartening GamerGate Campaign," *New York Times*, October 25, 2014, http://www.nytimes.com/2014/10/26/opinion/sunday/the-disheartening-gamergate-campaign.html; Paul Tassi, "Intel Apologizes for Pulling Ads Due to GamerGate Pressure," *Forbes*, October 4, 2014, http://www.forbes.com/sites/insertcoin/2014/10/04/intel-apologizes-for-pulling-ads-due-to-gamergate-pressure; Tom Watson, "What Fuels 'GamerGate' Anger and Outrage? Gender, Power and Money," *Washington Post*, October 20, 2014, http://www.forbes.com/sites/tomwatson/2014/10/20/what-fuels-gamergate-anger-and-outrage-gender-power-and-money; Nick Wingfield, "Intel Pulls Ads from Site after 'Gamergate' Boycott," *New York Times*, October 2, 2014, http://bits.blogs.nytimes.com/2014/10/02/intel-pulls-ads-from-site-after-gamergate-boycott; Wingfield, "Feminist Critics of Video Games Facing Threats in 'GamerGate' Campaign."

103. Jason Schreier, "Thousands Rally Online against Gamergate," *Kotaku*, October 15, 2014, http://kotaku.com/thousands-rally-online-against-gamergate-1646500492; YouTube, "MSNBC the Reid Report on #GamerGate."

104. Morgan Ramsay, "Are Feminists Taking Over Video Games?," Storify.com, September 12, 2014, https://storify.com/MorganRamsay/how-often-do-video-game-journalists-write-about-fe.

105. Holt, "GamerGate's Anniversary and the Rise of the VideoCons."

106. Christina Hoff Sommers, "What Critics of GamerGate Get Wrong," YouTube, October 27, 2014, http://www.youtube.com/watch?v=5RVlCvBd21w&list=PLytTJqkSQqtr7BqC1Jf4nv3g2yDfu7Xmd.

107. Wagner, "The Future of the Culture Wars Is Here, and It's Gamergate."

108. Alex Hern, "Lazy Coverage of Gamergate Is Only Feeding This Abusive Campaign," Guardian.co.uk, October 16, 2014, http://www.theguardian.com/technology/2014/oct/16/gamergate-abuse-feminist-new-york-times-anita-sarkeesian; Diver, "Does Someone Have to Actually Die before GamerGate Calms Down?"; Mytheos Holt, "GamerGate's Anniversary and the Rise of the VideoCons"; "#GamerGate: Misogyny or Corruption in the Gaming Community?," *The Federalist*, September 3, 2014; Samual Sales, "Another Take on the Anita Sarkeesian Controversy: Who's to Blame for This Madness?," *Gamer Headlines*, August 28, 2014, http://www.gamerheadlines.com/2014/08/another-take-anita-sarkeesian-whos-blame-madness; Pramath, "The ESA Finally Speaks Out in Response to GamerGate," GamingBolt.com, October 16, 2014, http://gamingbolt.com/the-esa-finally-speaks-out-in-response-to-gamergate.

109. Kain, "GamerGate: A Closer Look at the Controversy Sweeping Video Games."

110. Hamilton, "Competitive Gamer's Inflammatory Comments Spark Sexual Harassment Debate [Update]."

111. Alanna Bennett, "Let's Talk about That Law & Order: SVU Gamergate Episode," *The Mary Sue*, February 14, 2015, http://www.themarysue.com/svu-gamergate; Bernie Burton, "Gamergate Is the Latest Controversial Plot in 'Law & Order: SVU'—CNET," *C-Net*, February 9, 2015, http://www.cnet.com/news/gamergate-becomes-the-latest-law-order-svu-controversial-plot; "Law and Order SVU: The Intimidation Game," IGN, February 13, 2015, http://www.ign.com/boards/threads/law-and-order-svu-the-intimidation-game.454395022; Sam Machkovach, "Law & Order SVU Takes on GamerGate, Everyone Loses," *Ars Technica*, February 12, 2015, http://arstechnica.com/gaming/2015/02/law-order-svu-takes-on-gamergate-everyone-loses; Eddie Makuch, "Law & Order: SVU Gamer Harassment Episode Airs Tonight—GameSpot," *GameSpot*, February 11, 2015, http://www.gamespot.com/articles/law-order-svu-gamer-harassment-episode-airs-tonigh/1100-6425235; Danielle Reindeau, "The Cheesiest Lines from Law and Order: SVU's Gamer Episode," *Polygon*, February 12, 2015, http://www.polygon.com/2015/2/12/8024221/law-order-svu-gamergate-harassment; Jason Schreier, "So That Was Law & Order's GamerGate Episode," *Kotaku*, February 11, 2015, http://kotaku.com/so-that-was-law-orders-gamergate-episode-1685333828.

112. Joshua Rivera, "'Law & Order: SVU'S Take on Online Harassment Is Uncomfortably Accurate," *Entertainment Weekly*, February 11, 2015, http://www.ew.com/article/2015/02/11/law-order-svus-take-online-harassment-uncomfortably-accurate.

113. Anne Easton, "'Law & Order: SVU' 16x14 Recap: The Intimidation Game," *Observer*, February 12, 2015, http://observer.com/2015/02/law-order-svu-16x14-the-intimidation-game.

114. Dewey Caitlin, "This Is the Final Word on Gamergate—and It's From 'Law & Order: SVU,'" *Washington Post*, February 11, 2015, http://www.washingtonpost.com/news/the-intersect/wp/2015/02/11/this-is-the-final-word-on-gamergate-and-its-from-law-order-svu.

115. Ibid.

116. Wu, "I'm Brianna Wu, and I'm Risking My Life Standing Up to Gamergate."

117. Gray, *Race, Gender, and Deviance in Xbox Live: Theoretical Perspectives from the Virtual Margins*.

118. Patterson, "[PAX East] Exposing the Harassment Female Gamers Receive Online."

119. For research that acknowledges the unique harms of "technology-facilitated sexual violence," see Nicola Henry and Anastasia Powell, "Embodied Harms: Gender, Shame, and Technology-Facilitated Sexual Violence," *Violence against Women* 21, no. 6 (May 4, 2015): 758–79; Anastasia Powell and Nicola Henry, "Policing Technology-Facilitated Sexual Violence against Adult Victims: Police and Service Sector Perspectives," *Policing and Society*, March

8, 2016, 1–17; Crecente, "Game Dev Harassment Remains as Bad as It Was a Year Ago"; Mantilla, *Gendertrolling: How Misogyny Went Viral*; McNally, "[UPDATED] A Disheartening Account of the Harassment Going on in Gaming Right Now (and How Adam Baldwin Is Involved)"; Adi Robertson, "Trolls Drive Anita Sarkeesian Out of Her House to Prove Misogyny Doesn't Exist," *The Verge*, August 27, 2014, http://www.theverge.com/2014/8/27/6075179/anita-sarkeesian-says-she-was-driven-out-of-house-by-threats; Ortutay, "Four in 10 Adults Have Been Harassed Online, Majority Have Seen It, Study Finds"; Michael Pittaro, "Cyber Stalking: An Analysis of Online Harassment and Intimidation," *International Journal of Cyber Criminology* 1, no. 2 (2007): 180–97; Aja Romano, "The Sexist Crusade to Destroy Game Developer Zoe Quinn," *Daily Dot*, August 20, 2014, http://www.dailydot.com/geek/zoe-quinn-depression-quest-gaming-sex-scandal; Rott, "#Gamergate Controversy Fuels Debate on Women and Video Games"; Todd, "Video Games, Misogyny, and Terrorism: A Guide to Assholes."

120. Henry and Powell, "Embodied Harms: Gender, Shame, and Technology-Facilitated Sexual Violence."

121. Jamie Bartlett et al., "Misogyny on Twitter," Demos.co.uk, May 2014, http://www.demos.co.uk/files/MISOGYNY_ON_TWITTER.pdf?1399567516.

122. Ortutay, "Four in 10 Adults Have Been Harassed Online, Majority Have Seen It, Study Finds."

123. Sophie Gaston, "Male Celebrities Receive More Abuse on Twitter than Women," Demos.co.uk, August 24, 2014, http://www.demos.co.uk/press-release/demos-male-celebrities-receive-more-abuse-on-twitter-than-women-2.

124. Henry and Powell, "Embodied Harms: Gender, Shame, and Technology-Facilitated Sexual Violence"; Nathan Jurgenson, "The IRL Fetish," TheNewInquiry.com, June 28, 2012, http://thenewinquiry.com/essays/the-irl-fetish.

125. Vlad Chituc, "GamerGate: A Culture War for People Who Don't Play Video Games," *New Republic*, September 11, 2015, https://newrepublic.com/article/122785/gamergate-culture-war-people-who-dont-play-videogames; mrjohner, "Johner Rico on Twitter: "Twitter #Ferguson #SocialJusticeWarriors," Twitter.com, August 18, 2014, https://twitter.com/mrjohner/status/501469077370834946/photo/1; MrCappadocia, "Mr. Cappadocia on Twitter: '#GamerGate #SJW Victory against College Aged Men in CA. Males Now Guilty until Proven Innocent When Accused of Rape. No Due Process Prot.,'" Twitter.com, September 29, 2014, https://twitter.com/MrCappadocia/status/516498946508599296; David Ng, "Gamergate Advocate Milo Yiannopoulos Blames Feminists for SXSW Debacle," *Los Angeles Times*, October 29, 2015, http://www.latimes.com/entertainment/la-et-milo-yiannopoulos-gamergate-feminists-20151028-story.html; jordanowen, "Jordan Owen on Twitter: "Did You Think the #SJW Gang Would Stop at Ending Due Process? Now They're After Double Jeopardy as Well," Twitter.com, September 28, 2014, https://twitter.com/jordanowen42/status/516399112816979968; OldBones, "Old Bones on Twitter: "THIS Is What a War on Women Looks Like #SJW. Look at It Closely and Figure Out the Difference," Twitter.com, October 7, 2014, https://twitter.com/0LD_B0NES/status/519516560164421634; Young, "Blame

GamerGate's Bad Rep on Smears and Shoddy Journalism"; Leigh Alexander, "SXSW's GamerGate Debacle Shows It's Clueless on Diversity," *Wired*, October 28, 2015, http://www.wired.com/2015/10/sxsw-diversity-gamergate; Arthur Chu, "This Is Not a Game: How SXSW Turned GamerGate Abuse into a Spectator Sport," *Daily Beast*, October 27, 2015, http://www.thedailybeast.com/articles/2015/10/27/this-is-not-a-game-how-sxsw-turned-gamergate-abuse-into-a-spectator-sport.html; "SXSW Canceled Two Panels after Threats—but Did Nothing When Female Panelists Asked about Harassment," *Washington Post*, October 27, 2015, https://www.washingtonpost.com/news/the-intersect/wp/2015/10/27/sxsw-canceled-two-panels-after-threats-but-did-nothing-when-female-panelists-asked-about-harassment; Noah Kulwin, "SXSW Apologizes for Gamergate Panel Cancellations, Announces One-Day 'Online Harassment Summit' (Updated)," *Recode*, October 30, 2015, http://recode.net/2015/10/30/sxsw-apologizes-for-gamergate-panel-cancelations-announces-one-day-online-harassment-summit; "SXSW Cancels Gamergate-Related Panels after 'Threats of Violence,'" October 26, 2015; Caroline Sinders, "I Was on One of Those Canceled SXSW Panels. Here Is What Went Down," *Slate*, October 29, 2015, http://www.slate.com/articles/double_x/doublex/2015/10/sxsw_canceled_panels_here_is_what_happened.html; staff, "SXSW Facing Backlash over Gamer Panels, Threats," CNBC.com, October 27, 2015, http://www.cnbc.com/2015/10/27/sxsw-facing-backlash-over-canceled-panels.html; "Backlash Grows Over SXSW Interactive's Canceled Video Game Panels," *New York Times*, October 27, 2015, http://bits.blogs.nytimes.com/2015/10/27/backlash-grows-over-sxsws-canceled-video-game-panels; Julia Zorthian, "SXSW Apologizes for Canceling Gaming Panels and Announces Daylong Harassment Summit," *Time.com*, October 30, 2015, http://time.com/4094910/sxsw-gaming-harassment-daylong-summit; Helen Lewis, "The Hugo Awards Hijack Is Nasty and Dishonest—but It Just Proves Progressives Right," *Guardian*, April 18, 2015, http://www.theguardian.com/commentisfree/2015/apr/18/hugo-award-hijack-just-proves-progressives-right; Amy Wallace, "Who Won Science Fiction's Hugo Awards, and Why It Matters," *Wired.com*, August 23, 2015, http://www.wired.com/2015/08/won-science-fictions-hugo-awards-matters.

126. Holt, "GamerGate's Anniversary and the Rise of the VideoCons."

127. Sheena Goodyear, "Meet the Woman Getting a PhD in Gamergate and the Death Eaters Trying to Stop Her," *The Mary Sue*, June 15, 2015, http://www.themarysue.com/phd-in-gamergate.

128. Shira Chess and Adrienne Shaw, "A Conspiracy of Fishes, or, How We Learned to Stop Worrying about #GamerGate and Embrace Hegemonic Masculinity," *Journal of Broadcasting & Electronic Media* 59, no. 1 (March 11, 2015): 208–20.

5. GEEK SPACES

1. Suzanne Scott, "Fangirls in Refrigerators: The Politics of (in)Visibility in Comic Book Culture," *Transformative Works and Cultures* 13 (April 10, 2013); Rich Johnston, "One Possible Reason Why Fewer Women Work in Comic Stores than You Might Otherwise Expect," *Bleeding Cool*, September 3, 2014, http://www.bleedingcool.com/2014/09/03/one-possible-reason-why-less-women-work-in-comic-stores-than-you-might-otherwise-expect.

2. Paul Lopes, "Sequential Tarts: Gender Intervention in American Comic Book Culture" (paper presented at the American Sociological Association Annual Meeting, 2006), 1–35, http://citation.allacademic.com/meta/p_mla_apa_research_citation/3/7/1/6/6/p371663_index.html.

3. Scott, "Fangirls in Refrigerators: The Politics of (in)Visibility in Comic Book Culture."

4. Julie Brigham-Grette, Michelle Thaller, and G. Willow Wilson, "Conference on World Affairs," Colorado.edu, Boulder, CO, April 2015, http://www.colorado.edu/cwa/search_results.html?year=2015&words=G.+Willow+Wilson.

5. Natalie Zutter, "SDCC's 'Women Who Kick Ass' Panelists Only Want to Play Male Superheroes," Tor.com, July 28, 2013, http://www.tor.com/blogs/2014/07/sdcc-women-who-kick-ass-panel-highlights.

6. Brian Truitt, "In Superhero Genre, Movie Girl Power Is in Short Supply," *USA Today*, August 26, 2013. http://www.usatoday.com/story/life/movies/2013/08/25/female-superhero-movies/2651247; Kevin O'Keefe, "The Problem with How Superhero Movies Treat Women, in 11 Posters," Mic.com, August 7, 2015, http://mic.com/articles/123525/how-superhero-movies-treat-women-in-11-posters; Joan Hilty, "Wonder Girl's Head-Sized Breasts Illustrate the Sexism Problem in Comics," *Guardian*, May 3, 2014, http://www.theguardian.com/commentisfree/2014/may/03/wonder-girl-breasts-sexism-comics; Laurenn McCubbin, "Wonder Woman's Feminism Matters. So Why Would the Comic Industry Reject It?," Guardian.co.uk, July 3, 2014, http://www.theguardian.com/commentisfree/2014/jul/03/wonder-woman-feminism-comic-industry-inclusive.

7. DC and Marvel remain the dominant comic book publishers, comprising about 70 percent of the unit market share, and discourse around mainstream comics is the focus of this chapter (http://www.diamondcomics.com/Home/1/1/3/237?articleID=149506).

8. Noah Berlatsky, "Of Course Women Read Superhero Comics," *The Atlantic*, June 21, 2014, http://www.theatlantic.com/entertainment/archive/2014/07/just-how-many-women-read-comic-books/374736; Laura Hudson, "DC Comics Survey Reports 'New 52' Readership 93% Male, Only 5% New Readers [Updated]," *Comics Alliance*, February 10, 2014, http://comicsalliance.com/dc-comics-readers-survey-reports-new-52-readership-93-male.

9. Berlatsky, "Of Course Women Read Superhero Comics"; Brett Schenker, "Market Research Says 46.67% of Comic Fans Are Female," ComicsBeat.com, February 5, 2014, http://www.comicsbeat.com/market-research-

says-46-female; Trina Robbins, "Gender Differences in Comics by Trina Robbins," *Image & Narrative*, no. 4 (September 2002).

10. Yael Kohen, "Female Fans Give Boost to Comic Book Publishers," *Businessweek*, September 2, 2014, http://www.businessweek.com/articles/2014-09-04/female-comic-book-fans-rise-helps-publishers-profit.

11. Caitlin McGarry, "Good News, Dudes: Ladies Read Comics, Too," *Techhive*, October 9, 2013, http://www.techhive.com/article/2053313/good-news-dudes-ladies-read-comics-too.html; Dan Wickline, "ComiXology Shares Results from Reader Survey—Updated—Bleeding Cool Comic Book, Movie, TV News," *Bleeding Cool*, October 10, 2013, http://www.bleedingcool.com/2013/10/10/comixology-shares-results-from-reader-survey.

12. Schenker, "Market Research Says 46.67% of Comic Fans Are Female."

13. Nickie D. Phillips and Staci Strobl, *Comic Book Crime: Truth, Justice, and the American Way* (New York: New York University Press, 2013); Jennifer Stuller, *Ink-Stained Amazons and Cinematic Warriors* (New York: I. B. Tauris, 2010).

14. Phillips and Strobl, *Comic Book Crime: Truth, Justice, and the American Way*.

15. Ibid.; Crunkista, "Bringing Back Wonder Woman," *Crunk Feminist Collective*, May 23, 2013, http://www.crunkfeministcollective.com/2013/05/23/bringing-back-wonder-woman; Roz Kavency, *Superheroes! Capes and Crusaders in Comics and Films* (New York: I. B. Tauris, 2008); Danny Fingeroth, *Superman on the Couch: What Superheroes Really Tell Us about Ourselves and Our Society* (New York: Continuum, 2004); Tom Morris, *Superheroes and Philosophy: Truth, Justice, and the Socratic Way* (Peru, IL: Open Court, 2005); Matthew Pustz, *Comic Book Culture* (Jackson: University Press of Mississippi, 1999); Stuller, *Ink-Stained Amazons and Cinematic Warriors*; Kristy Guevara-Flanagan, *Wonder Women! The Untold Story of American Superheroines*, director, Kristy Guevara-Flanagan, 2012; Gret Garrett, *Holy Superheroes! Revised and Expanded Edition: Exploring the Sacred in Comics, Graphic Novels, and Film* (Louisville, KY: Westminster John Knox Press, 2008).

16. Some gender/diversity panels at cons have been called out for their underrepresentation of diverse panel participants. Janelle Asselin, "Con Organizers: Here's a Solution to Your Woman Problem," *Comics Alliance*, July 24, 2015, http://comicsalliance.com/comic-book-women-convention-resource; Amanda Marcotte, "Denver ComicCon Convenes a 'Women in Comics' Panel, Forgets to Invite Women," *Slate*, May 27, 2015, http://www.slate.com/blogs/xx_factor/2015/05/27/denver_comiccon_s_all_male_women_in_comics_panel.html; Natalie Wilson, "Women Attend Comic-Con but Don't Run the Show," MsMagazine.com, July 18, 2012, http://msmagazine.com/blog/2012/07/18/women-attend-comic-con-but-dont-run-the-show.

17. Guevara-Flanagan, *Wonder Women! The Untold Story of American Superheroines*.

18. "Publisher Market Shares: July 2014," DiamondComics.com, July 2014, http://www.diamondcomics.com/Home/1/1/3/237?articleID=149506.

19. Tim Hanley, "Gendercrunching July 2014—Plus Female Characters within and without Female-Led Books," *Bleeding Cool*, September 26, 2014, http://www.bleedingcool.com/2014/09/26/gendercrunching-july-2014-plus-female-characters-within-and-without-female-led-books.

20. Rich Johnston, "Ms Marvel, the Book That Was Meant to Get Cancelled by Issue 7," *Bleeding Cool*, September 28, 2014, http://www.bleedingcool.com/2014/09/28/ms-marvel-the-book-that-was-meant-to-get-cancelled-by-issue-7.

21. Jamie Lovett, "Ms. Marvel Trending on Twitter," ComicBook.com, February 5, 2014, http://comicbook.com/blog/2014/02/05/ms-marvel-trending-on-twitter.

22. Shehryar Warraich, "Marvel's Muslim Teenage Girl Superhero Spurs Mixed Pakistani Reactions," UPI, January 22, 2014, http://www.upi.com/Top_News/Special/2014/01/22/Marvels-Muslim-teenage-girl-superhero-spurs-mixed-Pakistani-reactions/21385611094776.

23. Ibid.

24. Ethan Sacks, "Ms. Marvel, a Muslim Teen, Set to Make History," *Daily News*, February 4, 2014, http://www.nydailynews.com/entertainment/comics/ms-marvel-aka-pakistani-american-teen-set-historic-comic-debut-article-1.1602320; Tammy Oler, "The Carol Corps and the Kamala Korps Are Changing the Way Marvel Thinks about Female Superheroes," *Slate*, April 7, 2014, http://www.slate.com/articles/arts/books/2014/04/kamala_khan_as_ms_marvel_and_carol_danvers_as_captain_marvel_female_nonwhite.html; Stephen Colbert, "Ms. Marvel's Reboot," *The Colbert Report*, November 6, 2013, http://thecolbertreport.cc.com/videos/rpo0ya/ms--marvel-s-reboot; Sabaa Tahir, "Ms. Marvel: Why Does Marvel's Latest Book Succeed? Because Its New Muslim Teen Superhero Is 'Sweet, Conflicted and Immensely Relatable,'" *Washington Post*, February 4, 2014, http://www.washingtonpost.com/blogs/comic-riffs/post/ms-marvel-why-does-marvels-new-reboot-succeed-because-its-muslim-teen-superhero-is-sweet-conflicted-and-utterly-relatable/2014/02/04/42908ac8-8dc6-11e3-95dd-36ff657a4dae_blog.html; Noah Berlatsky, "What Makes the Muslim Ms. Marvel Awesome: She's Just Like Everyone," *The Atlantic*, March 20, 2014, http://www.theatlantic.com/entertainment/archive/2014/03/what-makes-the-muslim-em-ms-marvel-em-awesome-shes-just-like-everyone/284517; Amanda Diehl, "Meet the New Ms. Marvel," *Islamic Monthly*, November 6, 2013, http://www.theislamicmonthly.com/meet-the-new-ms-marvel.

25. Matt Binder, "The New Gamergate: Angry White Men Are Trying to Shut Down Diverse Comics," *Salon*, March 24, 2015, http://www.salon.com/2015/03/24/the_new_gamergate_angry_white_men_are_trying_to_shut_down_diverse_comics.

26. Milo Yiannopoulos, "Female Thor Is What Happens When Progressive Hand-Wringing and Misandry Ruin a Cherished Art-Form," *Breitbart*, February 14, 2015, http://www.breitbart.com/london/2015/02/14/female-thor-is-what-happens-when-progressive-hand-wringing-and-misandry-ruin-a-cherished-art-form.

27. Lisette Mejia, "Surprise, Surprise: People Are Pissed That Thor Is a Lady," PopSugar.com, July 15, 2014, http://www.geeksugar.com/Tweets-About-Lady-Thor-35250906.

28. Mark Cassidy, "Twitter Buzz: Marvel's New Female THOR," Comic-BookMovie.com, July 16, 2014, http://www.comicbookmovie.com/fansites/not-yetamovie/news/?a=103706; Janey Tracey, "Best and Worst Fan Reactions to Female Thor and Black Captain America," OuterPlaces.com, July 17, 2014, http://outerplaces.com/buzz/news/item/4901-fan-reactions-to-female-thor-and-black-captain-america.

29. Marvel, "Marvel Proudly Presents Thor," July 15, 2014.

30. Jill Lepore, "Wonder Woman's Secret Past," *New Yorker*, September 22, 2014, http://www.newyorker.com/magazine/2014/09/22/last-amazon.

31. This also reflects the lack of diversity in Hollywood more generally. Bunche Center, "2015 Hollywood Diversity Report: Flipping the Script," BuncheCenter.ucla.edu, February 2015, http://www.bunchecenter.ucla.edu/wp-content/uploads/2015/02/2015-Hollywood-Diversity-Report-2-25-15.pdf; Gregg Kilday, "Women Filmmakers Held Just 19 Percent of Top Film Jobs in 2015," *The Hollywood Reporter*, January 12, 2016, http://www.hollywoodreporter.com/news/women-filmmakers-held-just-19-854852.

32. Dee Lockett, "DC Announces 10 New Superhero Films in Next Six Years, Including Stand-Alone Wonder Woman," *Slate*, October 15, 2014, http://www.slate.com/blogs/browbeat/2014/10/15/dc_comics_film_schedule_warner_bros_announces_at_least_10_new_superhero.html; Piya Sinha-Roy, "Marvel Expands with Dr. Strange, Female Captain Marvel Films," Reuters, October 28, 2014, http://www.reuters.com/article/2014/10/28/us-film-marvel-idUSKBN0IH21E20141028.

33. Mike Madrid, *The Supergirls: Fashion, Feminism, Fantasy, and the History of Comic Book Heroines* (Exterminating Angel Press, 2009); Jeffrey Brown, *Dangerous Curves: Action Heroines, Gender, Fetishism, and Popular Culture* (Jackson: University Press of Mississippi, 2011); Stuller, *Ink-Stained Amazons and Cinematic Warriors*.

34. Madrid, *The Supergirls: Fashion, Feminism, Fantasy, and the History of Comic Book Heroines*; Phillips and Strobl, *Comic Book Crime: Truth, Justice, and the American Way*.

35. Gail Simone, "Women in Refrigerators," *LBY3.com*, March 1999, http://lby3.com/wir.

36. Ibid.

37. Amy Kiste Nyberg, *Seal of Approval: The History of the Comics Code* (Jackson: University Press of Mississippi, 1998).

38. Walt Hickey, "Comic Books Are Still Made by Men, for Men and about Men," *FiveThirtyEight*, October 13, 2014, http://fivethirtyeight.com/features/women-in-comic-books.

39. Ibid.

40. Katie Schenkel, "'I Guess Comics Aren't for Me'—My Own Story of Childhood Gatekeeping and Why Just Making Girl-Friendly Comics Is Not

Enough," *The Mary Sue*, September 4, 2014, http://www.themarysue.com/comics-gatekeeping-why-making-girl-comics-isnt-enough.

41. Carolyn Cocca, "The 'Broke Back Test': A Quantitative and Qualitative Analysis of Portrayals of Women in Mainstream Superhero Comics, 1993–2013," *Journal of Graphic Novels and Comics* 5, no. 4 (October 14, 2014): 411–28, 411.

42. Chris Sims, "Artists Respond to DC's Back-Breaking 'Catwoman' #0 Cover," ComicsAlliance.com, June 12, 2012, http://comicsalliance.com/artists-respond-dc-comics-back-breaking-catwoman-0-cover; Jason Kerouac, "Op/Ed: The Catwoman #0 Cover," *Panels on Pages*, June 13, 2012, http://www.panelsonpages.com/?p=53203; Mark Langshaw, "'Catwoman' #0 Racy Cover Design Draws Criticism," *Digital Spy*, June 13, 2013, http://www.digitalspy.co.uk/displayarticle.php?id=387090; Matthew Meylikhov, "BOOM!'s Freelancers Parody Catwoman #0," *Multiversity Comics*, July 2, 2012, http://multiversitycomics.com/news/booms-freelancers-parody-catwoman-0; staff, "The Problem with Broke Back Catwoman #0," TheGeekTwins.com, June 23, 2012, http://www.thegeektwins.com/2012/06/problem-with-brokeback-catwoman-0.html.

43. Robo Panda, "The Internet Fittingly Lambasts the Ridiculous 'Catwoman #0' Cover," Uproxx.com, June 12, 2012, http://uproxx.com/gammasquad/2012/06/sexist-catwoman-0-cover-parodies/#page/1.

44. Kerouac, "Op/Ed: The Catwoman #0 Cover"; Rollin Bishop, "Catwoman Cover Changed after Internet Outrage," *The Mary Sue*, September 10, 2012, http://www.themarysue.com/catwoman-cover-changed; Robo Panda, "DC Listens to Internet Criticism, Fixes 'Catwoman' Zero Cover," Uproxx.com, September 10, 2012, http://uproxx.com/gammasquad/2012/09/catwoman-zero-cover-redo; Panda, "The Internet Fittingly Lambasts the Ridiculous 'Catwoman #0' Cover;"; Sims, "Artists Respond to DC's Back-Breaking 'Catwoman' #0 Cover."

45. Rebecca Pahle, "Is It Anatomically Possible to Do Milo Manara's Spider-Woman Cover? Three Gymnasts Test the Theory," *The Mary Sue*, August 28, 2014, http://www.themarysue.com/spider-woman-butt-cover-reeanacted.

46. Rob Bricken, "Check Out Spider-Woman #1, Starring Spider-Woman's Ass," io9.com, August 29, 2014, http://io9.com/check-out-spider-woman-1-starring-spider-womans-ass-1624535918; Alex Abad-Santos, "Spider-Woman Isn't Good for Women When She Looks Like This," Vox.com, August 20, 2014, http://www.vox.com/xpress/2014/8/20/6046577/marvel-spider-woman-cover-sexist; Gabe Bergado, "Marvel's 'Spider Woman #1' Cover Gives the Superhero a Majorly Sexist Treatment," Bustle.com, August 2014, http://www.bustle.com/articles/36524-marvels-spider-woman-1-cover-gives-the-superhero-a-majorly-sexist-treatment.

47. Jill Pantozzi, "Spider-Woman Cover Artist Milo Manara & Writer Dennis Hopeless Respond to Online Discussion," *The Mary Sue*, August 22, 2014, http://www.themarysue.com/manara-hopeless-respond-spider-woman-cover; Bea Kaye, "'Spider-Woman #1' Cover Artist Compares His Critics to Terror-

ists," Uproxx.com, August 25, 2014, http://uproxx.com/gammasquad/2014/08/spider-woman-cover-artist-milo-manara-compares-his-critics-to-terrorists.

48. Tom Brevoort, "Mr. Brevoort, What Is Your Opinion on the Debate over M. Manara's Variant Cover of Spider Woman?," *BrevoortForm-spring.Tumblr.com*, August 21, 2014, http://brevoortformspring.tumblr.com/post/95369504698/mr-brevoort-what-is-your-opinion-on-the-debate-over.

49. Joseph Darowski, *X-Men and the Mutant Metaphor: Race and Gender in the Comic Books* (Lanham, MD: Rowman & Littlefield, 2014), 121.

50. Ibid., 131.

51. Laura Hudson, "The Mad Max Furiosa Comic, Created Entirely by Men, Is Terrible about Women," Boingboing.net, June 25, 2015, http://boingboing.net/2015/06/25/the-furiosa-comic-is-terrible.html.

52. Lynn Stuart Parramore, "Why Imperator Furiosa, Not Mad Max, Is the Hero for Our Age," Reuters, November 6, 2007, blogs.reuters.com/great-debate/2015/05/22/why-imperator-furiosa-not-mad-max-is-the-hero-for-our-age.

53. Hayley Campbell, "Comic Artists Can't Stop Drawing 'Mad Max: Fury Road' and the Results Are Brilliant," *BuzzFeed*, May 26, 2015, http://www.buzzfeed.com/hayleycampbell/cant-stop-wont-stop-drawing-furiosa.

54. Ana Mardoll, "Review: We Need to Talk about the Furiosa Comic," *The Mary Sue*, June 20, 2015, http://www.themarysue.com/furiosa-comic-review.

55. Jesse Schedeen, "Mad Max: Fury Road—Furiosa #1 Review," IGN, June 17, 2015, http://www.ign.com/articles/2015/06/18/mad-max-fury-road-furiosa-1-review.

56. Teresa Jusino, "Mad Max Comic Co-Creator Thinks We Need Captivity Spelled Out for Us . . . with Rape Scenes," *The Mary Sue*, June 24, 2015, http://www.themarysue.com/mad-max-furiosa-mark-sexton-women-captivity.

57. Noelene Clark, "Mark Millar's Rape Comments, 'Superheroes' TCA Panel: The Comics World Responds," *Hero Complex*, August 8, 2013, http://herocomplex.latimes.com/comics/mark-millars-rape-comments-superheroes-tca-panel-the-comics-world-responds; Abraham Riesman, "'You're Done Banging Superheroes, Baby,'" *New Republic*, August 6, 2013, https://newrepublic.com/article/114150/mark-millar-kick-ass-2-author-comics-sickest-mind.

58. James Whitbrook, "The Furiosa Comic Undoes Everything Great about Mad Max: Fury Road," io9.com, June 23, 2015, http://io9.com/the-furiosa-comic-undoes-everything-great-about-mad-max-1713368243.

59. Jusino, "Mad Max Comic Co-Creator Thinks We Need Captivity Spelled Out for Us . . . with Rape Scenes."

60. Tammy S. Garland, Kathryn A. Branch, and Mackenzie Grimes, "Blurring the Lines: Reinforcing Rape Myths in Comic Books," *Feminist Criminology*, March 23, 2015, 1–21.

61. Michael Kimmel. *Angry White Men: American Masculinity at the End of an Era* (New York: Nation Books, 2015).

62. Joshua Rivera, "Here Is Why the Comics World Is Fighting over a 'Batgirl' Cover," *Entertainment Weekly*, March 19, 2015, http://www.ew.com/article/2015/03/19/here-why-comics-world-fighting-over-batgirl-cover.

63. David Barnett, "DC Comics Pull Cover of Batgirl Menaced by Joker after Online Protests," *Guardian*, March 17, 2015, http://www.theguardian.com/books/2015/mar/17/dc-comics-pull-batgirl-joker-cover-after-protests; Russ Burlingame, "Controversial Batgirl Variant Cover Cancelled," ComicBook.com, March 16, 2015, http://comicbook.com/2015/03/17/controversial-batgirl-variant-cover-cancelled; Rich Johnston, "The Batgirl Joker Variant Issue Goes Global as #SaveTheCover—Bleeding Cool Comic Book, Movie, TV News," *Bleeding Cool*, March 17, 2015, http://www.bleedingcool.com/2015/03/17/the-batgirl-joker-variant-issue-goes-global-as-savethecover; Teresa Jusino, "That Batgirl Variant Cover: What It Means to New Readers," *The Mary Sue*, March 16, 2015, http://www.themarysue.com/batgirl-variant-cover-problem; Tyler Kane, "Controversial Batgirl Variant Cover Canceled," *Paste*, May 17, 2015, http://www.pastemagazine.com/articles/2015/03/controversial-batgirl-variant-cover-canceled.html.

64. Albert Ching, "DC Comics Cancels 'Batgirl' Joker Variant Cover at Artist's Request," *Comic Book Resources*, March 16, 2015, http://www.comicbookresources.com/article/dc-comics-cancels-batgirl-joker-variant-at-artists-request.

65. James Butler, "Absolutely shocking you cancelled the Batgirl variant cover. So much for your 'je suis Charlie' statement," Twitter.com, March 17, 2015, https://twitter.com/Clock_punk/status/577854056863023104; David MacLean, "Remember when the right-on Twitter brigade chanted 'Je Suis Charlie'? A bunch of angry women just had a comic pulped," Twitter.com, March 17, 2015, https://twitter.com/GeordieStory/status/577846009792970752; Nancy Ing and Alastair Jamieson, "Charlie Hebdo Massacre Survivor: I Closed My Eyes and Waited for Bullet," NBC News, January 16, 2015, http://www.nbcnews.com/storyline/paris-magazine-attack/charlie-hebdo-massacre-survivor-i-closed-my-eyes-waited-bullet-n287396.

66. The Manc Geek, "THE MANC GEEK on Twitter," Twitter.com, March 17, 2015, https://twitter.com/BigA85GL/status/577922342954930176; Thunder, "Thunder on Twitter," Twitter.com, March 17, 2015, https://twitter.com/Thunder__Strike/status/577899286345617408; Cart5r, "CART5R on Twitter," Twitter.com, March 17, 2015, https://twitter.com/CART5R/status/577821930251759616; Young Gummy, "Young Gummy on Twitter," Twitter.com, March 17, 2015, https://twitter.com/MBIIdollabill/status/577891049592512512.

67. Daddy Warpig, "Daddy Warpig on Twitter," Twitter.com, March 17, 2015, https://twitter.com/Daddy_Warpig/status/577854805588115456.

68. Captain Privilege, "Captain Privilege on Twitter," Twitter.com, March 16, 2015, https://twitter.com/Capt_Privilege/status/577626987247722498.

69. "PC culture" has once again become a political rallying cry. Among Republican presidential candidates, Ted Cruz notably linked political correctness to terrorism and stated in a presidential debate on December 15, 2015, that "political correctness is killing people." Staff, "Cruz: 'Political Correctness Is Killing People,'" FoxNews.com, December 15, 2015, http://

www.foxnews.com/politics/2015/12/15/cruz-political-correctness-is-killing-people.html.

70. Brett White, "Learning from the #FireRickRemender Uproar," *Comic Book Resources*, July 9, 2014, http://www.comicbookresources.com/?page=article&id=53951.

71. Gloria Miller, "Why Marvel Needs to Fire Rick Remender," Examiner.com, July 3, 2014, http://www.examiner.com/article/why-marvel-needs-to-fire-rick-remender.

72. Heidi MacDonald, "'Fire Rick Remender'—a Timeout for the Internet's Outrage-O-Matic—UPDATE," July 7, 2014, http://comicsbeat.com/fire-rick-remender-a-timeout-for-the-internets-outrage-o-matic; Jill Pantozzi, "No, Rick Remender Did Not Write Falcon Having Sex with a 14-Year-Old in Captain America," *The Mary Sue*, July 7, 2014.

73. moneystcroix, "RE: Rick Remender, Alleged Statutory Rape, and Jet Black," *Moneystcroix*, July 3, 2013, http://moneystcroix.tumblr.com/post/90703508863/re-rick-remender-alleged-statutory-rape-and-jet.

74. Kieron Gillen, "Another Way to Breathe," July 8, 2014, http://kierongillen.tumblr.com/post/91144058367/do-you-understand-that-the-stuff-about-remenders-cap.

75. Ed Brubaker, "Seriously, people need to stop acting like fictional stories are how-to manuals showing the exact right way to be. Oh and #firerickremender," @brubaker, Twitter.com, July 8, 2014, https://twitter.com/brubaker/status/486517303370300166.

76. Tom Brennan, "The Brennanator Briefing: Why #FireRickRemender Should Outrage You," BrennanatorBriefing.Blogspot.com, July 7, 2014, http://brennanatorbriefing.blogspot.com/2014/07/why-firerickremender-should-outrage-you.html.

77. Jackie, "We Need All Voices in Comics (or, I Started the #FireRickRemender Twitter Tag and I'm Really Only Kind of Sorry About It)," *WeinerSoldier*, July 8, 2014, http://weinersoldier.tumblr.com/post/91160891783/we-need-all-voices-in-comics-or-i-started-the; Mark Waid, "Mark Waid on Twitter: 'If You're Replying to #FireRickRemender Supporters with Threats of Rape or Violence, Your Behavior Is Far More Inexcusable Than Theirs,'" Twitter.com, July 7, 2014, https://twitter.com/MarkWaid/status/486266533077725184.

78. Jackie, "We Need All Voices in Comics (or, I Started the #FireRickRemender Twitter Tag and I'm Really Only Kind of Sorry About It)."

79. Janelle Asselin, "Anatomy of a Bad Cover: DC's New "Teen Titans" #1—Comic Book Resources," *Comic Book Resources*, April 11, 2014, http://www.comicbookresources.com/?page=article&id=52103.

80. Ibid.; Janelle Asselin, "How Big of a Problem Is Harassment at Comic Conventions? Very Big," BitchMedia.org, July 22, 2014, https://bitchmedia.org/post/how-big-a-problem-is-harassment-at-comic-conventions-very-big-survey-sdcc-emerald-city-cosplay-consent.

81. Janelle Asselin, "Let's Talk about How Some Men Talk to Women in Comics," GimpNelly.Tumblr.com, April 14, 2014, http://gimpnel-

ly.tumblr.com/post/82704464182/lets-talk-about-how-some-men-talk-to-wom-en-in-comics.

82. Jude Terror, "Comics Smackdown: Is CBR in the Dog House with DC Comics after Teen Titans Hit Piece? (UPDATED)," *Outhousers*, April 11, 2014, http://www.theouthousers.com/index.php/news/127003-comics-smack-down-is-cbr-in-the-dog-house-with-dc-comics-after-teen-titans-hit-piece.html; Asselin, "Let's Talk about How Some Men Talk to Women in Comics."

83. Tauriq Moosa, "Female Journalist Gets Rape Threats over Comic Book Criticism," *Daily Beast*, April 21, 2014, http://www.thedailybeast.com/articles/2014/04/21/female-journalist-gets-rape-threats-over-comic-book-criti-cism.html.

84. Asselin, "Let's Talk about How Some Men Talk to Women in Comics."

85. Tim Hanley, "Gendercrunching DC Comics 1996–2011," *Bleeding Cool*, September 20, 2011, http://www.bleedingcool.com/2011/09/20/gender-crunching-dc-comics-1996-2011-by-tim-hanley.

86. Tim Hanley, "Gendercrunching: DC and Marvel September 2011—and Marvel 1996–2011," *Bleeding Cool*, November 11, 2011, http://www.bleedingcool.com/2011/11/11/gendercrunching-dc-and-marvel-septem-ber-2011-and-marvel-1996-2011; Tim Hanley, "Gendercrunching June 2014—Including Nationality and Ethnicity at the Big Two—Bleeding Cool Comic Book, Movie, TV News," *Bleeding Cool*, August 29, 2014, http://www.bleedingcool.com/2014/08/29/gendercrunching-june-2014-including-na-tionality-and-ethnicity-at-the-big-two.

87. "Publisher Market Shares: October 2015," DiamondComics.com, October 2015, http://www.diamondcomics.com/Home/1/1/3/237?artic-leID=170877; Heidi McDonald, "Is Image Just a Bunch of White Dudes? Yes and No," *The Beat*, January 10, 2014, http://www.comicsbeat.com/is-image-just-a-bunch-of-white-dudes-yes-and-no; Dan Wickline, "Image Expo Open-ing Triggers Gender and Race Diversity Conversations," *Bleeding Cool*, Janu-ary 9, 2014, http://www.bleedingcool.com/2014/01/09/image-expo-opening-triggers-gender-and-race-diversity-conversations.

88. Tess Fowler, "My Response," TessFowler.Tumblr.com, November 15, 2013, http://tessfowler.tumblr.com/post/67091692836/my-response; Beccator-ia, "Sleep-Speaker—Brian Wood: Because It Seems He Is Not the Man We Thought He Was," Beccatoria.LiveJournal.com, November 17, 2013, http://beccatoria.livejournal.com/179948.html.

89. Andy Kouri, "Brian Wood Releases Statement about Accusations of Sex-ual Harassment," *Comics Alliance*, November 15, 2013, http://comicsalli-ance.com/brian-wood-tess-fowler-sexual-harassment-accusations-statement.

90. Rich Johnston, "Tess Fowler and Modern Day Misogyny in the Comics Industry—Bleeding Cool Comic Book, Movie, TV News," *Bleeding Cool*, Oc-tober 28, 2013, http://www.bleedingcool.com/2013/10/28/tess-fowler-and-modern-day-misogyny-in-the-comics-industry; Laura Hudson, "Sexual Harass-ment in Comics: The Tipping Point," *Comics Alliance*, November 19, 2013, http://comicsalliance.com/sexual-harassment-women-in-comics; Noah Berlat-sky, "How to Dismantle the Comic-Books Boys' Club," *The Atlantic*, Novem-

ber 20, 2013, http://www.theatlantic.com/entertainment/archive/2013/11/how-to-dismantle-comic-books-boys-club-by-talking-about-it/281694.

91. Scott, "Fangirls in Refrigerators: The Politics of (in)Visibility in Comic Book Culture."

92. Rich Johnston, "The Shaming of Sexual Harassment by Social Media," *Bleeding Cool*, November 16, 2013, http://www.bleedingcool.com/2013/11/16/the-shaming-of-sexual-harassment-by-social-media.

93. Ibid.

94. automatickafka, "Opinion Piece on Brian Wood, Tess Fowler and Comic Harassment—/R/Comicbooks," Reddit.com, November 2013, http://www.reddit.com/r/comicbooks/comments/1qwzwz/opin-ion_piece_on_brian_wood_tess_fowler_and_comic.

95. Hudson, "Sexual Harassment in Comics: The Tipping Point."

96. Greg Rucka, "Front Toward Enemy," Ruckawriter.Tumblr.com, November 14, 2013, http://ruckawriter.tumblr.com/post/67037244257/reading-up-on-a-lot-on-social-media-on-how-the-comic.

97. Lisa Granshaw, "Comic Book Legend to Sexist Fan: 'You Have Major Issues,'" *Daily Dot*, September 19, 2013, http://www.dailydot.com/fandom/brian-michael-bendis-tumblr-response-sexist.

98. Rob Salkowitz, "How Many Fans??!! New York Comic Con Sets Attendance Record," *Forbes*, October 15, 2016, http://www.forbes.com/sites/robsalkowitz/2015/10/15/how-many-fans-new-york-comic-con-sets-attendance-record.

99. Henry Jenkins, "Superpowered Fans," *Boom: A Journal of California* 2, no. 2 (June 1, 2012): 22–36.

100. Anonymous, "I Was Sexually Harassed 3x at DC's Awesome Con Comic Convention," CollectiveActionDC.org, April 23, 2013, http://www.collectiveactiondc.org/2013/04/23/sexually-harassed-three-separate-times-at-dcs-awesome-con-comic-convention.

101. Noelle Micarelli, "Female Cosplayers Share Their Creeper Stories through Photos," *The Mary Sue*, October 18, 2013, http://www.themarysue.com/cosplay-creeper-quotes/2; Heidi MacDonald, "New York Comic-Con 2013: Creepy Camera Crews, Arizona's Big Cans, and Harassment," *The Beat*, October 15, 2013, http://comicsbeat.com/new-york-comic-con-2013-creepy-camera-crews-arizonas-big-cans-and-harassment.

102. Daily Mail Reporter, "America's Next Top Model Winner Adrianne Curry "Molested" at Star Wars Convention," *Daily Mail*, August 17, 2010, http://www.dailymail.co.uk/tvshowbiz/article-1303619/Americas-Next-Top-Model-winner-Adrianne-Curry-molested-Star-Wars-convention.html.

103. toofab, "Adrianne Curry Describes Horrific Groping Incident at Comic-Con," YouTube, July 28, 2014, http://www.youtube.com/watch?v=mXpFaHHyGek.

104. Pete Cashmore, "'Harrass a Booth Babe': A Twitter Contest Too Far?," *Mashable*, July 24, 2009, http://mashable.com/2009/07/24/danteteam-contest.

105. DanteTeam, "A Photo from @Danteteam," *Twitpic*, accessed November 9, 2014, http://twitpic.com/bityg.

106. Asselin, "How Big of a Problem Is Harassment at Comic Conventions? Very Big."

107. Girl-Wonder, "Girl-Wonder.org Founds Convention Anti-Harassment Project," Girl-Wonder.org, August 21, 2008, http://girl-wonder.org/2008/08/girl-wonderorg-founds-convention-anti-harassment-project.

108. Nicole Stark, "The Characteristics of Sexual Harassment Policies at Fan Conventions," unpublished, 2013, https://docs.google.com/document/d/1BDMxrXDfMNIVQcz6HJHn8vNtidP5wwRIEKRsBnUq8So/edit.

109. "Geeks for CONsent," GeeksForConsent.org, accessed October 31, 2014, http://www.geeksforconsent.org/who-we-are.

110. Jill Pantozzi, "New York Comic Con Has Asked Us to Help Draft Their Harassment Policy!," *The Mary Sue*, August 22, 2014, http://www.themarysue.com/new-york-comic-con-help-with-harassment-policy.

6. RAPE CULTURE ON CAMPUS

1. Chris Atmore, "Victims, Backlash, and Radical Feminist Theory (or, the Morning After They Stole Feminism's Fire)," in *New Versions of Victims Feminists Struggle with the Concept*, ed. Sharon Lamb (New York: New York University Press, 1999); Jody Raphael, *Rape Is Rape* (Chicago, IL: Chicago Review Press, 2013); Maria Bevacqua, *Rape on the Public Agenda: Feminism and the Politics of Sexual Assault* (Boston, MA: Northeastern University Press, 2000); Mary Koss, "Hidden, Unacknowledged, Acquaintance, and Date Rape: Looking Back, Looking Forward," *Psychology of Women Quarterly* 35, no. 2 (June 1, 2011): 348–54; Martin D. Schwartz and Walter S. DeKeseredy, *Sexual Assault on the College Campus: The Role of Male Peer Support* (Thousand Oaks, CA: Sage, 1997).

2. The Clery Act was passed in 1990 in response to the 1986 rape and murder of nineteen-year-old Jeanne Clery on Lehigh University campus. The fellow student, who raped and sodomized the victim before slashing her throat and strangling her, was subsequently arrested, convicted, and sentenced to death. The act was passed requiring "all colleges and universities that receive federal funding to collect data on violent crimes, share the information, and inform the public about crime occurring 'in or around campus' and to offer support for victims." Clery Center for Security on Campus, "Summary of the Jeanne Clery Act," CleryCenter.org, accessed August 17, 2015, http://clerycenter.org/summary-jeanne-clery-act. Title IX is defined as "a comprehensive federal law that prohibits discrimination on the basis of sex in any federally funded education program or activity." Department of Justice, "Overview of Title IX of the Education Amendments of 1972, 20 U.S.C. a§ 1681 Et. Seq.," Justice.gov, 1972. http://www.justice.gov/crt/overview-title-ix-education-amendments-1972-20-usc-1681-et-seq.

3. Sabrina Erdely, "A Rape on Campus: A Brutal Assault and Struggle for Justice at UVA," RollingStone.com, November 19, 2014.

4. Ibid. In the article, Seccuro stated that UVA administrators acted dismissively when she complained and that twenty years elapsed before one of the rapists was held to account for the crime. Erdely wrote of Seccuro's experience after her rape:

> "I went to the dean covered in scabs and with broken ribs," she remembers. "And he said, "Do you think it was just regrettable sex?" Seccuro wanted to call police, but she was incorrectly told Charlottesville police lacked jurisdiction over fraternity houses.

5. Ibid.
6. Erdely, "A Rape on Campus: A Brutal Assault and Struggle for Justice at UVA"; Robby Soave, "Campus Rape Expert Who Misrepresented His Work Faces Powerful New Criticism," *Reason*, August 11, 2015, https://reason.com/blog/2015/08/11/campus-rape-expert-who-misrepresented-hi; Kevin M. Swartout et al., "Trajectory Analysis of the Campus Serial Rapist Assumption," *JAMA Pediatrics*, 169, no. 12 (July 2015): 1148–54; David Lisak and Paul Miller, "Repeat Rape and Multiple Offending among Undetected Rapists," *Violence and Victims* 17, no. 1 (December 3, 2009): 73–84.
7. Andrew Elliott, "Students Claiming Responsibility for Phi Kappa Psi Vandalism Submit Anonymous Letter," *Cavalier Daily*, November 20, 2014, http://www.cavalierdaily.com/article/2014/11/letter-claiming-responsibility-for-phi-kappa-psi-vandalism-lists-anonymous-demands; Julianna Goldman, "Univ. of Va. Greek Activities Suspended in Wake of Rape Allegations," November 24, 2014, http://www.cbsnews.com/news/uva-greek-activities-suspended-in-wake-of-rape-allegations; Sandy Hausman, "Magazine Sheds Light on Allegations of Rape Culture at UVA," NPR, November 25, 2014, http://www.npr.org/2014/11/25/366504641/university-of-virginia-investigates-rape-allegations; Anthony Zurcher, "'Rape Culture' Investigation Shocks Virginia University," BBC News, November 24, 2014, http://www.bbc.com/news/blogs-echochambers-30153441; staff, "Rape at UVA: Readers Say Jackie Wasn't Alone," RollingStone.com, November 21, 2014, http://www.rollingstone.com/culture/news/rape-at-uva-readers-say-jackie-wasnt-alone-20141121.
8. Soraya Chemaly, "Our 'Rape Problem' Can't Be Solved by Colleges," *Huffington Post*, November 28, 2014, http://www.huffingtonpost.com/soraya-chemaly/the-college-rape-problem-_b_6228844.html.
9. Hausman, "Magazine Sheds Light on Allegations of Rape Culture at UVA"; Bonnie Gordon, "The UVA Gang Rape Allegations Are Awful, Horrifying, and Not Shocking at All," *Slate*, November 25, 2014, http://www.slate.com/blogs/xx_factor/2014/11/25/uva_gang_rape_allegations_in_rolling_stone_not_surprising_to_one_associate.html.
10. Melinda Skinner, "Skinner: Rape Culture Exists at More Places than U.Va.," *Richmond Times-Dispatch*, November 24, 2014, http://www.richmond.com/opinion/their-opinion/guest-columnists/article_0d477031-f320-5ef2-a6a0-05ce372542cc.html.

11. Richard Bradley, "Is the Rolling Stone Story True?," RichardBradley.net, November 24, 2014, http://www.richardbradley.net/shotsinthedark/2014/11/24/is-the-rolling-stone-story-true.

12. Jonah Goldberg, "Rolling Stone Rape Story Sends Shock Waves—and Stretches Credulity," *Los Angeles Times*, December 1, 2014, http://www.latimes.com/opinion/op-ed/la-oe-goldberg-uva-rape-rolling-stone-20141202-column.html; Robby Soave, "Is the UVA Rape Story a Gigantic Hoax?," *Reason*, December 1, 2014, http://social.reason.com/blog/2014/12/01/is-the-uva-rape-story-a-gigantic-hoax.

13. Erik Wemple, "Rolling Stone's Disastrous U-Va. Story: A Case of Real Media Bias," *Washington Post*, December 5, 2014, https://www.washingtonpost.com/blogs/erik-wemple/wp/2014/12/05/rolling-stones-disastrous-u-va-story-a-case-of-real-media-bias; Lindsay Beyerstein, "Rolling Stone's Bombshell Story about Campus Rape Comes under Fire," *Observer*, December 3, 2014, http://observer.com/2014/12/rolling-stones-bombshell-story-about-campus-rape-comes-under-fire; Paul Farhi, "Author of Rolling Stone Article on Alleged U-Va. Rape Didn't Contact Accused Assailants for Her Report," *Washington Post*, December 1, 2014, https://www.washingtonpost.com/lifestyle/style/author-of-rolling-stone-story-on-alleged-u-va-rape-didnt-talk-to-accused-perpetrators/2014/12/01/e4c19408-7999-11e4-84d4-7c896b90abdc_story.html; Paul Farhi, "Sabrina Rubin Erdely, Woman Behind Rolling Stone's Explosive U-Va. Alleged Rape Story," *Washington Post*, November 28, 2014, https://www.washingtonpost.com/lifestyle/style/sabrina-rubin-erdely-woman-behind-rolling-stones-explosive-u-va-alleged-rape-story/2014/11/28/89f322c2-7731-11e4-bd1b-03009bd3e984_story.html; T. Rees Shapiro, "Key Elements of Rolling Stone's U-Va. Gang Rape Allegations in Doubt," *Washington Post*, December 5, 2014, http://www.washingtonpost.com/local/education/u-va-fraternity-to-rebut-claims-of-gang-rape-in-rolling-stone/2014/12/05/5fa5f7d2-7c91-11e4-84d4-7c896b90abdc_story.html.

14. T. Rees Shapiro, "Key Elements of Rolling Stone's U-Va. Gang Rape Allegations in Doubt"; staff, "A Note to Our Readers," RollingStone.com, December 5, 2014, http://www.rollingstone.com/culture/news/a-note-to-our-readers-20141205; Alana Horowitz, "Rolling Stone Walks Back Contentious Apology Letter," *Huffington Post*, December 7, 2014, http://www.huffingtonpost.com/2014/12/07/rolling-stone-apology-uva-rape-jackie_n_6284100.html.

15. Krystal Ball, "Do We Cover Rape More When We Think Women Lie?," MSNBC, December 11, 2014, http://www.msnbc.com/the-cycle/do-we-cover-rape-more-when-we-think-women-lie.

16. Sheila Coronel, Steve Coll, and Derek Kravitz, "Rolling Stone and UVA: The Columbia University Graduate School of Journalism Report," *Columbia Journalism Review*, April 5, 2015, http://www.cjr.org/investigation/rolling_stone_investigation.php; Ravi Somaiya, "Rolling Stone Article on Rape at University of Virginia Failed All Basics, Report Says," *New York Times*, April 5,

2015, http://www.nytimes.com/2015/04/06/business/media/rolling-stone-re-tracts-article-on-rape-at-university-of-virginia.html.

17. Bradley, "Is the Rolling Stone Story True?"

18. Editorial Board, "Rolling Stone's 'Rape Culture,'" *New York Post*, December 15, 2014, http://nypost.com/2014/12/15/rolling-stones-rape-culture; David Weigel, "Rolling Stone, Lena Dunham, and the 'Rape Culture' Backlash—Bloomberg Politics," Bloomberg.com, December 9, 2014, http://www.bloomberg.com/politics/articles/2014-12-09/rolling-stone-lena-dunham-and-the-rape-culture-backlash; Elise Hilton, "'Rape Culture': Plausible, but Is It True?," *Acton Institute PowerBlog*, December 16, 2014, http://blog.acton.org/archives/74636-rape-culture-plausible-true.html; Matt Walsh, "Rape Culture Doesn't Exist and There Is No Rape Epidemic," *The Blaze*, December 9, 2014, http://www.theblaze.com/contributions/rape-culture-doesnt-exist-and-there-is-no-rape-epidemic.

19. Megan McArdle, "Moral Panics Won't End Campus Rape," *Bloomberg View*, January 28, 2015, http://www.bloombergview.com/articles/2015-01-28/moral-panics-won-t-end-campus-rape.

20. Heather Wilhelm, "Feminist Confusion and the UVA Rape Case," *Chicago Tribune*, December 8, 2014, http://www.chicagotribune.com/news/opinion/commentary/ct-rape-university-feminists-perspec-1209-20141208-story.html.

21. Camille Paglia, "The Modern Campus Cannot Comprehend Evil," Time.com, September 29, 2014, http://time.com/3444749/camille-paglia-the-modern-campus-cannot-comprehend-evil.

22. Kristen Lombardi and Kristin Jones, "Sexual Assault on Campus: A Frustrating Search for Justice," Center for Public Integrity, 2010, http://cloud-front-files-1.publicintegrity.org/documents/pdfs/Sexual%20Assault%20on%20Campus.pdf.

23. Ibid.

24. Shapiro, "Campus Rape Victims: A Struggle for Justice."

25. Russlynn Ali, "Dear Colleague Letter," U.S. Department of Education Office for Civil Rights, Washington, DC, April 4, 2011, http://www2.ed.gov/about/offices/list/ocr/letters/colleague-201104.pdf; Chris Krebs, Christine Lindquist, Tara Warner, Bonnie Fisher, and Sandra Martin, *The Campus Sexual Assault Study (CSA)* (Washington, DC: National Institute of Justice, 2007).

26. Katie Thomas, "Review Shows Title IX Is Not Significantly Enforced," *New York Times*, July 28, 2011, http://www.nytimes.com/2011/07/29/sports/review-shows-title-ix-is-not-significantly-enforced.html.

27. Nina Burleigh, "Confronting Campus Rape," RollingStone.com, June 4, 2014, http://www.rollingstone.com/politics/news/confronting-campus-rape-20140604; Tovia Smith, "How Campus Sexual Assaults Came to Command New Attention," NPR, August 12, 2014, http://www.npr.org/2014/08/12/339822696/how-campus-sexual-assaults-came-to-command-new-attention; Stacy Teicher Khadaroo, "Feds Warn Colleges: Handle Sexual Assault Reports Properly," Today.com, September 2, 2016, http://www.today.com/id/

44376767/ns/today-today_news/t/feds-warn-colleges-handle-sexual-assault-re-ports-properly.

28. Emily Suran, "Title IX and Social Media: Going Beyond the Law," *Michigan Journal of Gender and Law* 21, no. 2 (2014).

29. Ibid.

30. Jodi Cohen and Stacy St Clair, "Federal Authorities Investigating Sexual Violence Complaints at Several Area Colleges," March 1, 2016, http://www.chicagotribune.com/news/local/breaking/ct-universities-sexual-violence-investigations-20160301-story.html; Mary O'Toole, Brian Van Brunt, Brett Sokolow, Caitlin Flanagan, Monika Hostler, and Alison Kiss, "Sexual Assault on College and University Campuses," *Violence and Gender* 2, no. 1 (2015).

31. Tyler Kingkade, "Fewer Than One-Third of Campus Sexual Assault Cases Result in Expulsion," *Huffington Post*, September 29, 2014, http://www.huffingtonpost.com/2014/09/29/campus-sexual-assault_n_5888742.html.

32. Jon Krakauer, *Missoula: Rape and the Justice System in a College Town* (New York: Doubleday, 2015), 340.

33. Ibid., 338.

34. Kristin Bumiller, *In an Abusive State: How Neoliberalism Appropriated the Feminist Movement against Sexual Violence* (Durham, NC: Duke University Press, 2008); Susan Caringella, *Addressing Rape Reform in Law and Practice* (New York: Columbia University Press, 2009); Rose Corrigan, *Up Against a Wall: Rape Reform and the Failure of Success* (New York: New York University Press, 2013); Kathleen Daly and Brigitte Bouhours, "Rape and Attrition in the Legal Process: A Comparative Analysis of Five Countries," *Crime and Justice* 39, no. 1 (2010): 565–650; Susan Estrich, *Real Rape* (Cambridge, MA: Harvard University Press, 1988); Nicola Gavey, *Just Sex? The Cultural Scaffolding of Rape* (New York: Routledge, 2005); Barbara Krahé and Jennifer Tempkin, *Sexual Assault and the Justice Gap: A Question of Attitude* (Portland, OR: Hart Publishing, 2008); Kimberly Lonsway and Joanne Armchambault, "The 'Justice Gap' for Sexual Assault Cases: Future Directions for Research and Reform," *Violence against Women*, March 6, 2012; Stephen Schulhofer, *Unwanted Sex: The Culture of Intimidation and the Failure of Law* (Cambridge, MA: Harvard University Press, 1998).

35. Krakauer, *Missoula: Rape and the Justice System in a College Town*.

36. Barack Obama, "Weekly Address: Taking Action to End Sexual Assault," WhiteHouse.gov, 2014, http://www.whitehouse.gov/the-press-office/2014/01/24/weekly-address-taking-action-end-sexual-assault.

37. Ibid.

38. Anna Drezen, "The Six Best Colleges for Not Getting Raped," *Reductress*, 2014, http://reductress.com/post/the-six-best-colleges-for-not-getting-raped.

39. Burleigh, "Confronting Campus Rape."

40. Claire McCaskill, "Expanded Bipartisan Coalition Introduces Legislation to Prevent Sexual Assaults on College and University Campuses," McCaskill.senate.gov, February 26, 2015, http://www.mccaskill.senate.gov/media-cen-

ter/news-releases/expanded-bipartisan-coalition-introduces-legislation-to-prevent-sexual-assaults-on-college-and-university-campuses.

41. White House. "Not Alone: The First Report of the White House Task Force to Protect Students from Sexual Assault," White House Task Force, Washington, DC, April 2014; Krebs et al., *The Campus Sexual Assault Study (CSA) Final Report: Performance Period: January 2005 through December 2007*; Lombardi and Jones, "Sexual Assault on Campus: A Frustrating Search for Justice."

42. For example, in 2013, Caroline Kitchens wrote of the "one in five" statistic, "I have yet to see an article lamenting the campus rape culture that does not contain some iteration of this alarming statistic." Caroline Kitchens, "Statistics Don't Back Up Claims about 'Rape Culture.'" *U.S. News & World Report*, October 24, 2013, http://www.usnews.com/opinion/blogs/economic-intelligence/2013/10/24/statistics-dont-back-up-claims-about-rape-culture.

43. Glenn Kessler, "One in Five Women in College Sexually Assaulted: An Update on This Statistic," *Washington Post*, December 17, 2014, http://www.washingtonpost.com/blogs/fact-checker/wp/2014/12/17/one-in-five-women-in-college-sexually-assaulted-an-update.

44. Christopher Krebs and Christine Lindquist, "Setting the Record Straight on '1 in 5,'" Time.com, December 15, 2014, http://time.com/3633903/campus-rape-1-in-5-sexual-assault-setting-record-straight; see also Cantor et al. for an explanation as to why the "one in five" statistic is not nationally representative. David Cantor et al., "Report on the AAU Campus Climate Survey on Sexual Assault and Sexual Misconduct," Association of American Universities, Rockville, MD, September 21, 2015, https://www.aau.edu/uploadedFiles/AAU_Publications/AAU_Reports/Sexual_Assault_Campus_Survey/Report%20on%20the%20AAU%20Campus%20Climate%20Survey%20on%20Sexual%20Assault%20and%20Sexual%20Misconduct.pdf.

45. Christopher Krebs and Christine Lindquist, "Setting the Record Straight on '1 in 5.'"

46. Nick Anderson and Scott Clement, "Poll Shows That 20 Percent of Women Are Sexually Assaulted in College," *Washington Post*, June 12, 2015, http://www.washingtonpost.com/sf/local/2015/06/12/1-in-5-women-say-they-were-violated; Kessler, "One in Five Women in College Sexually Assaulted: An Update on This Statistic,"

47. George F. Will, "George Will: Colleges Become the Victims of Progressivism," *Washington Post*, 2014, http://www.washingtonpost.com/opinions/george-will-college-become-the-victims-of-progressivism/2014/06/06/e90e73b4-eb50-11e3-9f5c-9075d5508f0a_print.html; CNN, "Sexual Assault Survivor Lisa Sendrow Explains the Consequences of George Will's Rape Dismissal on CNN," *Media Matters for America*, 2014, http://mediamatters.org/video/2014/07/02/sexual-assault-survivor-lisa-sendrow-explains-t/199966; Steve Contorno, "Are 20 Percent of Women Sexually Assaulted before They Graduate College?," Politifact.com, May 2, 2015, http://www.politifact.com/truth-o-meter/article/2014/may/02/are-20-percent-women-sexually-assaulted-they-gra-

du; Ashe Schow, "No, 1 in 5 Women Have Not Been Raped on College Campuses," *Washington Examiner*, August 14, 2014, http://www.washingtonexaminer.com/no-1-in-5-women-have-not-been-raped-on-college-campuses/article/2551980.

48. Sofi Sinozich and Lynn Langton, "Rape and Sexual Assault Victimization among College-Age Females, 1995–2013," Bureau of Justice Statistics Washington, DC, December 2014; staff, "New DOJ Data on Sexual Assaults: Students Are Less Likely to Be Raped," *The Federalist*, December 11, 2014, http://thefederalist.com/2014/12/11/new-doj-data-on-sexual-assaults-college-students-are-actually-less-likely-to-be-victimized; Robin Wilson, "Study Challenges Notion That Risk of Sexual Assault Is Greater at College," *Chronicle of Higher Education*, December 12, 2014, http://chronicle.com/article/Study-Challenges-Notion-That/150817.

49. John Hinderaker, "'Rape Culture,' Debunked," *Powerline*, December 14, 2014, http://www.powerlineblog.com/archives/2014/12/rape-culture-de-bunked.php; Sierra Rayne, "We Will Never Know the Actual Rate of Sexual Assault," AmericanThinker.com, December 15, 2014, http://www.americanthinker.com/articles/2014/12/never_know_rate_sexual_assault.html; Wilson, "Study Challenges Notion That Risk of Sexual Assault Is Greater at College."

50. Cathy Young, "The Year the Crusade against 'Rape Culture' Stumbled," *Reason*, December 26, 2014, http://reason.com/archives/2014/12/26/the-year-the-crusade-against-rape-cultur.

51. Emily Yoffe, "The College Rape Overcorrection," *Slate*, December 7, 2014, http://www.slate.com/articles/double_x/doublex/2014/12/college_rape_campus_sexual_assault_is_a_serious_problem_but_the_efforts.html.

52. Morgan Baskin, "Q&A: Sen. Bob Casey on His Campus Sexual Assault Bill," *USA Today*, October 16, 2015, http://college.usatoday.com/2015/10/16/qa-sen-bob-casey-on-his-campus-sexual-assault-bill; Scott Greer, "Senators Exclude Statistics at Premiere of Campus Assault Documentary," *Daily Caller*, June 2, 2015, http://dailycaller.com/2015/06/02/senators-exclude-statistics-at-premiere-of-campus-assault-documentary; Chuck Ross, "Kirsten Gillibrand Admits 'We May Not Know' the Actual Rate of Campus Rape," *Daily Caller*, June 16, 2015, http://dailycaller.com/2015/06/16/kirsten-gillibrand-admits-we-may-not-know-the-actual-rate-of-campus-rape.

53. Bill Maher, "Real Time with Bill Maher: The Hunting Ground (HBO)," *Real Time with Bill Maher Blog*, March 17, 2015, https://www.youtube.com/watch?v=JINxoR-S5To.

54. David Cantor et al., "Report on the AAU Campus Climate Survey on Sexual Assault and Sexual Misconduct," Association of American Universities, Rockville, MD, September 21, 2015, https://www.aau.edu/uploadedFiles/AAU_Publications/AAU_Reports/Sexual_Assault_Campus_Survey/Report%20on%20the%20AAU%20Campus%20Climate%20Survey%20on%20Sexual%20Assault%20and%20Sexual%20Misconduct.pdf; Dean Kilpatrick and Kenneth J. Ruggiero, "Making Sense of Rape in America: Where Do the Num-

bers Come From and What Do They Mean?," National Crime Victims Research and Treatment Center, Medical University of South Carolina, Charleston, 2004; Mary P Koss, "The Under Detection of Rape: Methodological Choices Influence Incidence Estimates," *Journal of Social Issues* 48, no. 1 (April 1, 1992): 61–75; Krebs and Lindquist, "Setting the Record Straight on '1 in 5'"; Candace Kruttschnitt, William Kalsbeek, and Carole House, "Estimating the Incidence of Rape and Sexual Assault," Panel on Measuring Rape and Sexual Assault in Bureau of Justice Statistics Household Surveys, 2014; Schwartz and DeKeseredy, *Sexual Assault on the College Campus: The Role of Male Peer Support*.

55. In fact, it is through the use of behaviorally specific questions that researchers have discovered that a sizeable number of men deny that they would rape but readily report they would likely "use force to obtain intercourse" (191). Sarah Edwards, Kathryn Bradshaw, and Verlin Hinsz, "Denying Rape but Endorsing Forceful Intercourse: Exploring Differences among Responders," *Violence and Gender* 1, no. 4 (December 15, 2014): 188–93.

56. Cantor et al., "Report on the AAU Campus Climate Survey on Sexual Assault and Sexual Misconduct "; Kate Carey et al., "Incapacitated and Forcible Rape of College Women: Prevalence Across the First Year," *Journal of Adolescent Health* 56, no. 6 (June 1, 2015): 678–80; Bonnie Fisher, Leah Daigle, and Francis Cullen, *Unsafe in the Ivory Tower: The Sexual Victimization of College Women* (Thousand Oaks, CA: Sage, 2010); Bonnie Fisher, Francis Cullen, and Michael Turner, "The Sexual Victimization of College Women," Bureau of Justice Statistics, Washington, DC, 2000, https://www.ncjrs.gov/pdffiles1/nij/182369.pdf; Schwartz and DeKeseredy, *Sexual Assault on the College Campus: The Role of Male Peer Support*.

57. Christopher Krebs et al., "Campus Climate Survey Validation Study Final Technical Report," Bureau of Justice Statistics, Washington DC, January 19, 2016, http://www.bjs.gov/content/pub/pdf/ccsvsftr.pdf.

58. Cantor et al., "Report on the AAU Campus Climate Survey on Sexual Assault and Sexual Misconduct."

59. Fisher, Daigle, and Cullen, *Unsafe in the Ivory Tower: The Sexual Victimization of College Women*.

60. O'Toole et al., "Sexual Assault on College and University Campuses"; Fisher, Daigle, and Cullen, *Unsafe in the Ivory Tower: The Sexual Victimization of College Women*, 87.

61. Fisher, Daigle, and Cullen, *Unsafe in the Ivory Tower: the Sexual Victimization of College Women*, 180.

62. Ibid., 134.

63. Dick and Ziering are best known for their collaboration on the Academy Award–winning documentary *The Invisible War* (2012) that is credited with exposing the ongoing problem of sexual assault in the military and prompting a change in policies to address the lack of enforcement. Chris Lee, "Sundance 2015: 'The Hunting Ground' Exposes an 'Epidemic' of Rape in American Colleges," *Entertainment Weekly*, January 24, 2015, http://www.ew.com/arti-

cle/2015/01/24/sundance-2015-the-hunting-ground-exposes-an-epidemic-of-rape-in-american-colleges.

64. Sundance, "Sundance: The Hunting Ground," Sundance.org, 2014, http://www.sundance.org/projects/the-hunting-ground; Brooks Barnes, "'The Hunting Ground,' a Film about Rape Culture at Colleges," *New York Times*, January 25, 2015, http://www.nytimes.com/2015/01/26/movies/the-hunting-ground-a-film-about-rape-culture-at-colleges.html.

65. Neesha Arter, "'The Hunting Ground' Sheds New Light on Campus Rape Epidemic," *Daily Beast*, February 26, 2015, http://www.thedailybeast.com/articles/2015/02/26/the-hunting-ground-sheds-new-light-on-campus-rape-epidemic.html; Jeff Benedict, "Jameis Winston's Accuser Speaks in New Film about Sexual Assault," *Sports Illustrated*, February 26, 2015, http://www.si.com/college-football/2015/02/26/hunting-ground-sexual-assault-college-jameis-winston-florida-state-notre-dame; Ben Kenigsberg, "Sundance Film Review: 'The Hunting Ground,'" *Variety*, January 23, 2015, http://variety.com/2015/film/reviews/sundance-film-review-the-hunting-ground-1201413564; Manohla Dargis, "Review: 'The Hunting Ground' Documentary, a Searing Look at Campus Rape," *New York Times*, February 26, 2015, http://www.nytimes.com/2015/02/27/movies/review-the-hunting-ground-documentary-a-searing-look-at-campus-rape.html; Kate Fagan and Jane McManus, "OK, We Really Need to Talk about 'The Hunting Ground,'" ESPN, March 16, 2015, http://espn.go.com/espnw/news-commentary/article/12491771/ok-really-need-talk-hunting-ground; Sara Lipka, "Charges of Sexual-Assault 'Cover-Ups' Gain New Power on the Big Screen," *Chronicle of Higher Education*, March 9, 2015, http://chronicle.com/article/Charges-of-Sexual-Assault/228321; Tierney Sneed, "'The Hunting Ground' Subjects Defend Title IX Campaign," *U.S. News and World Report*, February 27, 2015, http://www.usnews.com/news/articles/2015/02/27/the-hunting-ground-subjects-defend-title-ix-campaign; Kenneth Turan, "Sundance 2015: In 'The Hunting Ground,' Jameis Winston's Accuser Goes Public," *Los Angeles Times*, January 23, 2015, http://www.latimes.com/entertainment/movies/la-et-mn-sundance-hunting-ground-20150124-column.html; Alexander Nazaryan, "'The Hunting Ground' Gives a Harrowing Look at College Rape," *Newsweek*, February 11, 2015, http://www.newsweek.com/hunting-ground-gives-harrowing-look-college-rape-305606; Chris Lee, "Sundance 2015: 'The Hunting Ground' Exposes an 'Epidemic' of Rape in American Colleges," *Entertainment Weekly*, January 24, 2015, http://www.ew.com/article/2015/01/24/sundance-2015-the-hunting-ground-exposes-an-epidemic-of-rape-in-american-colleges; Kelsey Miller, "New Doc Reveals the Alarming Truth about Campus Rape," *Refinery 29*, February 24, 2015, http://social.refinery29.com/2015/02/82798/hunting-ground-campus-sexual-assault-film; Vanessa Grigoriadis, "Sundance Smash the Hunting Ground Is Chasing a Tiger; in Its Rush to Theaters," VanityFair.com, February 26, 2015, http://www.vanityfair.com/hollywood/2015/02/the-hunting-ground-kirby-dick-amy-ziering-film-premieres.

66. Ibid.

67. Jason Bailey, "Our Brand Is Rape Skepticism: On Slate and Emily Yoffe's Weird 'Hunting Ground' Obsession," *Flavorwire*, June 2, 2015, http://flavorwire.com/521250/our-brand-is-rape-skepticism-on-slate-and-emily-yoffes-weird-hunting-ground-obsession; Richard Bradley, "Considering the Hunting Ground," RichardBradley.net, March 3, 2015, http://www.richardbradley.net/shotsinthedark/2015/03/03/considering-the-hunting-ground; Greer, "Senators Exclude Statistics at Premiere of Campus Assault Documentary"; Jake New, "Documentary on Campus Sexual Assault Drops Claim That 35 Colleges Declined Interviews," InsideHigherEd.com, March 2, 2015, https://www.insidehighered.com/news/2015/03/02/documentary-campus-sexual-assault-drops-claim-35-colleges-declined-interviews; Claire Potter, "What Movie Did You See? A Response to Emily Yoffe's Review of 'the Hunting Ground,'" *Chronicle of Higher Education*, March 3, 2015, http://chronicle.com/blognetwork/tenuredradical/2015/03/what-movie-did-you-see-a-response-to-emily-yoffees-review-of-the-hunting-ground; Sarah Seltzer, "Why Is 'The Hunting Ground' Driving a Campus Rape Activism Backlash?," *Flavorwire*, March 5, 2015, http://flavorwire.com/507958/why-is-the-hunting-ground-driving-a-campus-rape-activism-backlash; Ashe Schow, "The Continuing Collapse of 'The Hunting Ground,' a Campus Sexual Assault Propaganda Film," *Washington Examiner*, June 3, 2015, http://www.washingtonexaminer.com/the-continuing-collapse-of-the-hunting-ground-a-campus-sexual-assault-propaganda-film/article/2565464; Robby Soave, "Central Allegation in the Hunting Ground Collapses under Scrutiny," June 1, 2015; John Stossel, "Raping Culture," *Town Hall*, March 4, 2015, http://townhall.com/columnists/johnstossel/2015/03/04/raping-culture-n1965312; Emily Yoffe, "What's Wrong with the New Documentary about Rape on College Campuses," *Slate*, February 27, 2015, http://www.slate.com/articles/double_x/doublex/2015/02/the_hunting_ground_a_campus_rape_documentary_that_fails_to_provide_a_full.html.

68. "Transcript for CNN Program 'Sexual Assault on Campus,'" CNN.com, November 24, 2015, http://www.cnn.com/2015/11/24/us/the-hunting-ground-panel-discussion/index.html; Kareem Copeland, "Lawyers for Winston, Kinsman Unhappy ahead of 'Hunting Ground' Airing," BayNews9.com, November 22, 2015, http://www.baynews9.com/content/news/baynews9/sports/article.html/content/news/articles/bn9/2015/11/22/jameis_winston_cnn_hunting_ground.html; Eriq Gardner, "NFL Star Jameis Winston Sends Legal Threat to CNN over Rape Movie 'The Hunting Ground,'" *Hollywood Reporter*, November 20, 2015, http://www.hollywoodreporter.com/thr-esq/nfl-star-jameis-winston-sends-842572.

69. Amy Goodman, "'The Hunting Ground': Film Exposes How Colleges Cover Up Sexual Assault and Fail to Protect Students," DemocracyNow.org, January 28, 2015, http://www.democracynow.org/2015/1/28/the_hunting_ground_film_exposes_how.

70. Swartout et al., "Trajectory Analysis of the Campus Serial Rapist Assumption," 1153; Lisak and Miller, "Repeat Rape and Multiple Offending among Undetected Rapists"; Linda LeFauve, "The Misleading Video Inter-

view with a Rapist at the Heart of the Campus Sexual Assault Freakout,"
Reason, November 20, 2015, https://reason.com/archives/2015/11/20/lisak-
frank-interview-problem-rape; Robby Soave, "How the Hunting Ground
Spreads Myths about Campus Rape," *Reason*, November 20, 2015, https://
reason.com/blog/2015/11/20/how-the-hunting-ground-spreads-lies-abou; Robby Soave, "Junk Science and Campus Rape," *Reason*, October 20, 2015, https://
reason.com/archives/2015/10/20/junk-science-and-campus-rape; Swartout et
al., "Trajectory Analysis of the Campus Serial Rapist Assumption."

71. Daniel Fienberg, "Interview: 'Hunting Ground' Filmmakers Talk Campus Sexual Assault, Jameis Winston and More," *HitFix*, March 2, 2015, http://
www.hitfix.com/the-fien-print/interview-the-hunting-ground-filmmakers-talk-
campus-sexual-assault-jameis-winston-and-more; Brooke Jackson-Glidden,
"Exposing the Rape Problem—the Boston Globe," *Boston Globe*, March 7,
2015, https://www.bostonglobe.com/arts/movies/2015/03/07/exposing-rape-
problem/PXjMrmCREDekRpg5ZSVS7H/story.html; Ben Kenigsberg, "Sundance Film Review: 'The Hunting Ground.'"

72. Emily Yoffe, "What's Wrong with the New Documentary about Rape on
College Campuses," *Slate*, February 27, 2015, http://www.slate.com/articles/
double_x/doublex/2015/02/
the_hunting_ground_a_campus_rape_documentary_that_fails_to_provide_a_f
ull.html.

73. Matt Baker, "'The Hunting Ground' Puts a Face on Jameis Winston"s
Accuser," *Tampa Bay Times*, March 2, 2015, http://www.tampabay.com/sports/
college/the-hunting-ground-puts-a-face-on-jameis-winstons-accuser/2219779;
Copeland, "Lawyers for Winston, Kinsman Unhappy Ahead of 'Hunting
Ground' Airing"; Benedict, "Jameis Winston's Accuser Speaks in New Film
About Sexual Assault"; Perry Kostidakis, "Putting It in Perspective: Jameis
Winston, Rape Culture and Ourselves," FSUNews.com, May 20, 2015, http://
www.fsunews.com/story/sports/2015/01/26/jameis-winston-cleared-student-
code-of-conduct/22380791; Mark Schlabach, "Test Links Winston's DNA to
Accuser," ESPN, January 2, 2014, http://espn.go.com/ncf/story/_/id/10009077.

74. Baker, "'The Hunting Ground' Puts a Face on Jameis Winston's Accuser"; Marissa Payne, "Florida State President Criticizes 'The Hunting Ground'
over Its Portrayal of the Jameis Winston Case," *Washington Post*, March 3,
2015, https://www.washingtonpost.com/news/early-lead/wp/2015/03/03/florida-
state-president-criticizes-the-hunting-ground-over-its-portrayal-of-the-jameis-
winston-case; Jennifer Portman, "Thrasher Condemns CNN Broadcast of 'The
Hunting Ground,'" *Tallahassee Democrat*, November 16, 2015, http://
www.tallahassee.com/story/news/2015/11/16/thrasher-condemns-cnn-broad-
cast-hunting-grounds/75876676; David Robb, "University President Rips CNN
for Airing Campus Rape Docu 'The Hunting Ground,'" Deadline.com, November 16, 2015, http://deadline.com/2015/11/florida-state-president-cnn-
hunting-ground-campus-rape-documentary-1201626249.

75. Rachel Axon, "Florida State Agrees to Pay Winston Accuser $950,000 to
Settle Suit," *USA Today*, January 25, 2016, http://www.usatoday.com/story/

sports/ncaaf/2016/01/25/florida-state-settles-title-ix-lawsuit-erica-kinsman-ja-meis-winston/79299304.

76. Bailey, "Our Brand Is Rape Skepticism: On Slate and Emily Yoffe's Weird 'Hunting Ground' Obsession"; Yoffe, "A Closer Look at the Hunting Ground Reveals the Filmmakers Put Advocacy Ahead of Accuracy"; Cara Buckley, "Professors Dispute Depiction of Harvard Case in Rape Documentary," *New York Times*, November 13, 2015, http://www.nytimes.com/2015/11/14/movies/professors-dispute-depiction-of-harvard-case-in-rape-documentary.html.

77. Yoffe, "A Closer Look at the Hunting Ground Reveals the Filmmakers Put Advocacy Ahead of Accuracy."

78. Ibid.

79. Norman Zalkind, "Zalkind Duncan & Bernstein Press Release," Boston, MA, November 11, 2015, https://d28htnjz2elwuj.cloudfront.net/wp-content/uploads/2015/11/12125424/NZ-Press-Release.pdf; Radley Balko, "Why Do High-Profile Campus Rape Stories Keep Falling Apart?" *Washington Post*, June 2, 2015, https://www.washingtonpost.com/news/the-watch/wp/2015/06/02/why-do-high-profile-campus-rape-stories-keep-falling-apart; Christina Hoff Sommers, "The Media Is Making College Rape Culture Worse," *Daily Beast*, January 23, 2015, http://www.thedailybeast.com/articles/2015/01/23/the-media-is-making-college-rape-culture-worse.html; Robby Soave, "Blame Media, Government for Campus Rape Overreach," *Reason*, January 23, 2015, http://social.reason.com/blog/2015/01/23/blame-media-government-for-campus-rape-o; Guardian Sport, "Jameis Winston Threatens to Sue CNN over Rape Movie the Hunting Ground," *Guardian*, November 20, 2015, http://www.theguardian.com/sport/2015/nov/20/jameis-winston-threatens-to-sue-cnn-over-movie-the-hunting-ground.

80. Zalkind appeared on the CNN panel in November 2015 in defense of his client. CNN, "Transcript for CNN Program 'Sexual Assault on Campus'"; Gardner, "NFL Star Jameis Winston Sends Legal Threat to CNN over Rape Movie 'The Hunting Ground'"; Buckley, "Professors Dispute Depiction of Harvard Case in Rape Documentary"; Ashe Schow, "19 Harvard Law Professors Pen Letter Denouncing 'The Hunting Ground,'" *Washington Examiner*, November 11, 2015, http://www.washingtonexaminer.com/19-harvard-law-professors-pen-letter-denouncing-the-hunting-ground/article/2576140; Michael Shammas, "19 Harvard Law Professors Defend Law Student Brandon Winston, Denouncing His Portrayal in 'The Hunting Ground,'" HLRecord.org, November 13, 2015, http://hlrecord.org/2015/11/19-harvard-law-professors-defend-law-student-brandon-winston-denouncing-his-portrayal-in-the-hunting-ground; Hunting Ground, "Response to Statement by 19 Harvard Law Professors," TheHuntingGroundFilm.com, November 14, 2015, http://www.thehuntinggroundfilm.com/2015/11/response-to-statement-by-19-harvard-law-professors.

81. Meghan Daum, "How Grievance Culture Undercuts the Fight against Rape Culture," *Los Angeles Times*, March 4, 2015, http://www.latimes.com/

opinion/op-ed/la-oe-daum-hunting-ground-campus-rape-20150305-column.html.

82. Ibid.

83. Naomi Schaefer Riley, "The Real Rx for Campus Rape—Give Up on Liberal 'Answers,'" *New York Post*, May 6, 2014, http://nypost.com/2014/05/06/the-real-rx-for-campus-rape-give-up-on-liberal-answers; David Daley, "Camille Paglia: How Bill Clinton Is Like Bill Cosby," *Salon*, February 28, 2015, http://www.salon.com/2015/07/28/ca-mille_paglia_how_bill_clinton_is_like_bill_cosby; Caroline Kitchens, "Statistics Don't Back Up Claims about 'Rape Culture,'" *U.S. News World Report*, October 24, 2013, http://www.usnews.com/opinion/blogs/economic-intelligence/2013/10/24/statistics-dont-back-up-claims-about-rape-culture; Paglia, "The Modern Campus Cannot Comprehend Evil"; Erin Gloria Ryan, "'Rape Culture' Is Just Drunk College Sluts Lying, Says Major Magazine," *Jezebel*, October 25, 2013, http://jezebel.com/rape-culture-is-just-drunk-college-sluts-lying-says-1452312612?utm_campaign=socialfow_jezebel_twitter&utm_source=jezebel_twitter&utm_medium=socialflow; Ashe Schow, "The Left Is Still Looking for a Modern 'Rape Culture' Poster Child," *Washington Examiner*, January 27, 2015, http://www.washingtonexaminer.com/the-left-is-still-looking-for-a-modern-rape-culture-poster-child/article/2559283; Rich Lowry, "Rolling Stone vs. UVA," *Politico*, December 3, 2014, http://www.politico.com/magazine/story/2014/12/rolling-stone-vs-uva-113311.html; Heather MacDonald, "Neo-Victorianism on Campus," *Weekly Standard*, October 20, 2014, http://www.weeklystandard.com/neo-victorianism-on-campus/article/810871; Seltzer, "Why Is 'The Hunting Ground' Driving a Campus Rape Activism Backlash?"

84. Amanda Hess, "Student Journalists Exposed Columbia University's Rape Crisis. Then One of Their Own Was Accused," *Slate*, May 14, 2014, http://www.slate.com/blogs/xx_factor/2014/05/14/colum-bia_university_alleged_rapist_list_how_bwog_journalists_reported_on.html; Richard Pérez-Peña, "Students File Complaints on Sexual Assaults at Columbia University," *New York Times*, April 24, 2014, http://www.nytimes.com/2014/04/25/nyregion/accusations-over-assault-at-columbia.html.

85. Lawrence Crook III, "Alleged 'Rapist List' Appears around New York's Columbia University," CNN, May 15, 2014, http://www.cnn.com/2014/05/14/us/columbia-university-flier-rapes/index.html; Tara Culp-Ressler, "Columbia Students Are Writing the Names of Accused Rapists on Bathroom Walls," *Think Progress*, May 14, 2014, http://thinkprogress.org/health/2014/05/14/3437670/columbia-students-bathroom-lists; Eliana Dockterman, "Names of Alleged Sexual Predators Written on Columbia University Wall," Time.com, May 13, 2014, http://time.com/97764/columbia-bathroom-sexual-assault-names; Amanda Hess, "Student Journalists Exposed Columbia University's Rape Crisis. Then One of Their Own Was Accused"; George Joseph and Jon Swaine, "Behind Columbia's 'Rape Lists': 'When Existing Systems Fail, What Then?'" *Guardian*, June 26, 2014, http://www.theguardian.com/education/2014/jun/26/columbia-university-students-rape-list-mishandle-sexual-assault;

Rose Marcius and Sasha Goldstein, "Lists of Alleged Columbia University 'Rapists' Scrawled on Bathroom Walls," *Daily News*, May 15, 2014, http:// www.nydailynews.com/new-york/lists-alleged-columbia-university-rapists-scrawled-bathroom-walls-article-1.1793986; Kate Taylor, "List of Names in Sex Assaults Roils Columbia," *New York Times*, May 13, 2014, http:// www.nytimes.com/2014/05/14/nyregion/list-of-names-in-sex-assaults-roils-columbia.html.

86. Richard Pérez-Peña, "Students File Complaints on Sexual Assaults at Columbia University"; Roberta Smith, "In a Mattress, a Lever for Art and Political Protest," *New York Times*, September 21, 2014, http:// www.nytimes.com/2014/09/22/arts/design/in-a-mattress-a-fulcrum-of-art-and-political-protest.html.

87. Ibid.

88. Ibid.; Jerry Saltz, "The 19 Best Art Shows of 2014," *Vulture*, December 10, 2014, http://www.vulture.com/2014/12/19-best-art-shows-of-2014.html.

89. Daley, "Camille Paglia: How Bill Clinton Is Like Bill Cosby"; Emily Bazelon, "Have We Learned Anything from the Columbia Rape Case?," *New York Times*, May 29, 2015, http://www.nytimes.com/2015/05/29/magazine/ have-we-learned-anything-from-the-columbia-rape-case.html; Jessica Roy, "Posters around Columbia Campus Call Emma Sulkowicz a 'Pretty Little Liar,'" *NYMag*, May 20, 2015, http://nymag.com/thecut/2015/05/posters-around-columbia-emma-sulkowicz-lied.html; Emma Whitford, "Posters Go Up around Columbia Calling Mattress Rape Protester a 'Pretty Little Liar,' *Gothamist*, May 30, 2015, http://gothamist.com/2015/05/20/colum-bia_rape_protest_posters.php; Anna Merlan, "Posters on Columbia Campus Call Emma Sulkowicz a 'Pretty Little Liar,'" Jezebel.com, May 20, 2015, http:// jezebel.com/posters-on-columbia-campus-call-emma-sulkowicz-a-pretty-1705750162; Sarah Seltzer, "The Smearing of 'Carry That Weight' Activist Emma Sulkowicz Begins," *Flavorwire*, February 4, 2015, http://flavor-wire.com/502931/the-smearing-of-carry-that-weight-activist-emma-sulkowicz-begins; Caroline Williamson, "Our Role in the Unofficial Conviction of Paul Nungesser," *Columbia Spectator*, February 5, 2015, http://columbiaspecta-tor.com/opinion/2015/02/05/our-role-unofficial-conviction-paul-nungesser; Judith Shulevitz, "The Best Way to Address Campus Rape," *New York Times*, February 7, 2015, http://www.nytimes.com/2015/02/08/opinion/sunday/the-best-way-to-address-campus-rape.html.

90. Vanessa Grigoriadis, "Meet the College Women Who Are Starting a Revolution against Campus Sexual Assault," *NYMag*, September 21, 2014, http://nymag.com/thecut/2014/09/emma-sulkowicz-campus-sexual-assault-acti-vism.html.

91. Rebecca Solnit, "Listen Up, Women Are Telling Their Story Now," *Guardian*, December 30, 2014, http://www.theguardian.com/news/2014/dec/ 30/-sp-rebecca-solnit-listen-up-women-are-telling-their-story-now.

92. Nehi Gandhi, "We Asked Hillary Clinton Why She's Hopeful about Millennials—Here's Her Answer," *Refinery 29*, September 18, 2015, http:// social.refinery29.com/2015/09/94139/hillary-clinton-campus-sexual-assault-

interview; Grigoriadis, "Meet the College Women Who Are Starting a Revolution against Campus Sexual Assault"; Claire McCaskill, *S.590—114th Congress (2015–2016): Campus Accountability and Safety Act*, ed. Education Labor Committee on Health Pensions, n.d.; Katie Van Syckle, "Emma Sulkowicz Was 'Let Down' by Obama SOTU Speech," *NYMag*, January 21, 2015, http://nymag.com/daily/intelligencer/2015/01/sulkowicz-was-let-down-by-state-of-the-union.html.

93. Ariel Kaminer, "Accusers and the Accused, Crossing Paths at Columbia University," *New York Times*, December 21, 2014, http://www.nytimes.com/2014/12/22/nyregion/accusers-and-the-accused-crossing-paths-at-columbia.html.

94. Emma Bolger, "Frustrated by Columbia's Inaction, Student Reports Sexual Assault to Police," *Columbia Spectator*, May 16, 2015, http://columbiaspectator.com/news/2014/05/16/frustrated-columbias-inaction-student-reports-sexual-assault-police.

95. Bazelon, "Have We Learned Anything from the Columbia Rape Case?"; Kaminer, "Accusers and the Accused, Crossing Paths at Columbia University."

96. Bazelon, "Have We Learned Anything from the Columbia Rape Case?"

97. Alexandra Brodsky, "Fair Process, Not Criminal Process, Is the Right Way to Address Campus Sexual Assault," *American Prospect*, January 21, 2015, http://prospect.org/article/fair-process-not-criminal-process-right-way-address-campus-sexual-assault; Nancy Gertner, "How Harvard's Sexual Assault Policy Imperils Feminist Quest for Justice," *American Prospect*, 2015, http://prospect.org/article/sex-lies-and-justice; Shulevitz, "The Best Way to Address Campus Rape."

98. Ibid.

99. Schwartz and DeKeseredy, *Sexual Assault on the College Campus: The Role of Male Peer Support*; Fisher, Daigle, and Cullen, *Unsafe in the Ivory Tower: The Sexual Victimization of College Women*; Jed Rubenfeld, "Mishandling Rape," *New York Times*, November 15, 2015, http://www.nytimes.com/2014/11/16/opinion/sunday/mishandling-rape.html; Elizabeth Bartholet, Scott Brewer, Robert Clark, Alan Dershowitz, Christine Desan, Charles Donahue, Einer Elhauge, et al., "Rethink Harvard's Sexual Harassment Policy," *Boston Globe*, October 15, 2015, https://www.bostonglobe.com/opinion/2014/10/14/rethink-harvard-sexual-harassment-policy/HFDDiZN7nU2UwuUuWMnqbM/story.html.

100. Judith Shulevitz, "Regulating Sex," *New York Times*, June 27, 2015, http://www.nytimes.com/2015/06/28/opinion/sunday/judith-shulevitz-regulating-sex.html; Cathy Young, "Columbia Student: I Didn't Rape Her," *Daily Beast*, February 3, 2015, http://www.thedailybeast.com/articles/2015/02/03/columbia-student-i-didn-t-rape-her.html; Julie Zeilinger, "The Treatment of 'Mattress Girl' Emma Sulkowicz Proves We Still Have No Idea How to Talk about Rape," Mic.com, February 3, 2015, http://mic.com/articles/109446/the-treatment-of-emma-sulkowicz-proves-we-still-have-no-idea-how-to-talk-about-rape.

101. Cathy Young, "Exclusive: Brown University Student Speaks Out on What It's Like to Be Accused of Rape," *Daily Beast*, June 8, 2014, http://www.thedailybeast.com/articles/2014/06/08/exclusive-brown-university-student-speaks-out-on-what-it-s-like-to-be-accused-of-rape.html.

102. Caringella, *Addressing Rape Reform in Law and Practice*; Stephen Schulhofer, *Unwanted Sex: The Culture of Intimidation and the Failure of Law* (Cambridge, MA: Harvard University Press, 1998).

103. Emma Sulkowicz, "Ceci N'est Pas Un Viol," CeciNestPasUnViol.com, June 2015, http://www.cecinestpasunviol.com.

104. Blake Neff, "Is Mattress Girl Editing Her Sex Tape to Dodge a Lawsuit?," *Daily Caller*, June 8, 2015, http://dailycaller.com/2015/06/08/is-mattress-girl-editing-her-sex-tape-to-dodge-a-lawsuit.

105. Franklin Einspruch, "Oops, I Guess I Just Raped Emma Sulkowicz," *The Federalist*, June 15, 2015, http://thefederalist.com/2015/06/15/oops-i-guess-i-just-raped-emma-sulkowicz; Lizzie Crocker, "Why Has Columbia Rape Accuser Emma Sulkowicz Made a Sex Video?," *Daily Beast*, June 5, 2015, http://www.thedailybeast.com/articles/2015/06/05/why-has-columbia-rape-accuser-emma-sulkowicz-made-a-sex-video.html; Melissa Chan, "Anti-Rape Activist Emma Sulkowicz Releases Sex Video as Art," *Daily News*, June 6, 2015, http://www.nydailynews.com/news/national/anti-rape-activist-emma-sulkowicz-releases-sex-video-art-article-1.2247676; Mytheos Holt, "Mattress Girl Emma Sulkowicz Is a Typical Tyrannical Leftist. Here's Why," TheLibertarianRepublic.com, June 11, 2015, http://thelibertarianrepublic.com/mattress-girl-emma-sulkowicz-is-a-typical-authoritarian-leftist-heres-why; Milo Yiannopoulos, "Emma Sulkowicz Just Released a Sex Tape: Here's My Review," *Breitbart*, June 5, 2015, http://www.breitbart.com/big-hollywood/2015/06/05/mattress-girl-emma-sulkowicz-just-released-a-sex-tape-heres-my-review.

106. Sulkowicz, "Ceci N'est Pas Un Viol."

107. Hannah Rubin, "This Is Not about Emma Sulkowicz's Rape—It Is about You," Forward.com, June 9, 2015, http://forward.com/sisterhood/309709/this-is-not-about-my-rape-it-is-about-you.

108. RAINN, "RAINN Letter to White House Task Force to Protect Students from Sexual Assault," RAINN.org, February 28, 2014, https://rainn.org/images/03-2014/WH-Task-Force-RAINN-Recommendations.pdf.

109. In addition to "rape culture," RAINN also objected to the use of the term "date rape" in educational campaigns to reduce campus rapes. The organization disapproved of the term because it is not a legal term and therefore confusing rather than clarifying in terms of education around issues of consent.

110. Callie Beusman, "What RAINN's Recommendations on Campus Rape Get Wrong (and Right)," *Jezebel*, March 23, 2014, http://jezebel.com/what-rainns-recommendations-on-campus-rape-get-wrong-1548829646; story645, "RAINN Says Blame Rapists, Not Rape Culture," *Jezebel*, March 19, 2014, http://groupthink.jezebel.com/rainn-says-stop-blaming-rape-culture-for-rape-blame-ra-1547119242; Sandy Hingston, "Rape-Victim Advocacy Group: It's Not 'Rape Culture,'" Phillymag.com, March 24, 2014, http://www.phillymag.com/news/2014/03/24/nations-largest-rape-victim-advocacy-

group-sez-rape-culture-duh; Amanda Marcotte, "RAINN's Attack on the Concept of 'Rape Culture' Is Embarrassing and Misguided," *Slate*, March 18, 2014, http://www.slate.com/blogs/xx_factor/2014/03/18/rainn_attacks_the_phrase_rape_culture_in_its_recommendations_to_the_white.html; Matt Gurney, "America's Largest Rape Prevention Group Dodges 'Victim Blaming' Bullet," *National Post*, March 27, 2014, http://fullcomment.nationalpost.com/2014/03/27/matt-gurney-americas-largest-rape-prevention-group-dodges-victim-blaming-bullet; Megan Kovacs, "We're Not 'Hysterical' for Talking about Rape Culture," BitchMedia.org, March 26, 2014, https://bitchmedia.org/post/were-not-hysterical-for-talking-about-rape-culture-RAINN-response-feminist; Wagatwe, "RAINN's Recommendations Ignore Needs of Campus Survivors of All Identities," *Feministing*, March 14, 2014, http://feministing.com/2014/03/14/response-to-rainn-campus-rape-recommendations.

111. Caroline Kitchens, "It's Time to End 'Rape Culture' Hysteria," Time.com, March 20, 2014, http://time.com/30545/its-time-to-end-rape-culture-hysteria.

112. Zerlina Maxwell, "Rape Culture Is Real," Time.com, March 27, 2014, http://time.com/40110/rape-culture-is-real.

113. Tara Culp-Ressler, "Feminists Take to Twitter to Explain That Rape Culture Is Alive and Well," *Think Progress*, March 25, 2014, http://thinkprogress.org/health/2014/03/25/3418728/rape-culture-hashtag.

114. Balko, "Why Do High-Profile Campus Rape Stories Keep Falling Apart?"

115. Sara Darehshori; "Capitol Offenses: Police Mishandling of Sexual Assault Cases in the District of Columbia," Human Rights Watch, 2013, https://www.hrw.org/report/2013/01/24/capitol-offense/police-mishandling-sexual-assault-cases-district-columbia; John Eterno and Eli Silverman, *The Crime Numbers Game: Management by Manipulation* (Boca Raton, FL: CRC Press, 2012); Wendy Kaminer, "'Believe the Victim'? Maybe—but Protect the Rights of the Accused, Too," Cognoscenti.WBUR.org, February 4, 2014, http://cognoscenti.wbur.org/2014/02/04/campus-sexual-assault-wendy-kaminer; Marc Randazza, "Should We Always Believe the Victim?," CNN, December 7, 2014, http://www.cnn.com/2014/12/05/opinion/randazza-uva-rape-allegations/index.html; Jeannie Suk, "Shutting Down Conversations about Rape at Harvard Law," *New Yorker*, December 11, 2015, http://www.newyorker.com/news/news-desk/argument-sexual-assault-race-harvard-law-school; Corey Rayburn Yung, "How to Lie with Rape Statistics: America's Hidden Rape Crisis," *Iowa Law Review* 99, no. 1196 (March 4, 2014).

116. Dame Elish Angiolini, "Report of the Independent Review Into the Investigation and Prosecution of Rape in London," CPS.gov.uk, April 30, 2015, http://www.cps.gov.uk/publications/equality/vaw/dame_elish_angiolini_rape_review_2015.pdf; Laura Bates, "How the Police Are Letting Sexual Assault Victims Down," *Guardian*, accessed January 6, 2016, http://www.theguardian.com/lifeandstyle/womens-blog/2014/nov/21/police-letting-rape-victims-down-too; Katrin Hohl and Elisabeth Stanko, "Com-

plaints of Rape and the Criminal Justice System: Fresh Evidence on the Attrition Problem in England and Wales," *European Journal of Criminology* 12, no. 3 (April 9, 2015): 324–41; Helen Pidd, "Behind the Scenes at a Police Rape Team: 'We Start by Believing the Victim,'" *Guardian*, May 15, 2015, http://www.theguardian.com/society/2015/may/15/behind-the-scenes-at-a-police-rape-team-bbc-documentary.

117. Katie McDonough, "Virginia Police Department Policy Labeled All Rape Victims Liars," *Salon*, August 13, 2013, http://www.salon.com/2013/08/13/virgin-ia_police_department_policy_used_to_classify_all_rape_victims_as_liars; Patrick Wilson, "Victim's Ordeal Prompts Sex Assault Policy Shift," PilotOnline.com, August 13, 2013, http://pilotonline.com/news/local/crime/victim-s-ordeal-prompts-sex-assault-policy-shift/article_3ffc811d-163d-5a69-ba1a-62f5196e89c6.html.

118. T. Christian Miller and Tom Meagher, "Rape Is Rape, Isn't It?," *The Marshall Project*, December 18, 2015, https://www.themarshallproject.org/2015/12/18/rape-is-rape-isn-t-it.

119. Dame Elish Angiolini, "Report of the Independent Review into the Investigation and Prosecution of Rape in London," CPS.gov.uk, April 30, 2015, http://www.cps.gov.uk/publications/equality/vaw/dame_elish_angiolini_rape_review_2015.pdf; see also T. Christian Miller and Ken Armstrong, "An Unbelievable Story of Rape," ProPublica.org, December 16, 2015, https://www.propublica.org/article/false-rape-accusations-an-unbelievable-story.

120. A. J. Delgado, "Crying Rape," *National Review*, May 19, 2014, http://www.nationalreview.com/node/378310/print.

121. Philip Rumney, "False Allegations of Rape," *Cambridge Law Journal* 65, no. 1 (April 19, 2006): 128; Cassia Spohn, Clair White, and Katharine Tellis, "Unfounding Sexual Assault: Examining the Decision to Unfound and Identifying False Reports," *Law Society Review* 48, no. 1 (2014): 161–92.

122. Cassia Spohn, Clair White, and Katharine Tellis, "Unfounding Sexual Assault: Examining the Decision to Unfound and Identifying False Reports"; Kimberly Lonsway, "Trying to Move the Elephant in the Living Room: Responding to the Challenge of False Rape Reports," *Violence against Women*, 2010.

123. David Lisak et al., "False Allegations of Sexual Assault: An Analysis of Ten Years of Reported Cases," *Violence against Women* 16, no. 12 (December 1, 2010): 1318–34, 1319.

124. Candida Saunders, "The Truth, the Half-Truth, and Nothing Like the Truth: Reconceptualizing False Allegations of Rape," *British Journal of Criminology* 52, no. 6 (October 12, 2012): 1152–71, 1169.

125. Liz Kelly, "The (in)Credible Words of Women: False Allegations in European Rape Research," *Violence against Women* 16, no. 12 (December 16, 2010): 1345–55, 1351.

126. Joanne Belknap, "Rape: Too Hard to Report and Too Easy to Discredit Victims," *Violence against Women* 16, no. 12 (December 1, 2010): 1335–44.

127. Spohn, White, and Tellis, "Unfounding Sexual Assault: Examining the Decision to Unfound and Identifying False Reports," 186.

128. Robert Tracinski, "Rape Culture and Feminism's Sexual Exploitation of Women," February 10, 2015, *The Federalist*, http://thefederalist.com/2015/02/10/rape-culture-and-feminisms-sexual-exploitation-of-women.

129. Marjorie R. Sable et al., "Barriers to Reporting Sexual Assault for Women and Men: Perspectives of College Students," *Journal of American College Health* 55, no. 3 (November 2006): 157–62; Iva A. E. Bicanic et al., "Predictors of Delayed Disclosure of Rape in Female Adolescents and Young Adults," *European Journal of Psychotraumatology* 6 (May 11, 2015): 23645–49; Fisher, Daigle, and Cullen, *Unsafe in the Ivory Tower: The Sexual Victimization of College Women*; Gavey, *Just Sex? The Cultural Scaffolding of Rape*; Jennifer Baumgardner, *It Was Rape*, documentary (New York, 2013); Robin Warshaw, *I Never Called It Rape: The Ms. Report on Recognizing, Fighting, and Surviving Date and Acquaintance Rape* (New York: Harper Perennial, 1994).

130. Though much of the reaction to *Law & Order: SVU* continues to center on whether or not the episodes accurately represent reality, many of the actors participate in antiviolence activism through their involvement with the "No More" PSA celebrity campaign directed by Mariska Hargitay (founder of Joyful Heart) and launched in 2013. The campaign is designed to raise awareness of domestic violence and sexual assault and to encourage bystander intervention (http://nomore.org/about). For a critique of the program as nothing more than branding, see Diana Moskovitz's article in *Deadspin* (http://deadspin.com/no-more-the-nfls-domestic-violence-partner-is-a-sham-1683348576).

131. Katie J. M. Baker, "Law & Order: SVU Rips Story from Dozens of Campus Rape Headlines," *Jezebel*, April 25, 2013, http://jezebel.com/law-order-svu-airs-greatest-hits-compilation-of-camp-480867409.

132. Alexandra Brodsky, "Survivors Dishonored: A Response to SVU," *Feministing*, April 26, 2013, http://feministing.com/2013/04/26/survivors-dishonored-a-response-to-svu.

133. Ibid.; Chris Zimmer, "All Things Law and Order: Law & Order SVU 'Girl Dishonored' Recap & Review," AllThingsLawAndOrder.Blogspot.com, April 25, 2013, http://allthingslawandorder.blogspot.com/2013/04/law-order-svu-girl-dishonored-recap.html.

134. Allison Leotta, "SVU Shines a Light on the Rape Culture at College Campuses," *Huffington Post*, April 25, 2015, http://www.huffingtonpost.com/allison-leotta/post_4688_b_3151921.html.

135. Lisa Cuklanz and Sujata Moorti, "Television's 'New' Feminism: Prime-Time Representations of Women and Victimization," *Critical Studies in Media Communication* 23, no. 4 (October 2006): 302–21, 317; Stacey Hust et al., "Law & Order, CSI, and NCIS: The Association between Exposure to Crime Drama Franchises, Rape Myth Acceptance, and Sexual Consent Negotiation among College Students," *Journal of Health Communication*, September 29, 2015, 1–13.

136. Transcript, "Law & Order: Special Victims Unit S16e18 Episode Script, Devastating Story," SpringfieldSpringfield.co.uk, accessed November 15,

2015, http://www.springfieldspringfield.co.uk/view_episode_scripts.php?tv-show=law-and-order-special-victims-unit&episode=s16e18.

137. Melissa Chan, "'Law & Order: SVU' Airs Take on University of Virginia Rape," *Daily News*, April 2, 2015, http://www.nydailynews.com/news/national/law-order-svu-airs-university-virginia-rape-article-1.2171570.

138. Narsimha Chintaluri, "Law & Order SVU Season 16 Episode 18 Review: Devastating Story," TVFanatic.com, April 2, 2015, http://www.tvfanatic.com/2015/04/law-and-order-svu-season-16-episode-18-review-devastating-story.

139. Ibid.

140. Transcript, "Law & Order: Special Victims Unit S16e18 Episode Script, Devastating Story."

141. Sheila Burke, "Vanderbilt Gang-Rape Defense Points to Campus Culture," BigStory.ap.org, January 24, 2015, http://bigstory.ap.org/article/549b7fcf36c741aea9a9babdde958939/doc-player-was-so-drunk-hed-struggle-join-gang-rape.

142. Betsy Phillips, "A Word about Rape Culture," *Nashville Scene*, January 27, 2015, http://www.nashvillescene.com/pitw/archives/2015/01/27/a-word-about-rape-culture; Jennifer Gerson Uffalussy, "Vanderbilt Rape Trial: Ex-Football Players Found Guilty," *Yahoo!*, January 28, 2015, https://www.yahoo.com/health/vanderbilt-rape-trial-ex-football-players-found-109385887567.html; Erin Gloria Ryan, "GMA's Coverage of the Vanderbilt Rape Case Is Hot Buttered Garbage," *Jezebel*, January 21, 2015, http://jezebel.com/gmas-coverage-of-the-vanderbilt-rape-case-is-hot-butter-1680880279; Julie Zelinger, "Jury Convicts Vanderbilt Football Players in Powerful Blow to Rape Culture Apologists," Mic.com, January 28, 2015, http://mic.com/articles/109308/jury-convicts-vanderbilt-football-players-in-powerful-blow-to-rape-culture-apologists.

143. Leela Ginelle, "Vanderbilt Football Player's Attorney Blames 'Campus Drinking Culture' for Rape," BitchMedia.org, January 23, 2015, https://bitchmedia.org/post/vanderbilt-football-player-attorney-blames-campus-drinking-culture-for-rape; Jennifer Gerson Uffalussy, "What's Really behind College 'Rape Culture'?," *Yahoo!*, January 28, 2015, https://www.yahoo.com/health/whats-really-behind-college-rape-culture-109414596787.html.

144. ; Tim Ghianni, "Prosecutors Detail Assault as Vanderbilt University Rape Trial Opens," Reuters, January 14, 2015, http://www.reuters.com/article/2015/01/14/us-usa-tennessee-vanderbilt-idUSKBN0KN0D420150114.

145. Associated Press, "Vanderbilt Football Players in Rape Case Released from Jail," *New York Post*, June 24, 2015, http://nypost.com/2015/06/24/vanderbilt-football-players-in-rape-case-released-from-jail; Kavitha Davidson, "The Downside of the Vanderbilt Rape Convictions," *Bloomberg View*, January 29, 2015, http://www.bloombergview.com/articles/2015-01-28/the-downside-of-the-vanderbilt-rape-convictions; Uffalussy, "Vanderbilt Rape Trial: Ex-Football Players Found Guilty"; Uffalussy, "What's Really behind College 'Rape Culture'?"

7. RECONCILING PANIC AND POLICY

1. Frankie Y. Bailey and Donna Hale, eds., *Popular Culture, Crime, and Justice* (Belmont, CA: Wadsworth, 1997); Mathieu Deflem, ed., *Popular Culture, Crime and Social Control* (Bingley, UK: Emerald Group, 2010); Jeff Ferrell, Keith Hayward, and Jock Young, *Cultural Criminology: an Invitation* (Thousand Oaks, CA: Sage, 2008); Ray Surette, *Media, Crime, and Criminal Justice: Images, Realities and Policies*, 4 ed. (Belmont, CA: Wadsworth Publishing, 2010).

2. Chris Atmore, "Victims, Backlash, and Radical Feminist Theory (or, the Morning after They Stole Feminism's Fire)," in *New Versions of Victims Feminists Struggle with the Concept*, ed. Sharon Lamb (New York: New York University Press, 1999). See also Roxane Gay, *Bad Feminist Essays* (New York: HarperCollins, 2014).

3. Rhiannon Lucy Cosslett, "Have Accusations of Rape Victim Blaming Gone Too Far?," *Guardian*, August 28, 2014, http://www.theguardian.com/commentisfree/2014/aug/28/culture-rape-victim-blame-too-far.

4. Michelle Goldberg, "Feminism's Toxic Twitter Wars," *The Nation*, January 29, 2014, http://www.thenation.com/article/178140/feminisms-toxic-twitter-wars.

5. Michael Kimmel, *Angry White Men: American Masculinity at the End of an Era* (New York: Nation Books, 2015).

6. Karen Tumulty and Jenna Johnson, "Why Trump May Be Winning the War on 'Political Correctness,'" *Washington Post*, January 4, 2016, https://www.washingtonpost.com/politics/why-trump-may-be-winning-the-war-on-political-correctness/2016/01/04/098cf832-afda-11e5-b711-1998289ffcea_story.html; Jessica Chasmar, "Bill Maher: Political Correctness Could Cost Democrats the Election," *Washington Times*, February 10, 2016, http://www.washingtontimes.com/news/2016/feb/10/bill-maher-political-correctness-could-cost-democr; Emma Margolin, "The PC World Republicans Love, and Love to Hate," MSNBC, December 28, 2015, http://www.msnbc.com/msnbc/politically-correct-republicans.

7. Dorothy Chunn, Susan Boyd, and Hester Lessard, eds., *Reaction and Resistance: Feminism, Law, and Social Change* (Vancouver, Canada: UBC Press, 2007); Kimmel, *Angry White Men: American Masculinity at the End of an Era*; Abby Ohlheiser, "Why 'Social Justice Warrior,' a Gamergate Insult, Is Now a Dictionary Entry," *Washington Post*, October 7, 2015, https://www.washingtonpost.com/news/the-intersect/wp/2015/10/07/why-social-justice-warrior-a-gamergate-insult-is-now-a-dictionary-entry.

8. Stefanie Lohaus and Anne Wizorek, "Immigrants Aren't Responsible for Rape Culture in Germany," *Vice*, January 6, 2016, http://www.vice.com/read/rape-culture-germany-cologne-new-years-2016-876; Asche Schow, "Europe Is Enabling a Rape Culture," *New York Post*, January 10, 2016, http://nypost.com/2016/01/10/europe-is-enabling-a-rape-culture; Tom Tancredo, "Political Correctness Protects Muslim Rape Culture," *Breitbart*, January 2, 2016,

http://www.breitbart.com/big-government/2016/01/02/political-correctness-protects-muslim-rape-culture.

9. Carol Brown, "Articles: Refocusing the War on Women Where It Rightly Belongs," AmericanThinker.com, September 7, 2014, http://www.americanthinker.com/articles/2014/09/refocusing_the_war_on_women_where_it_rightly_belongs.html.

10. The Rotherham, UK, child sexual exploitation scandal refers to the incidents revealed in the August 2014 findings from the "Independent Inquiry into Child Sexual Exploitation in Rotherham, 1997–2013." The report concluded that an estimated 1,400 children were sexually exploited in Rotherham, South Yorkshire, England, during the time frame under study. The report described that although the abuse was well known by professionals working with the children, there was failure by officials and law enforcement to take appropriate action. The report's revelations about the sheer number of victims, the brutality of the victimizations, the time span, and the negligence by authorities created shock waves. The inquiry indicated that fear of racism was one factor in the lack of response to the abuse. Alexis Jay, "Independent Inquiry Into Child Sexual Exploitation in Rotherham (1997–2013) Rotherham Metropolitan Borough Council," Rotherham.gov.uk, Rotherham, UK, August 21, 2014, http://www.rotherham.gov.uk/downloads/file/1407/independent_inquiry_cse_in_rotherham.

11. Ian Tuttle, "Feminists' Failure on Rotherham," *National Review*, August 29, 2014, http://www.nationalreview.com/article/386651/feminists-failure-rotherham-ian-tuttle; see also streiff, "Rotherham and the Failure of Multiculturalism," *Red State*, September 8, 2014, http://www.redstate.com/2014/09/08/rotherham-failure-multiculturalism; Charlotte Hays, "IWF—Rotherham and the Shame of Western Feminists," IWF.org, September 2, 2014, http://www.iwf.org/blog/2794914/Rotherham-and-the-Shame-of-Western-Feminists.

12. Rich Lowry, "A Multicultural Rape Culture," *New York Post*, September 2, 2014, http://nypost.com/2014/09/02/a-multicultural-rape-culture.

13. Glenn Reynolds, "A Rape Epidemic—by Women?," *USA Today*, September 23, 2014, http://www.usatoday.com/story/opinion/2014/09/22/rape-cdc-numbers-misleading-definition-date-forced-sexual-assault-column/16007089.

14. Breanne Fahs, Mary Dudy, and Sarah Stage, eds., *The Moral Panics of Sexuality* (New York: Palgrave Macmillan, 2013); David Garland, "On the Concept of Moral Panic," *Crime, Media, Culture* 4, no. 1 (April 1, 2008): 9–30; Erich Goode and Ben-Yahuda Nachman, *Moral Panics: The Social Construction of Deviance*, 2nd ed. (West Sussex, UK: Blackwell, 2009); Gilbert Herdt, *Moral Panics, Sex Panics: Fear and the Fight over Sexual Rights* (New York: New York University Press, 2009); Roger Lancaster, *Sex Panic and the Punitive State* (Berkeley, CA: University of California Press, 2011); Debbie Nathan and Michael Snedeker, *Satan's Silence: Ritual Abuse and the Making of a Modern American Witch Hunt* (Lincoln, NE: Choice Press, 2001); Jock Young, "Moral Panic: Its Origins in Resistance, Ressentiment and the Translation of Fantasy into Reality," Special issue, *British Journal of Criminology* 49 (2009): 4–16.

In contrast, others have cautioned against the moral panic framework with regard to issues of child pornography and child sexual abuse. For example, when historian Philip Jenkins set out to study the issue of online child pornography, he initially believed the problem to be "bogus," but after further study he found himself "in the disconcerting position of seeking to *raise* public concern about a quite authentic problem that had been neglected." Philip Jenkins, *Beyond Tolerance: Child Pornography Online* (New York: New York University Press, 2001); see also Ross Cheit, *The Witch-Hunt Narrative: Politics, Psychology, and the Sexual Abuse of Children* (New York: Oxford University Press, 2014); Nancy Whittier, *The Politics of Child Sexual Abuse: Emotion, Social Movements, and the State* (New York: Oxford University Press, 2009).

15. Reynolds, "A Rape Epidemic—by Women?"

16. Nicola Gavey, *Just Sex? The Cultural Scaffolding of Rape* (New York: Routledge, 2005), 2.

17. Angela McRobbie and Sarah L. Thornton, "Rethinking 'Moral Panic' for Multi-Mediated Social Worlds," *British Journal of Sociology* 46, no. 4 (December 1, 1995): 559–74, 571; Garland, "On the Concept of Moral Panic."

18. Whittier usefully linked fears of wrongful convictions to moral panic analyses around victims of child sex abuse. She cautioned against a moral panic analysis of sexual violence in part by pointing out that prior claims of moral panic with regard to child sexual abuse are simply not supported by empirical evidence. Based on her research, she cautioned against using outliers—e.g., those cases in which a wrongfully convicted offender is placed on the sex registry—as representative of typical cases. She wrote, "In an ironic twist, they come to stand in for the more common and routine cases of child sexual abuse, in which charges and convictions are very rare" (8). Nancy Whittier, "Where Are the Children? Theorizing the Missing Piece in Gendered Sexual Violence," *Gender & Society*, October 22, 2015, 1–14.

19. Judith Levine, "Feminism Can Handle the Truth," BostonReview.net, December 6, 2014, http://bostonreview.net/blog/judith-levine-uva-rape-denialism-rolling-stone-hoax-feminism.

20. Mona Charen, "Who Really Created the 'Rape Culture'?," *National Review*, May 9, 2014, http://www.nationalreview.com/article/377565/who-really-created-rape-culture-mona-charen.

21. Rose Corrigan, *Up Against a Wall: Rape Reform and the Failure of Success* (New York: New York University Press, 2013), 4.

22. Ilene Seidman and Susan Vickers, "The Second Wave: An Agenda for the Next Thirty Years of Rape Law Reform," *Suffolk University Law Reform* 38 (2005): 467–91.

23. Kimberly Lonsway and Joanne Armchambault, "The 'Justice Gap' for Sexual Assault Cases: Future Directions for Research and Reform," *Violence against Women*, March 6, 2012, 156.

24. Ibid., 149; Barbara Krahé and Jennifer Tempkin, *Sexual Assault and the Justice Gap: A Question of Attitude* (Portland, OR: Hart Publishing, 2008).

25. Lonsway and Armchambault, "The 'Justice Gap' for Sexual Assault Cases: Future Directions for Research and Reform," 159; Seidman and Vick-

ers, "The Second Wave: An Agenda for the Next Thirty Years of Rape Law Reform."

26. Krahé and Tempkin, *Sexual Assault and the Justice Gap: A Question of Attitude*, 2.

27. Cassia Spohn and David Holleran, "Prosecuting Sexual Assault: a Comparison of Charging Decisions in Sexual Assault Cases Involving Strangers, Acquaintances, and Intimate Partners," *Justice Quarterly* 18, no. 3 (2001): 651–88; C. Spohn and K. Tellis, "The Criminal Justice System's Response to Sexual Violence," *Violence against Women* 18, no. 2 (March 20, 2012): 169–92.

28. Lisa Frohmann, "Discrediting Victims' Allegations of Sexual Assault: Prosecutorial Accounts of Case Rejections," *Social Problems* 38, no. 2 (1991): 214; Gavey, *Just Sex? The Cultural Scaffolding of Rape*.

29. Krahé and Tempkin, *Sexual Assault and the Justice Gap: A Question of Attitude*.

30. Susan Caringella, *Addressing Rape Reform in Law and Practice* (New York: Columbia University Press, 2009); Corrigan, *Up Against a Wall: Rape Reform and the Failure of Success*; Estelle Freedman, "Redefining Rape," *Chronicle of Higher Education*, September 16, 2013, 1–7; Emily Horowitz, *Protecting Our Kids? How Sex Offender Laws Are Failing Us* (New York: Praeger, 2014); Holly Johnson, Bonnie Fisher, and Veronique Jaquier, *Critical Issues on Violence against Women: International Perspectives and Promising Strategies* (New York: Routledge, 2015); Anastasia Powell, Nicola Henry, and Asher Flynn, *Rape Justice: Beyond the Criminal Law* (Hampshire, UK: Palgrave Macmillan, 2015); Seidman and Vickers, "The Second Wave: An Agenda for the Next Thirty Years of Rape Law Reform"; Whittier, "Where Are the Children? Theorizing the Missing Piece in Gendered Sexual Violence."

31. Kathleen Daly and Brigitte Bouhours, "Rape and Attrition in the Legal Process: A Comparative Analysis of Five Countries," *Crime and Justice* 39, no. 1 (2010): 565–650.

32. Caringella, *Addressing Rape Reform in Law and Practice*; Nancy Matthews, *Confronting Rape: The Feminist Anti-Rape Movement and the State* (New York: Taylor & Francis, 2005); Whittier, "Where Are the Children? Theorizing the Missing Piece in Gendered Sexual Violence."

33. Noreen Connell and Cassandra Wilson, eds., *Rape: The First Sourcebook for Women by New York Radical Feminists* (New York: Plume, 1974), 126.

34. Haley Clark, "A Fair Way to Go: Justice for Victim-Survivors of Sexual Violence," in *Rape Justice: Beyond the Criminal Law*, ed. Anastasia Powell, Nicola Henry, and Asher Flynn, 18–35 (Hampshire, UK: Palgrave Macmillan, 2015); Corrigan, *Up Against a Wall: Rape Reform and the Failure of Success*, 246.

35. Kristin Bumiller, *In an Abusive State: How Neoliberalism Appropriated the Feminist Movement against Sexual Violence* (Durham, NC: Duke University Press, 2008); Elizabeth Bernstein, "Carceral Politics as Gender Justice? The 'Traffic in Women' and Neoliberal Circuits of Crime, Sex, and Rights," *Theory and Society* 41, no. 3 (February 12, 2012): 233–59, doi:10.1007/s11186-

012-9165-9; Victoria Law, "Against Carceral Feminism," JacobinMag.com, October 17, 2014, https://www.jacobinmag.com/2014/10/against-carceral-feminism.

36. Lise Gotell, "Reassessing the Place of Criminal Law Reform in the Struggle against Sexual Violence: A Critique of the Critique of Carceral Feminism," in *Rape Justice: Beyond the Criminal Law*, ed. Anastasia Powell, Nicola Henry, and Asher Flynn, 53–71 (Hampshire, UK: Palgrave Macmillan, 2015).

37. Corrigan, *Up Against a Wall: Rape Reform and the Failure of Success*.

38. Todd Clear and Natasha A. Frost, *The Punishment Imperative: The Rise and Fall of Mass Incarceration in America* (New York: New York University Press, 2014).

39. Jon Krakauer, *Missoula: Rape and the Justice System in a College Town* (New York: Doubleday, 2015).

40. Katherine Beckett and Naomi Murakawa, "Mapping the Shadow Carceral State: Toward an Institutionally Capacious Approach to Punishment," *Theoretical Criminology* 16, no. 2 (2012): 221–44.

41. Kathleen Daly, "Sexual Violence and Justice: How and Why Context Matters," in *Rape Justice: Beyond the Criminal Law*, ed. Anastasia Powell, Nicola Henry, and Asher Flynn, 36–52 (Hampshire, UK: Palgrave Macmillan, 2015); David R. Karp, *Restorative Justice on the College Campus: Promoting Student Growth and Responsibility, and Reawakening the Spirit of Campus Community* (Springfield, IL: Charles C. Thomas, 2004).

APPENDIX

1. We excluded book reviews and letters to the editor.

INDEX

ABOUT THE AUTHOR

Nickie D. Phillips is an associate professor in the Department of Sociology and Criminal Justice at St. Francis College in Brooklyn, New York, and director of the college's Center for Crime and Popular Culture. Her research focuses on the intersection of crime, popular culture, and mass media.

CPSIA information can be obtained at www.ICGtesting.com
Printed in the USA
BVOW04*0504071016

464371BV00003B/6/P